A NEW SOCIAL ATLAS OF BRITAIN

DANIEL DORLING

University of Newcastle Upon Tyne, UK

JOHN WILEY & SONS
Chichester · New York · Brisbane · Toronto · Singapore

Other Wiley Editorial Offices

John Wiley & Sons, Inc., 605 Third Avenue,
New York, NY 10158–0012, USA

Jacaranda Wiley Ltd, 33 Park Road, Milton
Queensland 4064, Australia

John Wiley & Sons (Canada) Ltd, 22 Worcester Road,
Rexdale, Ontario M9W 1L1, Canada

John Wiley & Sons (SEA) Pte Ltd, 37 Jalan Pemimpin #05–04,
Block B, Union Industrial Building, Singapore 2057

British Library Cataloguing in Publication Data

A catalogue record for this book is available from the British Library

ISBN 0 471 94868 3

Produced from author's disks
Printed and bound in Great Britain by Alden Press, Oxford
This book is printed on acid-free paper responsibly manufactured from sustainable forestation,
for which at least two trees are planted for each one used for paper production.

Acknowledgements

The author and publisher gratefully acknowledge the following
copyright holders for permission to reproduce photographs on the
pages mentioned below:

Page xxxviii: © C. Hughes/Hutchinson Library
Page 24: © Hutchinson Library
Page 64: © Homer Sykes/Impact Photos
Page 100: © Lionel Derimais/Impact Photos
Page 134: © John Cole/Impact Photos
Page 168: © Gail Goodger/Hutchinson Library
Page 212: © Hutchinson Library

Information derived from the population censuses of Britain is reproduced
with the permission of the Controller of Her Majesty's Stationery Office.
© Crown Copyright.

Further details of data sources, research bodies providing funding towards the
production of this atlas and other acknowledgements are given on pages xvi
and xvii.

CONTENTS

2   Demography

5 Health

6 Society

7 Politics

Preface

Human Cartography and Social Geography

How many people live in your street? Fifty? One hundred? One thousand? What do those people do? How many of them are ill? How many children are there? Most of us could not answer these questions with any certainty, even about our nearest neighbours. If we were then asked how our lives and our communities compare with others, it may be even more difficult to answer with confidence. Are people in your street better off or worse off than average? Do many people of your age live where you live? Suppose you were asked how your neighbourhood has changed over recent years, would you be able to describe the changes and would you be able to say whether that change was unusual? Are more people in work? How do the changes that have occurred where you live compare with what has happened in other parts of this country? Who is losing? Who is gaining? How is the country changing? This atlas seeks to provide the answers to some of these questions by presenting a series of maps of the population of Britain drawn specifically to allow the geography of many aspects of the population to be studied in detail.

Human Cartography is a relatively new area of research which is concerned with mapping information about people (Szegö 1987, 1994, Öberg and Springfeldt 1991). It is difficult to compare the fortunes of millions of people individually. By comparing the experiences of people living in different neighbourhoods a picture of the population can be drawn in which everybody has a place and in which all places can be compared with each other. Where you live can affect what happens to you. Thus part of the study of society includes seeing how and where places differ, seeing society through the geographical patterns which social differences create.

Imagine that in your town or village a symbol were painted on every roof top showing the ages, occupations, wealth and political opinions of the people who lived in each home, and that you were given a detailed aerial photograph of the area. It would not take long to see where the most and least affluent areas are and what the people living there tended to do and how they vote. You may even be surprised by what you see. If, however, you were interested in the whole country, rather than just part of a town, this method would no longer work. The roof top signs would not be distinguishable, even on high resolution satellite pictures, and a collage of aerial photographs would cover many acres. You could get no overall impression. To be able to compare the population of a whole country a more subtle picture needs to be created, a picture which is not necessarily directly related to the physical geography of the country, but a picture which still shows the relationships between different people living in different places.

The publication of atlases mapping the social structure of Britain is becoming more frequent (Fielding 1993, Gordon & Forrest 1994, 1995). This is partly due to the increased availability of social data and the plethora of computer mapping programs which are now on the market (Beniger & Robyn 1978, Goodchild 1988). Most important in driving this trend, however, has been the growing awareness of the importance of human geography in understanding the working of society (Johnston 1986, Cliff & Haggett 1988). Initially this has resulted in an increase in the use of regional statistics and of mapping county or local authority district level averages. However, human geographers now see quite local differences as equally important for understanding the structure of society. The growing recognition of local patterns has resulted in social atlases being produced for small areas in different parts of the country (Dewdney & Rhind 1975, Bolsdon et al. 1994). This atlas is the first to put local differences in the context of the whole country, showing simultaneously both local and national patterns. This is done using equal population cartograms. These allow statistics for over ten thousand places to be viewed simultaneously, using an equitable method. The cartograms are scaled by the number of people living in each area, not the amount of land and therefore everyone is given equal prominence.

What is an Equal Population Cartogram?

A cartogram is a map or diagram showing geographical statistical information. More specifically, the word cartogram has been defined as a "combination map and graph" (Wilkie 1976: 1). In fact, ordinary maps are equal land area cartograms, equal areas of space being allocated on the map sheet to equal areas of land. Most of the cartograms in this atlas are equal population cartograms. These cartograms allocate equal areas of the map to equal numbers of people.

Imagine again attempting to view the spatial social structure of a country, but now you have some power and are not a passive spectator. Every person in Britain is sent to a small flat island three or four miles across providing standing room only. Each household is asked to keep together and to try to keep as near to its neighbours as possible, while allowing everyone equal room. A certain amount of pushing and shoving would be inevitable, but this simple rule would result in wards, towns, cities and regions remaining intact. If every person were then given coloured placards to hold overhead in reply to a question then a bird's eye view would show a population cartogram of the answer to that question. Obviously this could not actually be done, but a computer can simulate it. The cartograms in this atlas are just such a simulation. The rules which were used by the computer program which created the cartograms are as follows. First each ward (some cartograms use districts, some parliamentary constituencies) is represented by a circle, with the circle's area proportional to the population of that ward. Initially many of the circles overlap. The computer program moves each ward so that none overlap, but as many are kept near to their geographical neighbours as possible. In fact most neighbouring pairs of wards remain adjacent. The wards are also constrained to keep as near to their original positions as possible so that the north/south and east/west orientation of places is roughly correct. However the coastline is allowed to be elastic so that Scotland, which is relatively underpopulated, can shrink (so as to preserve the Scottish border). Geographical patterns can then be drawn on these cartograms showing the detail within, rather than between, district or county administrative boundaries.

Conventions Used in the Maps

A similar format is used in most of the maps in this atlas. The maps on page 11 can be taken as an example. On the left is a traditional equal land area map. The title of the map shows the subject and year. The year refers to the census or other data source used. The subtitle gives the type of statistic being mapped, here a proportion (average), and the group it refers to, in this case ward populations. The title to the key defines the statistic, in this case the "% of residents imputed". The text on the facing page 10 explains what is meant by "imputed" and provides a brief discussion of what the map contains. The keys are drawn as bar graphs which show what proportion of the map is shaded each colour. The actual percentages appear at the end of each bar and underneath the chart is stated what these figures refer to, in this case "% of the land area of Britain". Beneath that the scale is then given for an area of the map equal to a thousand square kilometres. County boundaries are drawn on the map to help in locating particular areas.

The equal population cartogram on the right of page 11 uses the same format for its key. It shows the same statistics and uses the same divisions. However, the percentages at the ends of the bar graphs refer to something very different and hence the bars in the key are of different lengths. On this cartogram it is the percentage of all residents in Britain who live in wards in each category, abbreviated on the key to "% of all residents in Britain". Beneath that the scale is then given for an area on the cartogram equal to a quarter of a million people. Thus the cartograms are quite literally drawn on a human scale. Because of this, the cartograms may appear to be a strange shape. London and the other metropolitan areas are huge (they contain many people), rural areas shrink and thinly populated highland areas appear as scattered dots. To help in learning this new geography county boundaries are also shown on each cartogram (see page 5 for maps of these). A set of index maps have also been provided at the end of this preface giving, for those who want it, the ward name, population, local authority district and parliamentary constituency for every circle on the cartograms.

The maps and cartograms usually show a single statistic in great detail. The unfamiliarity of the mapping technique, and the wealth of detail shown, results in an image which requires some experience to read. To acquire that experience the reader should first concentrate on subjects he or she is familiar with, which should then make this new format easier to understand.

The graphs accompanying the text usually show the relationship between two or more statistics, often at the national scale and using more traditional techniques. They may often appear complex because of the number of variables being compared. For instance Figure 1.10, which is drawn opposite the map and cartogram of imputation, shows the relationship between age, sex and geography as regards estimates of under-enumeration (a term explained in the text by the figure). Over 250 individual statistics are shown in this figure, arranged so that each can be compared with every other.

To make reading the graphs less difficult they also follow conventions similar to those used to draw the maps. The title, which is explained in the accompanying text, usually gives the overall areal unit used (e.g. "Britain" as, unlike a map, it is not obvious) as well as the subject and date. For graphs the title of the vertical axis is shown across the top of the graph and the title of the horizontal axis is given at the bottom. Once again "% of all residents in Britain" is often used as an abbreviation for "% of all residents in Britain who live in wards (or other areas) which fall into a particular category". Having learnt how to read the labelling of the maps and figures in this atlas the unfamiliar reader needs next to know how to appreciate what these pictures show.

Seeing Patterns and Change

Statistical methods and computer programs cannot identify unspecified patterns, they cannot interpret pictures. In contrast the human eye and brain excel in their ability to see patterns, and the more detailed a picture is, the more visible is the pattern (Tufte 1990). For instance, it is difficult to identify a face on a very low resolution photograph. As the resolution is increased the features of the face become more focused until it can be recognised. For similar reasons most of the maps and cartograms in this atlas are drawn at high resolution. If ten random numbers are selected and used to shade a map of the ten standard regions of Britain, there will often appear to be a geographical pattern to the map. However, if ten thousand random numbers are selected and used to shade a ward cartogram it is immediately apparent that there is no pattern in that map. Thus if some discernible pattern is seen on a ward cartogram, it is very unlikely to have arisen out of chance, and there is almost certainly an explanation for it and a process behind it. Many of the maps initially produced for this atlas showed no clear patterns. However, choice of an appropriate statistic and shading groups can greatly alter the clarity with which patterns are seen. Other maps initially showed patterns that were mainly a reflection of other statistics, such as crude mortality rates reflecting the distribution of pensioners. In these cases alternative statistics often had to be used which were independent of unwanted patterns such as underlying demography. Once two geographical distributions appeared to have a pattern in common, a scatterplot could be drawn to reveal the degree and nature of correlation (see Figure 1.9 for an example). Picture form is almost always the best way of presenting patterns.

Discovering patterns of change is often as interesting as uncovering the structure to the *status quo*. How is Britain changing? A series of maps or cartograms can be used to show change, but their comparison is difficult even when they are drawn side by side. It is often preferable to show change on a single map. Many of the basic statistics in this atlas are given as a percentage and then the changes in that percentage are mapped. The simple difference between two percentages is almost always used rather than a percentage of a percentage. For example, if the value of a statistic in one area increases from 1% to 2%, and another from 50% to 60%; these rises are shown as 1% and 10% respectively (not as 100% and 20% rises). This method diminishes the local impact of changes but allows better nationwide comparisons to be made.

How the Atlas was Produced

In 1989 the author created a computer-generated cartogram of British counties for a student dissertation. Many types of cartograms were developed in his subsequent PhD thesis on visualising spatial social structure (Dorling 1991) and some of the techniques developed there are used here. Work specifically on this atlas started in the summer of 1992 following the first releases of the new census data and the culmination of other research which involved the collection of large amounts of housing and voting data. In the end, however, the most time consuming aspect to drawing this atlas was still taken up by collecting more data to include. Few researchers realise just how much local information is available on Britain because of the difficulty of collecting it: "hardly any figures are available at a lower geographical scale than that of the local district or borough council" (Willmott 1994: 1). There are, in fact, thousands of figures available at detailed geographical scales. However, making these figures comparable, checking them, and then mapping what they show could not be done with commercial computer mapping software. Numerous short programs were written to transform, store, compress and retrieve the censuses and other data used here, to create and draw the maps, cartograms and other illustrations shown, and to calculate and check the statistics quoted. Files were produced to be compatible with the standard drawing program of an Acorn Archimedes computer which is used in many schools and which was used to produce all of this atlas. Numerous maps were created and viewed on screen, but only those which showed a pattern of interest were chosen. The text was then read by colleagues familiar with the various fields covered (see below). The information has been divided by subject and this structure reveals some of the areas of life in Britain about which detailed spatial information was available. Population, demography, economics, housing, health, society

and politics also reflect different areas of academic interest. Each chapter is relatively self-contained and the references are listed at the end of each. The final postscript files were also optimised to be as compact as possible. These still large files were then sent to the publishers to be printed at the high resolution necessary for all the detail to be visible. Throughout this process Wiley staff gave a great deal of advice and undertook numerous checks for quality, before proof-reading and printing the atlas.

Acknowledgements and Sources

The length of the following list is testimony to the debt of gratitude I owe to all those who helped me to write and draw this atlas, provided information for it and funded it. Most importantly the Economic and Social Research Council and the Joint Information Systems Committee purchased access to the census statistics and boundary data on behalf of the academic community. This information was prepared by the Office of Population Censuses and Surveys and is Crown Copyright. Members of this office have been most helpful providing the author with data and advice.

Most maps are based on data from the census *Small Area Statistics*, while most tables and graphs use the census *Local Base Statistics*. The referencing style of the latest *Social Trends* is followed here. Sources are only given when the data used is not census area statistics, and these are often given briefly in the text and in full in the references at the end of each chapter. Other census statistics are also used for Figures 1.14, 2.20, 4.20, 6.1, 6.2, 6.13, 6.15, 6.16 and 6.21 which are based on an analysis of the 1991 census *Sample of Anonymised Records*. *Mid Year Estimates* are used on pages 16, 17, 20 and 21 and in Figures 2.3, 2.4, 2.5, 2.6, 2.27 and 2.29. The data for these was also provided by the Office of Population Censuses and Surveys and was derived from estimates made by Helen Mounsey. The census data has been extensively analysed to create new datasets. David Atkins, Martin Charlton and David Choi helped correct the geography of the 1991 census enumeration district centroids shown on page 3, and link these to 1981 wards.

Other official statistics used in this atlas include data from the publications *Regional Trends* and *Social Trends,* which were sources for Figures 6.11, 6.30, 6.34, 6.35 6.36 and 6.37. The historical *Birth, Marriage and Mortality Statistical Series* were used for Figures 2.1, 2.2, 2.12, 2.13, 5.13, 5.17 and 5.21. More historical information is included in Figures 5.31 and 5.32 which incorporate information from past *Registrar General's Decennial Supplements and Statistical Reviews*. The *Labour Force Survey* was used in Figure 2.18. The *General Household Survey* and the *Housing and Construction Statistics* series were used in Figures 4.3 and 4.5. The homelessness figures shown on page 131 were derived from the *Local Housing Statistics* and the *Scottish Office Series*. Figures from the *Employment Gazette* were used in Figures 3.6 and 3.9 and data from the *National On-line Manpower Information System* were used for Figures 3.22, 3.23, 3.24,

3.25 3.26, 3.30 and 3.31 and the maps shown on pages 91 and 97.

Many other data sources have been drawn on for this atlas and many individuals have been very helpful to the author in accessing this information. Steve Carver provided the information on land-use shown on page 6. The Nationwide Building Society, via Tony Champion, provided the information on mortgages which was used to estimate house prices and equity levels in Figures 4.24, 4.25, 4.26, 4.27, 4.28, 6.28, 6.29 and 6.38 and in the maps on pages 125, 127, 129, 199, 205 and 207. Staff from the Office of Censuses and Population Survey's Medical Section and Brian Jarman, Madhavi Bajekal and Pat Davis of St. Mary's Hospital Medical School helped provide access to the mortality data used to produce most of the figures and maps in Chapter 5. The Department for Education and the Welsh Office were very helpful in providing the school exam results data used for Figure 6.12 and the maps on page 181. Stan Openshaw provided the information on share ownership used in Figure 6.31 and the maps on pages 201 and 203. Michael Thrasher provided the local government elections results used in Chapter 7. Steve Simpson allowed early access to the estimates being made of the locations of the missing million used on page 217. The general election data used in Chapter 7 was combined by James Cornford, Bruce Tether and the author from various sources and is deposited at the ESRC Data Archive at the University of Essex, along with the re-aggregated (to 1981 ward areas) 1991 census data which has been used here. Other sources are individually referenced in the text.

It has taken three years to complete this atlas and funding for the project has come from many sources. The work began under a Joseph Rowntree Foundation fellowship (to research housing) and has been completed while the author was funded by the British Academy to study the social transformation of Britain. The Economic and Social Research Council also provided financial support for this project through a grant to study social polarisation (H507255135), as, indirectly, did the Henley Centre and several other organisations interested in social change in Britain. Work requested by the Lord Commissioners of Her Majesty's Treasury in 1994 helped finance some of the computer equipment used to print this atlas. Thanks are also due to Norwich Computer Services for their continued support of this equipment, and to the production team at John Wiley & Sons for their patience in handling this complex project and in particular to Iain Stevenson for supporting it. I would also like to thank some of the people who read through and criticised earlier drafts of this atlas, in particular Ile Ashcroft, Tony Champion, James Cornford, Bronwen and David Dorling, Jenny Grundy, Stacy Hewitt, Ann Rooke and Rachel Woodward.

Most research is done by one person usually sitting alone at a desk or in front of a computer screen, and profound decisions about what to map, how when and in what way can depend as much on deciding when it is time to call it a day as on any grand theory.

My last words of thanks go to Anna Macdonald for understanding why I was always late drawing "one last map" and for encouraging me not to give it up.

With luck you will find something in this atlas of interest. In the end it is only possible to draw these pictures because most people diligently fill in census forms, voting slips, birth certificates, mortgage applications, unemployment cards and all the other paper work which is used to organise British society. Hopefully some of that information is being returned in these pages.

References

Beniger, J.R. & Robyn, D.L., 1978, Quantitative graphics in statistics: a brief history, *The American Statistician*, 32, 1, 1–11.

Bolsdon, D., King, D. & Musgrave, S., 1994, *Census Atlas of the Eastern Region: Housing, A Statistical Analysis based on the 1991 Census of Population*, PHRG information note 22, Chelmsford: Anglia Polytechnic University.

Cliff, A.D. & Haggett, P., 1988, *Atlas of Disease Distributions: Analytic Approaches to Epidemiological Data*, Oxford: Basil Blackwell Ltd.

Dewdney, J.C. & Rhind, D.W. (eds), 1975, *People in Durham — A Census Atlas*, University of Durham: Census Research Unit.

Dorling, D., 1991, *The Visualization of Spatial Social Structure*, Newcastle University: Unpublished PhD Thesis.

Fielding, A.J., 1993, *The Population of England and Wales in 1991: A Census Atlas*, Sheffield: Geographical Association.

Goodchild, M.F., 1988, Stepping over the line: technological constraints and the new cartography. *The American Cartographer*, 15, 3, 311–319.

Gordon, D. & Forrest, R., 1994, *People and Places 1: A 1991 Census Atlas of England*, Bristol: School for Advanced Urban Studies.

Gordon, D. & Forrest, R., 1995, *People and Places 2: Social and Economic Distinction in England*, Bristol: School for Advanced Urban Studies.

Johnston, R.J., 1986, A space for place (or a place for space) in British psephology: a review of recent writings with especial reference to the general election of 1983, *Environment and Planning A*, 18, 573–598.

Öberg, S. and Springfeldt, P., 1991, *The Population: The National Atlas of Sweden*, Stockholm: SNA publishing.

Szegö, J., 1987, *Human Cartography, Mapping the World of Man*, Stockholm: Swedish Council for Building Research.

Szegö, J., 1994, *Mapping Hidden Dimensions of the Urban Scene*, Stockholm: Swedish Council for Building Research.

Tufte, E.R., 1990, *Envisioning Information*, Cheshire, Connecticut: Graphics Press.

Wilkie, R.W., 1976, Maps and cartograms, *Statistical Abstract of Latin America*, 17, 1–23.

Willmott, P., (ed) 1994, *Urban Trends 2: A Decade in Britain's Deprived Urban Areas*, London: Policy Studies Institute.

Index Maps

The impact of cartograms based on the statistics for over 10 000 wards can be lost when the image is seen to occupy only half a page in this atlas. An advantage of high quality printing is the quantity of detail which can be seen on paper compared with any computer screen. A disadvantage is that it is not possible to zoom down on a particular area. The following pages of maps allow the reader to do the next best thing and identify individual wards. Each ward has a code in it. The number identifies the ward name in the relevant county list on the facing page. The capital letter in the code gives the ward's district and the lower case letter gives the ward's constituency. The names corresponding to these codes are given in a list like that printed directly below.

Although many ward names are unique, some such as "Central" and "North", are not. However, identifying the district from the capital letter in the ward circle makes the names more meaningful. Following the ward name in the lists is the 1991 resident population. This is for the 1981 ward geographical area. The cartograms use 1981 frozen ward boundaries for the reasons given on page 1. The ward names in the list are 1991 names. When only a proportion of a current ward's population is within the 1981 ward boundary, that proportion is given. When the 1981 ward has been split, more than one name is given in a short list. If a 1991 name appears to be unlisted in a particular county, it is because it appears in one of those short lists, usually before its alphabetical position in the full list. A few wards are also now in different districts or constituencies due to boundary changes that occurred in the 1980s. These are listed opposite the South West Region ward list to which most of the changes apply.

Scottish data is based on part-postcode-sectors, not wards. The postcode sectors have been allocated ward names to help location. The actual postcode of each sector is given after the population in the Scottish lists. For purposes of comparison cross area aggregation was used to assign local election data for Scotland from wards to part-postcode-sectors.

South East Region (part)

East Sussex
DISTRICTS
A Brighton
B Eastbourne
C Hastings
D Hove
E Lewes
F Rother
G Wealden
CONSTITUENCIES
a Bexhill and Battle
b Brighton Kemptown
c Brighton Pavilion
d Eastbourne
e Hastings and Rye
f Hove
g Lewes
h Wealden

Essex
DISTRICTS
A Basildon
B Braintree
C Brentwood
D Castle Point
E Chelmsford
F Colchester
G Epping Forest
H Harlow
I Maldon
J Rochford
K Southend-on-Sea
L Tendring
M Thurrock
N Uttlesford
CONSTITUENCIES
a Basildon
b Billericay
c Braintree
d Brentwood and Ongar
e Castle Point
f Chelmsford
g Epping Forest
h Harlow
i Harwich
j North Colchester
k Rochford
l Saffron Walden
m South Colchester and Maldon
n Southend East
o Southend West
p Thurrock

Greater London
DISTRICTS
A Barking and Dagenham
B Barnet
C Bexley
D Brent
E Bromley
F Camden
G City of London
H Croydon
I Ealing
J Enfield
K Greenwich
L Hackney
M Hammersmith and Fulham
N Haringey
O Harrow
P Havering
Q Hillingdon
R Hounslow
S Islington
T Kensington and Chelsea
U Kingston upon Thames
V Lambeth
W Lewisham
X Merton
Y Newham
Z Redbridge
A1 Richmond upon Thames
B1 Southwark
C1 Sutton
D1 Tower Hamlets
E1 Waltham Forest
F1 Wandsworth
G1 Westminster, City of
CONSTITUENCIES
a Barking
b Battersea
c Beckenham
d Bethnal Green and Stepney
e Bexley Heath
f Bow and Poplar
g Brent East
h Brent North
i Brent South
j Brentford and Isleworth
k Carshalton and Wallington
l Chelsea
m Chingford
n Chipping Barnet
o Chislehurst
p Croydon Central

q Croydon North East
r Croydon North West
s Croydon South
t Dagenham
u Dulwich
v Ealing Acton
w Ealing North
x Ealing Southall
y Edmonton
z Eltham
a1 Enfield North
b1 Enfield Southgate
c1 Erith and Crayford
d1 Feltham and Heston
e1 Finchley
f1 Fulham
g1 Greenwich
h1 Hackney North and Stoke Newington
i1 Hackney South and Shoreditch
j1 Hammersmith
k1 Hampstead and Highgate
l1 Harrow East
m1 Harrow West
n1 Hayes and Harlington
o1 Hendon North
p1 Hendon South
q1 Holborn and St. Pancras
r1 Hornchurch
s1 Hornsey and Wood Green
t1 Ilford North
u1 Ilford South
v1 Islington North
w1 Islington South and Finsbury
x1 Kensington
y1 Kingston-upon-Thames
z1 Lewisham Deptford
a2 Lewisham East
b2 Lewisham West
c2 Leyton
d2 Mitcham and Morden
e2 Newham North East
f2 Newham North West
g2 Newham South
h2 Norwood
i2 Old Bexley and Sidcup
j2 Orpington
k2 Peckham
l2 Putney
m2 Ravensbourne
n2 Richmond-upon-Thames and Barnes

o2 Romford
p2 Ruislip - Northwood
q2 Southwark and Bermondsey
r2 Streatham
s2 Surbiton
t2 Sutton and Cheam
u2 The City of London and Westminster South
v2 Tooting
w2 Tottenham
x2 Twickenham
y2 Upminster
z2 Uxbridge
a3 Vauxhall
b3 Walthamstow
c3 Wanstead and Woodford
d3 Westminster North
e3 Wimbledon
f3 Woolwich

Kent
DISTRICTS
A Ashford
B Canterbury
C Dartford
D Dover
E Gillingham
F Gravesham
G Maidstone
H Rochester upon Medway
I Sevenoaks
J Shepway
K Swale
L Thanet
M Tonbridge and Malling
N Tunbridge Wells
CONSTITUENCIES
a Ashford
b Canterbury
c Dartford
d Dover
e Faversham
f Folkestone and Hythe
g Gillingham
h Gravesham
i Maidstone
j Medway
k Mid Kent
l North Thanet
m Sevenoaks
n South Thanet
o Tonbridge and Malling
p Tunbridge Wells

Surrey
DISTRICTS
A Elmbridge
B Epsom and Ewell
C Guildford
D Mole Valley
E Reigate and Banstead
F Runnymede
G Spelthorne
H Surrey Heath
I Tandridge
J Waverley
K Woking
CONSTITUENCIES
a Chertsey and Walton
b East Surrey
c Epsom and Ewell
d Esher
e Guildford
f Mole Valley
g North West Surrey
h Reigate
i South West Surrey
j Spelthorne
k Woking

West Sussex
DISTRICTS
A Adur
B Arun
C Chichester
D Crawley
E Horsham
F Mid Sussex
G Worthing
CONSTITUENCIES
a Arundel
b Chichester
c Crawley
d Horsham
e Mid Sussex
f Shoreham
g Worthing

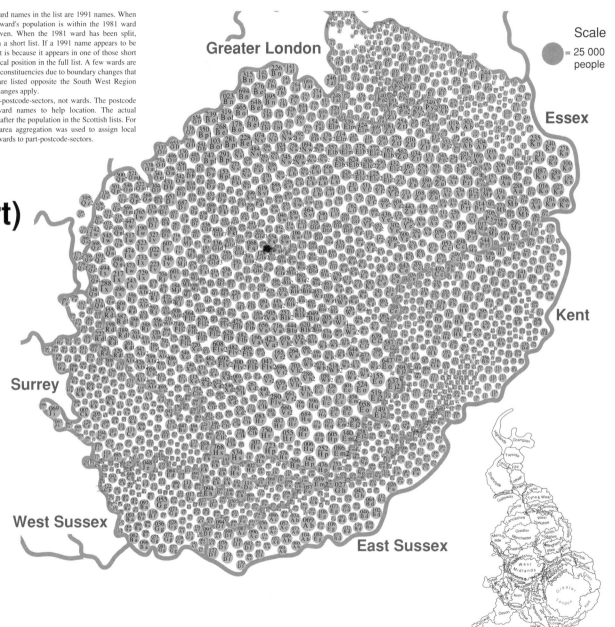

Scale
= 25 000 people

Greater London

Essex

Kent

Surrey

West Sussex

East Sussex

South East Region (part) Ward List

By County   *Format:*   Ward-number District-code Constituency-code Ward-name(s) : Population

East Sussex

Essex

Greater London

Kent

Surrey

West Sussex

South West Region and part of South East Region

Boundary Changes

Many ward boundaries were changed over the last decade. The 1991 names, sometimes split between 1981 wards, are listed. In 20 wards the majority of the population are now in another district due to these changes. The new districts are given by the new capital letter codes in the following list: Gloucestershire 080A, 081A, 105D, 116A and 104A; Gwent 058C; Hampshire 128J; Hereford and Worcester 044G; Kent 179C; Lancashire 247J; Nottinghamshire 142D; Oxfordshire 085B, 107B and 108B; and West Sussex 018D, 026D and 068D. The populations of three wards changed their county: Berkshire 006 to Hampshire district 'A'; Buckinghamshire 032 to Hertfordshire 'H' and Cambridgeshire 100 to Norfolk 'D'. Also, in Buckinghamshire, wards 116, 130 and 131 changed from Buckingham constituency 'c' to Milton Keynes constituency 'e' in 1990. The Milton Keynes Constituency was then divided into two new constituencies: Milton Keynes South West and North East Milton Keynes.

Avon
DISTRICTS
A Bath
B Bristol
C Kingswood
D Northavon
E Wansdyke
F Woodspring
CONSTITUENCIES
a Bath
b Bristol East
c Bristol North West
d Bristol South
e Bristol West
f Kingswood
g Northavon
h Wansdyke
i Weston-Super-Mare
j Woodspring

Berkshire
DISTRICTS
A Bracknell Forest
B Newbury
C Reading
D Slough
E Windsor and Maidenhead
F Wokingham
CONSTITUENCIES
a East Berkshire
b Newbury
c Reading East
d Reading West
e Slough
f Windsor and Maidenhead
g Wokingham

Buckinghamshire
DISTRICTS
A Aylesbury Vale
B Chiltern
C Milton Keynes
D South Bucks
E Wycombe
CONSTITUENCIES
a Aylesbury
b Beaconsfield
c Buckingham
d Chesham and Amersham
e Milton Keynes
f Wycombe

Cornwall
DISTRICTS
A Caradon
B Carrick
C Isles of Scilly
D Kerrier
E North Cornwall
F Penwith
G Restormel
CONSTITUENCIES
a Falmouth and Camborne
b North Cornwall
c South East Cornwall
d St. Ives
e Truro

Devon
DISTRICTS
A East Devon
B Exeter
C Mid Devon
D North Devon
E Plymouth
F South Hams
G Teignbridge
H Torbay
I Torridge
J West Devon
CONSTITUENCIES
a Exeter
b Honiton
c North Devon
d Plymouth Devonport
e Plymouth Drake
f Plymouth Sutton
g South Hams
h Teignbridge
i Tiverton
j Torbay
k Torridge and West Devon

Dorset
DISTRICTS
A Bournemouth
B Christchurch
C East Dorset (was Wimborne)
D North Dorset
E Poole
F Purbeck
G West Dorset
H Weymouth and Portland
CONSTITUENCIES
a Bournemouth East
b Bournemouth West
c Christchurch
d North Dorset
e Poole
f South Dorset
g West Dorset

Gloucestershire
DISTRICTS
A Cheltenham
B Cotswold
C Forest of Dean
D Gloucester
E Stroud
F Tewkesbury
CONSTITUENCIES
a Cheltenham
b Cirencester and Tewkesbury
c Gloucester
d Stroud
e West Gloucestershire

Hampshire
DISTRICTS
A Basingstoke and Deane
B East Hampshire
C Eastleigh
D Fareham
E Gosport
F Hart
G Havant
H New Forest
I Portsmouth
J Rushmoor
K Southampton
L Test Valley
M Winchester
CONSTITUENCIES
a Aldershot
b Basingstoke
c East Hampshire
d Eastleigh
e Fareham
f Gosport
g Havant
h New Forest
i North West Hampshire
j Portsmouth North
k Portsmouth South
l Romsey and Waterside
m Southampton Itchen
n Southampton Test
o Winchester

Isle of Wight
DISTRICTS
A Medina
B South Wight
CONSTITUENCIES
a Isle of Wight

Oxfordshire
DISTRICTS
A Cherwell
B Oxford
C South Oxfordshire
D Vale of White Horse
E West Oxfordshire
CONSTITUENCIES
a Banbury
b Henley
c Oxford East
d Oxford West and Abingdon
e Wantage
f Witney

Somerset
DISTRICTS
A Mendip
B Sedgemoor
C South Somerset (was Yeovil)
D Taunton Deane
E West Somerset
CONSTITUENCIES
a Bridgwater
b Somerton and Frome
c Taunton
d Wells
e Yeovil

Wiltshire
DISTRICTS
A Kennet
B North Wiltshire
C Salisbury
D Thamesdown
E West Wiltshire
CONSTITUENCIES
a Devizes
b North Wiltshire
c Salisbury
d Swindon
e Westbury

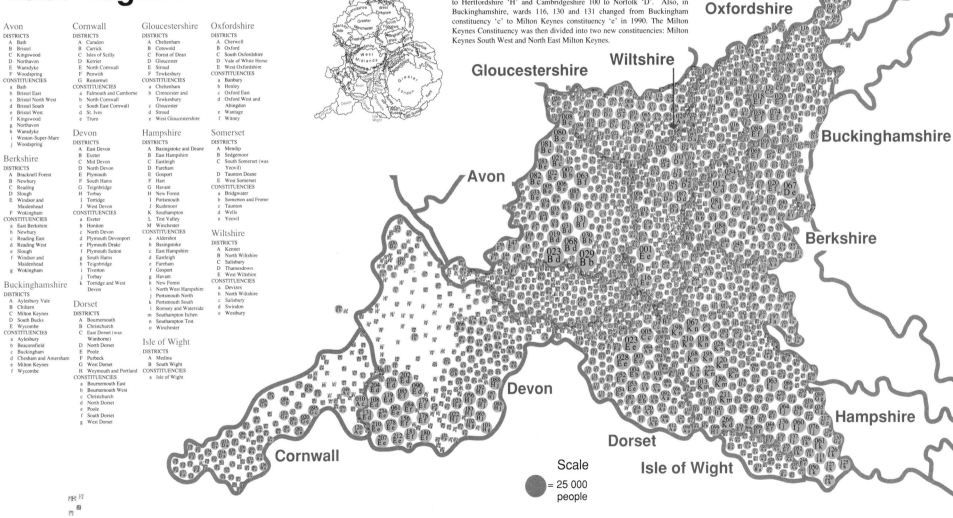

Scale
⬤ = 25 000 people

Oxfordshire

Wiltshire

Gloucestershire

Buckinghamshire

Avon

Berkshire

Devon

Dorset

Hampshire

Cornwall

Isle of Wight

South West Region and part of South East Region Ward List

By County   *Format:*   Ward-number District-code Constituency-code Ward-name(s) : Population

Avon

Berkshire

Buckinghamshire

Cornwall

Devon

Dorset

Gloucestershire

Hampshire

Isle of Wight

Oxfordshire

Somerset

Wiltshire

East Anglia Region, East Midlands Region, Bedfordshire and Hertfordshire

Bedfordshire
DISTRICTS
A Luton
B Mid Bedfordshire
C North Bedfordshire
D South Bedfordshire
CONSTITUENCIES
a Luton South
b Mid Bedfordshire
c North Bedfordshire
d North Luton
e South West Bedfordshire

Cambridgeshire
DISTRICTS
A Cambridge
B East Cambridgeshire
C Fenland
D Huntingdonshire
E Peterborough
F South Cambridgeshire
CONSTITUENCIES
a Cambridge
b Huntingdon
c North East Cambridgeshire
d Peterborough
e South East Cambridgeshire
f South West Cambridgeshire

Derbyshire
DISTRICTS
A Amber Valley
B Bolsover
C Chesterfield
D Derby
E Derbyshire Dales (was West Derbyshire)
F Erewash
G High Peak
H North East Derbyshire
I South Derbyshire
CONSTITUENCIES
a Amber Valley
b Bolsover
c Chesterfield
d Derby North
e Derby South
f Erewash
g High Peak
h North East Derbyshire
i South Derbyshire
j West Derbyshire

Hertfordshire
DISTRICTS
A Broxbourne
B Dacorum
C East Hertfordshire
D Hertsmere
E North Hertfordshire
F St.Albans
G Stevenage
H Three Rivers
I Watford
J Welwyn Hatfield
CONSTITUENCIES
a Broxbourne
b Hertford and Stortford
c Hertsmere
d North Hertfordshire
e South West Hertfordshire
f St. Albans
g Stevenage
h Watford
i Welwyn Hatfield
j West Hertfordshire

Leicestershire
DISTRICTS
A Blaby
B Charnwood
C Harborough
D Hinckley and Bosworth
E Leicester
F Melton
G North West Leicestershire
H Oadby and Wigston
I Rutland
CONSTITUENCIES
a Blaby
b Bosworth
c Harborough
d Leicester East
e Leicester South
f Leicester West
g Loughborough
h North West Leicestershire
i Rutland and Melton

Lincolnshire
DISTRICTS
A Boston
B East Lindsey
C Lincoln
D North Kesteven
E South Holland
F South Kesteven
G West Lindsey
CONSTITUENCIES
a East Lindsey
b Gainsborough and Horncastle
c Grantham
d Holland with Boston
e Lincoln
f Stamford and Spalding

Norfolk
DISTRICTS
A Breckland
B Broadland
C Great Yarmouth
D King's Lynn and West Norfolk (was West Norfolk)
E North Norfolk
F Norwich
G South Norfolk
CONSTITUENCIES
a Great Yarmouth
b Mid Norfolk
c North Norfolk
d North West Norfolk
e Norwich North
f Norwich South
g South Norfolk
h South West Norfolk

Northamptonshire
DISTRICTS
A Corby
B Daventry
C East Northamptonshire
D Kettering
E Northampton
F South Northamptonshire
G Wellingborough
CONSTITUENCIES
a Corby
b Daventry
c Kettering
d Northampton North
e Northampton South
f Wellingborough

Nottinghamshire
DISTRICTS
A Ashfield
B Bassetlaw
C Broxtowe
D Gedling
E Mansfield
F Newark and Sherwood
G Nottingham
H Rushcliffe
CONSTITUENCIES
a Ashfield
b Bassetlaw
c Broxtowe
d Gedling
e Mansfield
f Newark
g Nottingham East
h Nottingham North
i Nottingham South
j Rushcliffe
k Sherwood

Suffolk
DISTRICTS
A Babergh
B Forest Heath
C Ipswich
D Mid Suffolk
E St.Edmundsbury
F Suffolk Coastal
G Waveney
CONSTITUENCIES
a Bury St. Edmunds
b Central Suffolk
c Ipswich
d South Suffolk
e Suffolk Coastal
f Waveney

Scale

● = 25 000 people

East Anglia Region, East Midlands Region, Bedfordshire and Hertfordshire Ward List

By County   *Format:* Ward-number District-code Constituency-code Ward-name(s) : Population

Bedfordshire

Cambridgeshire

Derbyshire

Hertfordshire

Leicestershire

Lincolnshire

Norfolk

Northamptonshire

Nottinghamshire

Suffolk

Wales and the West Midlands Region

Clwyd
DISTRICTS
A Alyn and Deeside
B Colwyn
C Delyn
D Glyndwr
E Rhuddlan
F Wrexham Maelor
CONSTITUENCIES
a Alyn and Deeside
b Clwyd North West
c Clwyd South West
d Delyn
e Wrexham

Dyfed
DISTRICTS
A Carmarthen
B Ceredigion
C Dinefwr
D Llanelli
E Preseli Pembrokeshire
F South Pembrokeshire
CONSTITUENCIES
a Carmarthen
b Ceredigion and
   Pembroke North
c Llanelli
d Pembroke

Gwent
DISTRICTS
A Blaenau Gwent
B Islwyn
C Monmouth
D Newport
E Torfaen
CONSTITUENCIES
a Blaenau Gwent
b Islwyn
c Monmouth
d Newport East
e Newport West
f Torfaen

Gwynedd
DISTRICTS
A Aberconwy
B Arfon
C Dwyfor
D Meirionnydd
E Ynys Mon-Isle of
   Anglesey
CONSTITUENCIES
a Caernarfon
b Conwy
c Meirionnydd nant
   Conwy
d Ynys Mon

Hereford and Worcester
DISTRICTS
A Bromsgrove
B Hereford
C Leominster
D Malvern Hills
E Redditch
F South Herefordshire
G Worcester
H Wychavon
I Wyre Forest
CONSTITUENCIES
a Bromsgrove
b Hereford
c Leominster
d Mid Worcestershire
e South Worcestershire
f Worcester
g Wyre Forest

Mid Glamorgan
DISTRICTS
A Cynon Valley
B Merthyr Tydfil
C Ogwr
D Rhondda
E Rhymney Valley
F Taff-Ely
CONSTITUENCIES
a Bridgend
b Caerphilly
c Cynon Valley
d Merthyr Tydfil and
   Rhymney
e Ogmore
f Pontypridd
g Rhondda

Powys
DISTRICTS
A Brecknock
B Montgomeryshire
C Radnor
CONSTITUENCIES
a Brecon and Radnor
b Montgomery

Shropshire
DISTRICTS
A Bridgnorth
B North Shropshire
C Oswestry
D Shrewsbury and Atcham
E South Shropshire
F The Wrekin
CONSTITUENCIES
a Ludlow
b North Shropshire
c Shrewsbury and Atcham
d The Wrekin

South Glamorgan
DISTRICTS
A Cardiff
B Vale of Glamorgan
CONSTITUENCIES
a Cardiff Central
b Cardiff North
c Cardiff South and
   Penarth
d Cardiff West
e Vale of Glamorgan

Staffordshire
DISTRICTS
A Cannock Chase
B East Staffordshire
C Lichfield
D Newcastle-under-Lyme
E South Staffordshire
F Stafford
G Staffordshire Moorlands
H Stoke-on-Trent
I Tamworth
CONSTITUENCIES
a Burton
b Cannock and Burntwood
c Mid Staffordshire
d Newcastle-under-Lyme
e South East Staffordshire
f South Staffordshire
g Stafford
h Staffordshire Moorlands
i Stoke-on-Trent Central
j Stoke-on-Trent North
k Stoke-on-Trent South

Warwickshire
DISTRICTS
A North Warwickshire
B Nuneaton and Bedworth
C Rugby
D Stratford-on-Avon
E Warwick
CONSTITUENCIES
a North Warwickshire
b Nuneaton
c Rugby and Kenilworth
d Stratford-on-Avon
e Warwick and
   Leamington

West Glamorgan
DISTRICTS
A Lliw Valley
B Neath
C Port Talbot (was Afan)
D Swansea
CONSTITUENCIES
a Aberavon
b Gower
c Neath
d Swansea East
e Swansea West

West Midlands
DISTRICTS
A Birmingham
B Coventry
C Dudley
D Sandwell
E Solihull
F Walsall
G Wolverhampton
CONSTITUENCIES
a Aldridge – Brownhills
b Birmingham Edgbaston
c Birmingham Erdington
d Birmingham Hall Green
e Birmingham Hodge Hill
f Birmingham Ladywood
g Birmingham Northfield
h Birmingham Perry Barr
i Birmingham Selly Oak
j Birmingham Small
   Heath
k Birmingham Sparkbrook
l Birmingham Yardley
m Coventry North East
n Coventry North West
o Coventry South East
p Coventry South West
q Dudley East
r Dudley West
s Halesowen and
   Stourbridge
t Meriden
u Solihull
v Sutton Coldfield
w Walsall North
x Walsall South
y Warley East
z Warley West
a1 West Bromwich East
b1 West Bromwich West
c1 Wolverhampton North
   East
d1 Wolverhampton South
   East
e1 Wolverhampton South
   West

Scale

● = 25 000 people

Wales and the West Midlands Region Ward List

By County   *Format:*   Ward-number   District-code   Constituency-code   Ward-name(s)   :   Population

Clwyd

Dyfed

Gwynedd

Gwent

Hereford and Worcester

Powys

Mid Glamorgan

South Glamorgan

Shropshire

Staffordshire

Warwickshire

West Glamorgan

West Midlands

Yorkshire & Humberside, North West Region and Cumbria

Cheshire
DISTRICTS
A Chester
B Congleton
C Crewe and Nantwich
D Ellesmere Port and Neston
E Halton
F Macclesfield
G Vale Royal
H Warrington
CONSTITUENCIES
a City of Chester
b Congleton
c Crewe and Nantwich
d Eddisbury
e Ellesmere Port and Neston
f Halton
g Macclesfield
h Tatton
i Warrington North
j Warrington South

Cumbria
DISTRICTS
A Allerdale
B Barrow-in-Furness
C Carlisle
D Copeland
E Eden
F South Lakeland
CONSTITUENCIES
a Barrow and Furness
b Carlisle
c Copeland
d Penrith and the Borders
e Westmorland and Lonsdale
f Workington

Greater Manchester
DISTRICTS
A Bolton
B Bury
C Manchester
D Oldham
E Rochdale
F Salford
G Stockport
H Tameside
I Trafford
J Wigan
CONSTITUENCIES
a Altrincham and Sale
b Ashton-under-Lyne
c Bolton North East
d Bolton South East
e Bolton West
f Bury North
g Bury South
h Cheadle
i Davyhulme
j Denton and Reddish
k Eccles
l Hazel Grove
m Heywood and Middleton
n Leigh
o Littleborough and Saddleworth
p Makerfield
q Manchester Blackley
r Manchester Central
s Manchester Gorton
t Manchester Withington
u Manchester Wythenshawe
v Oldham Central and Royton
w Oldham West
x Rochdale
y Salford East
z Stalybridge and Hyde
a1 Stockport
b1 Stretford
c1 Wigan
d1 Worsley

Humberside
DISTRICTS
A Boothferry
B Cleethorpes
C East Yorkshire
D East Yorkshire Borough of Beverley (was Beverley)
E Glanford
F Great Grimsby
G Holderness
H Kingston upon Hull
I Scunthorpe
CONSTITUENCIES
a Beverley
b Booth Ferry
c Bridlington
d Brigg and Cleethorpes
e Glanford and Scunthorpe
f Great Grimsby
g Kingston-upon-Hull East
h Kingston-upon-Hull North
i Kingston-upon-Hull West

Lancashire
DISTRICTS
A Blackburn
B Blackpool
C Burnley
D Chorley
E Fylde
F Hyndburn
G Lancaster
H Pendle
I Preston
J Ribble Valley
K Rossendale
L South Ribble
M West Lancashire
N Wyre
CONSTITUENCIES
a Blackburn
b Blackpool North
c Blackpool South
d Burnley
e Chorley
f Fylde
g Hyndburn
h Lancaster
i Morecambe and Lunesdale
j Pendle
k Preston
l Ribble Valley
m Rossendale and Darwen
n South Ribble
o West Lancashire
p Wyre

Merseyside
DISTRICTS
A Knowsley
B Liverpool
C Sefton
D St. Helens
E Wirral
CONSTITUENCIES
a Birkenhead
b Bootle
c Crosby
d Knowsley North
e Knowsley South
f Liverpool Broadgreen
g Liverpool Garston
h Liverpool Mossley Hill
i Liverpool Riverside
j Liverpool Walton
k Liverpool West Derby
l Southport
m St. Helens North
n St. Helens South
o Wallasey
p Wirral South
q Wirral West

North Yorkshire
DISTRICTS
A Craven
B Hambleton
C Harrogate
D Richmondshire
E Ryedale
F Scarborough
G Selby
H York
CONSTITUENCIES
a Harrogate
b Richmond
c Ryedale
d Scarborough
e Selby
f Skipton and Ripon
g York

South Yorkshire
DISTRICTS
A Barnsley
B Doncaster
C Rotherham
D Sheffield
CONSTITUENCIES
a Barnsley Central
b Barnsley East
c Barnsley West and Penistone
d Don Valley
e Doncaster Central
f Doncaster North
g Rother Valley
h Rotherham
i Sheffield Attercliffe
j Sheffield Brightside
k Sheffield Central
l Sheffield Hallam
m Sheffield Heeley
n Sheffield Hillsborough
o Wentworth

West Yorkshire
DISTRICTS
A Bradford
B Calderdale
C Kirklees
D Leeds
E Wakefield
CONSTITUENCIES
a Batley and Spen
b Bradford North
c Bradford South
d Bradford West
e Calder Valley
f Colne Valley
g Dewsbury
h Elmet
i Halifax
j Hemsworth
k Huddersfield
l Keighley
m Leeds Central
n Leeds East
o Leeds North East
p Leeds North West
q Leeds West
r Morley and Leeds South
s Normanton
t Pontefract and Castleford
u Pudsey
v Shipley
w Wakefield

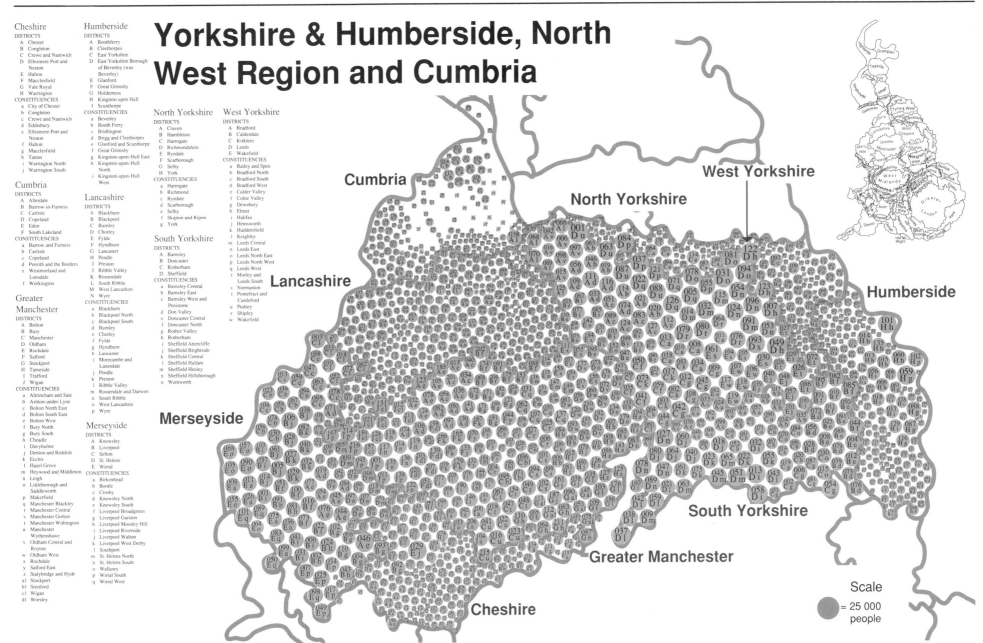

Cumbria

North Yorkshire

West Yorkshire

Lancashire

Humberside

Merseyside

South Yorkshire

Greater Manchester

Cheshire

Scale
● = 25 000 people

Yorkshire & Humberside, North West Region and Cumbria Ward List

By County   *Format:* Ward-number District-code Constituency-code Ward-name(s) : Population

Cheshire

Cumbria

Greater Manchester

Humberside

Lancashire

Merseyside

North Yorkshire

South Yorkshire

West Yorkshire

Scotland and part of Northern Region

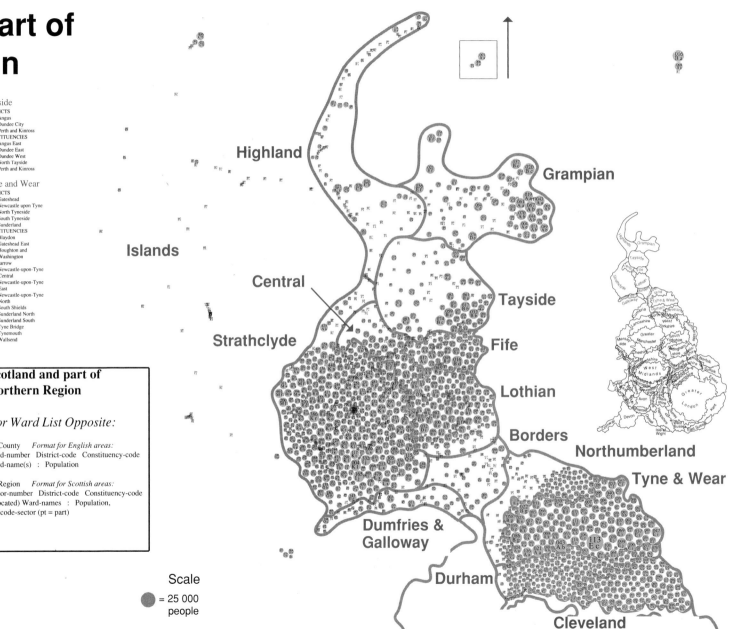

Borders
DISTRICTS
A   Berwickshire
B   Ettrick and Lauderdale
C   Roxburgh
D   Tweeddale
CONSTITUENCIES
a   Roxburgh and Berwickshire
b   Tweeddale, Ettrick and Lauderdale

Central
DISTRICTS
A   Clackmannan
B   Falkirk
C   Stirling
CONSTITUENCIES
a   Clackmannan
b   Falkirk East
c   Falkirk West
d   Stirling

Cleveland
DISTRICTS
A   Hartlepool
B   Langbaurgh-on-Tees
C   Middlesbrough
D   Stockton-on-Tees
CONSTITUENCIES
a   Hartlepool
b   Langbaurgh
c   Middlesbrough
d   Redcar
e   Stockton North
f   Stockton South

Dumfries and Galloway
DISTRICTS
A   Annandale and Eskdale
B   Nithsdale
C   Stewartry
D   Wigtown
CONSTITUENCIES
a   Dumfries
b   Galloway and Upper Nithsdale

Durham
DISTRICTS
A   Chester-le-Street
B   Darlington
C   Derwentside
D   Durham
E   Easington
F   Sedgefield
G   Teesdale
H   Wear Valley
CONSTITUENCIES
a   Bishop Auckland
b   City of Durham
c   Darlington
d   Easington
e   North Durham
f   North West Durham
g   Sedgefield

Fife
DISTRICTS
A   Dunfermline
B   Kirkcaldy
C   North East Fife
CONSTITUENCIES
a   Central Fife
b   Dunfermline East
c   Dunfermline West
d   Kirkcaldy
e   North East Fife

Grampian
DISTRICTS
A   Aberdeen City
B   Banff and Buchan
C   Gordon
D   Kincardine and Deeside
E   Moray
CONSTITUENCIES
a   Aberdeen North
b   Aberdeen South
c   Banff and Buchan
d   Gordon
e   Kincardine and Deeside
f   Moray

Highland
DISTRICTS
A   Badenoch and Strathspey
B   Caithness
C   Inverness
D   Lochaber
E   Nairn
F   Ross and Cromarty
G   Skye and Lochalsh
H   Sutherland
CONSTITUENCIES
a   Caithness and Sutherland
b   Inverness, Nairn and Lochaber
c   Ross, Cromarty and Skye

Islands
DISTRICTS
A   Orkney Islands
B   Shetland Islands
C   Western Isles Islands
CONSTITUENCIES
a   Orkney and Shetland
b   Western Isles

Lothian
DISTRICTS
A   East Lothian
B   Edinburgh City
C   Midlothian
D   West Lothian
CONSTITUENCIES
a   East Lothian
b   Edinburgh Central
c   Edinburgh East
d   Edinburgh Leith
e   Edinburgh Pentlands
f   Edinburgh South
g   Edinburgh West
h   Linlithgow
i   Livingston
j   Midlothian

Northumberland
DISTRICTS
A   Alnwick
B   Berwick-upon-Tweed
C   Blyth Valley
D   Castle Morpeth
E   Tynedale
F   Wansbeck
CONSTITUENCIES
a   Berwick-upon-Tweed
b   Blyth Valley
c   Hexham
d   Wansbeck

Strathclyde
DISTRICTS
A   Argyll and Bute
B   Bearsden and Milngavie
C   Clydebank
D   Clydesdale (was Lanark)
E   Cumbernauld and Kilsyth
F   Cumnock and Doon Valley
G   Cunninghame
H   Dumbarton
I   East Kilbride
J   Eastwood
K   Glasgow City
L   Hamilton
M   Inverclyde
N   Kilmarnock and Loudoun
O   Kyle and Carrick
P   Monklands
Q   Motherwell
R   Renfrew
S   Strathkelvin
CONSTITUENCIES
a   Argyll and Bute
b   Ayr
c   Carrick, Cumnock and Doon Valley
d   Clydebank and Milngavie
e   Clydesdale
f   Cumbernauld and Kilsyth
g   Cunninghame North
h   Cunninghame South
i   Dumbarton
j   East Kilbride
k   Eastwood
l   Glasgow Cathcart
m   Glasgow Central
n   Glasgow Garscadden
o   Glasgow Govan
p   Glasgow Hillhead
q   Glasgow Maryhill
r   Glasgow Pollock
s   Glasgow Provan
t   Glasgow Rutherglen
u   Glasgow Shettleston
v   Glasgow Springburn
w   Greenock and Port Glasgow
x   Hamilton
y   Kilmarnock and Loudoun
z   Monklands East
a1 Monklands West
b1 Motherwell North
c1 Motherwell South
d1 Paisley North
e1 Paisley South
f1 Renfrew West and Inverclyde
g1 Strathkelvin and Bearsden

Tayside
DISTRICTS
A   Angus
B   Dundee City
C   Perth and Kinross
CONSTITUENCIES
a   Angus East
b   Dundee East
c   Dundee West
d   North Tayside
e   Perth and Kinross

Tyne and Wear
DISTRICTS
A   Gateshead
B   Newcastle upon Tyne
C   North Tyneside
D   South Tyneside
E   Sunderland
CONSTITUENCIES
a   Blaydon
b   Gateshead East
c   Houghton and Washington
d   Jarrow
e   Newcastle-upon-Tyne Central
f   Newcastle-upon-Tyne East
g   Newcastle-upon-Tyne North
h   South Shields
i   Sunderland North
j   Sunderland South
k   Tyne Bridge
l   Tynemouth
m   Wallsend

Scotland and part of Northern Region

For Ward List Opposite:

By County   *Format for English areas:*
Ward-number   District-code   Constituency-code
Ward-name(s)   :   Population

By Region   *Format for Scottish areas:*
Sector-number   District-code   Constituency-code
(allocated) Ward-names   :   Population,
Postcode-sector (pt = part)

Scale

= 25 000 people

Ward List

Borders

Central

Cleveland

Durham

Dumfries and Galloway

Fife

Highland

Grampian

Lothian

Northumberland

Islands

Strathclyde

Tayside

Tyne and Wear

British Local Authority Districts

Format:
County-name (Region-code) County-population
County-number District-code District-name
(District-type-code) District Population

Avon (SW) 932674
01 A Bath (vi) 78689
01 B Bristol (v) 376144
01 C Kingswood (x) 89717
01 D Northavon (x) 130647
01 E Wansdyke (x) 80003
01 F Woodspring (x) 177472

Bedfordshire (SE) 524105
02 A Luton (vii) 171671
02 B Mid Bedfordshire (x) 109801
02 C North Bedfordshire (x) 133692
02 D South Bedfordshire (x) 108941

Berkshire (SE) 735326
03 A Bracknell Forest (viii) 95949
03 B Newbury (x) 137780
03 C Reading (vi) 128877
03 D Slough (vii) 101066
03 E Windsor & Maidenhead (x) 132465
03 F Wokingham (x) 139189

Borders (SC) 103881
04 A Berwickshire (xi) 19174
04 B Ettrick & Lauderdale (xi) 34038
04 C Roxburgh (xi) 35346
04 D Tweeddale (xi) 15323

Buckinghamshire
(SE) 634407
05 A Aylesbury Vale (x) 145931
05 B Chiltern (x) 89838
05 C Milton Keynes (viii) 176330
05 D South Bucks (x) 62482
05 E Wycombe (x) 157906

Cambridgeshire
(EA) 647089
06 A Cambridge (vi) 91933
06 B East Cambridgeshire (xi) 60416
06 C Fenland (xi) 75767
06 D Huntingdonshire (x) 144075
06 E Peterborough (viii) 153166
06 F South Cambridgeshire (x) 121732

Central (SC) 267492
07 A Clackmannan (vii) 47679
07 B Falkirk (vii) 140980
07 C Stirling (vi) 78833

Cheshire (NW) 956616
08 A Chester (x) 115458
08 B Congleton (x) 84525
08 C Crewe & Nantwich (vii) 103164
08 D Ellesmere Port & Neston (vii) 80873
08 E Halton (viii) 123716
08 F Macclesfield (x) 151590
08 G Vale Royal (x) 114605
08 H Warrington (viii) 182685

Cleveland (NO) 550293
09 A Hartlepool (vii) 90404
09 B Langbaurgh-on-Tees (vii) 145108
09 C Middlesbrough (vi) 140846
09 D Stockton-on-Tees (vii) 173912

Clwyd (WA) 408090
10 A Alyn & Deeside (vii) 73494
10 B Colwyn (ix) 55070
10 C Delyn (vii) 67849
10 D Glyndwr (xi) 41870
10 E Rhuddlan (ix) 54555
10 F Wrexham Maelor (vii) 115251

Cornwall (SW) 468425
11 A Caradon (xi) 76516
11 B Carrick (xi) 82707
11 C Isles of Scilly (xi) 2048
11 D Kerrier (xi) 87566
11 E North Cornwall (xi) 73800
11 F Penwith (xi) 59247
11 G Restormel (xi) 86519

Cumbria (NO) 483163
12 A Allerdale (vii) 95701
12 B Barrow-in-Furness (vii) 73122
12 C Carlisle (vii) 100562
12 D Copeland (vii) 71294
12 E Eden (xi) 45581
12 F South Lakeland (xi) 96897

Derbyshire (EM) 928636
13 A Amber Valley (vii) 113014
13 B Bolsover (vii) 70437
13 C Chesterfield (vii) 95885
13 D Derby (v) 218802
13 E Derbyshire Dales (was West Derbyshire) (xi) 67562
13 F Erewash (vii) 104984
13 G High Peak (vii) 85092
13 H North East Derbyshire (vii) 101088
13 I South Derbyshire (vii) 71772

Devon (SW) 1009950
14 A East Devon (ix) 115873
14 B Exeter (vi) 98125
14 C Mid Devon (xi) 64258
14 D North Devon (xi) 84800
14 E Plymouth (v) 243355
14 F South Hams (xi) 77565
14 G Teignbridge (ix) 108233
14 H Torbay (ix) 119670
14 I Torridge (xi) 52129
14 J West Devon (xi) 45895

Dorset (SW) 645166
15 A Bournemouth (ix) 151302
15 B Christchurch (ix) 40865
15 C East Dorset (was Wimborne) (ix) 78698
15 D North Dorset (xi) 52110
15 E Poole (ix) 133048
15 F Purbeck (xi) 42445
15 G West Dorset (xi) 85463
15 H Weymouth & Portland (ix) 61233

Dumfries & Galloway (SC) 147805
16 A Annandale & Eskdale (xi) 37087
16 B Nithsdale (x) 57012
16 C Stewartry (xi) 23629
16 D Wigtown (xi) 30077

Durham (NO) 593430
17 A Chester-le-Street (vii) 52224
17 B Darlington (vii) 98906
17 C Derwentside (vii) 86046
17 D Durham (vi) 81086
17 E Easington (viii) 97821
17 F Sedgefield (viii) 90530
17 G Teesdale (xi) 24068
17 H Wear Valley (vii) 62746

Dyfed (WA) 343543
18 A Carmarthen (xi) 55119
18 B Ceredigion (xi) 63094
18 C Dinefwr (xi) 38026
18 D Llanelli (vii) 75219
18 E Preseli Pembrokeshire (xi) 70157
18 F South Pembrokeshire (xi) 41886

East Sussex (SE) 690447
19 A Brighton (vi) 143582
19 B Eastbourne (ix) 81395
19 C Hastings (ix) 80820
19 D Hove (ix) 85364
19 E Lewes (ix) 87389
19 F Rother (ix) 81683
19 G Wealden (ix) 130214

Essex (SE) 1528577
20 A Basildon (viii) 161736
20 B Braintree (xi) 119160
20 C Brentwood (x) 70597
20 D Castle Point (x) 85948
20 E Chelmsford (x) 152418
20 F Colchester (x) 142507
20 G Epping Forest (x) 116027
20 H Harlow (viii) 74629
20 I Maldon (x) 52547
20 J Rochford (x) 75395
20 K Southend-on-Sea (ix) 158517
20 L Tendring (ix) 125813
20 M Thurrock (vii) 127795
20 N Uttlesford (xi) 65432

Fife (SC) 341199
21 A Dunfermline (vii) 127258
21 B Kirkcaldy (viii) 147053
21 C North East Fife (xi) 66888

Gloucestershire
(SW) 528370
22 A Cheltenham (vi) 86482
22 B Cotswold (xi) 73370
22 C Forest of Dean (xi) 75351
22 D Gloucester (vi) 94256
22 E Stroud (x) 110972
22 F Tewkesbury (x) 87937

Grampian (SC) 503888
23 A Aberdeen City (v) 204885
23 B Banff & Buchan (xi) 85303
23 C Gordon (xi) 76642
23 D Kincardine & Deeside (xi) 53442
23 E Moray (xi) 83616

Greater London
(SE) 6679699
24 A Barking & Dagenham (ii) 143680
24 B Barnet (ii) 293564
24 C Bexley (ii) 215615
24 D Brent (ii) 243025
24 E Bromley (ii) 290609
24 F Camden (i) 170444
24 G City of London (i) 4142
24 H Croydon (ii) 313510
24 I Ealing (ii) 275257
24 J Enfield (ii) 257417
24 K Greenwich (ii) 207650
24 L Hackney (i) 181248
24 M Hammersmith & Fulham (i) 148502
24 N Haringey (i) 202204
24 O Harrow (ii) 200100
24 P Havering (ii) 229492
24 Q Hillingdon (ii) 231602
24 R Hounslow (ii) 204397
24 S Islington (i) 164686
24 T Kensington & Chelsea (i) 138394
24 U Kingston upon Thames (ii) 132996
24 V Lambeth (i) 244834
24 W Lewisham (i) 230983
24 X Merton (ii) 168470
24 Y Newham (i) 212170
24 Z Redbridge (ii) 226218
24 A1 Richmond upon Thames (ii) 160732
24 B1 Southwark (i) 218541
24 C1 Sutton (ii) 168880
24 D1 Tower Hamlets (i) 161064
24 E1 Waltham Forest (ii) 212033
24 F1 Wandsworth (i) 252425
24 G1 Westminster, City of (i) 174814

Greater Manchester
(NW) 2499441
25 A Bolton (iv) 258584
25 B Bury (iv) 176760
25 C Manchester (iii) 404861
25 D Oldham (iv) 216531
25 E Rochdale (iv) 202164
25 F Salford (iv) 220463
25 G Stockport (iv) 284395
25 H Tameside (iv) 216431
25 I Trafford (iv) 212731
25 J Wigan (iv) 306521

Gwent (WA) 442212
26 A Blaenau Gwent (vii) 76468
26 B Islwyn (vii) 64525
26 C Monmouth (x) 74633
26 D Newport (vi) 136048
26 E Torfaen (viii) 90527

Gwynedd (WA) 235452
27 A Aberconwy (ix) 52972
27 B Arfon (xi) 53296
27 C Dwyfor (xi) 27070
27 D Meirionnydd (xi) 32965
27 E Ynys Mon-Isle of Anglesey (xi) 69149

Hampshire (SE) 1540467
28 A Basingstoke & Deane (x) 143710
28 B East Hampshire (x) 103460
28 C Eastleigh (x) 105999
28 D Fareham (x) 99262
28 E Gosport (x) 75061
28 F Hart (x) 87764
28 G Havant (x) 119697
28 H New Forest (ix) 160456
28 I Portsmouth (v) 174679
28 J Rushmoor (x) 75683
28 K Southampton (v) 196855
28 L Test Valley (x) 101428
28 M Winchester (x) 96386

Hereford & Worcester (WM) 676747
29 A Bromsgrove (x) 91544
29 B Hereford (x) 50234
29 C Leominster (xi) 39913
29 D Malvern Hills (xi) 86902
29 E Redditch (viii) 78106
29 F South Herefordshire (xi) 51763
29 G Worcester (vi) 80784
29 H Wychavon (xi) 102687
29 I Wyre Forest (vii) 94814

Hertfordshire (SE) 973286
30 A Broxbourne (x) 81449
30 B Dacorum (viii) 132240
30 C East Hertfordshire (x) 116266
30 D Hertsmere (x) 87590
30 E North Hertfordshire (x) 111371
30 F St.Albans (x) 126202
30 G Stevenage (viii) 74699
30 H Three Rivers (x) 78457
30 I Watford (x) 74566
30 J Welwyn Hatfield (viii) 92366

Highland (SC) 204004
31 A Badenoch & Strathspey (xi) 11008
31 B Caithness (xi) 26710
31 C Inverness (vi) 62186
31 D Lochaber (vii) 19310
31 E Nairn (xi) 10623
31 F Ross & Cromarty (xi) 48950
31 G Skye & Lochalsh (xi) 11754
31 H Sutherland (xi) 13216

Humberside (YH) 858040
32 A Boothferry (xi) 64158
32 B Cleethorpes (vii) 69066
32 C East Yorkshire (xi) 84072
32 D East Yorkshire Borough of Beverley (was Beverley) (x) 111699
32 E Glanford (xi) 71771
32 F Great Grimsby (vii) 90517
32 G Holderness (xi) 51000
32 H Kingston upon Hull (v) 254113
32 I Scunthorpe (vii) 61550

Islands (SC) 71734
33 A Orkney Islands (xi) 19612
33 B Shetland Islands (xi) 22522
33 C Western Isles Islands (xi) 29600

Isle of Wight (SE) 124577
34 A Medina (ix) 71104
34 B South Wight (ix) 53473

Kent (SE) 1508873
35 A Ashford (xi) 92331
35 B Canterbury (ix) 124435
35 C Dartford (vii) 76420
35 D Dover (ix) 102714
35 E Gillingham (x) 95358
35 F Gravesham (x) 93234
35 G Maidstone (x) 136209
35 H Rochester upon Medway (vii) 144857
35 I Sevenoaks (x) 111066
35 J Shepway (ix) 91486
35 K Swale (vii) 115766
35 L Thanet (ix) 123664
35 M Tonbridge & Malling (x) 101763
35 N Tunbridge Wells (x) 99538

Lancashire (NW) 1383998
36 A Blackburn (vii) 136612
36 B Blackpool (ix) 146069
36 C Burnley (vii) 92415
36 D Chorley (vii) 96366
36 E Fylde (ix) 70999
36 F Hyndburn (vii) 78390
36 G Lancaster (ix) 123850
36 H Pendle (vii) 85111
36 I Preston (vi) 126082
36 J Ribble Valley (x) 50482
36 K Rossendale (vii) 65681
36 L South Ribble (viii) 102139
36 M West Lancashire (viii) 107978
36 N Wyre (ix) 101818

Leicestershire
(EM) 867521
37 A Blaby (x) 82700
37 B Charnwood (x) 141806
37 C Harborough (x) 67607
37 D Hinckley & Bosworth (vii) 96201
37 E Leicester (v) 270493
37 F Melton (xi) 45112
37 G North West Leicestershire (vii) 80566
37 H Oadby & Wigston (x) 51547
37 I Rutland (x) 31489

Lincolnshire (EM) 584536
38 A Boston (xi) 53225
38 B East Lindsey (xi) 116957
38 C Lincoln (vi) 81987
38 D North Kesteven (x) 79942
38 E South Holland (xi) 67261
38 F South Kesteven (xi) 108945
38 G West Lindsey (xi) 76218

Lothian (SC) 726010
39 A East Lothian (x) 84114
39 B Edinburgh City (v) 418914
39 C Midlothian (vii) 78845
39 D West Lothian (viii) 144137

Merseyside (NW) 1403642
40 A Knowsley (iv) 152091
40 B Liverpool (iii) 452450
40 C Sefton (iv) 289538
40 D St. Helens (iv) 178764
40 E Wirral (iv) 330767

Mid Glamorgan
(WA) 534101
41 A Cynon Valley (vii) 65171
41 B Merthyr Tydfil (vii) 59317
41 C Ogwr (vii) 132442
41 D Rhondda (vii) 78344
41 E Rhymney Valley (vii) 103400
41 F Taff-Ely (vii) 95427

Norfolk (EA) 744272
42 A Breckland (xi) 107167
42 B Broadland (xi) 106292
42 C Great Yarmouth (ix) 87719
42 D King's Lynn & West Norfolk (was West Norfolk) (xi) 129118
42 E North Norfolk (xi) 90461
42 F Norwich (vi) 120895
42 G South Norfolk (xi) 102612

North Yorkshire
(YH) 702161
43 A Craven (xi) 49891
43 B Hambleton (xi) 79425
43 C Harrogate (x) 143526
43 D Richmondshire (x) 44179
43 E Ryedale (xi) 90746
43 F Scarborough (ix) 106221
43 G Selby (x) 89419
43 H York (vi) 98745

Northamptonshire
(EM) 578807
44 A Corby (viii) 53044
44 B Daventry (xi) 62886
44 C East Northamptonshire (vii) 67686
44 D Kettering (vii) 76150
44 E Northampton (viii) 180567
44 F South Northamptonshire (x) 70685
44 G Wellingborough (vii) 67789

Northumberland
(NO) 304694
45 A Alnwick (xi) 30081
45 B Berwick-upon-Tweed (xi) 26731
45 C Blyth Valley (vii) 79584
45 D Castle Morpeth (x) 50299
45 E Tynedale (xi) 57275
45 F Wansbeck (vii) 60724

Nottinghamshire
(EM) 993872
46 A Ashfield (vii) 108364
46 B Bassetlaw (vii) 103979
46 C Broxtowe (vii) 107137
46 D Gedling (vii) 106500
46 E Mansfield (vii) 100386
46 F Newark & Sherwood (vii) 106417
46 G Nottingham (v) 263522
46 H Rushcliffe (x) 97567

Oxfordshire (SE) 547584
47 A Cherwell (x) 117840
47 B Oxford (vi) 96853
47 C South Oxfordshire (x) 132718
47 D Vale of White Horse (x) 109922
47 E West Oxfordshire (x) 90251

Powys (WA) 117467
48 A Brecknock (xi) 41145
48 B Montgomeryshire (viii) 52692
48 C Radnor (xi) 23630

Shropshire (WM) 406387
49 A Bridgnorth (xi) 50511
49 B North Shropshire (xi) 52873
49 C Oswestry (xi) 33508
49 D Shrewsbury & Atcham (x) 91749
49 E South Shropshire (xi) 38230
49 F The Wrekin (viii) 139516

Somerset (SW) 460368
50 A Mendip (xi) 95603
50 B Sedgemoor (xi) 97763
50 C South Somerset (was Yeovil) (xi) 141655
50 D Taunton Deane (ix) 93696
50 E West Somerset (xi) 31643

South Glamorgan
(WA) 392780
51 A Cardiff (v) 279042
51 B Vale of Glamorgan (x) 113725

South Yorkshire
(YH) 1262630
52 A Barnsley (iv) 220937
52 B Doncaster (iv) 288854
52 C Rotherham (iv) 251637
52 D Sheffield (iii) 501202

Staffordshire
(WM) 1031135
53 A Cannock Chase (vii) 88833
53 B East Staffordshire (vii) 97105
53 C Lichfield (x) 92679
53 D Newcastle-under-Lyme (vii) 119091
53 E South Staffordshire (x) 105487
53 F Stafford (x) 117788
53 G Staffordshire Moorlands (vii) 95450
53 H Stoke-on-Trent (v) 244637
53 I Tamworth (vii) 70065

Strathclyde (SC) 2248706
54 A Argyll & Bute (xi) 65140
54 B Bearsden & Milngavie (iv) 40612
54 C Clydebank (iv) 45717
54 D Clydesdale (was Lanark) (x) 57588
54 E Cumbernauld & Kilsyth (viii) 62412
54 F Cumnock & Doon Valley (vii) 42594
54 G Cunninghame (viii) 136875
54 H Dumbarton (vii) 77173
54 I East Kilbride (iv) 82777
54 J Eastwood (iv) 59959
54 K Glasgow City (iii) 662853
54 L Hamilton (iv) 105202
54 M Inverclyde (vii) 90103
54 N Kilmarnock & Loudoun (vii) 79861
54 O Kyle & Carrick (x) 112658
54 P Monklands (iv) 102379
54 Q Motherwell (iv) 142632
54 R Renfrew (iv) 196980
54 S Strathkelvin (iv) 85191

Suffolk (EA) 636266
55 A Babergh (xi) 79632
55 B Forest Heath (x) 54843
55 C Ipswich (vii) 117365
55 D Mid Suffolk (xi) 78383
55 E St.Edmundsbury (xi) 91731
55 F Suffolk Coastal (xi) 107547
55 G Waveney (xi) 106750

Surrey (SE) 1018003
56 A Elmbridge (x) 114479
56 B Epsom & Ewell (x) 67007
56 C Guildford (x) 122378
56 D Mole Valley (x) 79220
56 E Reigate & Banstead (x) 117777
56 F Runnymede (x) 71789
56 G Spelthorne (x) 89987
56 H Surrey Heath (x) 79073
56 I Tandridge (x) 76969
56 J Waverley (x) 113212
56 K Woking (x) 86765

Tayside (SC) 383848
57 A Angus (xi) 94480
57 B Dundee City (v) 165873
57 C Perth & Kinross (xi) 123495

Tyne & Wear
(NO) 1095152
58 A Gateshead (iv) 199588
58 B Newcastle upon Tyne (iii) 259541
58 C North Tyneside (iv) 192278
58 D South Tyneside (iv) 154691
58 E Sunderland (iv) 289038

Warwickshire
(WM) 484247
59 A North Warwickshire (vii) 60747
59 B Nuneaton & Bedworth (vii) 117052
59 C Rugby (x) 84563
59 D Stratford-on-Avon (x) 105586
59 E Warwick (x) 116299

West Glamorgan
(WA) 361428
60 A Lliw Valley (vii) 63611
60 B Neath (vii) 65400
60 C Port Talbot (was Afan) (vii) 51023
60 D Swansea (v) 181303

West Midlands
(WM) 2551671
61 A Birmingham (iii) 961041
61 B Coventry (iv) 294387
61 C Dudley (iv) 304615
61 D Sandwell (iv) 290091
61 E Solihull (iv) 199859
61 F Walsall (iv) 259488
61 G Wolverhampton (iv) 242190

West Sussex (SE) 702290
62 A Adur (ix) 58016
62 B Arun (ix) 129357
62 C Chichester (xi) 101358
62 D Crawley (viii) 70711
62 E Horsham (x) 117680
62 F Mid Sussex (x) 128355
62 G Worthing (ix) 96157

West Yorkshire
(YH) 2013693
63 A Bradford (iv) 457344
63 B Calderdale (iv) 191585
63 C Kirklees (iv) 373127
63 D Leeds (iii) 680722
63 E Wakefield (iv) 310915

Wiltshire (SW) 564471
64 A Kennet (x) 68526
64 B North Wiltshire (x) 111974
64 C Salisbury (x) 105318
64 D Thamesdown (vii) 170850
64 E West Wiltshire (x) 107803

A ward is defined as an area of land. A district is a group of wards. A county is a group of districts. A standard region is a group of counties. The ward lists show which wards make up each district. The lists here show which districts make up each county and which counties make up each standard region. These are the regions which are later referred to in various tables and figures in the atlas:

Standard Regions

code	*name*	*census residents 1991*
NO	North	3 026 732
YH	Yorkshire & Humberside	4 836 524
EM	East Midlands	3 953 372
EA	East Anglia	2 027 627
SE	South East	17 207 641
SW	South West	4 609 424
WM	West Midlands	5 150 187
NW	North West	6 243 697
WA	Wales	2 835 073
SC	Scotland	4 998 567

Each district in Britain can also be assigned to one of eleven "district types" and these assignments are given on this page as the roman numerals which follow each district name. These alternative aggregations of districts are also used later in figures in the atlas. The eleven district types are:

District Types

code	*name*	*census residents 1991*
i	Inner London Boroughs	2 504 451
ii	Outer London Boroughs	4 175 248
iii	Principal Metropolitan Cities	3 922 670
iv	Other Metropolitan Districts	8 427 861
v	Large Nonmetropolitan Cities	3 492 772
vi	Small Nonmetropolitan Cities	1 826 303
vii	Districts with Industrial Areas	7 473 373
viii	Districts with New Towns	2 821 627
ix	Resort, Port & Retirement Districts	3 544 013
x	Urban & Mixed Urban / Rural	10 276 247
xi	Remoter Mainly Rural Districts	6 424 279

The populations given are the usual resident population counts of the 1991 census which, in total for Britain, included some 54 888 844 people, 97.4% of the number of people believed to be living in Britain on census night (see Figure 1.13, page 14).

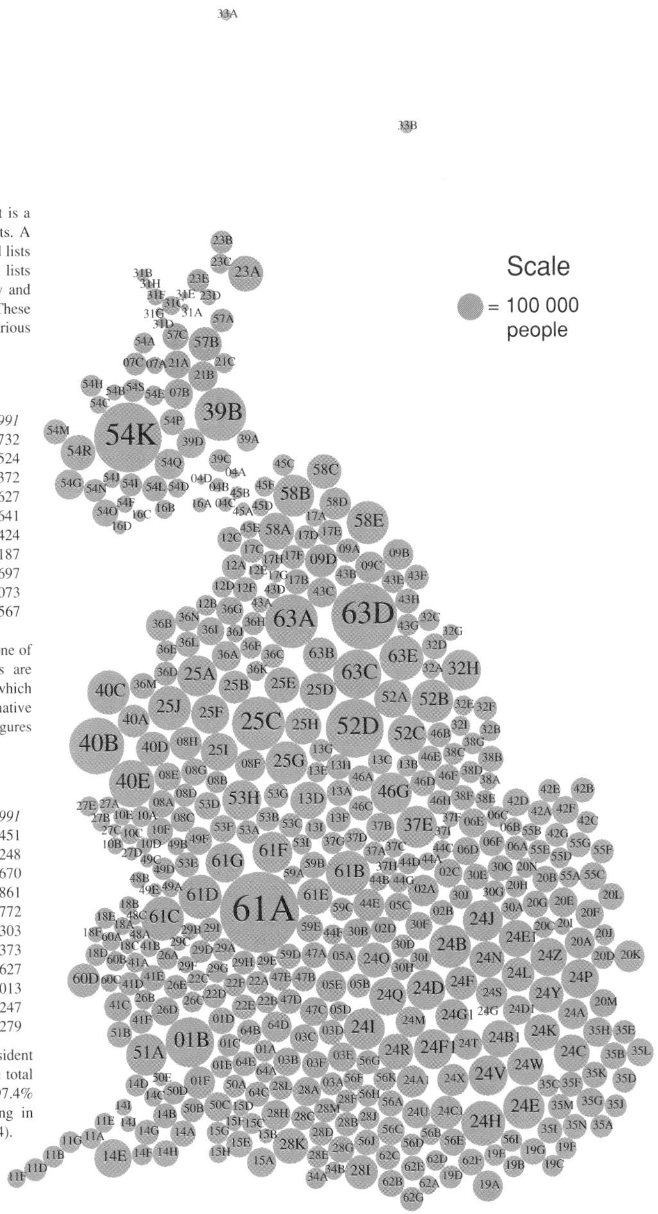

British Parliamentary Constituencies

Format:
County-name
County-number Constituency-code
Constituency-name : 1992 Electorate

Avon
01 a Bath: 63689
01 b Bristol East: 62577
01 c Bristol North West: 72726
01 d Bristol South: 64309
01 e Bristol West: 70579
01 f Kingswood: 71727
01 g Northavon: 83496
01 h Wansdyke: 77156
01 i Weston-Super-Mare: 78839
01 j Woodspring: 77534

Bedfordshire
02 a Luton South: 73016
02 b Mid Bedfordshire: 81864
02 c North Bedfordshire: 73789
02 d North Luton: 76857
02 e South West Bedfordshire: 79662

Berkshire
03 a East Berkshire: 90365
03 b Newbury: 80252
03 c Reading East: 72151
03 d Reading West: 67937
03 e Slough: 73889
03 f Windsor and Maidenhead: 77327
03 g Wokingham: 85914

Borders
04 a Roxburgh and Berwickshire: 43485
04 b Tweeddale, Ettrick and Lauderdale: 39493

Buckinghamshire
05 a Aylesbury: 79208
05 b Beaconsfield: 64268
05 c Buckingham (boundary altered slightly in 1990 see 05e): 56063
05 d Chesham and Amersham: 69895
05 e Milton Keynes (split into Milton Keynes South West and North East Milton Keynes on 10 July 1990 under statutory instrument no.1307): 129170
05 f Wycombe: 72564

Cambridgeshire
06 a Cambridge: 69022
06 b Huntingdon: 92913
06 c North East Cambridgeshire: 79935
06 d Peterborough: 87638
06 e South East Cambridgeshire: 78600
06 f South West Cambridgeshire: 84418

Central
07 a Clackmannan: 48963
07 b Falkirk East: 51918
07 c Falkirk West: 50126
07 d Stirling: 58266

Cheshire
08 a City of Chester: 63370
08 b Congleton: 70477
08 c Crewe and Nantwich: 74999
08 d Eddisbury: 75089
08 e Ellesmere Port and Neston: 71572
08 f Halton: 74906
08 g Macclesfield: 76548
08 h Tatton: 71085
08 i Warrington North: 78548
08 j Warrington South: 77694

Cleveland
09 a Hartlepool: 67968
09 b Langbaurgh: 79566
09 c Middlesbrough: 58844
09 d Redcar: 62494
09 e Stockton North: 69451
09 f Stockton South: 75959

Clwyd
10 a Alyn and Deeside: 60477
10 b Clwyd North West: 67351
10 c Clwyd South West: 60607
10 d Delyn: 66591
10 e Wrexham: 63720

Cornwall
11 a Falmouth and Camborne: 70702
11 b North Cornwall: 76844
11 c South East Cornwall: 73027
11 d St. Ives: 71152
11 e Truro: 75101

Cumbria
12 a Barrow and Furness: 67764
12 b Carlisle: 55140
12 c Copeland: 54911
12 d Penrith and the Borders: 73769
12 e Westmorland and Lonsdale: 71865
12 f Workington: 57597

Derbyshire
13 a Amber Valley: 70155
13 b Bolsover: 66693
13 c Chesterfield: 71783
13 d Derby North: 73176
13 e Derby South: 66328
13 f Erewash: 75627
13 g High Peak: 70793
13 h North East Derbyshire: 70707
13 i South Derbyshire: 82342
13 j West Derbyshire: 71201

Devon
14 a Exeter: 76723
14 b Honiton: 79223
14 c North Devon: 68998
14 d Plymouth Devonport: 65799
14 e Plymouth Drake: 51667
14 f Plymouth Sutton: 67430
14 g South Hams: 83061
14 h Teignbridge: 74892
14 i Tiverton: 71024
14 j Torbay: 71171
14 k Torridge and West Devon: 76933

Dorset
15 a Bournemouth East: 75089
15 b Bournemouth West: 74738
15 c Christchurch: 71438
15 d North Dorset: 76718
15 e Poole: 79221
15 f South Dorset: 75788
15 g West Dorset: 67256

Dumfries and Galloway
16 a Dumfries: 61145
16 b Galloway and Upper Nithsdale: 54474

Durham
17 a Bishop Auckland: 72572
17 b City of Durham: 68165
17 c Darlington: 66094
17 d Easington: 65061
17 e North Durham: 73694
17 f North West Durham: 61139
17 g Sedgefield: 61024

Dyfed
18 a Carmarthen: 68887
18 b Ceredigion and Pembroke North: 66180
18 c Llanelli: 65058
18 d Pembroke: 73187

East Sussex
19 a Bexhill and Battle: 65850
19 b Brighton Kemptown: 57646
19 c Brighton Pavilion: 57616
19 d Eastbourne: 76103
19 e Hastings and Rye: 71838
19 f Hove: 67450
19 g Lewes: 73918
19 h Wealden: 74665

Essex
20 a Basildon: 67585
20 b Billericay: 80388
20 c Braintree: 78880
20 d Brentwood and Ongar: 65830
20 e Castle Point: 66229
20 f Chelmsford: 83441
20 g Epping Forest: 67585
20 h Harlow: 68615
20 i Harwich: 80260
20 j North Colchester: 86479
20 k Rochford: 76869
20 l Saffron Walden: 74878
20 m South Colchester and Maldon: 86410
20 n Southend East: 56708
20 o Southend West: 64198
20 p Thurrock: 69171

Fife
21 a Central Fife: 56152
21 b Dunfermline East: 50179
21 c Dunfermline West: 50948
21 d Kirkcaldy: 51762
21 e North East Fife: 53747

Gloucestershire
22 a Cheltenham: 79808
22 b Cirencester and Tewkesbury: 88299
22 c Gloucester: 80578
22 d Stroud: 82553
22 e West Gloucestershire: 80007

Grampian
23 a Aberdeen North: 60217
23 b Aberdeen South: 58881
23 c Banff and Buchan: 64873
23 d Gordon: 80103
23 e Kincardine and Deeside: 66617
23 f Moray: 63255

Greater London
24 a Barking: 50454
24 b Battersea: 68218
24 c Beckenham: 59440
24 d Bethnal Green and Stepney: 55675
24 e Bexley Heath: 57684
24 f Bow and Poplar: 56685
24 g Brent East: 53319
24 h Brent North: 58917
24 i Brent South: 56034
24 j Brentford and Isleworth: 70880
24 k Carshalton and Wallington: 65179
24 l Chelsea: 42371
24 m Chingford: 55401
24 n Chipping Barnet: 57153
24 o Chislehurst: 53782
24 p Croydon Central: 55798
24 q Croydon North East: 64405
24 r Croydon North West: 57241
24 s Croydon South: 64768
24 t Dagenham: 59645
24 u Dulwich: 55141
24 v Ealing Acton: 58687
24 w Ealing North: 63528
24 x Ealing Southall: 65574
24 y Edmonton: 63052
24 z Eltham: 51989
24 a1 Enfield North: 67421
24 b1 Enfield Southgate: 64311
24 c1 Erith and Crayford: 59213
24 d1 Feltham and Heston: 81221
24 e1 Finchley: 52907
24 f1 Fulham: 52740
24 g1 Greenwich: 47789
24 h1 Hackney North and Stoke Newington: 54655
24 i1 Hackney South and Shoreditch: 57935
24 j1 Hammersmith: 47229
24 k1 Hampstead and Highgate: 58203
24 l1 Harrow East: 74733
24 m1 Harrow West: 69616
24 n1 Hayes and Harlington: 54449
24 o1 Hendon North: 51513
24 p1 Hendon South: 48401
24 q1 Holborn and St. Pancras: 64480
24 r1 Hornchurch: 60522
24 s1 Hornsey and Wood Green: 73491
24 t1 Ilford North: 58670
24 u1 Ilford South: 55741
24 v1 Islington North: 56270
24 w1 Islington South and Finsbury: 55541
24 x1 Kensington: 42129
24 y1 Kingston-upon-Thames: 51077
24 z1 Lewisham Deptford: 57014
24 a2 Lewisham East: 57674
24 b2 Lewisham West: 59317
24 c2 Leyton: 57271
24 d2 Mitcham and Morden: 63723
24 e2 Newham North East: 59555
24 f2 Newham North West: 46471
24 g2 Newham South: 51143
24 h2 Norwood: 52496
24 i2 Old Bexley and Sidcup: 49449
24 j2 Orpington: 57318
24 k2 Peckham: 58269
24 l2 Putney: 61914
24 m2 Ravensbourne: 57259
24 n2 Richmond-upon-Thames and Barnes: 53081
24 o2 Romford: 54001
24 p2 Ruislip - Northwood: 54151
24 q2 Southwark and Bermondsey: 60251
24 r2 Streatham: 56825
24 s2 Surbiton: 42421
24 t2 Sutton and Cheam: 60949
24 u2 The City of London and Westminster South: 55021
24 v2 Tooting: 68306
24 w2 Tottenham: 68319
24 x2 Twickenham: 63072
24 y2 Upminster: 64138
24 z2 Uxbridge: 61744
24 a3 Vauxhall: 62473
24 b3 Walthamstow: 49140
24 c3 Wanstead and Woodford: 55821
24 d3 Westminster North: 58847
24 e3 Wimbledon: 61917
24 f3 Woolwich: 55977

Greater Manchester
25 a Altrincham and Sale: 65897
25 b Ashton-under-Lyne: 58701
25 c Bolton North East: 58659
25 d Bolton South East: 65600
25 e Bolton West: 71344
25 f Bury North: 69529
25 g Bury South: 65793
25 h Cheadle: 66131
25 i Davyhulme: 61679
25 j Denton and Reddish: 68463
25 k Eccles: 64910
25 l Hazel Grove: 64302
25 m Heywood and Middleton: 57176
25 n Leigh: 70064
25 o Littleborough and Saddleworth: 65576
25 p Makerfield: 71425
25 q Manchester Blackley: 55234
25 r Manchester Central: 56446
25 s Manchester Gorton: 62410
25 t Manchester Withington: 63838
25 u Manchester Wythenshawe: 53548
25 v Oldham Central and Royton: 61333
25 w Oldham West: 54063
25 x Rochdale: 69522
25 y Salford East: 52616
25 z Stalybridge and Hyde: 68189
25 a1 Stockport: 58095
25 b1 Stretford: 54467
25 c1 Wigan: 72739
25 d1 Worsley: 72244

Gwent
26 a Blaenau Gwent: 55638
26 b Islwyn: 51079
26 c Monmouth: 59147
26 d Newport East: 51603
26 e Newport West: 54871
26 f Torfaen: 61104

Gwynedd
27 a Caernarfon: 46468
27 b Conwy: 53576
27 c Meirionnydd nant Conwy: 32413
27 d Ynys Mon: 53412

Hampshire
28 a Aldershot: 81754
28 b Basingstoke: 82952
28 c East Hampshire: 92139
28 d Eastleigh: 91736
28 e Fareham: 81124
28 f Gosport: 69638
28 g Havant: 74217
28 h New Forest: 75413
28 i North West Hampshire: 73101
28 j Portsmouth North: 79592
28 k Portsmouth South: 77645
28 l Romsey and Waterside: 82628
28 m Southampton Itchen: 72104
28 n Southampton Test: 72932
28 o Winchester: 79218

Hereford and Worcester
29 a Bromsgrove: 71111
29 b Hereford: 69676
29 c Leominster: 70873
29 d Mid Worcestershire: 84269
29 e South Worcestershire: 80423
29 f Worcester: 74211
29 g Wyre Forest: 73550

Hertfordshire
30 a Broxbourne: 72116
30 b Hertford and Stortford: 76654
30 c Hertsmere: 69951
30 d North Hertfordshire: 80066
30 e South West Hertfordshire: 70836
30 f St. Albans: 74188
30 g Stevenage: 70233
30 h Watford: 72291
30 i Welwyn Hatfield: 72146
30 j West Hertfordshire: 78573

Highland
31 a Caithness and Sutherland: 30905
31 b Inverness, Nairn and Lochaber: 69468
31 c Ross, Cromarty and Skye: 55524

Humberside
32 a Beverley: 81198
32 b Booth Ferry: 80747
32 c Bridlington: 84829
32 d Brigg and Cleethorpes: 82377
32 e Glanford and Scunthorpe: 73479
32 f Great Grimsby: 67427
32 g Kingston-upon-Hull East: 69036
32 h Kingston-upon-Hull North: 71363
32 i Kingston-upon-Hull West: 56111

Islands
33 a Orkney and Shetland: 31472
33 b Western Isles: 22784

Isle of Wight
34 a Isle of Wight: 99838

Kent
35 a Ashford: 71767
35 b Canterbury: 75181
35 c Dartford: 72366
35 d Dover: 68962
35 e Faversham: 81977
35 f Folkestone and Hythe: 65856
35 g Gillingham: 71851
35 h Gravesham: 70740
35 i Maidstone: 72834
35 j Medway: 61736
35 k Mid Kent: 74459
35 l North Thanet: 70978
35 m Sevenoaks: 71050
35 n South Thanet: 62441
35 o Tonbridge and Malling: 77292
35 p Tunbridge Wells: 76808

Lancashire
36 a Blackburn: 73251
36 b Blackpool North: 58087
36 c Blackpool South: 56801
36 d Burnley: 68952
36 e Chorley: 78531
36 f Fylde: 63573
36 g Hyndburn: 58539
36 h Lancaster: 58714
36 i Morecambe and Lunesdale: 56426
36 j Pendle: 64063
36 k Preston: 64158
36 l Ribble Valley: 64996
36 m Rossendale and Darwen: 76909
36 n South Ribble: 78173
36 o West Lancashire: 77462
36 p Wyre: 67778

Leicestershire
37 a Blaby: 81790
37 b Bosworth: 80234
37 c Harborough: 76514
37 d Leicester East: 63434
37 e Leicester South: 71120
37 f Leicester West: 65510
37 g Loughborough: 75450
37 h North West Leicestershire: 72414
37 i Rutland and Melton: 80976

Lincolnshire
38 a East Lindsey: 80026
38 b Gainsborough and Horncastle: 72038
38 c Grantham: 83463
38 d Holland with Boston: 67900
38 e Lincoln: 78905
38 f Stamford and Spalding: 75153

Lothian
39 a East Lothian: 66699
39 b Edinburgh Central: 56527
39 c Edinburgh East: 45687
39 d Edinburgh Leith: 56520
39 e Edinburgh Pentlands: 55567
39 f Edinburgh South: 61355
39 g Edinburgh West: 58998
39 h Linlithgow: 61082
39 i Livingston: 61092
39 j Midlothian: 60255

Merseyside
40 a Birkenhead: 62682
40 b Bootle: 69308
40 c Crosby: 82537
40 d Knowsley North: 48761
40 e Knowsley South: 62260
40 f Liverpool Broadgreen: 60080
40 g Liverpool Garston: 57538
40 h Liverpool Mossley Hill: 60409
40 i Liverpool Riverside: 49595
40 j Liverpool Walton: 70102
40 k Liverpool West Derby: 56718
40 l Southport: 71443
40 m St. Helens North: 71261
40 n St. Helens South: 67507
40 o Wallasey: 65676
40 p Wirral South: 61116
40 q Wirral West: 62453

Mid Glamorgan
41 a Bridgend: 58531
41 b Caerphilly: 64529
41 c Cynon Valley: 49695
41 d Merthyr Tydfil and Rhymney: 58430
41 e Ogmore: 52195
41 f Pontypridd: 61685
41 g Rhondda: 59955

Norfolk
42 a Great Yarmouth: 68263
42 b Mid Norfolk: 80336
42 c North Norfolk: 73780
42 d North West Norfolk: 77438
42 e Norwich North: 63308
42 f Norwich South: 63603
42 g South Norfolk: 81647
42 h South West Norfolk: 77652

North Yorkshire
43 a Harrogate: 76250
43 b Richmond: 82879
43 c Ryedale: 87048
43 d Scarborough: 76364
43 e Selby: 77178
43 f Skipton and Ripon: 75628
43 g York: 79242

Northamptonshire
44 a Corby: 68333
44 b Daventry: 71824
44 c Kettering: 67853
44 d Northampton North: 69139
44 e Northampton South: 83477
44 f Wellingborough: 73875

Northumberland
45 a Berwick-upon-Tweed: 54919
45 b Blyth Valley: 60913
45 c Hexham: 57812
45 d Wansbeck: 63457

Nottinghamshire
46 a Ashfield: 75075
46 b Bassetlaw: 58583
46 c Broxtowe: 73123
46 d Gedling: 68953
46 e Mansfield: 66964
46 f Newark: 68801
46 g Nottingham East: 67939
46 h Nottingham North: 69494
46 i Nottingham South: 72796
46 j Rushcliffe: 76253
46 k Sherwood: 73354

Oxfordshire
47 a Banbury: 71840
47 b Henley: 64702
47 c Oxford East: 63075
47 d Oxford West and Abingdon: 72328
47 e Wantage: 68328
47 f Witney: 78521

Powys
48 a Brecon and Radnor: 51509
48 b Montgomery: 41386

Shropshire
49 a Ludlow: 68935
49 b North Shropshire: 82675
49 c Shrewsbury and Atcham: 70620
49 d The Wrekin: 90892

Somerset
50 a Bridgwater: 71567
50 b Somerton and Frome: 71354
50 c Taunton: 78036
50 d Wells: 69833
50 e Yeovil: 73057

South Glamorgan
51 a Cardiff Central: 57716
51 b Cardiff North: 56721
51 c Cardiff South and Penarth: 61484
51 d Cardiff West: 58898
51 e Vale of Glamorgan: 66672

South Yorkshire
52 a Barnsley Central: 55373
52 b Barnsley East: 54051
52 c Barnsley West and Penistone: 63374
52 d Don Valley: 76327
52 e Doncaster Central: 68890
52 f Doncaster North: 74732
52 g Rother Valley: 68303
52 h Rotherham: 60937
52 i Sheffield Attercliffe: 69177
52 j Sheffield Brightside: 63810
52 k Sheffield Central: 59059
52 l Sheffield Hallam: 76584
52 m Sheffield Heeley: 70953
52 n Sheffield Hillsborough: 77343
52 o Wentworth: 64914

Staffordshire
53 a Burton: 75292
53 b Cannock and Burntwood: 72600
53 c Mid Staffordshire: 73414
53 d Newcastle-under-Lyme: 66595
53 e South East Staffordshire: 70199
53 f South Staffordshire: 82758
53 g Stafford: 74663
53 h Staffordshire Moorlands: 75036
53 i Stoke-on-Trent Central: 65527
53 j Stoke-on-Trent North: 73141
53 k Stoke-on-Trent South: 71316

Strathclyde
54 a Argyll and Bute: 47894
54 b Ayr: 65481
54 c Carrick, Cumnock and Doon Valley: 55330
54 d Clydebank and Milngavie: 47337
54 e Clydesdale: 61878
54 f Cumbernauld and Kilsyth: 46489
54 g Cunninghame North: 54803
54 h Cunninghame South: 49010
54 i Dumbarton: 57222
54 j East Kilbride: 64080
54 k Eastwood: 63685
54 l Glasgow Cathcart: 44689
54 m Glasgow Central: 48107
54 n Glasgow Garscadden: 41289
54 o Glasgow Govan: 45822
54 p Glasgow Hillhead: 57223
54 q Glasgow Maryhill: 48426
54 r Glasgow Pollock: 46139
54 s Glasgow Provan: 36560
54 t Glasgow Rutherglen: 52709
54 u Glasgow Shettleston: 51910
54 v Glasgow Springburn: 45842
54 w Greenock and Port Glasgow: 52053
54 x Hamilton: 61531
54 y Kilmarnock and Loudoun: 62002
54 z Monklands East: 48391
54 a1 Monklands West: 49269
54 b1 Motherwell North: 57290
54 c1 Motherwell South: 50042
54 d1 Paisley North: 46403
54 e1 Paisley South: 47889
54 f1 Renfrew West and Inverclyde: 58122
54 g1 Strathkelvin and Bearsden: 61116

Suffolk
55 a Bury St. Edmunds: 79967
55 b Central Suffolk: 82735
55 c Ipswich: 67261
55 d South Suffolk: 84833
55 e Suffolk Coastal: 79333
55 f Waveney: 84181

Surrey
56 a Chertsey and Walton: 70465
56 b East Surrey: 57878
56 c Epsom and Ewell: 68138
56 d Esher: 58840
56 e Guildford: 77265
56 f Mole Valley: 66949
56 g North West Surrey: 83648
56 h Reigate: 71853
56 i South West Surrey: 72288
56 j Spelthorne: 69343
56 k Woking: 80842

Tayside
57 a Angus East: 63170
57 b Dundee East: 58959
57 c Dundee West: 59953
57 d North Tayside: 55969
57 e Perth and Kinross: 65410

Tyne and Wear
58 a Blaydon: 66044
58 b Gateshead East: 64355
58 c Houghton and Washington: 79325
58 d Jarrow: 62611
58 e Newcastle-upon-Tyne Central: 59973
58 f Newcastle-upon-Tyne East: 57165
58 g Newcastle-upon-Tyne North: 66187
58 h South Shields: 59392
58 i Sunderland North: 72874
58 j Sunderland South: 72607
58 k Tyne Bridge: 53079
58 l Tynemouth: 74955
58 m Wallsend: 77941

Warwickshire
59 a North Warwickshire: 71473
59 b Nuneaton: 70906
59 c Rugby and Kenilworth: 77766
59 d Stratford-on-Avon: 82824
59 e Warwick and Leamington: 71259

West Glamorgan
60 a Aberavon: 51650
60 b Gower: 57231
60 c Neath: 56392
60 d Swansea East: 59196
60 e Swansea West: 59785

West Midlands
61 a Aldridge - Brownhills: 63404
61 b Birmingham Edgbaston: 53041
61 c Birmingham Erdington: 52398
61 d Birmingham Hall Green: 60091
61 e Birmingham Hodge Hill: 57651
61 f Birmingham Ladywood: 56970
61 g Birmingham Northfield: 70533
61 h Birmingham Perry Barr: 72161
61 i Birmingham Selly Oak: 72150
61 j Birmingham Small Heath: 55213
61 k Birmingham Sparkbrook: 51677
61 l Birmingham Yardley: 54749
61 m Coventry North East: 64787
61 n Coventry North West: 50670
61 o Coventry South East: 48796
61 p Coventry South West: 63474
61 q Dudley East: 75355
61 r Dudley West: 86632
61 s Halesowen and Stourbridge: 77644
61 t Meriden: 76994
61 u Solihull: 77303
61 v Sutton Coldfield: 71410
61 w Walsall North: 69604
61 x Walsall South: 65642
61 y Warley East: 51717
61 z Warley West: 57164
61 a1 West Bromwich East: 56940
61 b1 West Bromwich West: 57655
61 c1 Wolverhampton North East: 62695
61 d1 Wolverhampton South East: 56158
61 e1 Wolverhampton South West: 67288

West Sussex
62 a Arundel: 79241
62 b Chichester: 82124
62 c Crawley: 78277
62 d Horsham: 84158
62 e Mid Sussex: 80827
62 f Shoreham: 71252
62 g Worthing: 77540

West Yorkshire
63 a Batley and Spen: 76417
63 b Bradford North: 66719
63 c Bradford South: 69914
63 d Bradford West: 70016
63 e Calder Valley: 74417
63 f Colne Valley: 72043
63 g Dewsbury: 72839
63 h Elmet: 70558
63 i Halifax: 73401
63 j Hemsworth: 55679
63 k Huddersfield: 67604
63 l Keighley: 66358
63 m Leeds Central: 62058
63 n Leeds East: 61695
63 o Leeds North East: 64372
63 p Leeds North West: 69406
63 q Leeds West: 67084
63 r Morley and Leeds South: 63107
63 s Normanton: 65562
63 t Pontefract and Castleford: 64648
63 u Pudsey: 70847
63 v Shipley: 68816
63 w Wakefield: 69794

Wiltshire
64 a Devizes: 89745
64 b North Wiltshire: 85851
64 c Salisbury: 75916
64 d Swindon: 90067
64 e Westbury: 87356

also on cartogram:
Northern Ireland
65 a Antrim East: 62839
65 b Antrim North: 69124
65 c Antrim South: 68013
65 d Belfast East: 52833
65 e Belfast North: 55062
65 f Belfast South: 52032
65 g Belfast West: 54609
65 h Down North: 68662
65 i Down South: 76093
65 j Fermanagh and South Tyrone: 70192
65 k Foyle: 74585
65 l Lagan Valley: 72645
65 m Londonderry East: 75559
65 n Newry and Armagh: 67508
65 o Strangford: 68870
65 p Ulster Mid: 69071
65 q Upper Bann: 67446

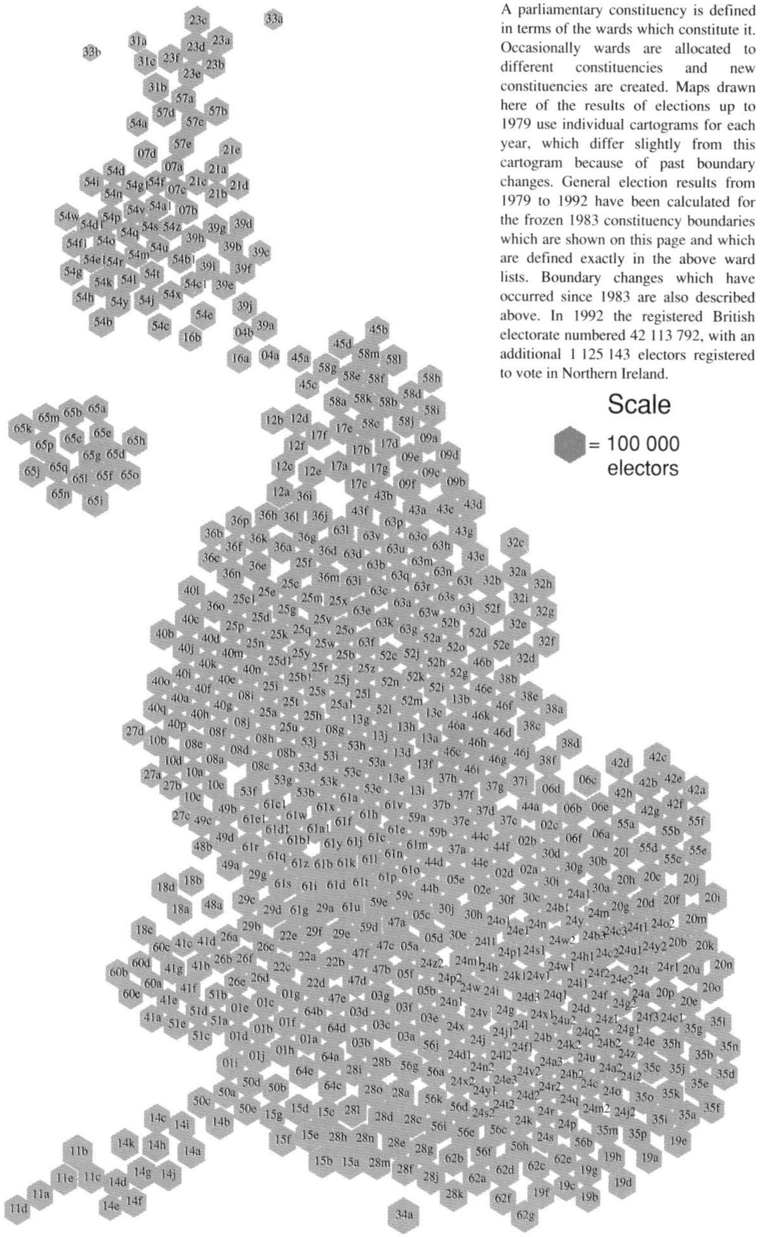

A parliamentary constituency is defined in terms of the wards which constitute it. Occasionally wards are allocated to different constituencies and new constituencies are created. Maps drawn here of the results of elections up to 1979 use individual cartograms for each year, which differ slightly from this cartogram because of past boundary changes. General election results from 1979 to 1992 have been calculated for the frozen 1983 constituency boundaries which are shown on this page and which are defined exactly in the above ward lists. Boundary changes which have occurred since 1983 are also described above. In 1992 the registered British electorate numbered 42 113 792, with an additional 1 125 143 electors registered to vote in Northern Ireland.

Looking at the Maps in the Atlas

Why the Maps Look Strange

Opposite are two pictures; Colour Print A looks familiar while Colour Print B looks strange. They both show the relationship between people and land. Colour Print A is a ward land map; a ward land map with all ward boundaries drawn and a county key is shown on page 5. On Colour Print A only the county boundaries are shown, with each ward area shaded to show its density of population. Wards are the smallest administrative areas used to elect politicians in Britain. There are ten thousand of them and an average ward now contains over 5000 people. Wards vary greatly in land area. This atlas uses boundaries which were in place in 1981, but statistics taken from different times.

The population density of a ward is the number of people living in that ward divided by its land area. The key shows that in Britain this ranges from under 1 to over 10 000 people per square kilometre. It is easy to see on the map the areas where the density of population is low, but there is a problem with areas of high density. The wards are often too small to see on a map of this size. This is a problem if it is people which are of interest because a great many people live in those wards. Half the people of Britain live on only 3% of the land shown in Colour Print A.

Colour Print B is a ward population cartogram where each ward is shown as a circle of size in proportion to its population. The cartogram would be of little use if most of these circles overlapped, so in making the cartogram a map is first drawn with circles so small that none overlap and all these circles are placed at the centres of wards on a land map. The circles are then allowed to expand slowly, and if they touch they push each other out of the way. The shape of the map becomes distorted, but it is still possible to draw county boundaries, districts, towns and villages upon it. On Colour Print B the county boundaries are again drawn and there is a key to these boundaries on page 5.

On Colour Print B each ward is shaded to show the density of population, as in Colour Print A. It uses the same key with the same colours. The separate coloured bars on the key are drawn differing lengths to show what proportion of each picture is shaded each colour — the percentage is given at the end of each bar. Colour Print A shows that most of the country has few people living in it. Colour Print B shows that most of the people live in places where many other people live. Both of these facts are true, but the first focuses on the land and the second focuses on the people. This atlas is concerned with people and so cartograms are used throughout. This is because population cartograms give prominence to people depending not on how much land they occupy, but on their numbers. Each of the eight colour prints which follow refers to the page on which it is described. All the other maps and cartograms in this atlas are described in the text on the page facing them.

Other Cartograms in the Atlas

On page xxx is a population cartogram of the 459 1981 British local authority districts. It is possible to identify each one because each has a number giving its county and a capital letter code showing which district it is (within that county on the accompanying list). Districts vary greatly in population. Like the ward cartograms in this atlas, every area is proportional to the size of its population. The district cartogram is used repeatedly in the atlas, partly because many of these cartograms can be placed on one page. For instance, it is used to show where people born in different parts of the world live in Britain on page 55 by drawing a cartogram for each group and to show how levels of unemployment changed over sixteen years using fifteen cartograms on page 97.

Opposite the key to the district cartogram is a key to the 633 1983 British parliamentary constituencies (and the 17 constituencies in Northern Ireland). On each constituency is a number giving the county and a lower-case letter code used to identify the constituency on the accompanying list. The constituency cartogram is used to show general election statistics. Hexagons are used in place of circles to make these cartograms stand out as they are based on the number of people registered to vote in each area rather than on the number of people living there. The constituency level results of the last eleven general elections are shown on page 229 and illustrate how much detail can be included when using small cartograms of these relatively large areas.

Finding an Area on the Ward Cartogram

The index map which includes the county of interest has first to be located from the six subdivisions of the country shown on the previous pages. In each ward circle a capital letter identifies its district, a lower case letter identifies its constituency and a number identifies its name on the list opposite for its county. To locate a named ward, find its name on the ward list for the county and read its full code. The capital letter district and lower-case constituency codes can be used to find districts and constituencies as well as to home in on the part of the county containing the ward, before identifying its particular numbered circle. Parts of the population of some new wards have been assigned to two or three different 1981 wards on these cartograms, but the ward indexes list all the parts (and details of the wards which changed district in the 1980s are given on page xx).

Although it is possible to use cartograms to identify individual statistics, they are not designed for that. Instead they provide a visual overview of a detailed spatial distribution. For example, Colour Print A shows that most of the country is countryside, but Colour Print B shows that the experience of most people is not to be living in the countryside. This atlas is about people's lives viewed from a human perspective.

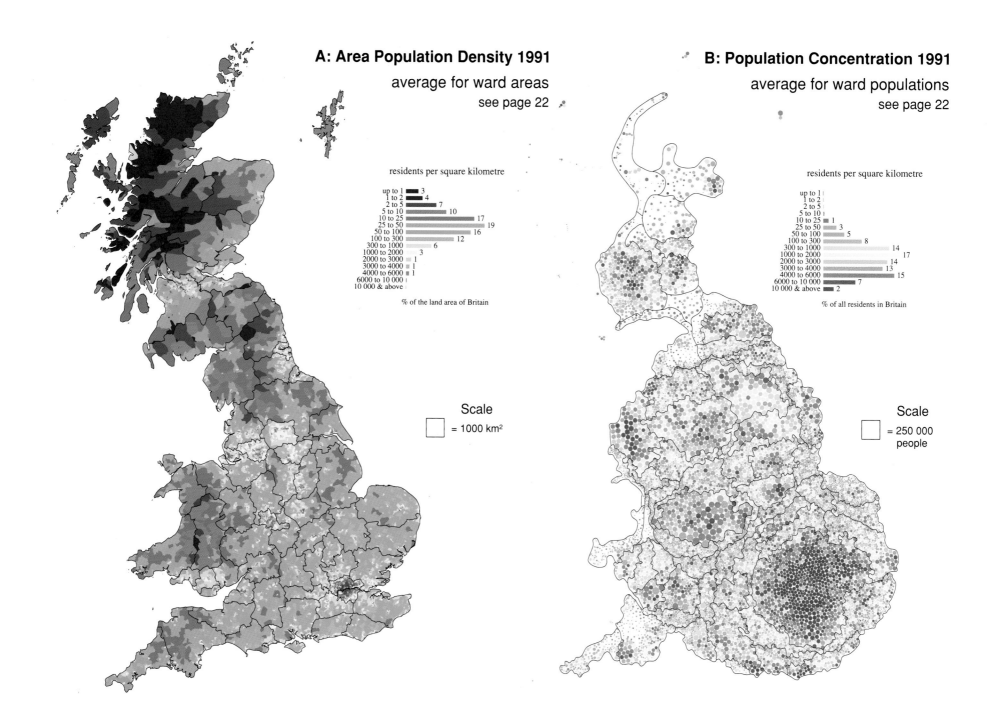

A: Area Population Density 1991

average for ward areas

see page 22

residents per square kilometre

up to 1	3
1 to 2	4
2 to 5	7
5 to 10	10
10 to 25	17
25 to 50	19
50 to 100	16
100 to 300	12
300 to 1000	6
1000 to 2000	3
2000 to 3000	1
3000 to 4000	1
4000 to 6000	1
6000 to 10 000	
10 000 & above	

% of the land area of Britain

Scale

☐ = 1000 km²

B: Population Concentration 1991

average for ward populations

see page 22

residents per square kilometre

up to 1	
1 to 2	
2 to 5	
5 to 10	
10 to 25	1
25 to 50	3
50 to 100	5
100 to 300	8
300 to 1000	14
1000 to 2000	17
2000 to 3000	14
3000 to 4000	13
4000 to 6000	15
6000 to 10 000	7
10 000 & above	2

% of all residents in Britain

Scale

☐ = 250 000 people

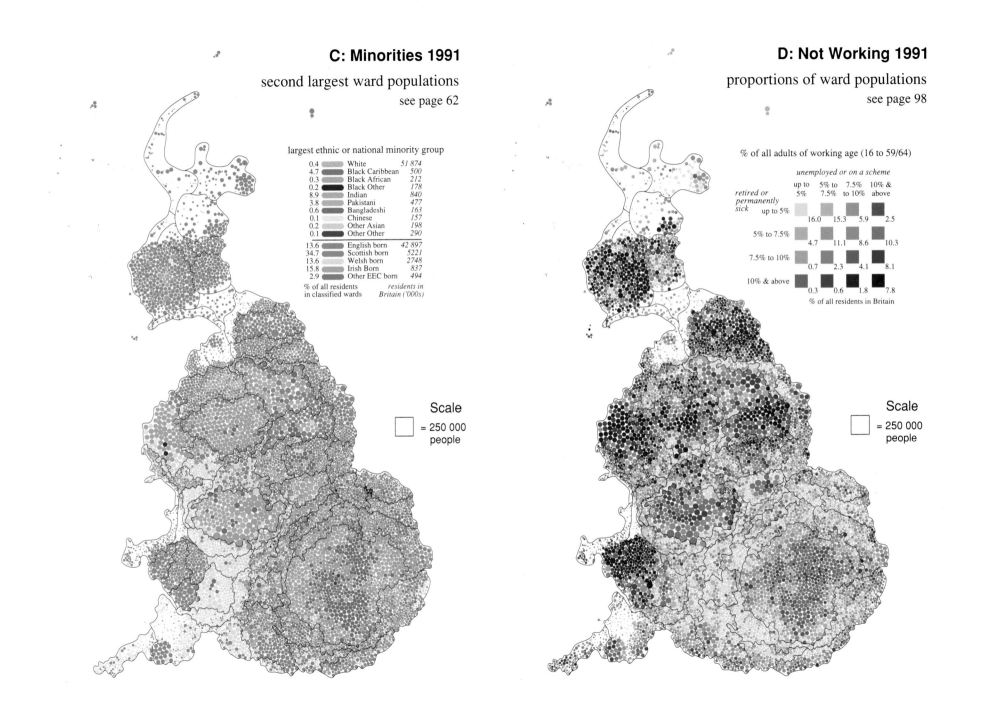

C: Minorities 1991

second largest ward populations

see page 62

largest ethnic or national minority group

0.4	White	*51 874*
4.7	Black Caribbean	*500*
0.3	Black African	*212*
0.2	Black Other	*178*
8.9	Indian	*840*
3.8	Pakistani	*477*
0.6	Bangladeshi	*163*
0.1	Chinese	*157*
0.2	Other Asian	*198*
0.1	Other Other	*290*
13.6	English born	*42 897*
34.7	Scottish born	*5221*
13.6	Welsh born	*2748*
15.8	Irish Born	*837*
2.9	Other EEC born	*494*

% of all residents   *residents in*
in classified wards   *Britain ('000s)*

Scale

☐ = 250 000
people

D: Not Working 1991

proportions of ward populations

see page 98

% of all adults of working age (16 to 59/64)

unemployed or on a scheme

retired or permanently sick	up to 5%	5% to 7.5%	7.5% to 10%	10% & above
up to 5%	16.0	15.3	5.9	2.5
5% to 7.5%	4.7	11.1	8.6	10.3
7.5% to 10%	0.7	2.3	4.1	8.1
10% & above	0.3	0.6	1.8	7.8

% of all residents in Britain

Scale

☐ = 250 000
people

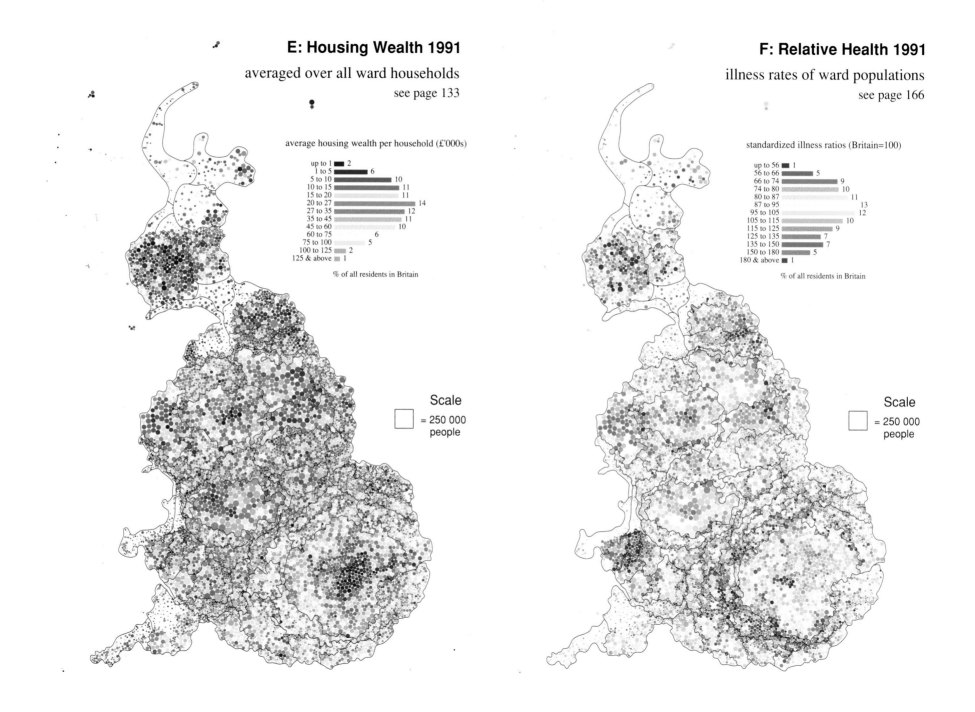

E: Housing Wealth 1991

averaged over all ward households

see page 133

average housing wealth per household (£'000s)

up to 1	2
1 to 5	6
5 to 10	10
10 to 15	11
15 to 20	11
20 to 27	14
27 to 35	12
35 to 45	11
45 to 60	10
60 to 75	6
75 to 100	5
100 to 125	2
125 & above	1

% of all residents in Britain

Scale

☐ = 250 000 people

F: Relative Health 1991

illness rates of ward populations

see page 166

standardized illness ratios (Britain=100)

up to 56	1
56 to 66	5
66 to 74	9
74 to 80	10
80 to 87	11
87 to 95	13
95 to 105	12
105 to 115	10
115 to 125	9
125 to 135	7
135 to 150	7
150 to 180	5
180 & above	1

% of all residents in Britain

Scale

☐ = 250 000 people

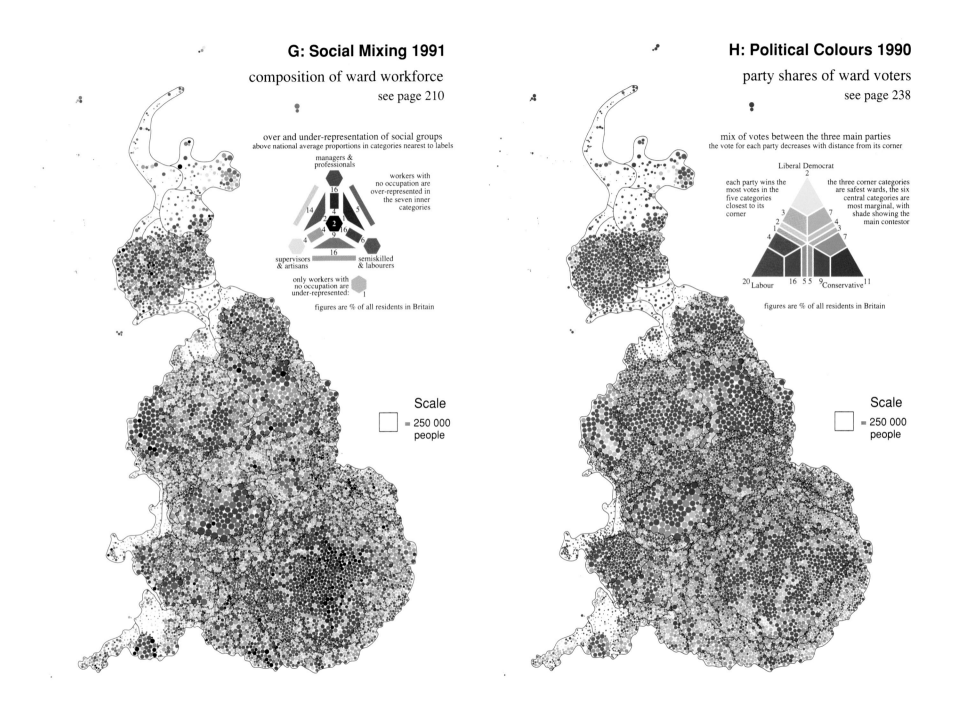

G: Social Mixing 1991

composition of ward workforce

see page 210

over and under-representation of social groups
above national average proportions in categories nearest to labels

managers &
professionals

workers with
no occupation are
over-represented in
the seven inner
categories

14   4   5
2   1
4   16
4   9   6
16

supervisors
& artisans

semiskilled
& labourers

only workers with
no occupation are
under-represented: 1

figures are % of all residents in Britain

Scale

☐ = 250 000
people

H: Political Colours 1990

party shares of ward voters

see page 238

mix of votes between the three main parties
the vote for each party decreases with distance from its corner

Liberal Democrat

each party wins the
most votes in the
five categories
closest to its
corner

the three corner categories
are safest wards, the six
central categories are
most marginal, with
shade showing the
main contestor

3   7
2   4
1   3
4   7

20 Labour   16   5 5   9 Conservative 11

figures are % of all residents in Britain

Scale

☐ = 250 000
people

Selected Districts on the Ward Cartogram

one area shown in each county and Scottish Region

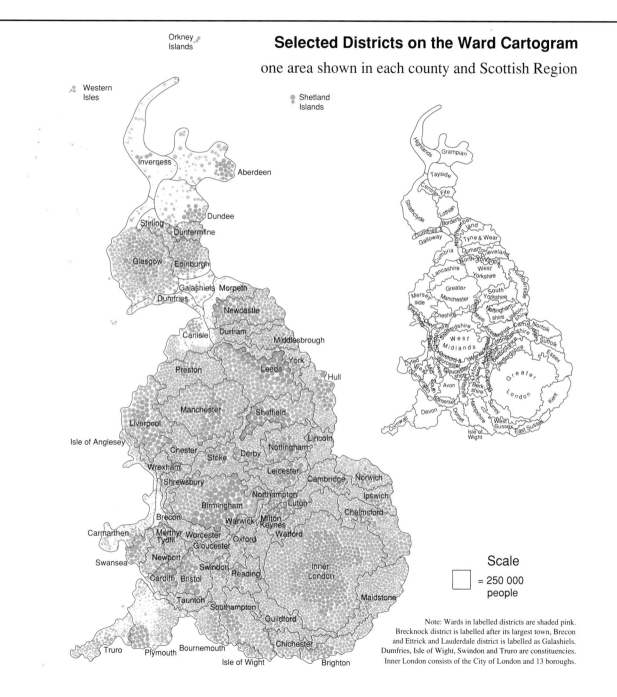

Orkney Islands

Western Isles

Shetland Islands

Inverness

Aberdeen

Dundee

Stirling

Dunfermline

Glasgow

Edinburgh

Galashiels Morpeth

Dumfries

Newcastle

Carlisle Durham

Middlesbrough

Preston

Leeds

York

Hull

Manchester

Sheffield

Liverpool

Lincoln

Isle of Anglesey

Chester

Stoke Derby

Nottingham

Wrexham

Leicester

Shrewsbury

Cambridge

Norwich

Northampton

Ipswich

Birmingham

Luton

Brecon

Warwick Milton Keynes

Chelmsford

Carmarthen

Merthyr Tydfil Worcester

Watford

Swansea

Gloucester Oxford

Newport

Swindon Reading

Inner London

Cardiff Bristol

Taunton

Maidstone

Southampton

Guildford

Truro Plymouth Bournemouth

Chichester

Isle of Wight Brighton

Highlands Grampian

Tayside

Central Fife

Strathclyde Lothian

Borders

Dumfries & Galloway Northumberland

Cumbria Tyne & Wear

Durham Cleveland

Lancashire North Yorkshire

West Yorkshire Humberside

Merseyside Greater Manchester South Yorkshire

Cheshire Nottinghamshire Lincolnshire

Derbyshire Norfolk

Gwynedd Clwyd Staffordshire Leicestershire Cambridgeshire Suffolk

West Midlands Warwickshire Northamptonshire Bedfordshire Essex

Hereford & Worcester Gloucestershire Oxfordshire Buckinghamshire Hertfordshire

Dyfed Gwent Greater London

West Glamorgan South Glamorgan Avon Wiltshire Berkshire Surrey Kent

Somerset Hampshire West Sussex East Sussex

Cornwall Devon Dorset Isle of Wight

Scale

☐ = 250 000 people

Note: Wards in labelled districts are shaded pink.
Brecknock district is labelled after its largest town, Brecon
and Ettrick and Lauderdale district is labelled as Galashiels.
Dumfries, Isle of Wight, Swindon and Truro are constituencies.
Inner London consists of the City of London and 13 boroughs.

1: Population

The subject of this atlas is the population of Great Britain. Although this may appear a simple concept, saying precisely who is living in this country at any one time and where they are, let alone determining how that pattern is changing, is not necessarily easy. This chapter lays the foundation for the rest of the atlas by defining those who constitute British society, where they are and how their numbers have been changing.

The boundary of Great Britain delimits the population studied for statistical and geographical convenience. *Britain* is used to refer to England, Scotland and Wales, and therefore excludes the populations of Northern Ireland, the Isle of Man and the Channel Islands. It is difficult to collate comparable information for these areas. This is because data from the decennial censuses and other official statistics are used in the maps drawn here, and these data do not cover the United Kingdom in a uniform fashion.

To compare the population of a place over time it is necessary that the boundaries of that place do not alter, and if these boundaries have been constrained not to alter they are termed *frozen*. For most of the maps which follow, Britain is divided geographically into 9289 frozen local government wards in England and Wales and 1155 part postcode sectors in Scotland. These were the areas used for the 1981 census. *Wards* is used as shorthand for these areas even though they have changed in some parts of the country and differ from local government wards in Scotland. Small area statistics from the 1971 and 1991 censuses have been recalculated for these boundaries so that reliable comparisons of population change can be made over time (Atkins *et al.* 1993). The 459 frozen local government districts are also used as a geographical base in some maps.

The boundaries of both these sets of areas have their own geography which is shown in this chapter. These boundaries are again chosen for convenience rather than designed. The choice of boundaries and map projection can affect the patterns shown as much as the characteristics of the population being studied. However, where a number of contiguous areas show similar characteristics, that impression is unlikely to be an artefact of the boundaries. This is one reason why the detailed geography of wards is used so often in these maps, because such small places provide the greatest flexibility for producing robust patterns from contiguous areas showing similar characteristics.

The populations of larger or smaller wards, both in terms of land and people, have followed particularly distinctive changes over time. Ward size also tends to correlate strongly with land use, which is shown here in conjunction with population density, the most basic statistic to be calculated from a census.

This chapter begins with traditional equal area maps of Britain to show the distributions of people over the land and then progresses to equal population cartograms to show how that population is made up and how it is changing. The two types of projection are placed side by side in many of the prints so that the different impressions given can be compared and a feeling gained for how the use of cartograms alters the visual impression, even when the places depicted and their shading are identical.

The censuses are by far the most important source of geographically disaggregated social information on Britain; but even censuses can miss people. It is possible only to estimate from where people were missed, but the distribution of where people are difficult to contact for enumeration can be shown. Censuses also classify people in different ways depending on whether they were enumerated in their home or elsewhere. The characteristics of the population on census night who were not residents at a private address which was their usual home — visitors or the residents of communal establishments — are also often omitted from local statistics, so their geographical distributions and social characteristics are also presented here as the experiences of these groups cannot be included in most of the maps which appear later in this atlas.

The precise definition of the population being considered is important when changes in the size of population in different places are being compared over time. If the raw census figures are used the total resident population of Britain appears to have fallen in the 1980s by over half a million people. This was due to problems with data collection. In fact, the number of people living in Britain on census night is thought to have actually increased by one and a third million people between 1981 and 1991. The definition of the population employed in defining statistics makes as crucial a difference to the maps produced, as does the choice of boundaries and map projection.

Three aspects of change and three population definitions are used by the end of the chapter. The *population present* on census night is presented, as is the geography of its changes over the course of this century in local authority districts (with their boundaries frozen). The change in the numbers of people *usually resident* in wards between the 1971, 1981 and 1991 censuses is then depicted. Finally, the annual changes from 1981 to 1990 in the official *mid-year estimates* of the population of each district are shown. All these definitions count the night-time (or more correctly the bedtime) population in every place — where people are sleeping. Daytime population can be very different from the night-time count so it is important to realise which areas people are allocated to. The most extreme example of this daily oscillation is found in central London.

First, however, the geographical distribution of where people currently live in Britain is presented, both in its raw form and then using two more sophisticated mapping techniques. To understand the more subtle social characteristics of the population it is necessary first to know what that population is and where it is located. To comprehend changes in the social make-up of the population, changes in the geographical distribution of that population must be taken into account.

1.1: Equal Population Grid Squares

Each black "square" contains 30 000
people, each red "square" contains up
to 3 million people (100 black "squares").

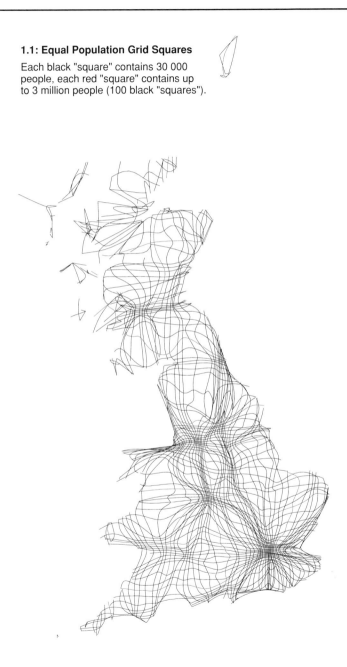

Distribution

The most basic distribution for any social atlas is of the population over the land. 55 889 000 people were identified as being present in the 151 700 enumeration districts and output areas of the 1991 census. Each of these areas is drawn as a dot on the map of population distribution shown opposite with county boundaries superimposed. Local features are apparent even at this scale, such as the unpopulated Lea Valley which splits north London in two. From this image, however, it is difficult to gain an overview of how concentrated the population is in different places and how concentrated it is overall. Most of the map is coloured white, showing where people do not live. The total area covered by black is less than the size of a one penny piece.

To understand the implications of population distribution it is useful to calculate a statistic such as population potential (Clarke 1987: 38) and use that to shade a map. The *population potential* of a ward is the total of the populations of all the other wards in Britain each divided by their distance from the centre of that ward. This is expressed in the rather abstract units of "residents per metre" which is highest at 1152 in Bayswater ward in the City of Westminster and lowest at 67 in postcode sector ZE2 9 in the Shetland islands. In the map each ward is classified into one of five groups which each contain a fifth of the total resident population of Britain.

Only Greater London and the centres of the West Midlands and Greater Manchester fall in the highest quintile. The next quintile covers the hinterlands of these three centres, much of Merseyside, West Yorkshire, South Yorkshire, Chesterfield, Stoke-on-Trent, Derby, Nottingham and Leicester. The third quintile fills in the gaps between these places completing the belt from London to Liverpool within which over half the people of Britain live — the half who are closest to each other. Tyne & Wear, Cleveland and Glasgow are the only areas in the North of England and Scotland not shown in the bottom quintile.

What both maps also highlight is how little land the majority of the population occupy. In the next few pages the relationship between the people and the land is explored. Here an alternative method is used to show another way of looking at the basic distribution of people across the land. In Figure 1.1 almost 2000 "squares" cover the land area of Britain in a grid. The lines of this grid are curved so that each "square" contains the same number of people (Dorling 1993). Large cities pull the net inwards. Smaller ones, such as Norwich, can also be seen to have an effect. When the lines of the grid are pulled straight the map of Britain is transformed to form an equal population cartogram. Curved, as they are here, they give a graphical impression of the relative influence of the populations of different areas over the surface of the land.

Note that in Figure 1.1 the Shetland Islands are shown in their true position. On the far map opposite (and in all the other maps in this atlas) they have been moved southwards.

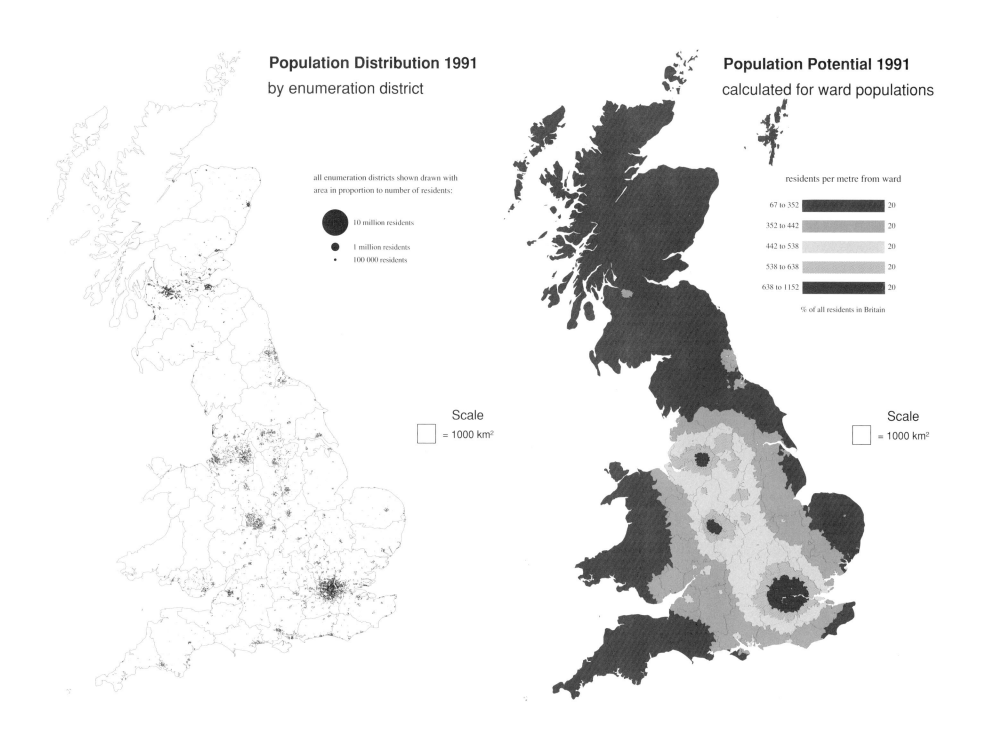

Population Distribution 1991

by enumeration district

all enumeration districts shown drawn with
area in proportion to number of residents:

10 million residents

1 million residents

100 000 residents

Scale

☐ = 1000 km²

Population Potential 1991

calculated for ward populations

residents per metre from ward

67 to 352	20
352 to 442	20
442 to 538	20
538 to 638	20
638 to 1152	20

% of all residents in Britain

Scale

☐ = 1000 km²

Boundaries

Maps are about boundaries. Many maps do not show the boundaries which are used in their creation but all maps present spatial boundaries of one form or another. In this atlas administrative boundaries are used to create the maps, and then the boundaries between areas with different levels of a variable are depicted. If the boundaries of too many areas are shown then parts of the map always appear black from the concentration of lines, as can be seen opposite. To avoid this only county boundaries are shown on subsequent ward equal area maps and population cartograms. These lines are included to provide a visual key to the areas.

The pattern of the boundaries is in itself interesting. As wards are designed for electing local councillors, they vary little in population within the same district. Because of this they tend to vary greatly in area. On the equal land area map, cities and market towns can be identified in England and Wales just from the dense clustering of their wards. In Scotland the boundaries were designed simply for the convenience of the Post Office (being part postcode sectors) and so vary more in population. The variations in population size and land area across all these small parts of Britain are shown in Figures 1.2 and 1.3.

On the ward cartogram "no man's lands" are to be found in the least populated places where the algorithm which reprojected the map did not pull such sparsely settled wards together. The three Island Areas have been individually identified. Shetland on the cartogram is displaced similarly to the equal area map. Small islands which are parts of other administrative areas are not shown here. What is most evident (from the boundaries on the cartogram) is how much larger are urban wards, in terms of people, than rural wards. Rural wards tend to be much larger in physical area and, as Figure 1.4 shows, it is these wards which have been growing most in population over the last twenty years.

The 64 counties and Scottish regions are labelled in the two insets to provide a key for the maps. Far more detailed keys are given at the start of this atlas to all the cartograms used. The detailed keys also describe how administrative and political boundaries changed in Britain over the last decade and how those changes are dealt with here. The only boundaries which have hardly been altered at all have been county boundaries. On the cartogram opposite the county boundaries allow the relative populations of these large areas to be crudely compared. The shape of Britain when drawn like this is also enlightening. London dominates the country surrounded by the Home Counties which are wrapped tightly around it. The large conurbations of the North West and Yorkshire, centred on Manchester, counter-balance London to an extent, while sandwiched between the two is Birmingham in the centre of the West Midlands. All other places are attached around this central belt. Wales is split north and south while Scotland is only held onto England by a thread of wards across the Borders.

1.2: Residents by Ward Population 1991

% of all residents in Britain

1.3: Residents by Ward Area 1991

% of all residents in Britain

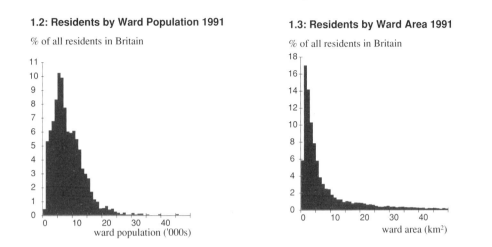

1.4: Population Resident Change 1981–1991 and 1971–1981

% change in the number of residents by ward in Britain

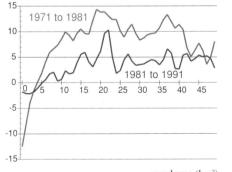

ward area (km²)

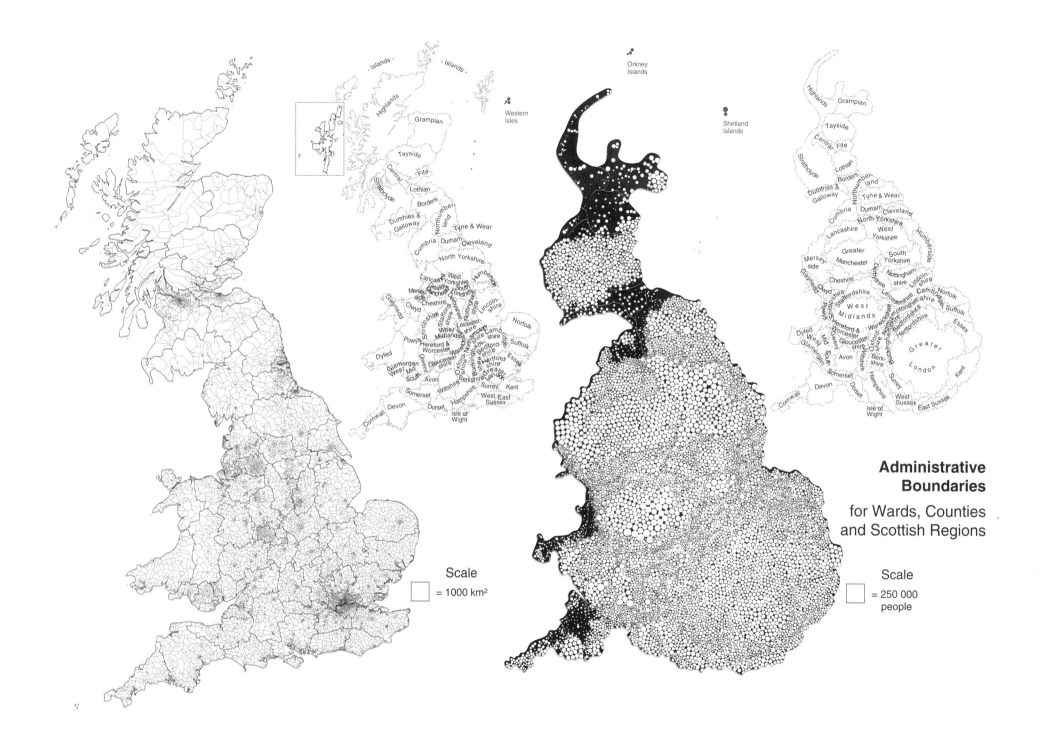

**Administrative
Boundaries**

for Wards, Counties
and Scottish Regions

Scale

☐ = 1000 km²

Scale

☐ = 250 000
people

Map labels (counties and Scottish regions):

Orkney Islands, Shetland Islands, Western Isles, Highlands, Grampian, Tayside, Central, Fife, Lothian, Strathclyde, Borders, Dumfries & Galloway, Northumberland, Tyne & Wear, Cumbria, Durham, Cleveland, North Yorkshire, Lancashire, West Yorkshire, Humberside, Merseyside, Greater Manchester, South Yorkshire, Cheshire, Nottinghamshire, Lincolnshire, Gwynedd, Clwyd, Derbyshire, Staffordshire, Shropshire, Leicestershire, West Midlands, Norfolk, Powys, Hereford & Worcester, Warwickshire, Northamptonshire, Cambridgeshire, Suffolk, Dyfed, Gloucestershire, Oxfordshire, Buckinghamshire, Bedfordshire, Essex, Glamorgan West, Mid Glamorgan, South Glamorgan, Gwent, Avon, Wiltshire, Berkshire, Hertfordshire, Greater London, Kent, Somerset, Hampshire, Surrey, West Sussex, East Sussex, Devon, Dorset, Isle of Wight, Cornwall

1.5: Ward Population by Area Shaded by Land Use Classification

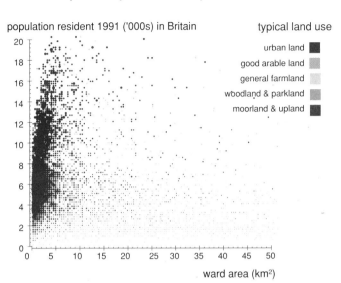

population resident 1991 ('000s) in Britain

typical land use

urban land ■
good arable land ▨
general farmland ▨
woodland & parkland ▨
moorland & upland ▨

ward area (km²)

1.6: Population Change by Land Use Classification 1971–1991

residents in wards in 1991 ('000s) in Britain

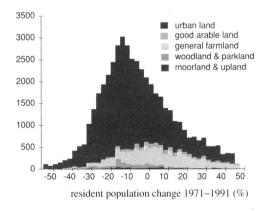

■ urban land
▨ good arable land
▨ general farmland
▨ woodland & parkland
■ moorland & upland

resident population change 1971–1991 (%)

Land Use

The most widely used classification by which the population of Britain is divided is "urban and rural". It is also one of the worst defined. As these two terms are used repeatedly elsewhere in this atlas, an attempt is made here to define which areas are which. This divide is also used to describe the basic population distribution just outlined, and the distribution of population density covered next.

All the one kilometre grid squares of Britain can be classified by land use using remote sensing (Carver 1990). Here each ward is assigned to one of six aggregations of these land use classes on the basis of the activity in its most central grid-square. Almost exactly half the land area of Britain is categorised as general farmland by this method. Only one in six people (17%) live on that land. As the cartogram makes abundantly clear, three quarters of all the residents of Britain live in wards which are classified as urban, although these only cover 14% of the land. Both the map and the cartogram show how county boundaries tend to follow farmland.

Agricultural land varies in quality so one subgroup has been extracted here — good arable land. In many countries it was the initial distribution of the best farmland which influenced many later developments, and Britain is no exception. The best agricultural land is to be found predominantly around the lowlands of the rivers Humber, Severn and the Ouse, in Kent and amid the claylands of East Anglia. This land is also more densely populated than farmland in general.

The land which contains the least people per hectare is moorland and upland. Together with the "other" category this constitutes one fifth of the land area of Britain but houses only 1% of the population. The "other" category includes wards with large lakes in their centres and other such oddities. The final category of land shown here is woodland and parkland. More than two dozen wards in London, as the cartogram shows, fall into this group when classified using remote sensing techniques.

Land use and ward area are closely related as Figure 1.5 illustrates. Urban wards tend to be high in population and low in area; the converse is true for rural wards. However, the divide between the two is not sharp. Rural wards are also more likely to have seen population growth over the last twenty years. Figure 1.6 shows the twenty year trend. The modal point for urban wards is a fall of 8% to 10% of their population over twenty years (2.5 million people live in wards which have experienced this). For the two agricultural categories combined the modal point is a rise of 8% to 10% over twenty years in areas where over half a million people now live. The distribution for woodland and parkland is bimodal but the median change is a fall of 7%, while for moorland and upland areas the population change has, on average, been static. However, these statistics hide a great deal of variation as is illustrated in Figure 1.6 which depicts most clearly the width of the range of population changes which have occurred on each type of land.

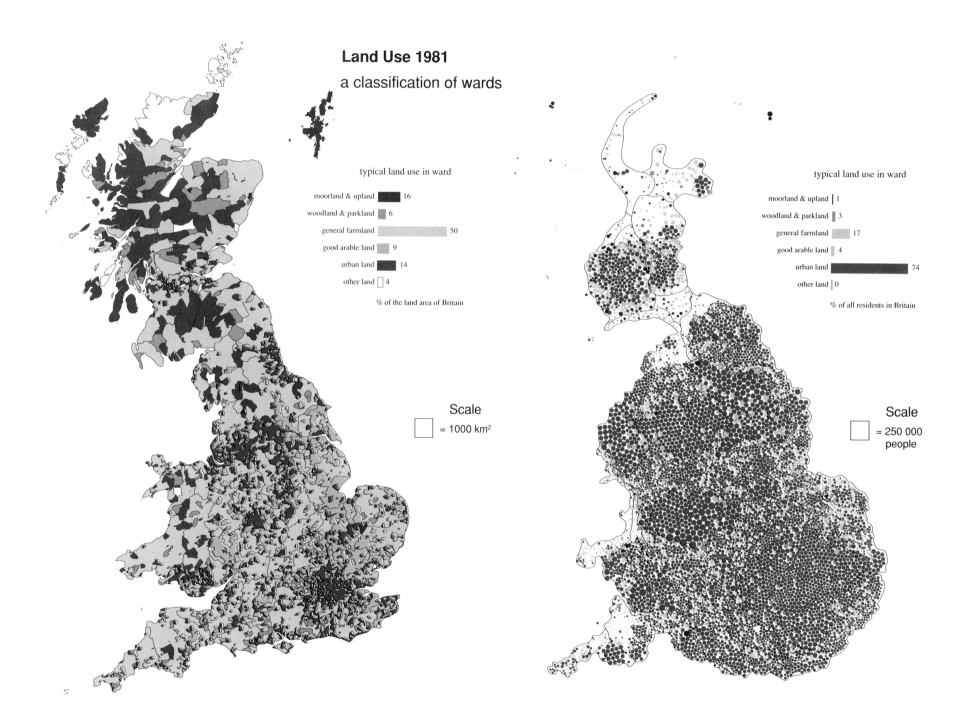

Land Use 1981

a classification of wards

typical land use in ward

moorland & upland	16
woodland & parkland	6
general farmland	50
good arable land	9
urban land	14
other land	4

% of the land area of Britain

Scale

= 1000 km²

typical land use in ward

moorland & upland	1
woodland & parkland	3
general farmland	17
good arable land	4
urban land	74
other land	0

% of all residents in Britain

Scale

= 250 000 people

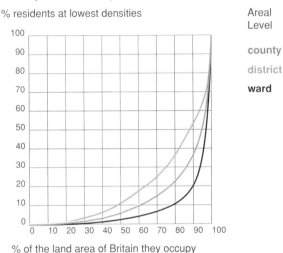

% residents at lowest densities

Areal Level

county

district

ward

% of the land area of Britain they occupy

1.8: Population Density Change 1981–1991 and 1971–1981

absolute change in the number of residents in Britain by ward ('000s)

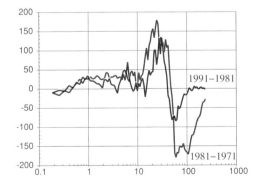

1991–1981

1981–1971

residents per hectare (log scale, using 100 divisions)

Density

Ten percent of the people live on eighty percent of the land — true? It depends on the areas you use to count the people. This is the basic problem with population density (Craig 1985). The *population density* of a place is simply its population divided by its area. For all of Britain in 1991 this was 245 people per km^2. The median population density for all wards, however, is 1775 residents per km^2, while 15% of the population live at ward densities of more than 5000 residents per km^2 (on only 0.5% of the land).

The map and cartogram opposite show the detailed distribution of population density. Although the density of individual wards depends as much on how the boundaries are drawn as on how many people live there, where a group of contiguous wards have similar densities the pattern is likely to be more robust. The largest cluster of wards of the highest density is in Inner London, the next largest is in Liverpool, both ends of the belt of high population potential. This map and cartogram can be compared to Colour Prints A and B respectively.

Inside cities the areas of low density often coincide with the places where the most affluent people live. These can be identified from the cartogram. Elsewhere the rings of very low densities, which on the cartogram circle the conurbations and on the map dominate the image, are also interesting. The large clusters of low density wards (in terms of population and hence area on the cartogram) are to be found around Norwich in Norfolk, in Lincolnshire and in North Wales. Here are where the largest expanses of people living at low densities in Britain are to be found.

So do just 10% of the people live on 80% of the land? The answer is yes, but only if wards are used to calculate this. Figure 1.7 contains three Gini curves (Lorenz 1905) which show how much land the groups of people living at the lowest densities live on. It illustrates that if the same statistics were calculated for the populations of counties, they would show that the 10% of the people who were least densely concentrated lived on just 50% of the land. For districts, that figure rises to 60%. For wards the figure rises again to 80%. If the curve were calculated using any areas taken from a cartogram a straight line would be the result. On the cartogram everybody is, in this sense, equal.

What is required to produce an unequivocal answer to the question first posed is an unambiguous set of areas — the land areas which people actually own or lease. Unfortunately, the spatial boundaries of these areas are not generally available. What they might well have shown, if they were digitised, is the gradual redistribution of land indicated by Figure 1.8, as the most dense areas have declined in population and the least dense have risen (in absolute terms as shown here, and even more so relatively). However, this process of counterurbanisation (Champion 1989) is slowing down. Precisely where and when this occurred is of great interest, and is a subject dealt with later in this chapter.

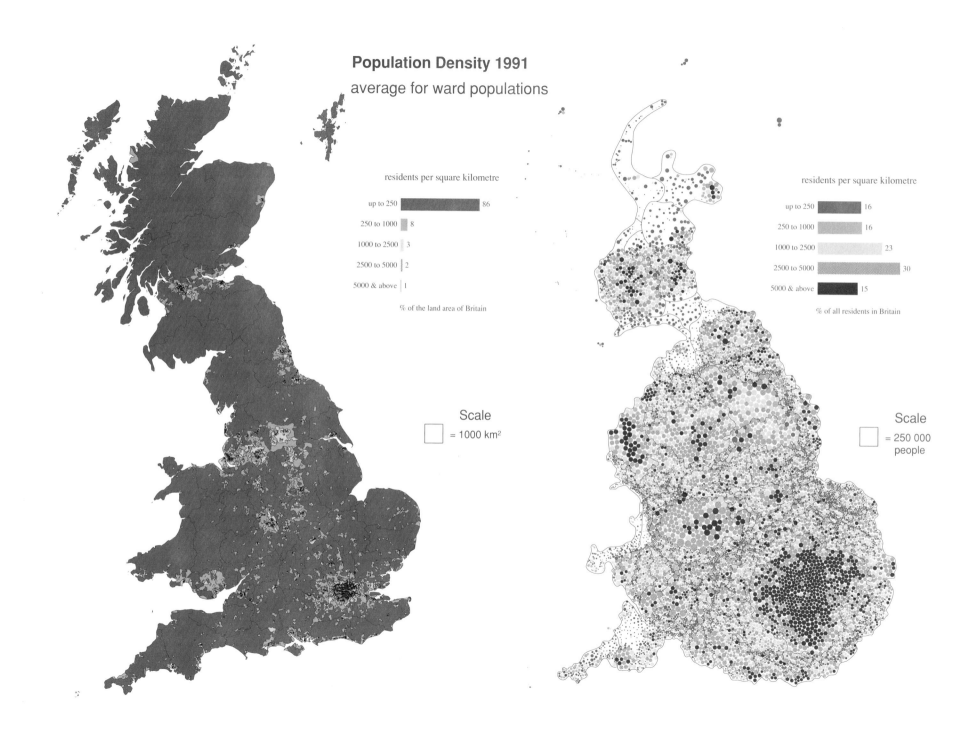

Population Density 1991
average for ward populations

residents per square kilometre

up to 250	86
250 to 1000	8
1000 to 2500	3
2500 to 5000	2
5000 & above	1

% of the land area of Britain

residents per square kilometre

up to 250	16
250 to 1000	16
1000 to 2500	23
2500 to 5000	30
5000 & above	15

% of all residents in Britain

Scale

= 1000 km²

Scale

= 250 000 people

1.9: Residents Imputed and Population Density in Britain 1991

% residents imputed in each ward

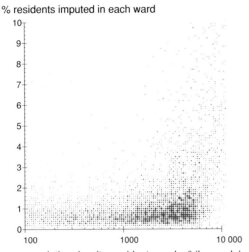

population density: residents per km² (log scale)

1.10: OPCS 1991 Census Under-enumeration Rates in England and Wales

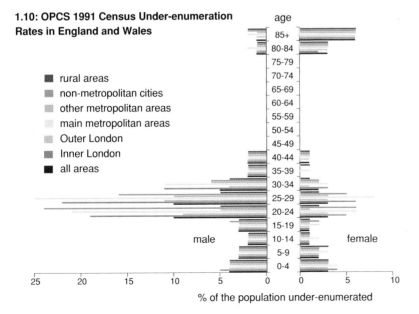

- rural areas
- non-metropolitan cities
- other metropolitan areas
- main metropolitan areas
- Outer London
- Inner London
- all areas

% of the population under-enumerated

Imputation

The 1991 census was the first British census in which some people were imputed. Where the census enumerator thought a household was absent, and a census form was left but not completed, values estimated by the enumerator were used to impute the residents of that household. *Imputation* was achieved for wholly absent households by duplicating the characteristics of the last household input which lived in similar accommodation (OPCS 1992: 5). Nationwide 450 000 households within which 870 000 people were thought to be living were imputed (1.6%). The fabricated characteristics of these people are contained in all the maps shown here which are based on the 1991 census small area statistics.

Fortunately, the proportion of households which were imputed (2.1%) is low enough to have only a marginal effect on the bias of the census sample. However, it is useful to know the geographical distribution of places where people are unwilling to answer the door or to return forms, or where they tend not to be at home. The cartogram emphasises large concentrations of more than one in twenty residents imputed in some urban areas although, as Figure 1.9 shows, the rise with population density is not uniform. The map over-emphasises high rates of imputation in a few rural wards with very low populations.

Unfortunately, the imputation procedure failed to compensate fully for all the people and households which were not enumerated. Nationally, 1 202 000 more people are thought to have been missed entirely by the 1991 census. This is a larger proportion of people (2.2%) than those imputed, but more importantly it is not a typical subgroup of people. Figure 1.10 gives the factors by which census users are advised to allow for under-enumeration in terms of age, sex and broad geographical area (OPCS 1994). This single diagram contains all the official information available at the time of writing on the characteristics of the "missing million" in England and Wales (see, however, page 217 for an as yet unofficial view of where they might have been living). We are told that, on average, a quarter of men aged between 25 and 29 who lived in the "main metropolitan areas" were not included in the census, but we do not know whether these young men were more likely to be out of work, to be in ethnic minorities, or were more likely to be the partners of "lone mothers", than their enumerated counterparts.

Inferences and assumptions can be made and it does appear likely that the people and households not represented in the remaining pages of this atlas tend to belong to particular social groups (Simpson *et al.* 1993). At a detailed geographical level they may follow the pattern of those who have been imputed (shown opposite). The census statistics are now a 96.4% sample of the population — fine for most purposes, although ward level mapping relies on particularly accurate data sources. In 1981, 99.6% of the people of Britain were found, although for operational reasons only 97.8% were included in the 1981 small area statistics (see Figure 1.13).

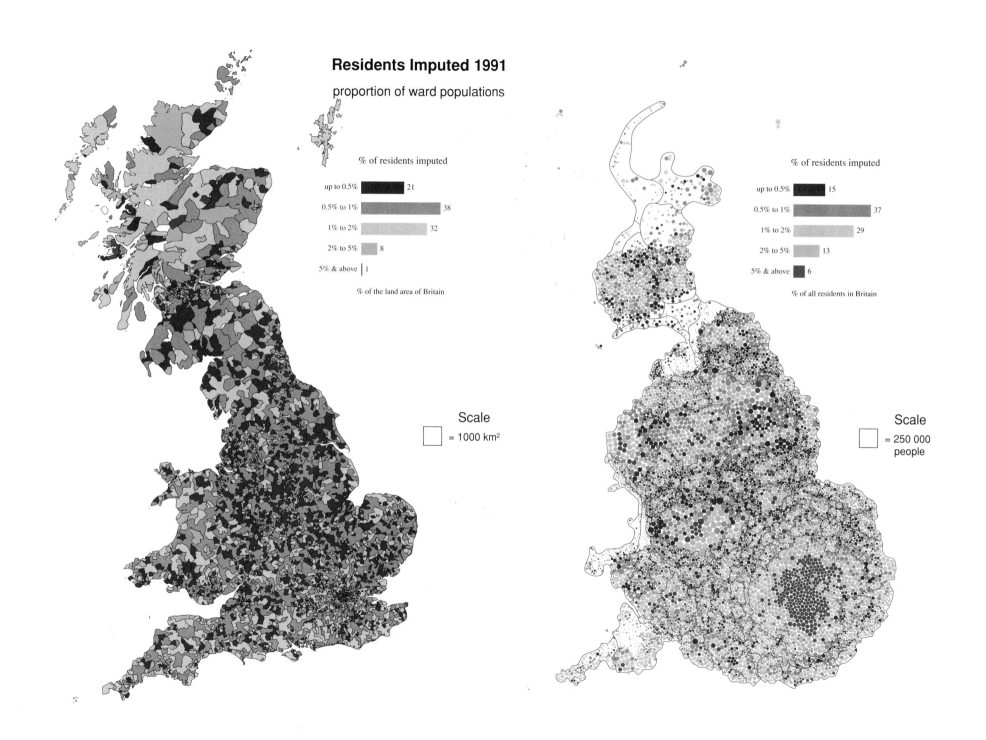

Residents Imputed 1991

proportion of ward populations

% of residents imputed

up to 0.5%		21
0.5% to 1%		38
1% to 2%		32
2% to 5%		8
5% & above		1

% of the land area of Britain

Scale

= 1000 km²

% of residents imputed

up to 0.5%		15
0.5% to 1%		37
1% to 2%		29
2% to 5%		13
5% & above		6

% of all residents in Britain

Scale

= 250 000 people

1.11: Some Characteristics of Residents Living in Communal Establishments in Britain 1991

Type of Establishment	Total	Male	Female	Children 16-44		44 -P.A.	P.A.+	White	Black Groups	South Asian	Chinese & other
All Residents in Britain	**54 888 800**	**48%**	**52%**	**20%**	**42%**	**19%**	**19%**	**95%**	**2%**	**3%**	**1%**
communal residents (non-staff)	735 700	41%	59%	3%	28%	8%	61%	95%	2%	1%	2%
residential home (private)	175 700	26%	74%	0%	7%	5%	87%	99%	0%	0%	0%
nursing home (private)	134 000	24%	76%	0%	2%	3%	95%	99%	0%	0%	0%
Local Authority home	113 600	31%	69%	1%	11%	6%	82%	99%	1%	0%	0%
hospital (NHS — other)	58 400	39%	61%	1%	36%	14%	49%	96%	2%	1%	1%
defence establishment	49 600	87%	13%	0%	98%	1%	1%	95%	2%	0%	3%
hotels and boarding houses	48 600	64%	36%	12%	62%	17%	10%	84%	8%	4%	4%
psychiatric hospital (NHS)	30 500	47%	53%	0%	19%	18%	63%	97%	2%	1%	1%
schools and colleges	26 700	61%	39%	6%	86%	4%	4%	64%	10%	5%	22%
other misc. establishments	22 600	42%	58%	11%	53%	12%	25%	90%	4%	3%	2%
Housing Association home	21 100	46%	54%	1%	34%	13%	51%	93%	4%	1%	2%
hostels and lodging houses	19 400	70%	30%	9%	54%	24%	13%	86%	8%	3%	4%
prison service establishment	15 300	96%	4%	0%	86%	13%	1%	82%	12%	4%	2%
children's home	9400	56%	44%	100%	0%	0%	0%	88%	8%	2%	3%
hospital (private — other)	4500	39%	61%	1%	28%	17%	54%	95%	3%	1%	2%
psychiatric hospital (private)	2700	51%	49%	1%	27%	19%	53%	95%	3%	1%	2%
persons sleeping rough	1900	84%	16%	0%	73%	25%	2%	98%	2%	0%	0%
ships, boats and barges	1200	85%	15%	2%	75%	22%	1%	89%	5%	1%	6%
campers	300	49%	51%	23%	41%	10%	26%	97%	0%	0%	3%

Note: percentages between bars sum to 100%; P.A. stands for Pensionable Age; see page 40 for the definitions of ethnic group categories used here.

1.12: People Living in Communal Establishments by Sex in Britain, 1971–1981–1991

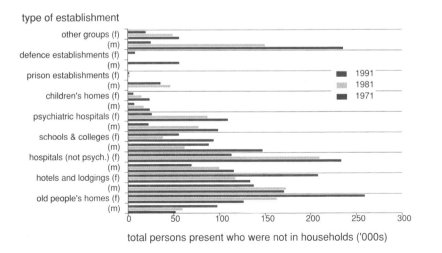

type of establishment

total persons present who were not in households ('000s)

Communal Establishments

There is a second reason, besides under-enumeration, why some British people's characteristics will not appear in the following pages of this atlas — they live in communal establishments, not households. Although these people were enumerated by the census, most of the census tables omit them as being "uncharacteristic of the general population". In total, as can be ascertained from Figure 1.11, the non-staff residents of communal establishments constitute only 1.3% of the enumerated population; the majority of these people are elderly. Apart from tending to be old and hence to include more women, there are significant ethnic minority concentrations in particular establishments. For instance, as Figure 1.11 indicates, the census shows that young black men are seven times more likely to be in prison than their white counterparts.

Prison populations are some of the most dispersed and smallest communities shown on the district based population cartograms opposite. Only in two small south coast districts do the residents of prisons number just over 1% of the total population. The residents of educational establishments reach this proportion only in the City of London, Cambridge and Oxford. The (non-staff) population in hotels exceeds the 1% level in the City, Westminster, Kensington and Chelsea. As well as highlighting these exceptional cases, the cartograms show overall geographical patterns. Nursing and residential homes are spread around the coast; psychiatric hospitals tend to be located in rural areas; other hospitals are more numerous (in terms of patients in beds) in central London and eastern Scotland (see Figure 5.12). It is defence establishments, however, that show the most concentration — among the populations of East Anglia and the South West.

Successive census counts of people in communal establishments provide a good record of how their populations have changed over time, although prisoners were not distinguished in 1971 and (some) defence establishments were admitted to exist only in 1991. Figure 1.12 shows the changing absolute populations of different types of establishment subdivided by sex. The biggest rise is of women in old people's homes, while the biggest fall is of men in unidentified establishments (due largely to the recent declassification of so many military bases). What is most probably a switch from falling boarding school numbers to rising university residence is demonstrated by this figure, as are the declines of the populations of hospitals, childrens' homes and prisons. The counts used in this figure include all people present in communal establishments, so the rise of women in hotels is due to fewer men working there as well as more women guests.

As well as people living in communal establishments the census also attempted to count travellers and campers, people sleeping rough and civilians on ships in dock. Only the last category was enumerated with any accuracy. Special "shipping" wards were created for each of the last three censuses. The total number of people present in these has fallen from 37 500 in 1971, to 11 900 in 1981 and then to 4700 in 1991.

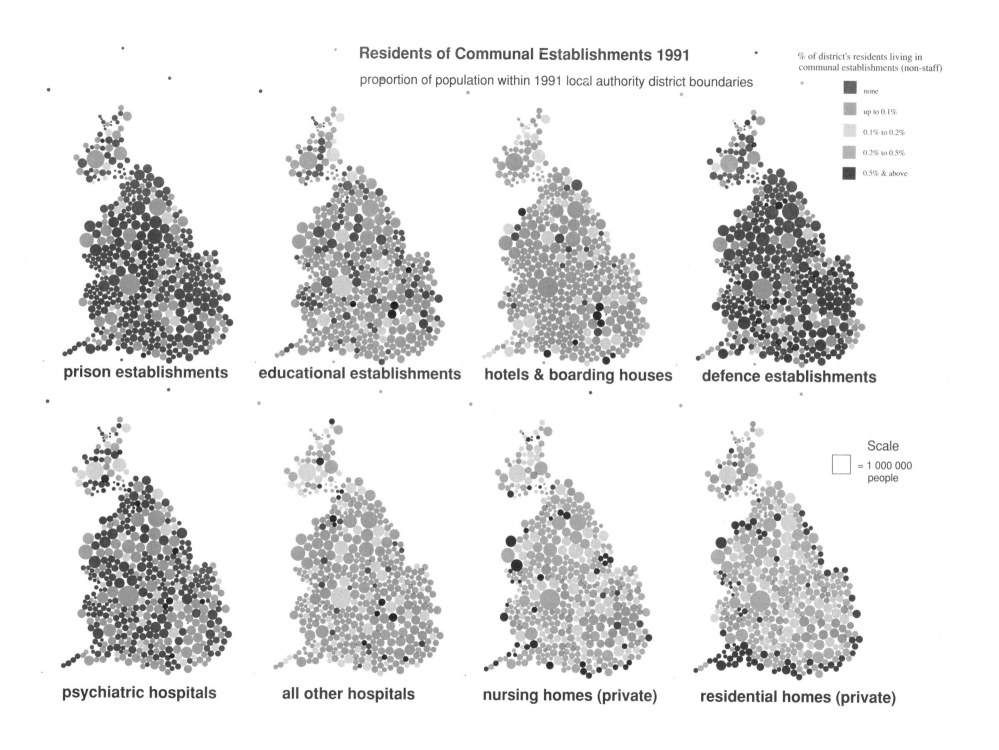

Residents of Communal Establishments 1991

proportion of population within 1991 local authority district boundaries

% of district's residents living in communal establishments (non-staff)

- none
- up to 0.1%
- 0.1% to 0.2%
- 0.2% to 0.5%
- 0.5% & above

prison establishments

educational establishments

hotels & boarding houses

defence establishments

psychiatric hospitals

all other hospitals

nursing homes (private)

residential homes (private)

Scale

☐ = 1 000 000 people

1.13: Number of People in Britain on Census Night

	1971		1981		1991	
Residents	("000s)		("000s)		("000s)	
Resident present in private households at enumeration	51 658	95.7%	52 077	94.7%	51 533	91.5%
Absent residents (part of household present)	—	—	684	1.2%	974	1.7%
Absent residents (wholly absent households)	—	—	1005[1]	1.8%	680	1.2%
Imputed residents (wholly absent households)	—	—	—	—	869[2]	1.5%
Present residents of communal establishments	909	1.7%	797	1.4%	833	1.5%
Residents (enumerated and imputed)	52 567	97.4%	54 562	99.2%	54 889	97.4%
Visitors						
Visitors resident in the United Kingdom	1257	2.3%	(1222)	(2.2%)	(1535)[3]	(2.7%)
Visitors resident outside the United Kingdom	155	0.3%	190	0.3%	255	0.5%
Total Population Present (enumerated and imputed)	53 979	100.0%	54 752	99.6%	55 144	97.9%
Under-enumeration						
Accounted for by validation survey	—	—	215	0.4%	299	0.5%
Not accounted for by validation survey	—	—	26	0.0%	899	1.6%
Total Population						
Estimated number of people in Britain on census night	53 979	100.0%	54 993	100.0%	56 342	100.0%

Source: Champion 1995, and the 1971 and 1981 Small Area Statistics files
Note 1: 1005 000 residents from wholly absent households were not in the 1981 small area statistics
Note 2: Imputed residents will include some households who were out of the country on census night
Note 3: 249 000 visitors were not included in the 1991 enumeration district small area census statistics

1.14: Age and Sex Distribution of People not Resident in Households in Britain 1991

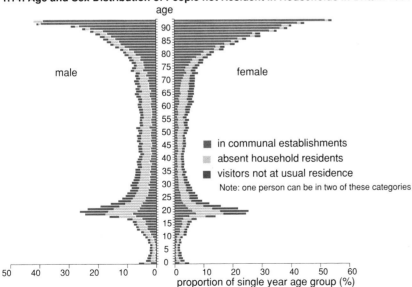

Visitors

After those who were not enumerated and the residents of communal establishments the final group of people living in Britain who are often forgotten are visitors. *Visitors* are people who are not usually resident at the address at which they are enumerated. Only 14% of all visitors have a usual residence outside the United Kingdom. However, these people have a very marked geographical distribution, as is evident opposite.

Visitors are seen as a great annoyance for census takers; some no doubt wish it were still possible to order the population to move back "home" for census night (The Bible, Luke 2:1-3). Figure 1.13 shows how visitors have been dealt with at successive censuses to try to estimate more accurately how many people usually live in each place. The figure also shows how many people were actually thought to be in Britain at the time of each census, which has increased between 1971 and 1991 even though the number of people enumerated at home each year has decreased. This is due partly to an increase in the rate of visiting, as mobility has risen overall.

Visitors are not a uniform cross section of the population, they tend to be young; in 1991 half were aged between 18 and 30. Figure 1.14, derived from the Sample of Anonymised Records, shows that when the population of communal establishments, absent residents and visitors are combined a quite dramatic age–sex profile is established (although these categories may overlap somewhat). Over half of the very old live in communal establishments, while over a quarter of 21 year-olds in the sample were not recorded as being present at their usual residence on census night.

An unusual category of visitors are those living in a household where everyone said they were a visitor. These *visitor households* were specifically identified because it was thought that they would "give an approximate measure of those in second homes..." (OPCS 1992: 24). A significant proportion of students (10%) was recorded as visitors on census night so it is perhaps not surprising that those wards with the highest proportions of people in visitor households should cluster around universities — see opposite. Indeed, one in three of these households contains only students. Some people with second homes may be classifying their "country residence" as their usual residence but this is unlikely to account for the remainder of the pattern.

Combined, the distribution of wholly absent households and imputed residents may give an indication of where the missing million are most likely to be, because these are the areas where census taking is most difficult. Unofficial estimates (page 217) have also used the distribution of unemployment (page 89) as an indicator. The rise in the proportion of the population in Britain who are overseas visitors begs the question: how many young and old people who are now thought to be in Britain are actually overseas visitors elsewhere? As national and international mobility increases, the traditional methods of enumerating the population become increasingly inadequate.

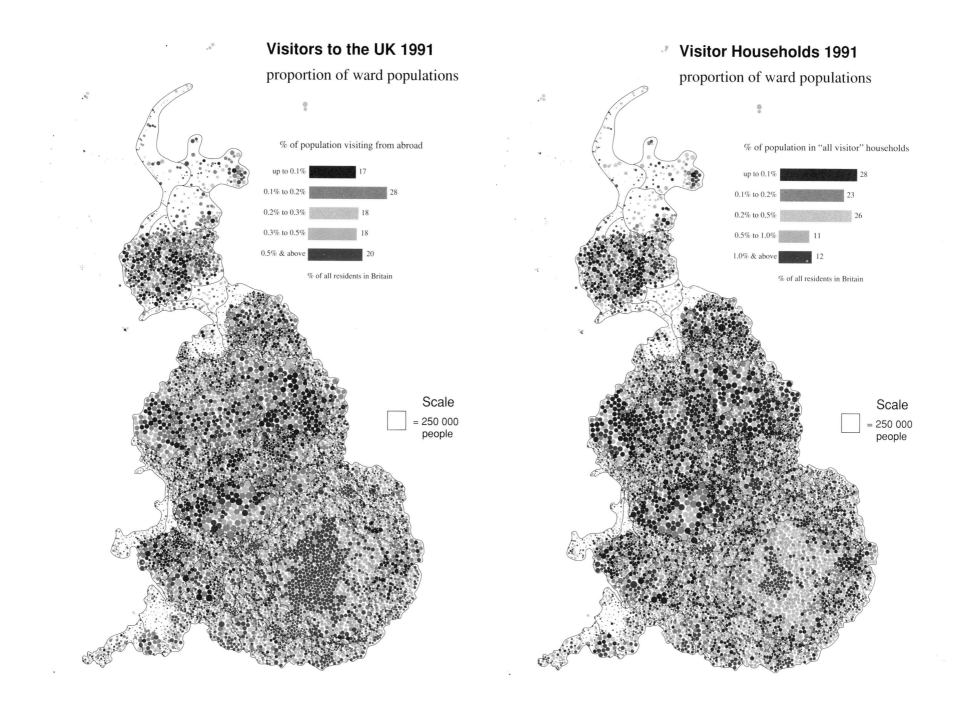

Visitors to the UK 1991

proportion of ward populations

% of population visiting from abroad

up to 0.1%	17
0.1% to 0.2%	28
0.2% to 0.3%	18
0.3% to 0.5%	18
0.5% & above	20

% of all residents in Britain

Scale

☐ = 250 000 people

Visitor Households 1991

proportion of ward populations

% of population in "all visitor" households

up to 0.1%	28
0.1% to 0.2%	23
0.2% to 0.5%	26
0.5% to 1.0%	11
1.0% & above	12

% of all residents in Britain

Scale

☐ = 250 000 people

1.15: Average and Extreme Population Present Changes in Britain 1901–1991

Change Period	National Average	District and County Growing Most Quickly	Total Growth	District and County Declining Most Quickly	Total Decline
1901–1911	10.4%	Southend-on-Sea	102.8%	City of London	-27.0%
		Mid Glamorgan	37.2%	Scottish Islands	-3.0%
1911–1921	4.7%	Crawley	117.9%	Eastwood	-52.7%
		Gwent	13.6%	Highland	-8.3%
1921–1931	4.7%	Barking and Dagenham	209.2%	Argyll and Bute	-22.7%
		Hertfordshire	20.1%	Scottish Islands	-12.1%
1931–1951	9.1%	Corby	283.4%	Tower Hamlets	-52.8%
		Hertfordshire	50.4%	Mid Glamorgan	-10.3%
1951–1961	5.0%	Harlow	830.2%	Richmondshire	-20.7%
		Hertfordshire	40.3%	Scottish Islands	-9.2%
1961–1971	5.2%	Cumbernauld and Kilsyth	144.5%	Islington	-22.7%
		Buckinghamshire	26.0%	Scottish Islands	-7.0%
1971–1981	0.6%	Milton Keynes	86.1%	Kensington and Chelsea	-26.2%
		Scottish Islands	21.6%	Merseyside	-8.7%
1981–1991	-0.4%	Milton Keynes	39.2%	City of London	-32.2%
		Cambridgeshire	11.8%	Scottish Islands	-9.8%

1.16: Population Change by District Type in Britain 1901–1991

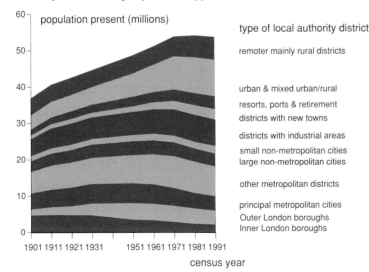

population present (millions)

type of local authority district

remoter mainly rural districts

urban & mixed urban/rural

resorts, ports & retirement

districts with new towns

districts with industrial areas

small non-metropolitan cities
large non-metropolitan cities

other metropolitan districts

principal metropolitan cities
Outer London boroughs
Inner London boroughs

census year

Population Present 1901–1991

Few series of British social statistics extend back before the 1970s with any degree of geographical detail. The 1971 census was the first to be made available in digital form, which is why that marks the earliest date in many of the maps shown here. Total population figures have, however, been estimated for a single set of small places using census figures back to 1901 (Mounsey 1982). These places are local authority districts with their boundaries frozen in 1981. The only definition of the population which is consistent across this time period is of the population present and enumerated in each district on census night. There was no census held in 1941 due to the war. The spatial patterns of almost all that is known of ninety years of population change in Britain are shown opposite.

A consistent set of shades is used so that different times can be compared. It should be remembered that the period from 1931 to 1951 is twice the length of the others so it is not surprising that shading categories then tend to be more extreme. The decline of the population of Inner London had begun even before the century started, in sharp contrast to the strong growth of other urban areas in the first decade. By the last decade the pattern shown for London is deceptive as so many of its people were not enumerated on census night in 1991 (see page 10). The capital is actually thought to have grown in size by 84 300 people over the decade to 1991, once under-enumeration has been taken into account. The only indication of this from the illustration is the rise in the population present in Tower Hamlets.

Seventy years ago the buzz-word was suburbanisation, which the red rings of districts surrounding the centres of the major cities show. Over the twenty years around the Second World War the population decline of the capital accelerated along with ports like Liverpool, South Tyneside and Portsmouth, and the Welsh coalfield. The 1950s and 1960s saw a new phenomenon — counterurbanisation — which became even more distinct by the 1970s and 1980s as so many more cities began to lose large numbers of people when national population growth stabilised. Figure 1.15 lists those districts and counties which saw the most extreme changes in each period. The last period of change is covered in greater detail below.

A useful way to summarise the detailed changes shown opposite is to use a categorisation of districts into types based largely on the urban–rural dichotomy following Craig (1987). Figure 1.16 shows how the change in the total population of Britain is built up from the changes in eleven types of districts. Local features, such as the reversal of the sizes of Inner and Outer London, are evident as well as the general trend towards growth in rural areas and decline of the cities. However, with smaller households who prefer cities (page 105) predicted (Figure 4.6), these trends, which can already be seen to be slowing down, could eventually move into reverse.

Population Change 1901–1991

change in district populations

1901–1911

1911–1921

1921–1931

1931–1951

1951–1961

1961–1971

1971–1981

1981–1991

% change in population present

up to -5%

-5% to 0%

0% to 5%

5% to 10%

10% & above

Scale

= 1 000 000
people in 1981

1.17: Distributions of Population Change 1971–1981 and 1981–1991

1.18: Population Change in Britain 1971–1981 / 1981–1991 Shaded by Density

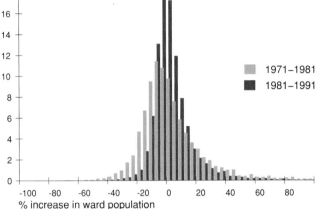

Usual Residents 1971–1991

Figures for how many people are usually resident in wards have only been available since 1971. This is often seen as a better measure to use when looking at population change as it is not influenced by temporary moves. In theory, when the usual resident definition is used the timing of the census should not affect the population sizes of, for instance, university cities with very mobile populations. In 1971 only usual residents who were present on census night were counted, representing 97.4% of the population. However, this proportion is comparable with those enumerated in 1991 (see Figure 1.13).

Both cartograms opposite use the same shading categories to highlight the greater diversity of changes in the 1970s compared with the 1980s. These are also the same categories as used previously to show the changes at district level. The variety of experiences within cities is highlighted here, particularly in the second period. Distinct clusters of wards in almost all large cities can be seen to have lost more than one in twenty of their population in the 1970s, while 30% of people now live in areas which then saw a net population growth of more than one in ten.

The extremes of change were less marked by the 1980s but were often still in the same general direction. However, many wards across Inner London experienced rapid growth due to redevelopment and immigration. The other conurbations did not experience a similar turnabout. Figure 1.17 shows how less variable were the changes in 1981–91 compared to the previous decade. In 1971–81, three quarters of all people lived in wards with changes of more than 5% either way; that proportion fell to just over a half.

Although side-by-side the two cartograms suggest that wards which saw a rise of population in one period were likely to see a rise in the next, this is not necessarily true. Figure 1.18 illustrates the relationship between the two changes, showing how variable it is. The figure also shows, for both decades, a strong relationship between high population increases and low population density. It may well be that, although individual wards were not especially likely to see a high increase in the 1970s followed by an increase a decade later, their neighbouring wards may (if they did not grow in the first period). This is because population growth often requires new dwellings to be constructed, and one development may well preclude another in the same very local area.

It is important to remember that we are not comparing the same people or even the same number of people when rates of social characteristics are compared across areas over time. Places which have lost people are likely to have lost particular sub-groups of people, predominantly the mobile and the old, this will change their social make-up. Similarly, Inner London in the 1990s does not contain the same mix of people as it did in the 1980s, not because the people there have changed, but because different people have moved in and others have left. When we compare the populations of areas over time we are charting the evolution of communities which are themselves changing shape.

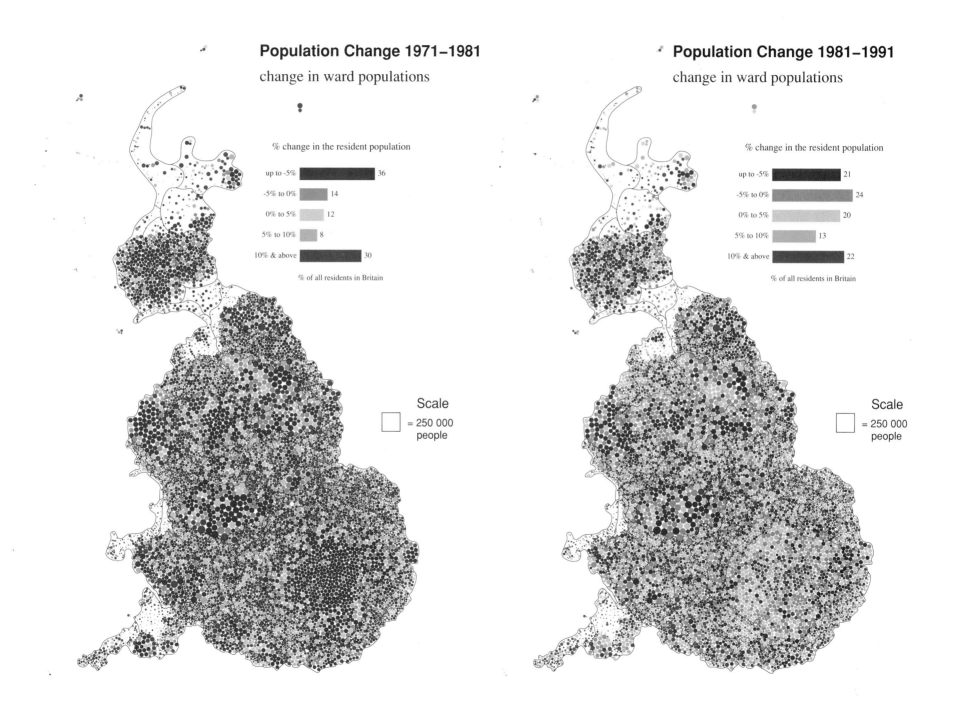

Population Change 1971–1981

change in ward populations

% change in the resident population

up to -5%	36
-5% to 0%	14
0% to 5%	12
5% to 10%	8
10% & above	30

% of all residents in Britain

Scale

☐ = 250 000 people

Population Change 1981–1991

change in ward populations

% change in the resident population

up to -5%	21
-5% to 0%	24
0% to 5%	20
5% to 10%	13
10% & above	22

% of all residents in Britain

Scale

☐ = 250 000 people

1.19: Components of Mid-Year Estimated Population Change 1981–1991

proportion of district populations   % change from 1981

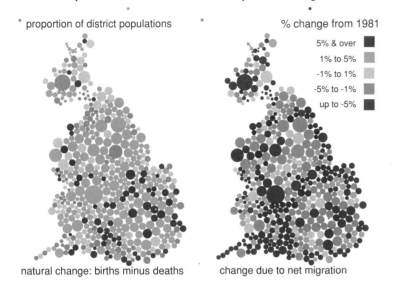

5% & over	■
1% to 5%	■
-1% to 1%	■
-5% to -1%	■
up to -5%	■

natural change: births minus deaths   change due to net migration

1.20: Annual Population Change by District Type 1981–1990

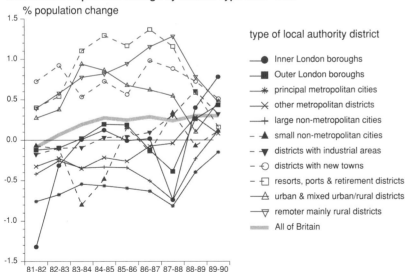

% population change

type of local authority district

— ● Inner London boroughs
— ■ Outer London boroughs
— ✳ principal metropolitan cities
— ✕ other metropolitan districts
— ＋ large non-metropolitan cities
– ▲ small non-metropolitan cities
– ▼ districts with industrial areas
– ⊙ districts with new towns
– ⊟ resorts, ports & retirement districts
– △ urban & mixed urban/rural districts
– ▽ remoter mainly rural districts
▬ All of Britain

81-82 82-83 83-84 84-85 85-86 86-87 87-88 88-89 89-90
mid-year to mid-year

Mid-Year Estimates 1981–1991

This chapter ends with a more detailed look at trends during the 1980s using a different source and a somewhat different definition of the population. *Mid-year estimates* are made by the Government Statistical Service for the number of people resident in each local authority on the 30th of June each year. Not only does the timing of these statistics differ from the census, but there are other significant differences. Students are taken to be at their term-time residence; estimates are made of the number of people missed by the censuses, and birth, death and migration statistics are all incorporated in updating these figures annually.

Because the components of population change are included in these calculations they are also made available for study. Figure 1.19 shows the geographical distributions of the changes *in situ* (births and deaths) and those due to migration in each district over the last decade (GRO(S) 1993, OPCS 1993). The latter can be seen to be very much more important than the former. Deaths outweigh births in those areas with an older population, hence the coast is grey. Migration shows a more varied and extreme pattern. Only one central London borough has had an overall population rise through net migration. This is not because migration into the capital is low, just that out-migration is greater (although less in net effect than the number of births over deaths resulting from an influx of so many younger in-migrants). In terms of migration the coast is coloured red, as old people move there, while the major northern conurbations on the west of the country have been losing people through out-migration.

The annual geographical anatomy of these changes is shown opposite for each of the nine pairs of years 1981–82 to 1989–90. The counterurbanisation of 1981–82 is hardly evident by 1989–90, with some Inner London boroughs having the largest rises by then. This may well be due to the recession, but there was also a recession in the early 1980s. In between these two periods the sustained growth of the districts of the South West and East Anglia is most evident, along with the relentless decline of Liverpool and Glasgow.

Finally, the changes are shown in a single illustration — Figure 1.20. Here the same eleven types of district are used as for charting change over the century (see Figure 1.16). Until 1988 the four most rural types (shown by red lines) were always growing faster than the national average and the seven more urban types (in grey) growing slower. Suddenly the lines converged in the last two years and there may even be an indication that some are crossing over. The dramatic rise of Inner London is clear, but so too is the fall in population of the ports and retirement districts. These figures are to be updated following the findings of the 1991 census (hence they stop in 1990, see page 23) but they do illustrate how much diversity of change there was over the period which is being studied here. Will the 1990s see the reversal of the population deconcentration which has predominated since 1951 or a continuation of the post-war exodus to the countryside?

Population Change 1981–1990

change in mid-year district populations

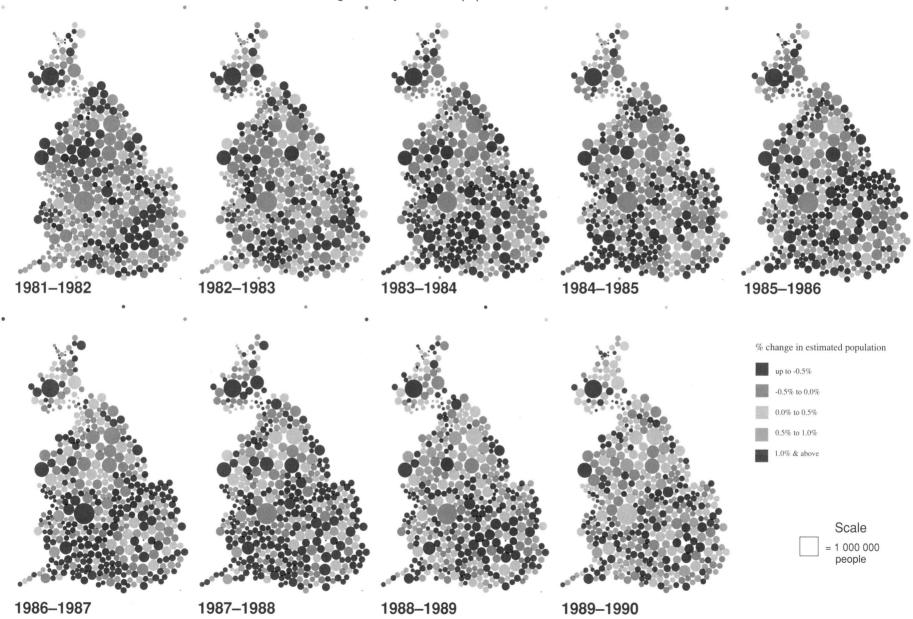

1981–1982

1982–1983

1983–1984

1984–1985

1985–1986

1986–1987

1987–1988

1988–1989

1989–1990

% change in estimated population

up to -0.5%

-0.5% to 0.0%

0.0% to 0.5%

0.5% to 1.0%

1.0% & above

Scale

= 1 000 000 people

Conclusion: People and Land

Distribution

The population of Britain is highly concentrated. A third of the population live in the seven metropolitan counties which occupy only 3% of the land. With the exception of Tyne & Wear these counties are in the central belt of Britain running from London to Liverpool. The majority of people in Britain live within the cities of this belt. Colour Print A shows the locations of these cities in detail, illustrating how the boundaries of metropolitan counties have been drawn around the most densely populated areas. The map also shows how the locations of physical features such as mountain tops and navigable harbours are reflected by the detailed distribution of the population. Colour Print B shows this same detailed distribution of population densities drawn upon the cartogram using identical colour shading. The majority of the population live in wards at densities of over two thousand people per square kilometre. On the cartogram the detailed patterns of density to be found within these peoples' cities are revealed. For instance, the most dense wards in London form a ring around the centre of that city. The cartogram also shows how the boundaries of non-metropolitan counties often traverse the least densely populated parts of the country. Different levels of population density can be crudely associated with many social distributions, such as the chance of children living with their married parents (Figure 6.5), or the likelihood of people not filling in census forms (Figure 1.9). This is because population density acts as a useful surrogate for social divisions between urban and rural Britain.

Mapping People: Colour Prints A and B

The maps in Colour Prints A and B should be compared with the maps on page 9, which show the same dataset over the same areas using the same projections. The maps drawn in full colour show much greater detail, and convey more information by using fifteen categories of density ordered on an approximate logarithmic scale. Full colour maps can also be more confusing to read than two colour maps because of the more complex patterns they can show. To make these maps most legible, a rainbow shading scheme is used to colour them as that allows a greater number of categories to be differentiated on an intuitively ordered spectral scale. Maps inevitably simplify, and the cartographic choices of shading, categorisation and projection determine what can be revealed in them. Similarly the statistics on which maps are based can also simplify, and sometimes misrepresent, the situation. These maps are based on the density lived at by people who were successfully enumerated or imputed by the 1991 census, treating the missing million as if they were invisible. Inclusion of the best estimates of where the missing million residents live would make some of the densest areas much denser.

Population Change

Another misleading impression which may be read from some maps and cartograms is that the pattern they show is static. In 1901 the population of Britain consisted of just under 37 million people. Ninety years later it exceeded 56 million residents. The population grew most slowly in the depressions of the 1930s and 1980s. Although initially the most remote areas lost people, later the most accessible inner city districts were experiencing the greatest declines. Growth before the second world war was typically suburban, but since then it has been progressively more rural and orientated towards small market towns. A decentralisation of the population has been seen to have occurred. The components of this decentralisation can be illustrated by considering the post war changes in the sizes of three different geographical definitions of the same fraction of the population. In 1951 the least densely populated 314 districts contained 40% of the population, their share rose to 42% in 1961, 45% in 1971, 49% in 1981 and to 50% by 1991. The areas which are currently constituted as metropolitan counties contained 40% of the population of Britain in 1951, 38% in 1961, 36% in 1971, 33% in 1981 and 32% in 1991. There has also been a gradual southwards shift of the population. The counties which make up the three southernmost standard regions contained 40% of the population in 1951. This share rose to 41% in 1961, 42% in 1971, and to 43% by 1991. People in Britain are being spread more evenly over the available land, and most of this under-occupied but easily habitable land is in the south of England. They are also following the migration of employment in Britain which has moved southwards at a faster rate than people over the last two decades (page 69).

Missing Million

The figures given above for population change are based upon mid-year estimates of the population for 1991, rather than on census counts. This is because more than a million people avoided being enumerated by the last census, with just under a million more not being available to complete their census forms (which were completed for them by imputation, see page 10). These factors mean that the characteristics of young men are under-represented in metropolitan areas on many of the maps which follow. A further three quarters of a million communal establishment residents and one quarter of a million visitors from abroad are also often omitted from social statistics. This practice is also followed here as most of the maps in this atlas are about "usual residents in private households". Because of this, the locations and some of the characteristics of visitors and of people who live in communal establishments have been presented in some detail in this chapter. Only the maps based on mid-year estimates of the population show all the population. A rough impression of whose social characteristics are most under-estimated by the 1991 census can be gained by knowing where people lived who were missing from the census. The precise location of the missing million is returned to in a section on electoral registration in the concluding chapter of the atlas (page 216).

Recent Change

Analysis of the most recent trends in population shows that, in general, population decentralisation is continuing, but with some interesting exceptions. Until 1988 the four most rural district types were growing most quickly (Figure 1.20), but this situation had changed by 1990 so that — after over fifty years of continuous decline (Figure 1.16) — the population of Inner London boroughs rose to become the fastest growing of the eleven district types. More recent mid-year estimates (which became available just before this book was printed) show that the revival of the Inner London population has continued through to 1993, but also that the three most rural district types have reinstated their position of having the strongest growth following the unusual circumstances of 1991. Large and small non-metropolitan cities have also experienced above average population growth. This is due to high inward migration rather than a large excess of births over deaths (as has occurred in London). All other types of district have grown less rapidly than the national average. In particular, principal metropolitan cities — Manchester, Liverpool, Sheffield, Newcastle upon Tyne, Birmingham, Leeds and Glasgow — have, as a group, continued to grow most slowly due to continually high rates of out-migration. Because of this, the national share of the population living in metropolitan counties has continued to decline since 1991, despite the growth of Inner London. Inner London's growth has, however, helped the southwards shift of population to continue unabated, but the overall shift to less dense areas has also continued. At the local authority district level it is affluent areas which have experienced the strongest population growth in the first two years following the last census, with seven districts experiencing rises of at least four people in every hundred (Cotswold, Cambridge, Forest Heath, Hertsmere, Three Rivers, Kincardine & Deeside, and Northavon).

Population Projections

Much more information is available on population numbers than on any other aspect of the social geography of Britain because these statistics are required in order to interpret most other information. This is also true in terms of future projections, which are made first for population and then for other social statistics. The population of Britain is projected to grow by 3.4% between 1991 and 2001, by 2.4% in the decade up to 2011, by 1.5% in the decade up to 2021 and to grow by less than 0.2% per decade by 2031, after which it is projected to fall (CSO 1995). These projections assume net immigration over the next four decades They also show that the population of Scotland is due to start declining by the start of next century, while East Anglia and the South West are projected to grow most quickly. Population estimates and projections can thus provide a context for other social statistics which are available for much more limited periods. For instance, population mobility was very low at the time of the 1991 census, and statistics derived from that source used later in this atlas, such as migration rates, may not be typical of more usual times. By studying population changes around census dates it is possible to gain an impression of how unusual are the census years which we are often obliged to use to analyse social change. Similarly, by observing where the population missing or excluded from other sources resides, an estimate can be made of the direction and importance of the biases introduced by these factors. Studying simple population distribution and change is an essential prerequisite to understanding more complex patterns and developments in the social geography of a country.

References

Atkins, D., Charlton, M., Dorling, D. & Wymer, C., 1993, Connecting the 1981 and 1991 Censuses, *North East Regional Research Laboratory Working Paper* 93/9, Department of Geography, University of Newcastle upon Tyne.

Carver, S.J., 1990, *Application of Geographic Information Systems to Siting Radioactive Waste Disposal Facilities*, Unpublished PhD Thesis, University of Newcastle upon Tyne.

Champion, A.G., 1989, *Counterurbanisation: The Changing Pace and Nature of Population Deconcentration*, London: Edward Arnold.

Champion, A.G., 1995, Analysis of Change Through Time, in S. Openshaw (ed.) *A Census Users' Handbook*, London: Longman.

Clarke, J., 1987, *Population Geography*, Oxford: Pergamon Press.

Craig, J., 1985, Better Measures of Population Density, *Population Trends*, 42: 30–35.

Craig, J., 1987, An Urban-Rural Categorization for Wards and Local Authorities, *Population Trends*, 47: 6–11.

CSO, 1995, *Social Trends* 25, London: HMSO.

Dorling, D., 1993, Map Design for Census Mapping, *The Cartographic Journal*, 30/2: 167–183.

GRO(S), 1993, *Mid 1991 Population Estimates*, Scotland, London: HMSO.

Lorenz, M.O., 1905, Methods of Measuring the Concentration of Wealth, *Publications of the American Statistical Association*, 9: 209–219.

Mounsey, H.M. 1982, *The Cartography of Time-Changing Phenomena: the Animated Map*, Unpublished PhD Thesis, Department of Geography, University of Durham.

OPCS, 1992, *1991 Census Definitions*, London: HMSO.

OPCS, 1993, *Mid-1991 Population Estimates*, England and Wales, London: HMSO.

OPCS, 1994, Undercoverage in Great Britain, *1991 Census User Guide* 58, London: HMSO.

Simpson, S., March, C. & Sandhu, A., 1993, Validation of Census Coverage by Other Means, *Manchester Census Group Occasional Paper*, University of Manchester.

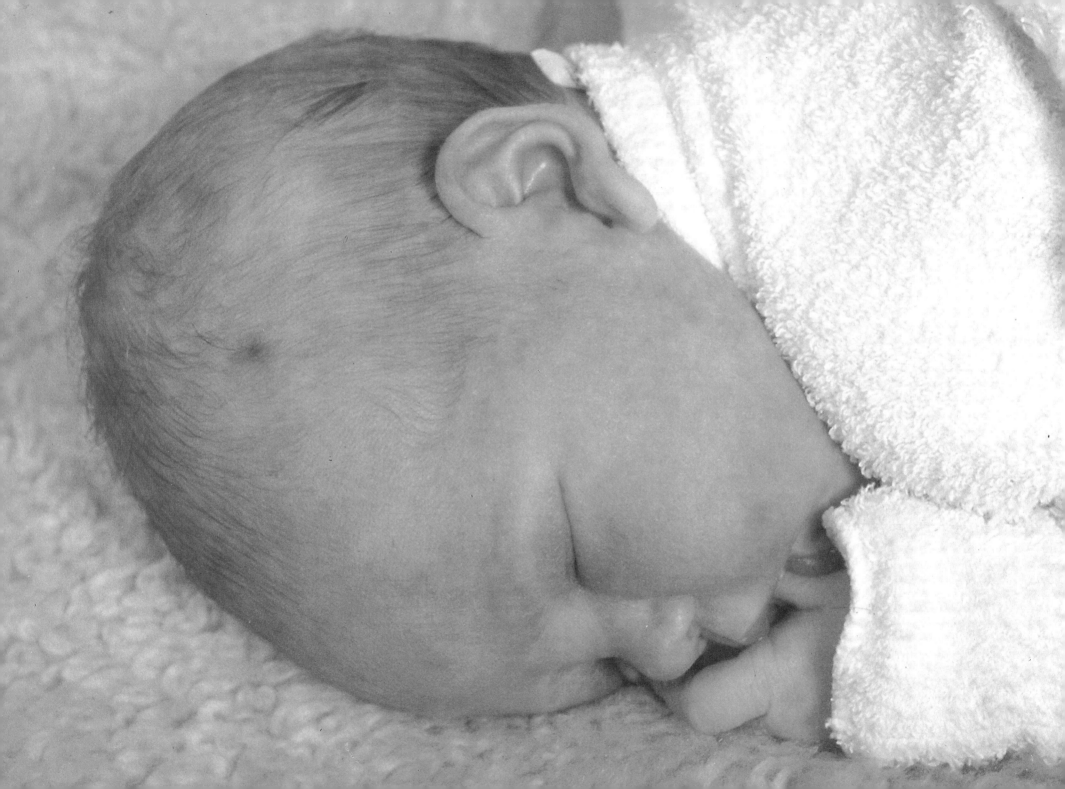

2: Demography

Demography is used here to mean the study of the most basic aspects of society other than population distribution. This includes things people cannot change such as their birthplace, sex, age, ethnic group — and some closely related phenomena which they can and do alter — their marital status, nationality, language and location. Illness and mortality are usually studied under the heading of demography, but so much information is available about these subjects that a separate chapter is reserved for health issues.

Basic demographic patterns underlie many of the more topical economic, social and political subjects covered later and they are included here to show the underlying distributions of people upon which economic circumstances, social choices and political movements prey. It is the changes in these basic patterns which most affect other distributions. An ageing population in one area or a high birth rate in another will increase the "dependency ratio" as easily as a fall in employment rates.

As many of the statistics in this chapter concern aspects which change only over generations, whenever a map of change is shown the twenty year perspective from 1971 is used if suitable figures are available. In graphing national changes, figures back to the last century are included where these are available. Demographic statistics rely more heavily on censuses than any other subject so almost all the information shown here is derived from the 1971, 1981 or 1991 censuses of population.

The chapter begins in life-cycle order with birth and fertility statistics. Next the simple ratios of women to men are shown, given the close connection of the ratio of the sexes to the age distribution — women being closely related to the very young and more likely to be (or to be caring for) the very old. The very different spatial distributions of two age groups of children are then examined. The geography of toddlers is shown just before they are old enough to go to nursery school or playgroup. This distribution is contrasted with that of adolescents who have just finished compulsory schooling. Keeping on the theme of education, the location of students and how that has changed over the last two decades is presented. The propensity of all young adults to marry or bring up children on their own is then depicted, followed by the changing geographical distribution of the likelihood of marriage for adults aged over 25. The section on age distribution is drawn to a close by showing the changing locational preferences of, or constraints on, pensioners in Britain.

The 1991 census was the first British census to ask people explicitly which ethnic group they thought they belonged to. Unfortunately, "white" ethnic groups were not differentiated, so 95% of the population fall into this bland group. The distributions of those people completing the "non-white" answers can be shown, both on map and cartogram for each of the particular categories in which they felt themselves to be. For the bulk of the population, the nearest measure of their ethnic make-up is country of birth, so the locations of the English, Irish, Scots and Welsh *nations*, defined in this way, are plotted. Statistics on birthplace were collected in almost all censuses and so the changing locations over time for people from many other countries are also shown.

These changes in the distribution of people by birthplace and ethnic group occur almost exclusively because of population movement, hence the simple net patterns of migration are shown next, both within Britain and from abroad. One of the most interesting maps to plot would be emigration rates by area but it is not possible to find out how many people have left the country from each place. Changes in the patterns of lifetime migration to Britain can be shown over twenty years, by each group of migrants' present location in this country.

Finally, the distributions of the languages people speak are given in detail for Scottish Gaelic and Welsh speakers on maps which just show Scotland and Wales. Limitations on the questions which are asked in the census mean that the locations of other people who can speak languages other than English are not known. However, these two peripheral groups provide interesting patterns, particularly of the changes which have occurred in a generation, and also illustrate just how diverse are the group of people, here referred to with the apparently unambiguous phrase "British residents".

Among the key results it is shown that in some cities almost twice as many children are born for every woman living there as in others. More children are born per woman where there are fewer than average young men. Most toddlers are growing up in cities, but a disproportionate number of school leavers live in the countryside (to which many of their parents have presumably migrated). At the age of 18 a large proportion of people are suddenly concentrated in the centre of cities again, but now as students, living in the middle of areas where people of their ages tend not to marry. In the cities the proportion of young lone parents is many times higher than in the more rural areas. It is in rural areas that the highest proportions of married people are found. Marriage is going out of fashion fastest in metropolitan areas, particularly in London. By the time people become pensioners many have moved even further from the cities in which most were born. But people in ethnic minority groups live almost exclusively in cities, as do people born in Ireland, despite belonging to a rapidly ageing population. Geographically, however, the most peripheral groups in Britain are those who speak Welsh or Scottish Gaelic.

In the chapters that follow, as the maps of unemployment rates, household overcrowding, ill health, poverty, wealth and votes are shown, the diagrams presented here should be referred back to. Remember that certain social circumstances, if geographically unevenly spread, are not distributed among a uniform society, but are highly concentrated within certain communities and are almost unheard of in others.

2.1: Fertility Ratios in England and Wales 1838–1991

relative number of births per year

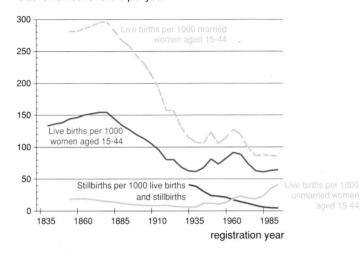

registration year

2.2: Outcome of Conceptions in England and Wales 1969–1991

total conceptions other than miscarriages and stillbirths ('000s)

Fertility

Fertility measures the propensity of an adult to have children. Although it would be interesting to know how many children each man in Britain thinks he is the father of, statistics have only been collected nationally for women. Annual statistics on births have been collected for over one hundred and fifty years as Figure 2.1 shows. This figure depicts the ratio of births to various groups of women, not the fertility rate (which is how many children each woman tends to have). The high point over this period was an average of one birth every six years per woman (aged 15–44) in 1876; the low points were one every 17 years in both 1941 and 1977 (OPCS 1987). The baby boom of the 1960s and the smaller boom twenty years before that are clear, as is the recent increase in births outside marriage (rising to above 30% of all births in 1991). Another dramatic change has been in the decline of stillbirths. One in twenty five babies was born dead in the 1930s; today that figure is less than one in two hundred.

It is interesting to see where the twenty-somethings of today were most likely to have been born, and as the number of children each woman had ever had was last asked in the 1971 census, that year is chosen for the distribution shown opposite. Women in southern and some Scottish cities tended to have had the least children, while the rate was generally over average in northern cities (this has been the case at least since 1850 when the ethnicity factor of a "Danish influence" was cited as one possible explanation by the census authorities of those times! Population Trends 1977: 27). Fertility is lower, measured in this way, where there are disproportionately more younger women. A more independent standardised fertility ratio which allows for age structure could have been used but the interpretation would not have been so simple.

Today it is possible to calculate only a crude fertility ratio of the number of children to women by age. This is illustrated in the right-hand map opposite, showing changes in the spatial pattern of fertility between 1971 and 1991 . Fertility has fallen everywhere except for central London and a few other distinctive clusters of wards, which together contain only 6% of the British population. The fall has been led by areas in between cities.

Figure 2.2 shows that between 1971 and 1991 the total number of conceptions rose from 836 000 to 854 000 per year. This is a fall when divided by the number of women aged 15 to 44, which increased by 15% over that period. The increase in legal abortions only accounts for a small part of the fall in fertility. Women are now becoming pregnant less frequently than their mothers. Of those who are having babies, more are choosing to do so outside marriage, but this rise is due mainly to an increase in the number of registrations by two unmarried parents. There has also been a marked decrease in the number of women getting married within eight months of conception and an increase in the number of children being born to a woman in her second or subsequent marriage. By 1991 only 56% of recorded conceptions were within marriage.

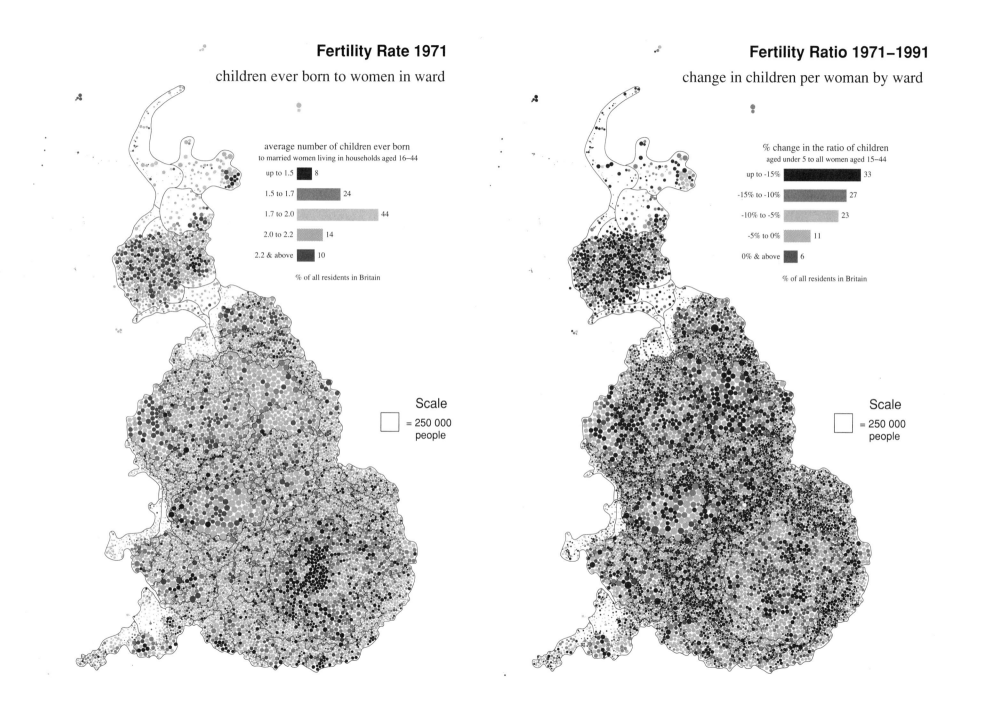

Fertility Rate 1971

children ever born to women in ward

average number of children ever born
to married women living in households aged 16–44

up to 1.5 8
1.5 to 1.7 24
1.7 to 2.0 44
2.0 to 2.2 14
2.2 & above 10

% of all residents in Britain

Scale

☐ = 250 000
people

Fertility Ratio 1971–1991

change in children per woman by ward

% change in the ratio of children
aged under 5 to all women aged 15–44

up to -15% 33
-15% to -10% 27
-10% to -5% 23
-5% to 0% 11
0% & above 6

% of all residents in Britain

Scale

☐ = 250 000
people

Sex

The imbalance of the sexes is another basic geographical distribution. Any other aspect of society in which men are more or less likely to be engaged than women will partly reflect this distribution. It is interesting that in London, where the fertility rate of women is lowest, there are least men. However, one reason fewer men appear to be in the capital is that more men than women avoided census enumeration, particularly young men living in cities (see Figure 1.10 and the map on page 217).

Nationally, slightly more men than women are born (5% more in 1991), but by the age of 40 the ratios are even as men are more likely to die young than women. Figure 2.3 shows how, from then on, the ratio of women to men rises, there being two women for every man aged 82. The ratio has been decreasing for men aged between 20 and 30 (there has been greater male net immigration than deaths in recent years) but increasing for men aged between 30 and 50. Beyond age 50, due to improvements in men's health, the ratio has been falling over time (OPCS 1983, 1993, GRO(S) 1983, 1993).

The national distribution of men in the population (first map) shows concentrations of over 50% around the Home Counties, in central Birmingham and in the Potteries and Coalfields. Women dominate in London, Liverpool, Scottish cities and on the coast (where they tend to be either elderly or caring for the elderly). When the "young adult" age group is considered in isolation (far right), many of these patterns become clearer although here, it must be remembered, the effects of under-enumeration are most strong. The coast is now a much less clear cut entity, but the cities show even stronger divisions, being the only places likely to have more women enumerated in this age range.

In the graphs that accompany the maps in this atlas people are often disaggregated by their sex. This is done because there are often significant differences between the situations of men and women. Figure 2.4 shows the population pyramid of Britain shaded to indicate which parts are growing in size over time and which are declining. The baby boom generation (the birthplaces of the last of which are shown on the previous page) was, in 1991, in its late 20s. Below them the cohort in the first ten years of life is also rising and above them a peak can be seen of people who were born in 1947. The number of men aged 50 and 51 is increasing. The sudden drop in both sexes is for those few born before 1919, before which men tail away far faster than women, mostly because of natural causes, but also because so many men born before 1920 died in the Second World War. Premature deaths, like baby booms, influence the numbers in education, the size of the workforce and the numbers of pensioners for generations to come. The "spikes" at the top of the graph represent all people aged over 90.

The size of the baby boom generation today, the make-up of elderly people's households and the high numbers of people now approaching retirement age are all the result of specific differences in the life-chances and behaviour of men and women.

2.3: Single Year Sex Ratio in 1991 (showing change from 1981)

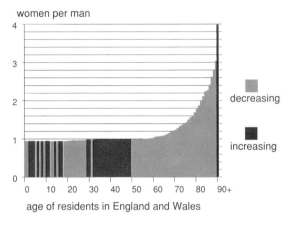

women per man

decreasing

increasing

age of residents in England and Wales

2.4: Age–Sex Distribution in 1991 (showing change from 1981)

single year of age

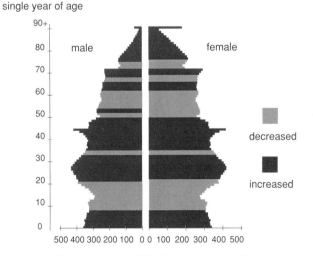

male   female

decreased

increased

numbers of residents ('000s) in England and Wales

Male Residents 1991

proportion of ward populations

% of residents who are male

up to 47%	12
47% to 48%	23
48% to 49%	33
49% to 50%	22
50% & above	10

% of all residents in Britain

Scale

☐ = 250 000 people

Young Men 1991

proportion of ward populations

% of single residents aged 18–24 who are male

up to 50%	22
50% to 52%	21
52% to 53%	12
53% to 55%	23
55% & above	22

% of all residents in Britain

Scale

☐ = 250 000 people

2.5: Change in Single Year Sex Ratios 1981–1991

% point increase in men per woman

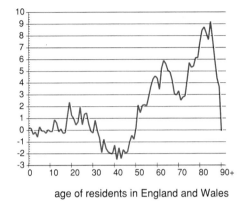

age of residents in England and Wales

2.6: Change in the Size of Age Bands 1981–1991

% increase or decrease

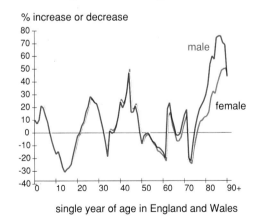

single year of age in England and Wales

Children

Children present a great diversity of geographical patterns because adults are at their most mobile when their children are growing up. It would therefore make little sense to map children as a whole. Instead two narrow age ranges are concentrated on here: those aged 1 or 2 and those aged 16 or 17, both in 1991. The former have been termed "toddlers" here and show where the families of very young children live in disproportionate numbers. There tends to be significantly more toddlers growing up in East London and towards the centres of many large cities. In more rural areas, Inner London and on the coast, families tend to have fewer small children. These are also often the areas where young men are unlikely to be found (or enumerated). The close correspondence between this distribution and that of fertility rates twenty years earlier (page 27) shows, with some exceptions, how the same places are reserved for bringing up children over generations.

The same shading categories have been used to plot the cohort which has just passed through eleven years of schooling and usually one or more home moves. This group is 8% smaller in size than the toddlers and so very few areas have over 3.5% of their populations in this age band. The rings around Glasgow and London are particularly distinctive, however. Adolescents are least likely to be living where they are most often portrayed — in inner cities. Again this could be partly due to under-enumeration, but this age range is not thought to have been missed in high numbers (Figure 1.10). What this distribution represents is the movement of parents out into the suburbs and the countryside as their children grow up. It may also show where the few boarding schools and remand centres containing children of this age tend to be located.

There have been no great national changes in the proportion of children by sex over the 1980s as Figure 2.5 shows. The figures shown here are based on the mid-year estimates to avoid problems of under-enumeration (OPCS 1983, 1993). During the last decade men were more likely to have migrated to Britain in their 20s than women, but were also more likely to have emigrated or returned abroad in their 30s and 40s. Improvements in men's health over the age of 50 has increased the age–sex ratio rapidly. The dip by age 70 is due to these improvements not being so significant for men who were in their 20s during the last world war. Between 1981 and 1991 the proportion of the population aged 20 who were men rose by 2%.

The dramatic swings in the sizes of various age bands over just ten years is illustrated in Figure 2.6. These swings have repercussions for school class sizes, social security payments, the job and housing markets, future pension arrangements and so on. In 1991 school-leavers were having to compete with a much smaller number of people to find work than in 1981. When today's toddlers leave school there will be many thousands more people looking for work and homes.

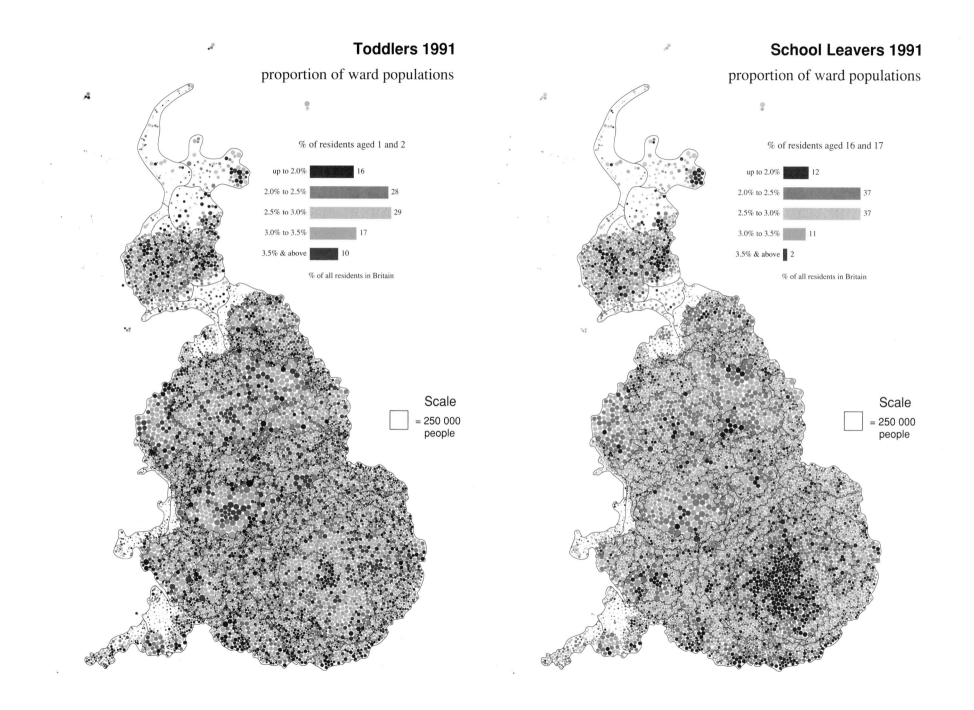

Toddlers 1991

proportion of ward populations

% of residents aged 1 and 2

up to 2.0%		16
2.0% to 2.5%		28
2.5% to 3.0%		29
3.0% to 3.5%		17
3.5% & above		10

% of all residents in Britain

Scale

☐ = 250 000 people

School Leavers 1991

proportion of ward populations

% of residents aged 16 and 17

up to 2.0%		12
2.0% to 2.5%		37
2.5% to 3.0%		37
3.0% to 3.5%		11
3.5% & above		2

% of all residents in Britain

Scale

☐ = 250 000 people

2.7: Proportion of the Population Who Were Students by Age and Sex 1991

% of their age group in Britain (log scale)

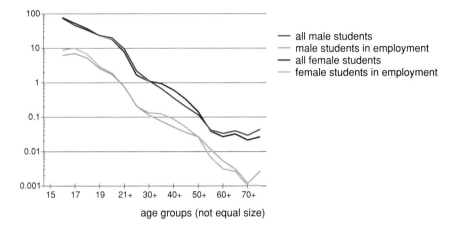

— all male students
— male students in employment
— all female students
— female students in employment

age groups (not equal size)

2.8: Proportion of Students in Each Ethnic Minority Group by Sex in Britain 1991

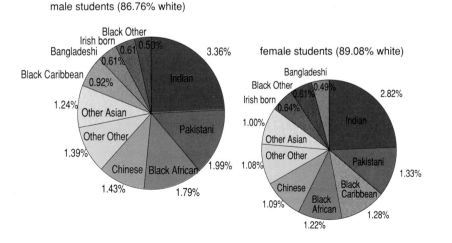

Students

Students are generally defined as anyone aged 16 or over who was at school or in full time education at the time of the census. A more familiar sub-group of students is used in the first map opposite, which shows the distribution of students aged 18 or over at their "term-time address". This definition clearly picks out the country's universities and the local neighbourhoods in which their students tend to live (students living in halls are also included here). London dominates the country having by far the largest number of students. On the map Edinburgh and Manchester appear to vie for second place. The bright red wards constitute the "student lands" of Britain. Only one in twenty people live there, but one in twenty of them go to college.

Nationally almost two million people said they were students of some description in 1991, a rise of 11% on the total of twenty years ago. That increase has been concentrated in certain areas. In particular, it is inner cities which have seen the proportion of their student populations rise fastest. This would be partly due to residents who were not students leaving. The decline of boarding school populations around London and in the Scottish cities is also apparent (as Figure 1.12 indicated). When reading this map it is worth remembering that term times differed in different places over twenty years, that the population base is slightly different and that many students were not enumerated.

Nevertheless, the rise in numbers shows clear local clustering around specific universities. For example, the wards of the west end of Newcastle saw an extra 2% or more of their population become students over the two decades so that now more than 5% of that population is in full time education. Increasing rates of school-leavers "staying on" are one reason for the general rise. As Figure 2.7 shows, 78% of girls aged 16 and 73% of boys aged 16 were in full time education in 1991; by the age of 18 these two figures are 37% and 32%, respectively (more women now go on to take degrees or diplomas), but by the age of 20 these proportions are 18% and 19%, respectively. The current increase in student numbers can be seen working its way through the system in the census year through this changing balance of the sexes. Although there are now more mature students than before, a log scale is still needed to show them on the graph. Between the ages of 30 and 50 more students are women; aged over 50 they are more likely to be men. The figure also shows the variation in the number of students "working their way" through college. At age 16 one in nine girls and one in twelve boys are working as well as studying; by the age of 18 these figures are one in five and one in six, respectively.

Finally, the ethnic group composition of all non-white students is shown in Figure 2.8. Because a larger proportion of people in ethnic minorities tend to be in the younger age ranges a disproportionate number are in full time education, but this varies considerably among the groups and also by sex as the figure shows.

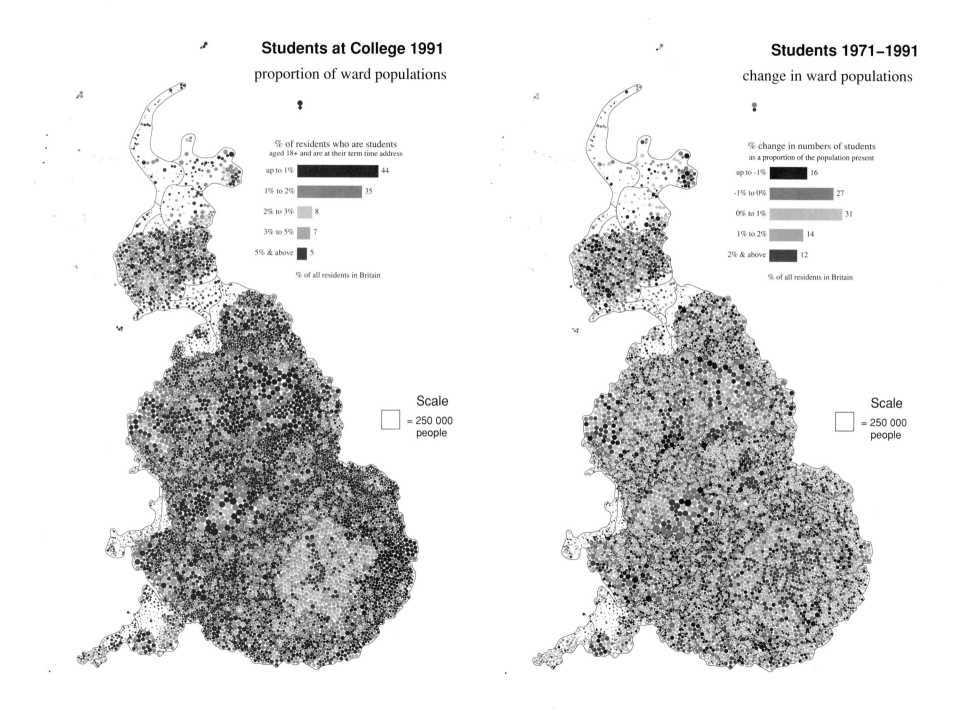

Students at College 1991

proportion of ward populations

% of residents who are students
aged 18+ and are at their term time address

up to 1%	44
1% to 2%	35
2% to 3%	8
3% to 5%	7
5% & above	5

% of all residents in Britain

Scale

☐ = 250 000 people

Students 1971–1991

change in ward populations

% change in numbers of students
as a proportion of the population present

up to -1%	16
-1% to 0%	27
0% to 1%	31
1% to 2%	14
2% & above	12

% of all residents in Britain

Scale

☐ = 250 000 people

2.9: Marital Status by Age in Britain 1991

■ female   ■ male

% of residents in each category

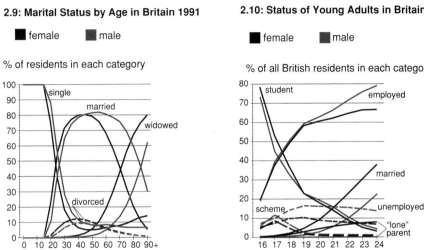

five year age bands

2.10: Status of Young Adults in Britain 1991

■ female   ■ male

% of all British residents in each category

single year age band

Young Adults

In demographic terms the eight years of life from 16 to 24 are often the most turbulent. It is then that people will probably get a job, leave home and may get married. Figure 2.9 shows the likely marital status of individuals given their age and sex. Men are likely to remain single for slightly longer than women. Four out of every five people are married by their 50th birthday but less than one in three is married by the time they are 24. Spatially there are huge variations in the proportion of young people who have chosen to marry, as the map opposite highlights, with threefold variations between wards being commonplace. London and Liverpool have some of the lowest rates of marriage despite, or perhaps because of, also having few young men who are single. South Manchester, Bristol and Guildford also see very few young adults getting married.

Marriage is an important demographic influence on the population because of its association with having children. Lone parenthood is shown here as one alternative to married life for some young people, but the map of where young adults are lone parents is not the mirror image of where they choose to marry. In the ribbon that runs down the centre of London most young people are neither married nor lone parents. It is of course possible to be both married and a "lone parent" simultaneously as a *lone parent* is defined here, following the census, as an adult living on his/her own with child or children aged 0-15. Figure 2.10 shows how almost all young lone parents are women, but only 8% of all young women fall into this category by the age of 24 (this figure may well be inflated by young men excluding themselves from the census enumeration).

Young adults are most likely to be on a government scheme at the age of 17, and 17% of all men are unemployed at the age of 19 (although the proportion of those available to work, the unemployment rate, is 21%, with a further 3% being on government training schemes). Despite this, 79% of men and 67% of women are in work by the time they reach 24. This is very similar to the situation ten years ago, apart from a 10% increase in the proportion of 24 year old women in the workforce and a 2% rise in the proportion of 24 year old men not in work. The changes for all ages are shown in Figure 2.11, which cannot easily be summarised in the space available here. The dramatic changes in the sizes of these groups of people is due partly to the level of under-enumeration. Nevertheless, there are far fewer teenagers now than ten years ago. Despite this, 41% of 16 year old boys in 1991 who were available for work could not find it, compared to just 23% in 1981. The proportions of students who are women has risen fastest. Most dramatic are the falls in the number of people getting married at these ages. In 1981 a quarter of women aged 20 were married; a decade later that proportion had fallen to 9%. Choices over marriage affect decisions to have children and are affected by employment and educational opportunities. It is difficult to disassociate demographic changes from other changes that are happening in society.

2.11: The Changing Circumstances of Young Adults in Britain 1981–1991

Age	All Resident Persons		Married		Students		In the Workforce		Out of Work	
	1991	1981–91	1991	1981–91	1991	1981–91	1991	1981–91	1991	1981–91
Male	'000s	%change	% of all	change%	% of all	change%	% of all	change%	% workforce	change%
16	348	-25%	0%	-0%	73%	5%	32%	1%	41%	18%
17	352	-21%	0%	-0%	45%	13%	62%	-6%	36%	17%
18	367	-15%	1%	-1%	33%	11%	71%	-6%	29%	10%
19	379	-10%	1%	-3%	23%	7%	78%	-5%	24%	5%
20	391	-5%	3%	-6%	20%	4%	81%	-3%	22%	3%
21	384	-3%	6%	-10%	16%	3%	84%	-2%	21%	2%
22	394	2%	10%	-15%	11%	2%	88%	-2%	19%	2%
23	397	4%	16%	-20%	6%	1%	92%	-1%	17%	2%
24	411	11%	23%	-22%	4%	0%	94%	-1%	16%	2%
Female										
16	330	-26%	0%	-0%	79%	5%	29%	4%	34%	10%
17	339	-23%	1%	-1%	53%	13%	54%	-4%	30%	11%
18	356	-16%	2%	-4%	37%	13%	64%	-6%	23%	6%
19	376	-8%	5%	-10%	23%	8%	70%	-5%	17%	2%
20	394	-2%	9%	-16%	18%	5%	71%	-2%	14%	1%
21	391	2%	15%	-21%	14%	4%	71%	1%	13%	0%
22	409	7%	23%	-24%	9%	3%	73%	3%	12%	0%
23	416	10%	30%	-26%	5%	2%	74%	7%	11%	0%
24	429	17%	38%	-26%	3%	1%	74%	10%	10%	-0%

Young and Married 1991

proportion of ward populations

% residents aged 16–24 who are married

up to 5%	12
5% to 7.5%	18
7.5% to 10%	19
10% to 15%	33
15% & above	17

% of all residents in Britain

Scale

☐ = 250 000 people

Young Lone Parents 1991

proportion of ward populations

% residents aged 16–24 who are lone parents

up to 0.5%	23
0.5% to 1%	16
1% to 2%	23
2% to 4%	22
4% & above	16

% of all residents in Britain

Scale

☐ = 250 000 people

2.12: Marriages by Manner of Solemnization 1837–1991

number of weddings per year in England and Wales ('000s)

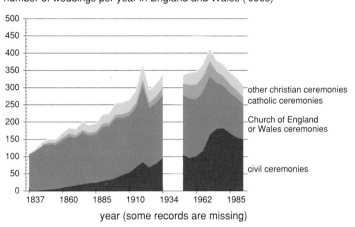

other christian ceremonies
catholic ceremonies

Church of England
or Wales ceremonies

civil ceremonies

year (some records are missing)

2.13: Divorces by Partners' Previous Marital Conditions 1957–1991

number of divorces in England and Wales ('000s)

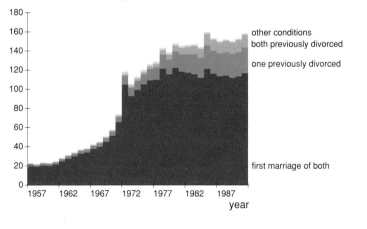

other conditions
both previously divorced

one previously divorced

first marriage of both

year

Marriage

Marriage is one of the few indicators available (at a detailed geographical level) of religious and cultural attitudes, although it is also important for purely demographic reasons. It is included here because the propensity of people to marry influences the age structure as well as changing peoples' economic circumstances. Married people tend to live longer and have more children. A more detailed examination of the different forms families can take is reserved for a later chapter on society in general.

Marriage is currently in decline, particularly as solemnized through the established Church which, in 1991, conducted its lowest number of ceremonies ever recorded at just over one hundred thousand (despite a much larger population eligible to marry: OPCS 1990). Figure 2.12 shows how the absolute number of marriages has fluctuated over the last century and a half. The first peak was in 1919 and the second highest peak was in 1970. No doubt there would also be a peak at the end of the Second World War if figures for that period were available. Given the large numbers of 1960s baby boomers who are now young adults, it is even more remarkable that so few people are getting married in the 1990s. Marriages solemnized under religions which are not Christian are recorded as civil ceremonies. Jewish weddings are recorded separately, but the numbers are too small to be visible on a graph of this scale (the highest number of Jewish weddings ever recorded in England and Wales was just over 2000 in 1906). The increase in civil ceremonies since the 1960s will have been due mainly to the remarriage of divorcees and changes in social attitudes to religious ceremonies.

The cartogram opposite shows a marked urban–rural divide in the propensity of adults to be married. The group aged between 25 and 64 has been chosen to reduce the influence of different population structures in different areas. In a large number of London wards, and in pockets of other cities, over half the adults of these ages are single (however, these areas only contain 3% of the national population). The second map shows how it is the cities which have led the national decline in the proportion of the population marrying over the last two decades. The decline in the number of people who are married is partly due to fewer people marrying in the first place, but it is also due to an increasing number of divorces.

Divorce rates accelerated in 1972 following the implementation of the 1969 Divorce Reform Act (Coleman and Salt 1992: 196). They appear to have stabilised at around 150 000 per year, although this includes an increasing number of previous divorcees, with the absolute number of first marriage break ups falling slightly from 1981 to 1991. There are much more sophisticated methods of analysing divorce and marriage rates. Here, however, the basic patterns have been shown because it is these that need to be held in mind to form an overall picture of the population of Britain and the geographical differences between areas.

Married Residents 1991

proportion of ward populations

% of residents aged 25–65 who are married

up to 50%	3
50% to 60%	6
60% to 70%	15
70% to 80%	47
80% & above	29

% of all residents in Britain

Scale
☐ = 250 000
people

Married 1971–1991

change in ward populations

% change in the proportion who are married
of those aged 25–64 who are living in private households

up to -20%	8
-20% to -15%	13
-15% to -10%	25
-10% to -5%	35
-5% & above	20

% of all residents in Britain

Scale
☐ = 250 000
people

2.14: Marital and Residential Status by Age in Britain 1991

2.15: Proportion of Pensioners by Age and Type of District 1971, 1981, 1991

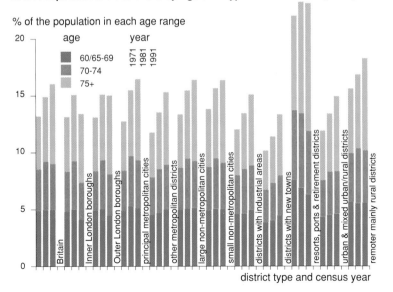

Pensioners

Progressing chronologically, the distribution of people of pensionable age has been reserved for the end of this half of the chapter. The maps opposite show the proportion of people of pensionable age or older (65 for men, 60 for women) in 1991, and how that proportion has changed since 1971. The coastal concentration is well established although particular areas of large cities also contain high concentrations of pensioners: the centre of Glasgow, for example. More surprising perhaps is the pattern of change. The elderly are no longer moving to the coasts in such large numbers, with well known resorts like Blackpool and Eastbourne seeing some of the greatest falls in the proportion of their populations who are elderly, as pensioners who die are not replaced. Instead it is to the outer suburbs and market towns that the elderly now appear to be migrating to in their greatest numbers. The elderly continue to leave the city centres.

Figure 2.14 provides a combined view of people's likely marital and residential status (from Figures 1.14 and 2.9). The pensionable years can be seen to provide the next most turbulent set of circumstances after young adulthood. Fewer pensioners are divorced because marriages made in the 1930s and 1940s have proved to be stable. More elderly women have been single all their lives than subsequent generations of women are likely to be; due partly to the two world wars. By the time women reach 75 (and when men reach 90) most have been widowed and have not remarried. The majority of elderly people living in institutions are widows.

The changing distribution of pensioners over time is important because they make up such a large and growing part of the population so that changes in their aspirations can have a marked overall effect. Figure 2.15 shows how, ironically, apart from London boroughs, the only category of districts to have seen a fall in their proportion of pensioners are labelled "resort ports and retirement districts". The sharpest rise in the proportion of pensioners has been in districts with new towns, reflecting the ageing of their previously young populations. The youngest group of pensioners shows this pattern most clearly. The proportion of the population aged 75 and over increased by exactly 50% from 1971 to 1991. It has grown most in the principal metropolitan districts and least in Inner London.

The cartogram of these changes shows that this is partly a result of how the boundaries are drawn. Around each major metropolis there is a ring of high rates of increases in proportions of the elderly. In the case of London that ring falls just outside the boundary, while in Merseyside, Tyne and Wear, Avon and the West Midlands it clearly falls just within the metropolitan area boundary. The advantage of showing distributions nationally, at the ward level, is that artifacts of administrative boundaries have less effect. A similar advantage is seen for spatially concentrated groups which are also only well represented at ward level, some of which are described next.

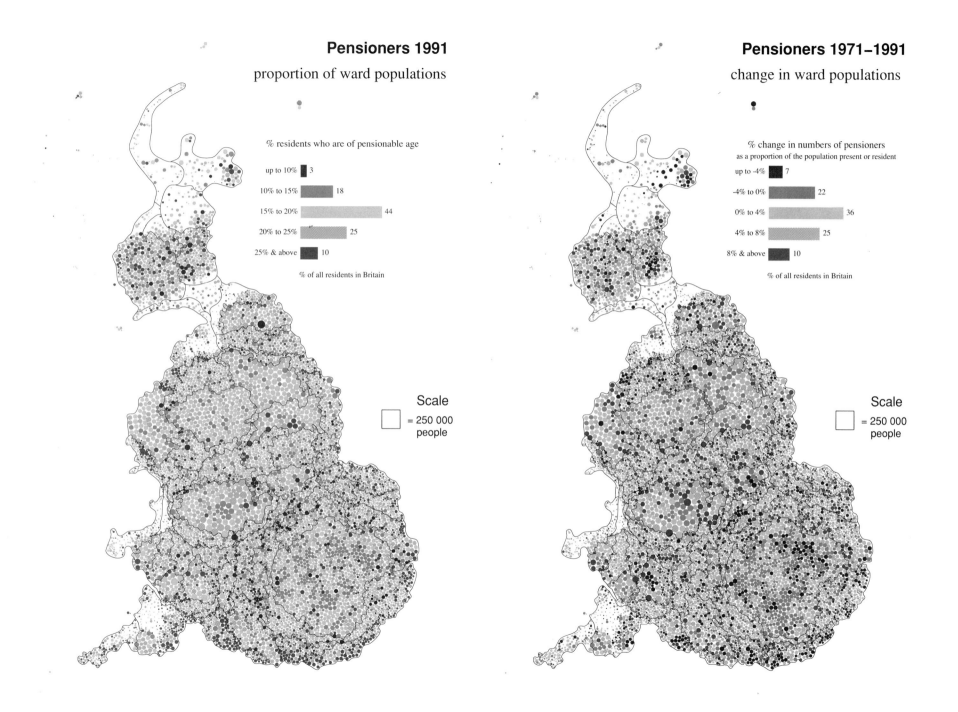

Pensioners 1991

proportion of ward populations

% residents who are of pensionable age

	% of all residents in Britain
up to 10%	3
10% to 15%	18
15% to 20%	44
20% to 25%	25
25% & above	10

% of all residents in Britain

Scale

☐ = 250 000 people

Pensioners 1971–1991

change in ward populations

% change in numbers of pensioners
as a proportion of the population present or resident

	% of all residents in Britain
up to -4%	7
-4% to 0%	22
0% to 4%	36
4% to 8%	25
8% & above	10

% of all residents in Britain

Scale

☐ = 250 000 people

2.16: Distribution of Ethnic Groups by Region and Metropolitan County 1991

% of residents of each group in each subregion

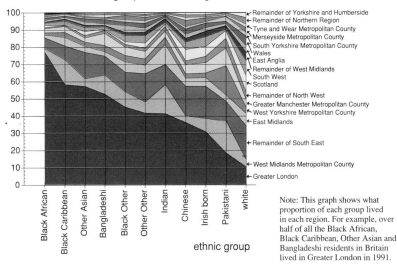

Remainder of Yorkshire and Humberside
Remainder of Northern Region
Tyne and Wear Metropolitan County
Merseyside Metropolitan County
South Yorkshire Metropolitan County
Wales
East Anglia
Remainder of West Midlands
South West
Scotland
Remainder of North West
Greater Manchester Metropolitan County
West Yorkshire Metropolitan County
East Midlands
Remainder of South East
West Midlands Metropolitan County
Greater London

ethnic group

Note: This graph shows what proportion of each group lived in each region. For example, over half of all the Black African, Black Caribbean, Other Asian and Bangladeshi residents in Britain lived in Greater London in 1991.

2.17: People Resident in Britain, Born in the New Commonwealth 1971–1991

change in the proportion of district populations

% change over 10 years

1.0% & over
0.5% to 1.0%
0.2% to 0.5%
0% to 0.2%
up to 0%

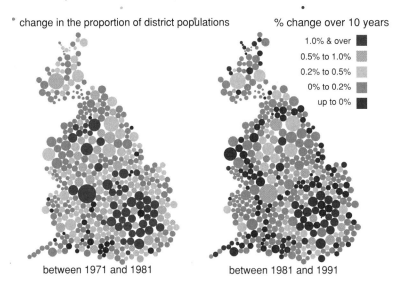

between 1971 and 1981   between 1981 and 1991

Ethnic Minority Residents

Before 1991 people in Britain had, nationally, not been asked to which ethnic group they thought they belonged. Assumptions had been made on the basis of small surveys and on the birthplace of immigrants, but these were not thought to be particularly reliable because the groups being studied were so small. The idea that there are distinguishable ethnic groups is more contentious than the claim that it is useful to categorise people by their sex and age when looking at how society is constituted. It is unfortunate that the census office only used labels for groups associated with relatively recent waves of immigration. Nevertheless, the answers that people gave provide a wealth of information about these groups of people, if not about the ethnicity of the population as a whole.

A person is defined as a member of an *ethnic minority* if they ticked any box other than "white" on the census form. The map and cartogram opposite have been placed together so that the degree of concentration of ethnic minorities within only a few cities is made clear. Three distinct parts of London, and the centres of Birmingham, Leicester, Manchester and Bradford, contain most people belonging to ethnic minorities. Seventy seven percent of people in Britain live in wards where less than 5% of the population are in these groups. In this sense much of our society is only minimally "multi-racial".

A nine-fold subdivision of ethnic groups is used in many of the diagrams which follow. Most labels should be self explanatory even though they are based on a mixture of skin colour, country of origin, religion and so on. The three which may not be clear are: "Black Other", which includes people who wrote "Black British", "Black/White" or similar; "Other Asian", which includes people who filled in none of the specific black categories but wrote "Black Asian", "East African", or included a nationality elsewhere in Asia; and "Other Other" which includes "Arab", "Asian/White" and numerous other possibilities. The census volumes should be consulted for more precise definitions (OPCS 1992).

The regional (and sub-regional) geography for each of these nine groupings of ethnic minorities is shown in Figure 2.16. Nationally, just over three million people ticked something other than white, 5.5% of the population. The cartogram shows that the spatial concentrations within regions are at least as distinct as those between them.

Figure 2.17 gives some indication of how these patterns arose over time but also highlights the inadequacies of using country of birth indicators as a proxy for ethnicity. For these maps Pakistan has been included with the New Commonwealth countries in 1981. The most distinctive features are the actual falls in the numbers born in the New Commonwealth countries living in rural districts in recent years. This is almost certainly not due to falls in ethnic minority populations, but to falls in the number of white people who were born in what were then the colonies, and who chose (and were able) to live in these rural areas. These people represent a white ex-colonial minority in decline.

Ethnic Minority Residents 1991

proportion of ward populations

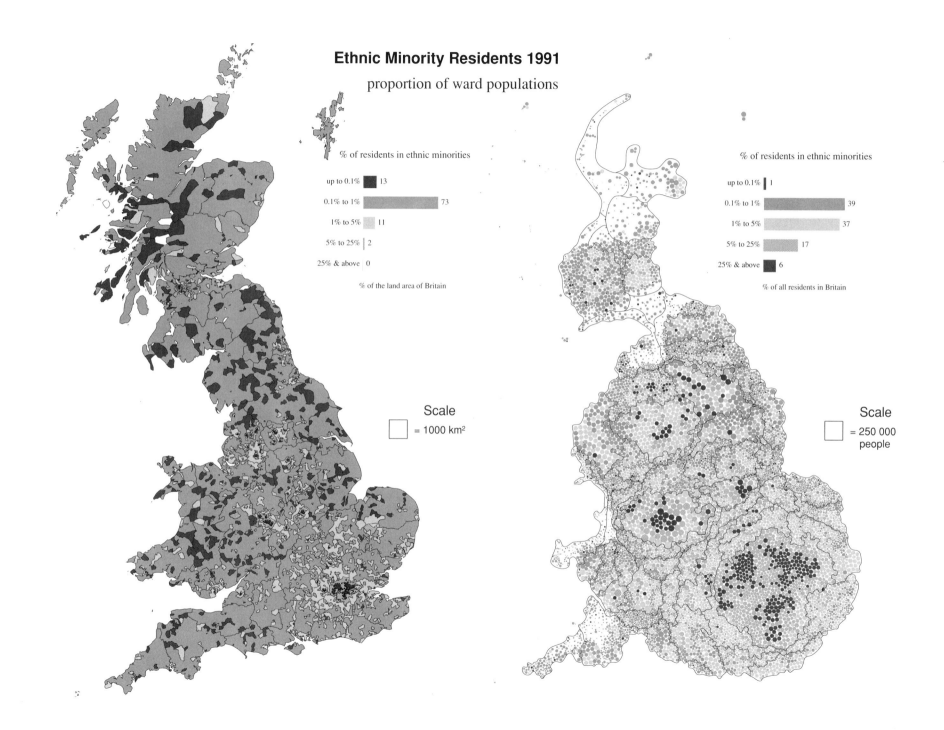

% of residents in ethnic minorities

up to 0.1%	▮	13
0.1% to 1%	▬	73
1% to 5%	▬	11
5% to 25%	▮	2
25% & above		0

% of the land area of Britain

Scale

☐ = 1000 km²

% of residents in ethnic minorities

up to 0.1%	▮	1
0.1% to 1%	▬	39
1% to 5%	▬	37
5% to 25%	▬	17
25% & above	▮	6

% of all residents in Britain

Scale

☐ = 250 000 people

2.18: Residents born outside the UK by Year of Entry and Country of Birth 1989–1991

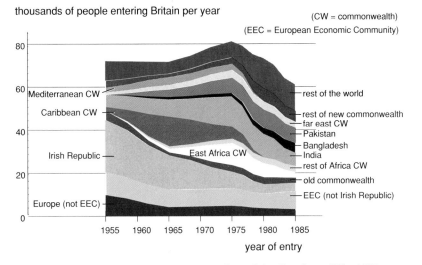

thousands of people entering Britain per year

(CW = commonwealth)
(EEC = European Economic Community)

Labels: Mediterranean CW, Caribbean CW, Irish Republic, East Africa CW, Europe (not EEC); rest of the world, rest of new commonwealth, far east CW, Pakistan, Bangladesh, India, rest of Africa CW, old commonwealth, EEC (not Irish Republic)

year of entry

Source: Labour Force Survey 1990 and 1991

2.19: % in Each Ethnic Group by People's Own and their Head of Household's Birthplace, 1991

Country of Birth (by household head in brackets)	white	Black Caribbean	Black African	Black Other	Indian	Pakistani	Bangladeshi	Chinese	Other Asian	Other Other
Total Persons in Britain ('000s)	51 086	493	202	176	835	474	161	152	191	285
England	80% (79%)	53% (32%)	35% (19%)	82% (52%)	41% (7%)	48% (6%)	36% (3%)	26% (10%)	22% (12%)	56% (39%)
Scotland	10% (10%)		1% (1%)	1% (2%)	1%	2%		2% (1%)	(1%)	2% (2%)
Wales	5% (5%)		1% (1%)	2% (2%)		1%	1%	1%		2% (2%)
Northern Ireland	(1%)									
Rest of United Kingdom										
Irish Republic	1% (2%)			1% (1%)						(1%)
Old Commonwealth										1% (1%)
Eastern Africa Commonwealth			8% (8%)	1% (1%)	17% (25%)	1% (2%)			6% (8%)	1% (3%)
Other Africa Commonwealth			38% (51%)	1% (4%)						1% (1%)
Caribbean Commonwealth		45% (65%)	1% (2%)	3% (23%)	1% (1%)			1% (1%)	1% (1%)	2% (6%)
Bangladesh							62% (94%)		1% (1%)	(1%)
India			(1%)	1% (1%)	37% (61%)	3% (7%)	(1%)	(1%)	3% (6%)	5% (8%)
Pakistan				(1%)	1% (1%)	45% (83%)	1% (1%)		2% (4%)	1% (3%)
South-East Asia Commonwealth					1% (1%)			46% (57%)	6% (5%)	2% (2%)
Cyprus					1% (1%)					
Other New Commonwealth				1% (2%)	1% (1%)			1% (2%)	22% (26%)	1% (3%)
Other European Community	1% (1%)			1% (1%)					(1%)	1% (1%)
Other Europe										
United States of America			1% (1%)	3% (3%)					(1%)	1% (1%)
China								12% (15%)		
Vietnam								6% (8%)	5% (6%)	
Rest of the World	(1%)	(1%)	14% (14%)	3% (3%)	1% (2%)			3% (3%)	32% (27%)	23% (25%)

Black and Asian

Although members of all ethnic minorities are more likely to live in cities than whites, they are also likely to live in distinct parts of those cities. Two broad groupings have been used in the maps opposite. *Afro-Caribbean* consists of the three groups prefixed "Black-", and *South-Asian* consists of people identifying with India, Pakistan or Bangladesh. Only in parts of London and in one ward in Manchester are more than a quarter of the population Afro-Caribbean, while in many wards in Wales, Scotland and the North practically nobody identifies with this category. The largest concentration of people of South-Asian ethnic origin now live in Birmingham, but many more smaller clusters of people with these backgrounds are visible even as far north as Dundee.

One reason for the very different spatial patterns is that many of these people's parents or grandparents entered Britain at different times. Figure 2.18 shows an estimate of when and from where people who migrated to this country and were living here in 1991 came. By 1977 most migration from the Caribbean had ceased, whereas migration from Bangladesh had only just begun. The sudden influx of East African Asians from Uganda in the 1970s is particularly distinctive. People migrating from the Irish Republic form the largest single group. By defining Irish-born as another ethnic group it is possible to subdivide the white majority slightly so this has been done, where possible, below.

Immigration and ethnicity are very strongly linked despite 47% of people in ethnic minorities having been born in the United Kingdom. Only 19% of their household heads were born here and so it can be assumed that the majority of those who are "British-born" are the children of people who migrated. Figure 2.19 gives, in detail, the breakdown of all individuals in each ethnic group both by country of birth and by the country of birth of household head (the person who put his/her name first on the census form). All the percentages are rounded to the nearest whole number and are not shown when that is zero. The figures for all individuals are shown in brackets when they are classified by the country of birth of the head of household. Thus, for instance, 1% of whites were born in the Irish Republic but 2% live in households in which the head of the household was born in the Irish Republic. Household head is not a very robust concept, but here it does help to show how strong the social links with various parts of the world may be for different groups, and how that is likely to alter according to their ages (household heads must be older than 16). For example, most of the almost half million people who see themselves as belonging to a "Black Caribbean" ethnic minority were born in Britain, 45% of them were born in the (New Commonwealth part of the) Caribbean, but 65% of them live in households whose head's country of birth was in the Caribbean. The other way in which this table can be used is to look across a region of the world to see which groups in Britain are most closely associated with these countries, East Africa, for example.

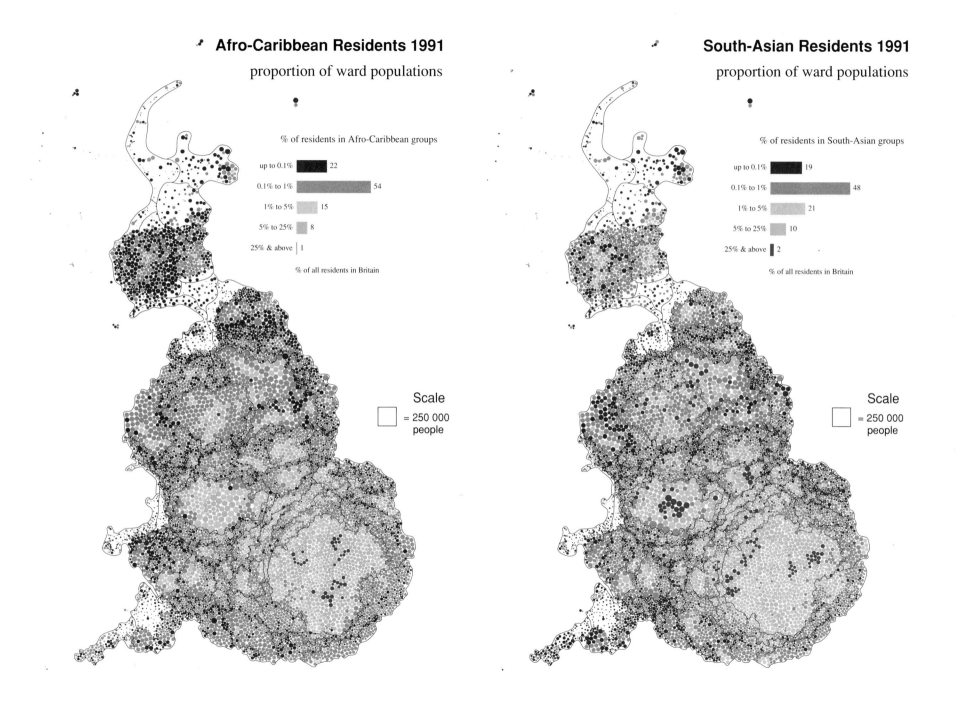

Afro-Caribbean Residents 1991

proportion of ward populations

% of residents in Afro-Caribbean groups

up to 0.1%   22
0.1% to 1%   54
1% to 5%   15
5% to 25%   8
25% & above   1

% of all residents in Britain

Scale

☐ = 250 000
people

South-Asian Residents 1991

proportion of ward populations

% of residents in South-Asian groups

up to 0.1%   19
0.1% to 1%   48
1% to 5%   21
5% to 25%   10
25% & above   2

% of all residents in Britain

Scale

☐ = 250 000
people

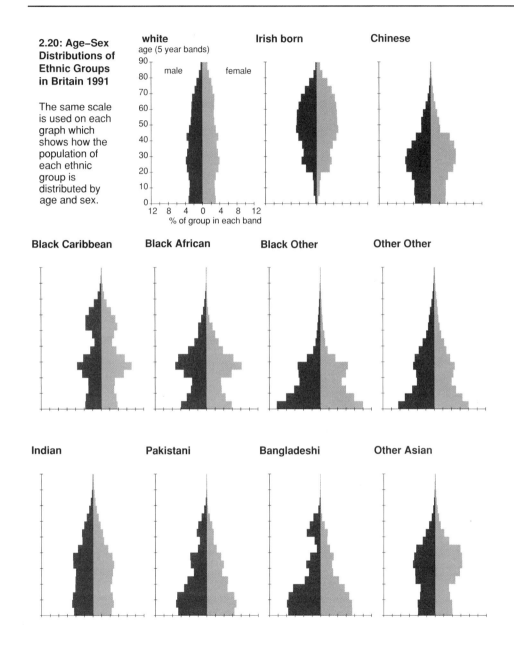

2.20: Age–Sex Distributions of Ethnic Groups in Britain 1991

The same scale is used on each graph which shows how the population of each ethnic group is distributed by age and sex.

Ethnic Minority Groups

Each of the ethnic minority groups given in census output has a very distinct geographical pattern. These are shown here by local authority district because the numbers involved are often very small and because of the space which would otherwise be required. The key to each of the maps is the same so that the relative sizes of each ethnic group can be compared. Here people born in the Irish Republic are included as a surrogate ethnic group representative of those who would have classified themselves as Irish if this had been suggested. The areas of highest concentration are very different for different groups as should be evident opposite. The degrees of spatial variation in the places where practically nobody identifies with a particular group are also interesting. Very few areas contain nobody of Chinese origin, while there are unusually low numbers of people born in Ireland living in the Welsh Valleys or in Tyneside.

Coastal districts contain low numbers of all ethnic groups. One reason for this is the age distribution of people identifying with ethnic minorities which should be studied in conjunction with these maps. Figure 2.20 shows the age and sex population pyramids for each ethnic group including whites (which is close to that for the population as a whole). Only the Irish born tend to have an older structure, although that tapers quickly, possibly due to emigration in old age. The Irish born are also the only group to have significant numbers of people living among the population on the south coast.

All the non-white ethnic minorities have younger population structures than whites, explained largely by the periods when they or their parents migrated (Figure 2.18). Differences between the sex ratios are also apparent, there being more older Bangladeshi men than women in this country and fewer middle-aged "Other Asian" men than women. The "Black Other" and "Other Other" categories have the youngest age structures reflecting the increasing heterogeneity of ethnic identity in Britain. Ethnic categories are usually only defined when groups who think they are different mix, thus through the process by which ethnicity is defined there cannot be robust ways of classification.

One other reason why ethnic minority groups have been included here is that they are often used later on to show how, for instance, employment and housing are distributed unequally among people from these nine or ten backgrounds. When looking at those statistics it is important to bear in mind the different age structures of each of these groups. Young groups of people, for example, are more likely to be unemployed regardless of their ethnicity. It is possible, with census data, to standardise every statistic in a variety of ways; for instance, to show the standardised geographical distribution of people in ethnic minorities allowing for the prevailing age and sex structure of each group. While such statistics can enhance information it is most important to realise what the basic underlying patterns are before looking for more subtle variations. Here only those basic patterns are shown.

Ethnic Minority Groups 1991

proportions of district populations

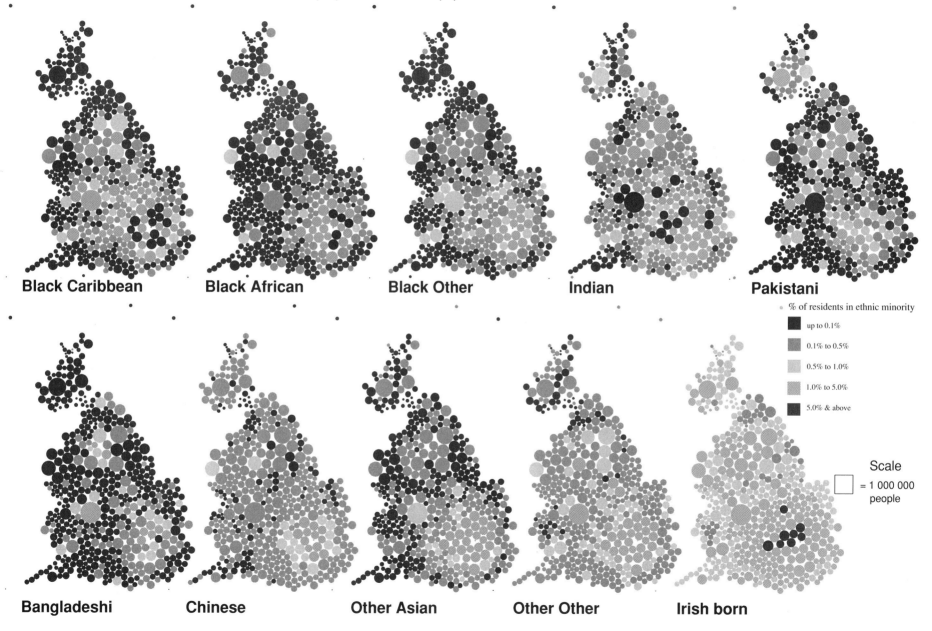

Black Caribbean

Black African

Black Other

Indian

Pakistani

Bangladeshi

Chinese

Other Asian

Other Other

Irish born

% of residents in ethnic minority

up to 0.1%

0.1% to 0.5%

0.5% to 1.0%

1.0% to 5.0%

5.0% & above

Scale

= 1 000 000
people

2.21: Change in % of Residents Born in England 1971–1991 by 1960s Immigration by Ward

change in % of residents born in England 1971–1991 (for all wards in Britain)

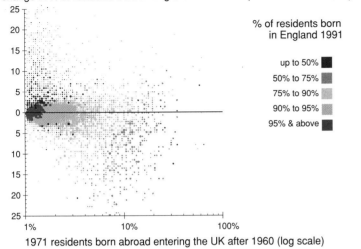

% of residents born
in England 1991

| up to 50% |
| 50% to 75% |
| 75% to 90% |
| 90% to 95% |
| 95% & above |

1971 residents born abroad entering the UK after 1960 (log scale)

2.22: English Born Living in Scotland 1971–1991

% of all residents in each region born in England

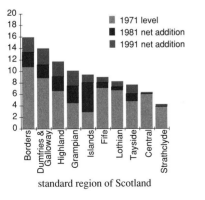

standard region of Scotland

2.23: English Born Living in Wales 1971–1991

% of all residents in each county born in England

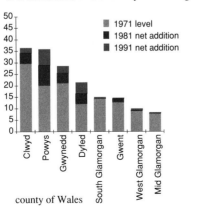

county of Wales

Born in England

Birthplace was the traditional indicator of ethnic origin in British censuses before 1991. Knowing how many people living in one place were born in another gives an indication both of lifetime migration rates and of the national origins of different populations. Unfortunately, no geographical detail below the country level is recorded by the census, but even this information can produce some very striking distributions.

Just over three quarters of British residents were born in England; this is by far the largest group by birthplace and it has grown very slightly in proportion since 1971, as fewer people have entered the country from abroad. For obvious reasons most people living in Scotland and Wales were not born in England, although in a few wards on the Welsh border just over half of residents were born in England. Inside England itself, as the map opposite shows, it is people living in London who are least likely to have been born in England. The "English" are most prevalent in the north of England, concentrated at very high proportions in particularly distinct localities (see opposite).

The map of change shows how the pattern of 1991 is different from that of a generation ago. The two striking features are the decline in the proportion of Outer London's population who were born in England and the rise of English born people choosing to live in Scotland and Wales. These changes are only slight in comparison with the size of the English born population but they are very clearly clustered.

There will be many reasons to explain why this overall shift of people has occurred away from the capital and towards the periphery. The change is composed of both out-migration of the English and immigration from other countries (principally from Scotland and Wales) to London. Figure 2.21 plots the distribution of change against the proportion of people living in each ward in 1971 who were not born in Britain and who entered the country in the preceding ten years. Each ward in the graph is shaded identically to the shade used in the static distribution shown opposite. Although English born people are more likely to have left areas in the 1970s and 1980s where the rate of immigration was high in the 1960s, this is partly due to the absolute increase in those areas of the number of people who were born abroad. Their children, if born in these same wards, have an influence on the trend in the opposite direction.

The largest group of immigrants in Britain are the English in Scotland and Wales. Since 1971 in every county and region in these countries the proportion of people born in England has increased (see Figures 2.22 and 2.23). The number of English born people resident in these two countries has risen by 40% since 1971 to now stand at 893 000. This is the greatest increase of any group now living in a country other than that of its birth in Britain. In the more rural counties and regions of Wales and Scotland the rises have been even greater. English born people used to migrate more to live in the industrial areas of these two countries, now they migrate to their countryside.

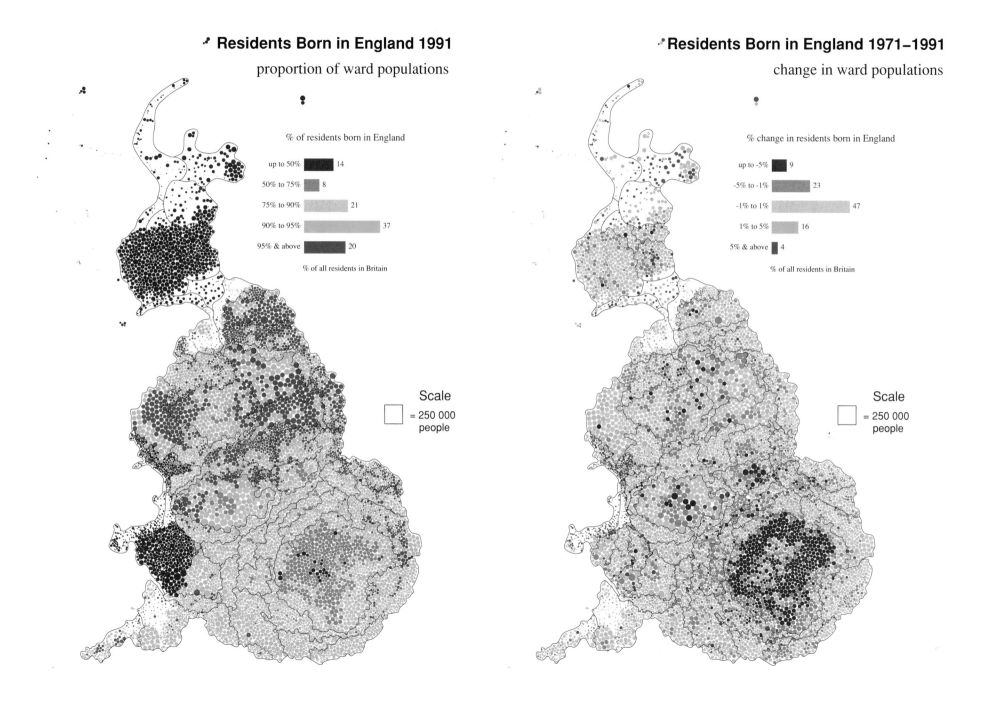

Residents Born in England 1991

proportion of ward populations

% of residents born in England

up to 50%	14
50% to 75%	8
75% to 90%	21
90% to 95%	37
95% & above	20

% of all residents in Britain

Scale

☐ = 250 000 people

Residents Born in England 1971–1991

change in ward populations

% change in residents born in England

up to -5%	9
-5% to -1%	23
-1% to 1%	47
1% to 5%	16
5% & above	4

% of all residents in Britain

Scale

☐ = 250 000 people

2.24: Change in the Proportion of Residents Born in Ireland by Region 1971–1991

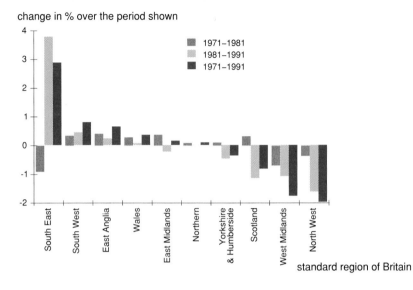

change in % over the period shown

Legend:
- 1971–1981
- 1981–1991
- 1971–1991

standard region of Britain

Regions (left to right): South East, South West, East Anglia, Wales, East Midlands, Northern, Yorkshire & Humberside, Scotland, West Midlands, North West

2.25: Ratio of Irish Republic Born to Northern Irish Born 1991, 1971–1991

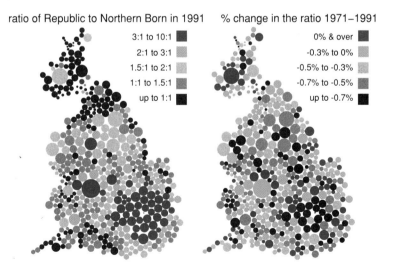

ratio of Republic to Northern Born in 1991

- 3:1 to 10:1
- 2:1 to 3:1
- 1.5:1 to 2:1
- 1:1 to 1.5:1
- up to 1:1

% change in the ratio 1971–1991

- 0% & over
- -0.3% to 0%
- -0.5% to -0.3%
- -0.7% to -0.5%
- up to -0.7%

Born in Ireland

Monitoring the number of people migrating to Britain from Ireland has been a major preoccupation of the British census for the last one hundred and fifty years (Craig 1987: 33). As Figure 2.20 shows, Irish born people are the only group, distinguished by the census authorities along with ethnic groups, to have a significantly older age profile than the population as a whole. Also the Irish born population in Britain is declining.

Nationally, only one in every 65 British residents was born in Ireland, with London and very distinct parts of the West Midlands and Manchester containing most of these, as the first map indicates. It is most probably the ageing of the Irish population which has led to the pattern of change shown since 1971. Irish born people have moved from the inner city to the outer city and have not been replaced by young Irish born migrants.

Figure 2.24 gives the broad regional changes. The same graphical format is used later to show the movements of the Welsh and Scottish born populations. Over the 1970s the South East saw the largest proportionate loss of its Irish born population closely followed by the West Midlands. For the former region that pattern was dramatically reversed in the 1980s so that by the end of the twenty year period three more people in every hundred living in London were born in Ireland than at the beginning. From the censuses it is not possible to say whether this was due to people moving from regions which lost large numbers of people born in Ireland or to immigration. The regions in the graph are shown ordered by the overall change from 1971 to 1991.

A further subdivision of the statistics for the Irish born population living in Britain is possible into those born in the Irish Republic and those born in Northern Ireland. The ratio of south to north nationally is 2.42:1 but this statistic disguises sharp differences even at the local authority district level, as Figure 2.25 shows. People born in the Irish Republic are more likely to be living in the south of Britain, while those born in Northern Ireland outnumber the Irish Republic born in most of the north of Britain. This difference is slowly decreasing as the second map in the figure shows — with the Northern Irish born increasing most rapidly in London while the strongest area of growth of the Irish Republic born living in Britain was around Glasgow, albeit both from low initial numbers. Later the geographical distributions of each group and their separate growth rates are shown (pages 55 and 57). Disentangling the effects of an ageing population from the influence of new young migrants and older Irish born emigrants is not easily possible as the age of the Irish born population was not calculated in census statistics before 1991. There is evidence that the Irish born in Britain are a rapidly ageing population (King and Shuttleworth 1989), but because no question was asked about Irish ethnicity in the census we do not know how many younger people who were born in Britain identify with Ireland and how many born in Ireland do not see themselves as "Irish".

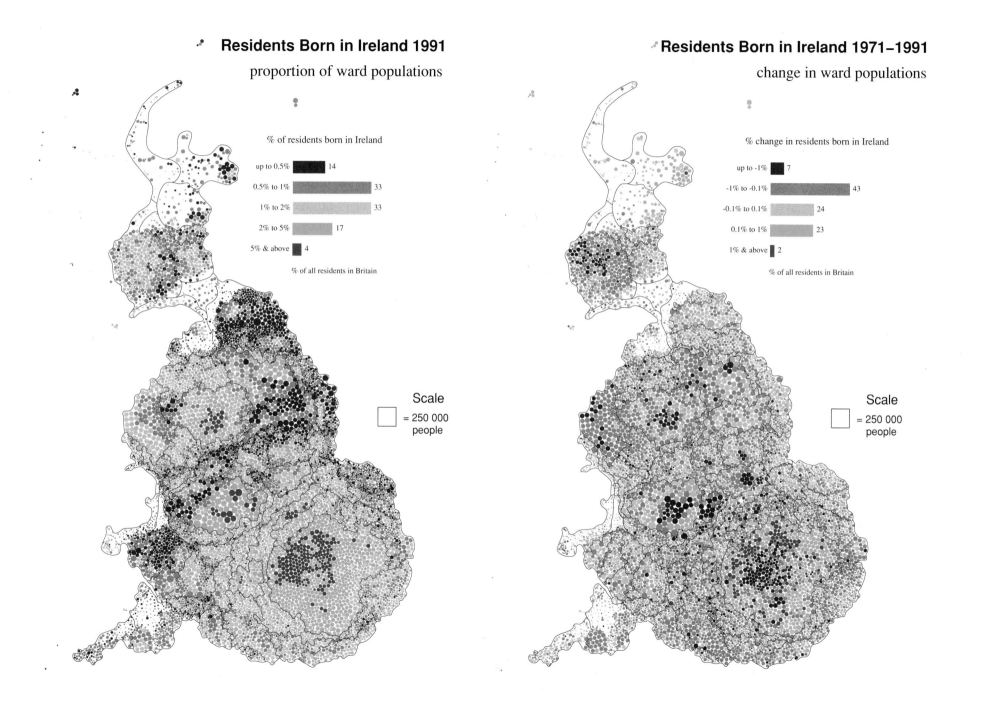

Residents Born in Ireland 1991

proportion of ward populations

% of residents born in Ireland

up to 0.5%	14
0.5% to 1%	33
1% to 2%	33
2% to 5%	17
5% & above	4

% of all residents in Britain

Scale

☐ = 250 000 people

Residents Born in Ireland 1971–1991

change in ward populations

% change in residents born in Ireland

up to -1%	7
-1% to -0.1%	43
-0.1% to 0.1%	24
0.1% to 1%	23
1% & above	2

% of all residents in Britain

Scale

☐ = 250 000 people

2.26: Change in the Proportion of Residents Born in Scotland by Region 1971–1991

change in % over the period shown

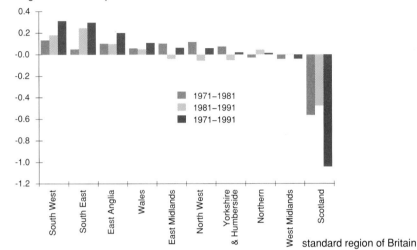

1971–1981
1981–1991
1971–1991

standard region of Britain

2.27: Change in the Number of Residents Living in Scottish Regions 1901–1991

percentage change from 1901

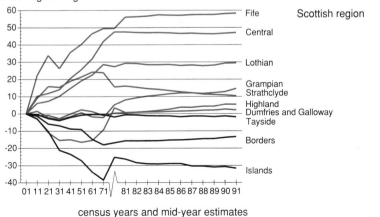

census years and mid-year estimates

Born in Scotland

As Scotland is the second largest country in Britain, people born in Scotland are the second largest group by birthplace, comprising just under 10% of the population. Out of every seven people born in Scotland, one is now living in England. The map opposite shows precisely where these lifetime migrants are likely to be. The proportions of Scottish born people in England are high near the border, particularly in Carlisle, Barrow in Furness and Blackpool. Further south, Scottish born people are most likely to be found in the west of London and across the Home Counties as well as in particular places such as Corby. The geographical patterns suggest that Scottish born migrants tend to end up in more affluent areas. The very low numbers of Scottish born people in most of the West Midlands, South Wales, Merseyside and South Yorkshire are also noticeable.

As the map of a generation of change shows, it is the older industrial areas to which Scottish born migrants are least likely to come to or to be replaced in. There is also a distinct ring in Outer London from which there has been a net reduction in the proportion born in Scotland, who now appear in greater numbers further afield. Most dramatic, however, are the changes which have taken place within Scotland itself. It is important to note that changes in the proportion of people born in Scotland can be produced by the movements and mortality of people born outside Scotland as well as by Scottish born people themselves; but at least one extra person in every hundred now living in the north, east and south of Scotland was not born in that country (as compared to twenty years ago). Only around Glasgow, but not in its centre, has the proportion of Scottish born people risen, and only then because there has been a greater proportionate decline in people born elsewhere living there.

Figure 2.26 shows just how dramatic the twenty year change has been for Scotland and how it has been sustained over the last two decades. The fact that it is the South West which has seen the highest rise in its Scottish born population suggests that it may be the retirement migration of people who left Scotland many years ago which is accounting for many of the patterns shown here. This figure allows the changes which occurred in the 1970s to be contrasted with those of the 1980s and also compared to the regional changes in the proportions of people born in Ireland (Figure 2.24). The explanation for the declining proportion of Scottish born people living in Scotland can be provided by looking at the rates of English born immigration shown in Figure 2.22.

Although here changes over the last twenty years are being highlighted, the changes over the last century have been much more dramatic. This is particularly the case in Scotland itself. Figure 2.27 shows the relative changes in population for each Scottish region and the island areas. Three of these areas still contain less people now than they did a century ago despite overall growth of the population nationally. The source of the data used in this figure is the same as that used in the maps shown on page 17.

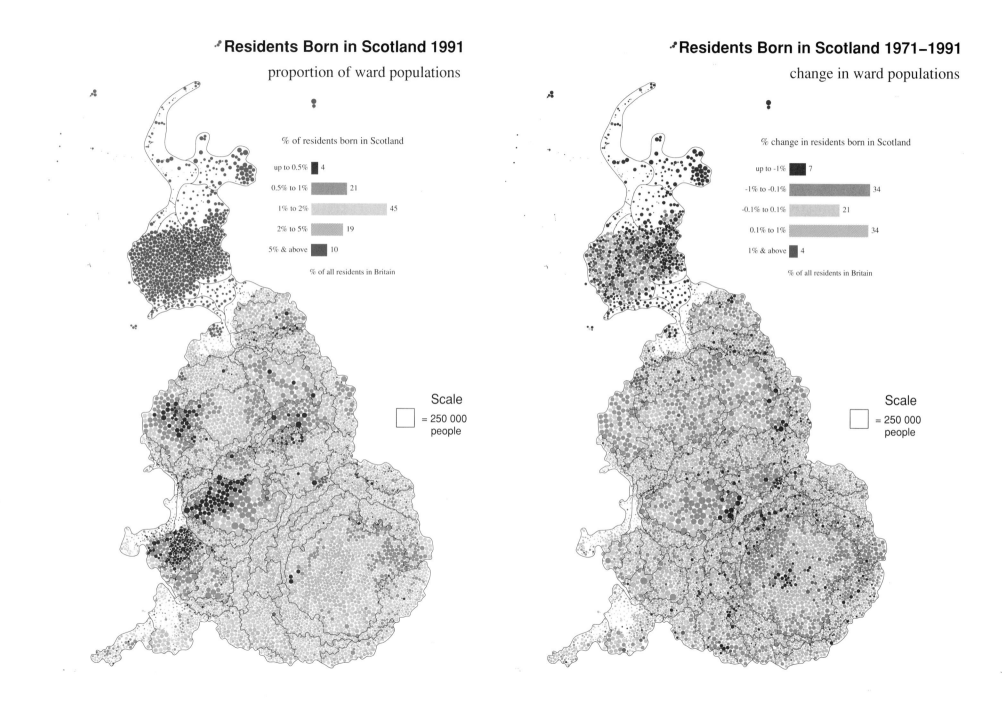

Residents Born in Scotland 1991

proportion of ward populations

% of residents born in Scotland

up to 0.5%	4
0.5% to 1%	21
1% to 2%	45
2% to 5%	19
5% & above	10

% of all residents in Britain

Scale

☐ = 250 000 people

Residents Born in Scotland 1971–1991

change in ward populations

% change in residents born in Scotland

up to -1%	7
-1% to -0.1%	34
-0.1% to 0.1%	21
0.1% to 1%	34
1% & above	4

% of all residents in Britain

Scale

☐ = 250 000 people

2.28: Change in the Proportion of Residents Born in Wales by Region 1971–1991

change in % over the period shown

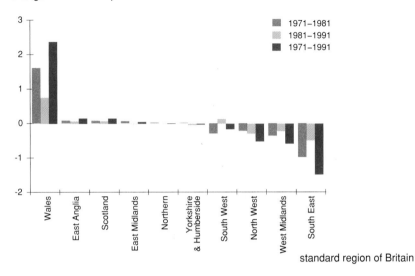

standard region of Britain

2.29: Change in the Number of Residents Living in Welsh Counties 1901–1991

percentage change from 1901

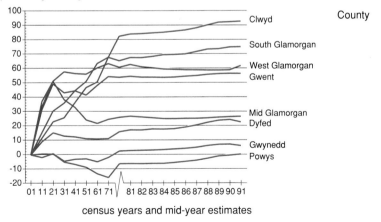

census years and mid-year estimates

Born in Wales

One in twenty people living in Britain in 1991 was born in Wales, but only 80% of these people were living in Wales at that time. One simple reason why a higher proportion of the Welsh live in England than the Scots is that the Welsh border is much longer and Wales is smaller. The map shows the geographical diffusion of Welsh born people out from Wales into Avon, Gloucestershire, Wiltshire and beyond. It also shows how Wales is very clearly split north and south; diffusion from the north being very much less evident than from the south. In terms of where people were born, it is the Valleys which have been becoming most "Welsh" over the last two decades. Their influence has lead to the overall increase in the proportion of the total Welsh born population living in Wales shown in Figure 2.28. This has occurred despite the dramatic increases in the number of people born in England now living in Wales shown in Figure 2.23. Fewer Welsh born people are now leaving Wales than was the case twenty years ago.

Again the changes over the last ninety years have been more dramatic than those of recent decades as parts of Wales experienced rapid industrial expansion at the start of this century similar to the experience in parts of Scotland. In many ways, however, the Welsh experience of population change is now very different to that of Scotland. Figure 2.29 shows that the population of every Welsh County is now higher than it was a century ago despite significant rural depopulation. Powys has only just reached this state, however, but is now the fastest growing county. It is also the county which saw the highest proportionate increase in its English born population during the 1980s, followed by Dyfed, Gywnedd and Clwyd (Figure 2.23).

One reason for the increasing proportion of Welsh born people living in Wales is the low out-migration rates of the Welsh which were reported in detail after the 1981 census (Brant 1984: 24, Devis 1983: 17, Kennett 1983: 223). Changes above or below 1% shifts in the proportion born in Wales are not that dramatic in areas where the majority of the population are born in Wales, whereas the falls of over 1% seen in parts of west London often represent a fall of more than half the Welsh born populations of those areas over twenty years. The Welsh born are, on average, becoming more concentrated in Wales and in the Valleys in particular. At the same time a new generation of people born in Wales whose parents came from England is now emerging. Figure 2.29 is testimony to the degree to which the influence of immigration is diluted over time. The populations of the areas which are now Gwent, Mid Glamorgan and West Glamorgan grew in population by an additional 50% from 1901 to 1921. It is somewhat ironic that at the start of this century largely English immigration fuelled the population growth of the Valleys which are now seen, in the simple demographic terms used here, as the most Welsh parts of Wales. Country of birth information can only be used as a poor proxy for "white" people's ethnic identities.

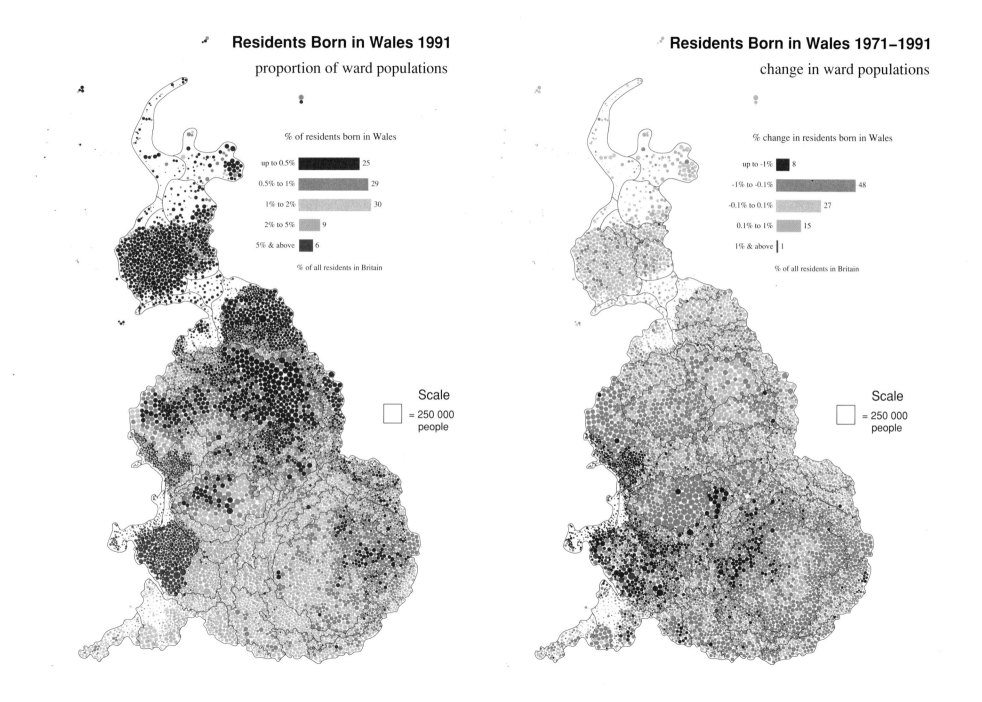

Residents Born in Wales 1991

proportion of ward populations

% of residents born in Wales

up to 0.5%	25
0.5% to 1%	29
1% to 2%	30
2% to 5%	9
5% & above	6

% of all residents in Britain

Scale

☐ = 250 000
people

Residents Born in Wales 1971–1991

change in ward populations

% change in residents born in Wales

up to -1%	8
-1% to -0.1%	48
-0.1% to 0.1%	27
0.1% to 1%	15
1% & above	1

% of all residents in Britain

Scale

☐ = 250 000
people

2.30: Country of Birth of all Residents in Britain 1991

Countries of Birth	Population	prop-ortion	District with highest proportion	
UNITED KINGDOM	51 114 048	93.12%	Blaenau Gwent	99.05%
England	42 897 179	78.15%	Easington	97.83%
Scotland	5 221 038	9.51%	Monklands	96.44%
Wales	2 747 790	5.01%	Rhondda	93.83%
Northern Ireland	244 914	0.45%	Corby	1.64%
Rest of United Kingdom	3127	0.01%	Epsom & Ewell	0.25%
OUTSIDE UK	3 774 796	6.88%	Brent	42.14%
Channel Islands	18 714	0.03%	Southampton	0.20%
Isle of Man	9960	0.02%	Wirral	0.09%
Irish Republic	592 020	1.08%	Brent	8.19%
Ireland (part not stated)	530	0.00%	Brent	0.01%
Old Commonwealth	177 355	0.32%	Kensington & Chelsea	3.17%
Australia	73 217	0.13%	Kensington & Chelsea	1.63%
Canada	63 153	0.12%	Kensington & Chelsea	0.71%
New Zealand	40 985	0.07%	City of London	0.89%
New Commonwealth	1 688 396	3.08%	Brent	23.89%
Africa	331 313	0.60%	Brent	7.41%
Eastern Africa	220 605	0.40%	Harrow	6.95%
Kenya	112 422	0.20%	Harrow	3.89%
Malawi	10 697	0.02%	Leicester	1.04%
Tanzania	29 825	0.05%	Harrow	1.00%
Uganda	50 903	0.09%	Harrow	1.76%
Zambia	16 758	0.03%	Leicester	0.22%
Southern Africa	23 253	0.04%	Kensington & Chelsea	0.18%
Zimbabwe	21 252	0.04%	Kensington & Chelsea	0.17%
Botswana, Lesotho & Swaziland	2001	0.00%	Isles of Scilly	0.10%
West Africa	87 455	0.16%	Southwark	3.57%
Gambia	1388	0.00%	City of London	0.05%
Ghana	32 672	0.06%	Lambeth	1.09%
Nigeria	47 085	0.09%	Southwark	2.44%
Sierra Leone	6310	0.01%	Southwark	0.27%
Caribbean	264 591	0.48%	Lambeth	5.87%
Barbados	22 294	0.04%	Reading	0.62%
Jamaica	142 483	0.26%	Lambeth	4.16%
Trinidad and Tobago	17 620	0.03%	Haringey	0.33%
Other Independent States	44 045	0.08%	Hackney	1.60%
Caribbean Dependent Territories	6338	0.01%	Hackney	0.36%
West Indies (so stated)	10 123	0.02%	Hackney	0.27%
Belize	1210	0.00%	Argyll and Bute	0.02%
Guyana	20 478	0.04%	Lambeth	0.49%
Asia	937 937	1.71%	Tower Hamlets	16.19%
South Asia	787 528	1.43%	Tower Hamlets	15.61%
Bangladesh	105 010	0.19%	Tower Hamlets	14.63%
India	409 022	0.75%	Leicester	7.70%
Pakistan	234 107	0.43%	Bradford	4.69%
Sri Lanka	39 387	0.07%	Brent	1.23%
South East Asia	150 409	0.27%	Westminster, City of	1.59%
Hong Kong	72 937	0.13%	Westminster, City of	0.60%
Malaysia	43 511	0.08%	Westminster, City of	0.74%
Singapore	33 961	0.06%	City of London	0.34%
New Commonwealth Remainder	154 555	0.28%	Enfield	4.99%
Cyprus	78 031	0.14%	Enfield	4.40%
Gibraltar	11 391	0.02%	Gosport	0.21%
Malta & Gozo	31 237	0.06%	Gosport	0.48%
Mauritius	23 450	0.04%	Haringey	0.76%
Seychelles	2967	0.01%	Hounslow	0.17%
Other New Commonwealth	7479	0.01%	Westminster, City of	0.15%

Countries of Birth	Population	prop-ortion	District with highest proportion	
Europe including UK	52 403 308	95.47%	Blaenau Gwent	99.51%
European Community+UK	52 200 488	95.10%	Blaenau Gwent	99.45%
European Community−UK	493 890	0.90%	Kensington & Chelsea	9.06%
Belgium	16 416	0.03%	Kensington & Chelsea	0.29%
Denmark	14 226	0.03%	City of London	0.41%
France	53 443	0.10%	Kensington & Chelsea	2.25%
Germany	215 534	0.39%	Richmondshire	2.98%
Greece	14 610	0.03%	Westminster, City of	0.53%
Italy	91 010	0.17%	North Bedfordshire	1.87%
Luxembourg	705	0.00%	Kensington & Chelsea	0.02%
Netherlands	29 442	0.05%	Elmbridge	0.53%
Portugal	19 775	0.04%	Kensington & Chelsea	1.03%
Spain	38 729	0.07%	Kensington & Chelsea	1.67%
Remainder of Europe (−EC)	174 146	0.32%	Kensington & Chelsea	2.98%
Albania	161	0.00%	Kensington & Chelsea	0.01%
Austria	20 645	0.04%	Camden	0.32%
Bulgaria	1710	0.00%	Ross and Cromarty	0.48%
Czechoslovakia	8720	0.02%	Camden	0.22%
Finland	5285	0.01%	Kensington & Chelsea	0.14%
Hungary	12 487	0.02%	City of London	0.24%
Norway	8684	0.02%	City of London	0.31%
Poland	73 738	0.13%	Ealing	1.32%
Romania	3960	0.01%	City of London	0.19%
Sweden	11 054	0.02%	Kensington & Chelsea	0.53%
Switzerland	12 613	0.02%	Kensington & Chelsea	0.36%
Yugoslavia	13 813	0.03%	Hammersmith & Fulham	0.39%
Other Europe	1276	0.00%	Shetland	0.05%
Turkey	26 597	0.05%	Hackney	2.64%
(former) U.S.S.R.	27 011	0.05%	Bradford	0.32%
Africa	146 869	0.27%	Kensington & Chelsea	3.06%
Algeria	3672	0.01%	Kensington & Chelsea	0.13%
Egypt	22 849	0.04%	Kensington & Chelsea	0.59%
Libya	6604	0.01%	Westminster, City of	0.09%
Morocco	9073	0.02%	Kensington & Chelsea	0.70%
Tunisia	2417	0.00%	Westminster, City of	0.06%
Republic of South Africa	68 059	0.12%	Camden	0.92%
Other Africa	34 195	0.06%	Haringey	1.15%
America	185 033	0.34%	Forest Heath	18.64%
United States of America	143 484	0.26%	Forest Heath	18.47%
Caribbean	2504	0.00%	Forest Heath	0.07%
Central America	4449	0.01%	Kensington & Chelsea	0.14%
South America	34 596	0.06%	Kensington & Chelsea	1.26%
Asia	231 045	0.42%	Westminster, City of	6.67%
Middle East	101 719	0.19%	Westminster, City of	4.36%
Iran	32 262	0.06%	Kensington & Chelsea	1.18%
Israel	12 195	0.02%	Barnet	0.73%
Other Middle East	57 262	0.10%	Westminster, City of	2.93%
Remainder of Asia	129 326	0.24%	Kensington & Chelsea	2.69%
Burma (Union of Myanmar)	10 608	0.02%	Croydon	0.15%
People's Republic of China	23 784	0.04%	Cambridge	0.33%
Japan	28 235	0.05%	Barnet	1.38%
Philippines	21 836	0.04%	Kensington & Chelsea	1.09%
Vietnam	20 119	0.04%	Southwark	0.82%
Other Asia	24 744	0.05%	Hart	0.92%
Remainder	3230	0.01%	Leicester	0.08%

Born Abroad

Although the largest group of people living in Britain who were born abroad were from Ireland, the Irish born make up only 21% of all British residents who were not born in Britain. The complete breakdown (that is available for every ward in Britain) of the numbers of people born abroad is shown in Figure 2.30 by country. Countries are grouped first by whether they are members of the Commonwealth or not, then by continent and then region. The total number of people who claimed to be born in each country and are now resident in Britain is shown, followed by the percentage of all residents which that number represents, then the name of the local authority district which has the highest proportion from that country, and then that proportion. Local clusters can be surprising. For instance, the results of the return to Britain of the children of members of the armed forces born overseas may well be reflected through the unusual numbers of people born in Belize and Gibraltar who now live in Argyll & Bute and Gosport. Cambridge has the highest proportion of people born in China.

The geographical spread for ten of the largest and most distinctive countries or groupings of countries at the district level is shown opposite. These groupings were chosen so that comparisons could be made with figures taken from the 1971 census, shown later. The letters "CW" stand for "Commonwealth" and indicate that only countries that were members of the Commonwealth are included in the definition.

Most people live in wards where less than one in one hundred of the population were born in any of these distinct regions. The proportions that are shown here are very small, which is one reason for using this level of geographical aggregation. The geographical distributions of the Irish have already been mentioned; here Northern and Republic are shown separately. People born in the "Rest of Europe" (excluding Britain and Ireland) and the "Rest of the World" (excluding all the other groups shown) are the most numerous, comprising 670 000 and 810 000 people, respectively. They also have the most marked tendency to live in the south of England. The smallest group shown here is of those born in the South East Asian commonwealth comprising Hong Kong (49%), Malaysia (29%) and Singapore (22%) (see Figure 2.30). Geographically their distribution is similar to the next smallest group who were born in the "old commonwealth". The next two groups, which are similar, are those born in the Caribbean commonwealth and Pakistan or Bangladesh, as they both tend not to live near the coast. The pattern of Indian born settlement is most like that of people who were born in African Commonwealth countries (34% of whom were born in Kenya, most probably being "East African Asian" migrants, originally from India). Some of these maps can be compared with the district based distributions of ethnic minority groups shown earlier. Much of the difference in the patterns shown will be due to the number of people who were born in Britain but whose parents were born abroad.

Residents Born Abroad 1991

proportions of district populations

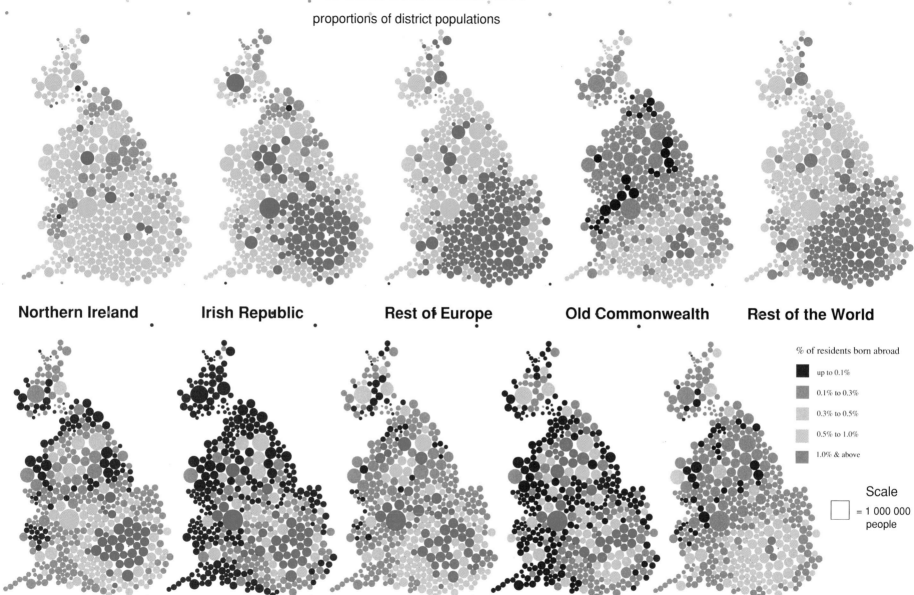

Northern Ireland

Irish Republic

Rest of Europe

Old Commonwealth

Rest of the World

African CW

Caribbean CW

India

Pakistan and Bangladesh

South East Asian CW

% of residents born abroad

up to 0.1%

0.1% to 0.3%

0.3% to 0.5%

0.5% to 1.0%

1.0% & above

Scale

= 1 000 000 people

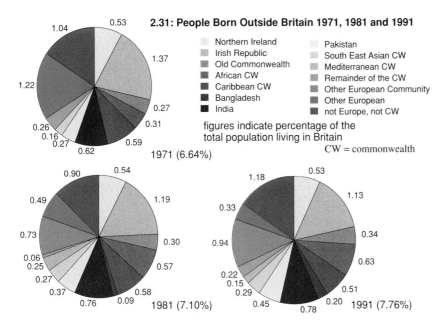

2.31: People Born Outside Britain 1971, 1981 and 1991

Northern Ireland
Irish Republic
Old Commonwealth
African CW
Caribbean CW
Bangladesh
India

Pakistan
South East Asian CW
Mediterranean CW
Remainder of the CW
Other European Community
Other European
not Europe, not CW

figures indicate percentage of the
total population living in Britain

CW = commonwealth

1971 (6.64%)

1981 (7.10%)

1991 (7.76%)

2.32: Residents Born in the UK by Age and Head of Household's Birthplace 1981–1991

HoH = head of household

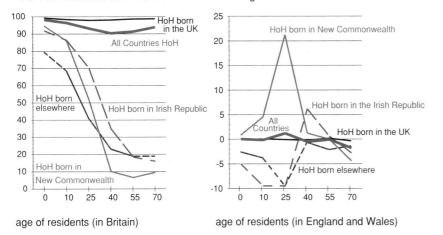

% of 1991 residents born in the UK

% change 1981–1991 in residents born in the UK

age of residents (in Britain)

age of residents (in England and Wales)

Changing Countries

Because people were not asked their affiliations to ethnic groups at censuses before 1991, the change in the locations of people born outside Britain has often been used as a proxy for ethnic group changes, although, as Figure 2.17 suggested, this is unwise. Country of birth changes indicate more about the changing patterns of lifetime migration and the movements of an ageing group of immigrants to Britain, within Britain. Figure 2.31 shows how the proportions of people living in Britain who were born overseas have not changed dramatically over the last twenty years. Countries such as Bangladesh did not exist in 1971, and the European Community was not differentiated by the census then, so some care is needed when reading this figure. Here, for comparability, Northern Ireland includes all people born in other parts of the United Kingdom outside Britain. The pie charts increase slightly in size as the overseas born population has increased to include an additional 1% of the population between 1971 and 1991.

The geographical distribution of these changes for the ten groups used earlier is shown opposite. More people are living in districts which have seen a fall in the proportions of people born in the Irish Republic and the Caribbean Commonwealth than a rise. Places where there have been increases in the proportion of a district's population born in a particular country (or group of countries) often display very strong geographical proximity within Britain. A large proportion of many of these groups will, in 1991, have been students, which may account for some of the clusters. There have also been large differences in the ratios of men to women in some of these groups in earlier years. For instance, there were 2.58 men born in Pakistan to every woman born there living in Britain in 1971. That figure is now 0.95 to one, although this may be influenced by disparate rates of under-enumeration in the 1991 census.

The other use to which country of birth information can be put, in this context, is to estimate how many people living in Britain are the offspring of people who migrated to this country. A key assumption is that members of a household are related to the person stated on the census form to be the "head" of that household. Figure 2.32 shows the probability that a person was born in the United Kingdom given both his/her age and the country of birth of his/her household head. The figure also shows how that relationship has changed over the 1980s. The most striking change is that an extra one out of every five 25 year olds whose head of household was born in the New Commonwealth (including Pakistan) was born in the UK in 1991 as compared to 1981. By 1991 a majority (52%) of all those aged between 16 and 29 whose head of household was born in the New Commonwealth were themselves born in the UK. This change could well be the result of immigration controls which have made it more difficult for people born in the New Commonwealth to come to Britain in recent years. Their experiences contrast markedly with those of migrants from other countries outside Britain.

Residents Born Abroad 1971–1991

change in district populations

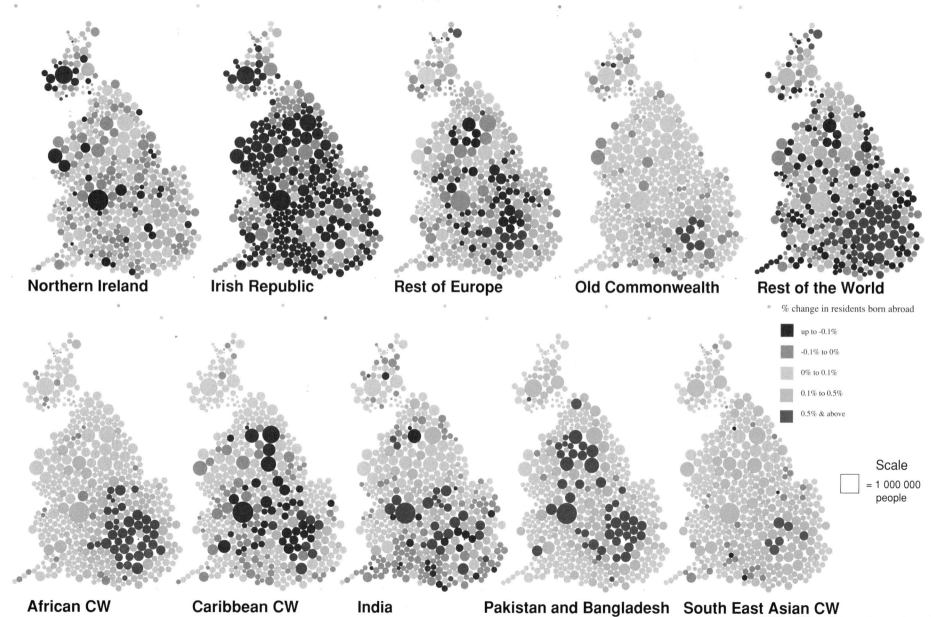

Northern Ireland

Irish Republic

Rest of Europe

Old Commonwealth

Rest of the World

African CW

Caribbean CW

India

Pakistan and Bangladesh

South East Asian CW

% change in residents born abroad

- up to -0.1%
- -0.1% to 0%
- 0% to 0.1%
- 0.1% to 0.5%
- 0.5% & above

Scale

□ = 1 000 000 people

2.33: Migrants in Britain by Age and Administrative Area of Origin 1991

% of residents moving within each type of area since 1990

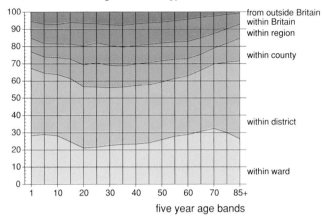

five year age bands

2.34: Migrants by Age and Sex in Britain 1971, 1981 and 1991

% of age and sex group migrating in the year to census day

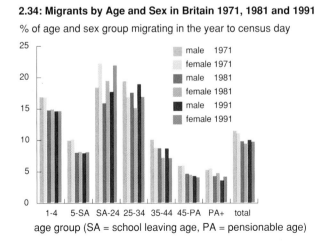

age group (SA = school leaving age, PA = pensionable age)

Migration

The first map opposite shows the cumulative effect of people migrating to Britain over the years, through depicting the proportion of each ward's population which was born abroad. This map shows the results of a pattern of life-time migration. The similarities with the distribution of students at their term time addresses are worth noting (see page 33). Only in a very few wards are less than 1% of the population born abroad.

The second map gives an indication of the turnover of the population by showing how many residents had a different address a year before census day. Thus this map shows the rate of annual migration. Again the similarities with concentrations of students are noteworthy, often coinciding with wards where more than one in six of the population moves every year. This contrasts strongly with large parts of Merseyside and Essex where less than one in sixteen people move per year.

Aspects of the movement of people both from outside and within Britain could consume many more pages of this atlas, but here there is only room for one. For migrants of all ages most moves are to new addresses within the same local authority district as is shown by Figure 2.33. Moves within the same ward are most likely when people are either young or very old, while moves from abroad occur with greatest frequency between the ages of 35 and 39 (7.7% of all moves for this age band are from abroad). It is important to know that the origin of migrants in this figure is taken as the place which they put as their usual address a year before census day, and a person is assumed to be a migrant if that address is different from their current usual address.

The rate at which people move depends not only on their age, family and educational circumstances, but also on general economic conditions (there are more migrants when there are more jobs). Thus, as Figure 2.34 shows, a higher proportion of the population moved home between 1970 and 1971 than between either 1980 and 1981 or 1990 and 1991. In all cases men are slightly more likely to move than women, although for any particular age group the rates are similar. Under 25, however, women are more likely to change address than men; over 25 it is men who are more likely to be moving. This difference may be associated with differences in the average age of marriage. A recent change that has occurred for both sexes is an increase in the proportion of people migrating in their 20s, recovering almost to 1971 levels.

Migration is often the most important influence on other demographic changes. The changes in the distributions of people by age are also due largely to changes in the destinations of migrants. Even patterns of fertility are altered by migration as new cohorts of potential parents move to slightly different areas, in different decades, to have children. Divorce and marriage both often cause moves to take place, as does retirement or becoming a student at a university. Migration can also have more subtle influences, for instance on the proportion of people speaking different languages in an area.

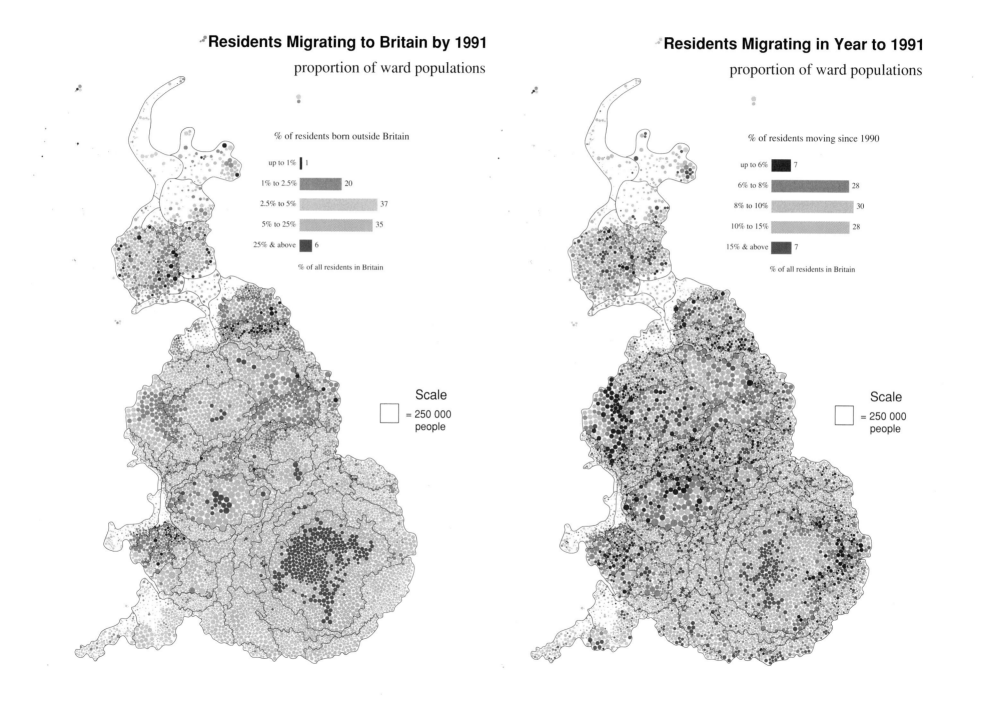

Residents Migrating to Britain by 1991

proportion of ward populations

% of residents born outside Britain

up to 1%	1
1% to 2.5%	20
2.5% to 5%	37
5% to 25%	35
25% & above	6

% of all residents in Britain

Scale

☐ = 250 000 people

Residents Migrating in Year to 1991

proportion of ward populations

% of residents moving since 1990

up to 6%	7
6% to 8%	28
8% to 10%	30
10% to 15%	28
15% & above	7

% of all residents in Britain

Scale

☐ = 250 000 people

2.35: Residents Who Speak Welsh in Wales by County 1981, 1991

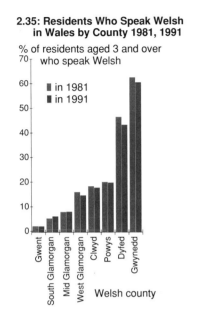

% of residents aged 3 and over who speak Welsh

- in 1981
- in 1991

Welsh county

2.36: Residents Who Can Speak Gaelic in Scotland by Region 1981, 1991

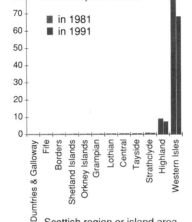

% of residents aged 3 and over who can speak Gaelic

- in 1981
- in 1991

Scottish region or island area

2.37: Welsh Speakers by Age and Sex 1991

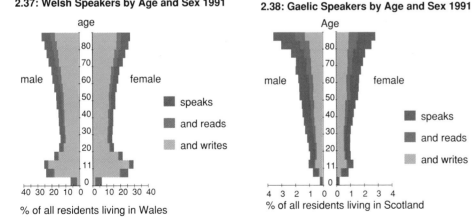

age

male   female

- speaks
- and reads
- and writes

40 30 20 10 0 0 10 20 30 40

% of all residents living in Wales

2.38: Gaelic Speakers by Age and Sex 1991

Age

male   female

- speaks
- and reads
- and writes

4 3 2 1 0 0 1 2 3 4

% of all residents living in Scotland

Language

Demography does not traditionally include the study of language, but as this is so closely related to birthplace, migration, age and ethnicity, that subject is included to end this chapter. Questions were asked about only two languages in the 1991 British census, Welsh and Scottish Gaelic, and these questions were only asked in Wales and Scotland, respectively. Hence only these two countries are used in the maps shown here using both equal area and equal population projections. Similar questions were asked in the 1981 census so the geographical distributions of the changes over time in the proportions of the population speaking these languages can also be shown here.

In Wales 508 000 people speak Welsh, while in Scotland only 66 000 people *can* speak Gaelic (the question is worded slightly differently as applied to the two countries). Figure 2.35 shows how dramatically the proportion who speak Welsh varies even at the county scale. The wards of most counties only fall into two shading bands as the map and cartogram opposite show. Most Welsh residents live in wards where less than one in ten people can speak Welsh.

On the equal land area map of Scotland the distribution of Gaelic speakers is shown most clearly although the cartogram and graph are reminders of how few people live in those areas. Ninety nine per cent of Scottish residents live in wards where less than 10% of the people can speak Scottish Gaelic. Figure 2.36 demonstrates how concentrated the Gaelic speakers are in Scotland. The Western Isles contains only 0.6% of the population of Scotland but 29.6% of all the Scottish people who can speak Gaelic.

In Wales the proportion of people who speak Welsh has fallen from 19.0% to 18.7% between 1981 and 1991. This is due largely to the age structure of people who speak Welsh, which is shown in Figure 2.37 (which includes a breakdown of the proportions who can read and write Welsh additionally). It is only the teaching of Welsh to children in schools which has averted a much steeper decline in the proportion of Welsh speakers. The map and cartogram of change show how this policy has resulted in actual rises in the proportion of people speaking Welsh living in areas where very few people used to be able to speak that language.

In Scotland, however, the age profile is even more marked, as Figure 2.38 makes clear. Although there is a slight rise between the ages of 11 and 15 this will be no compensation in the coming years for the relatively high proportions of very elderly people who can speak Gaelic. In 1981 1.64% of people in Scotland aged over 3 could speak Scottish Gaelic; now that figure is 1.37%. The decline has been most marked in those areas where the highest proportions of people can speak Gaelic. Elsewhere there is no appreciable level from which to decline except just to the north of Glasgow city centre, where a small but noticeable proportion used to claim to be able to speak Scottish Gaelic in 1981.

Residents Speaking Gaelic or Welsh 1991

proportion of ward populations

Residents Speaking Gaelic or Welsh 1981–1991

change in ward populations

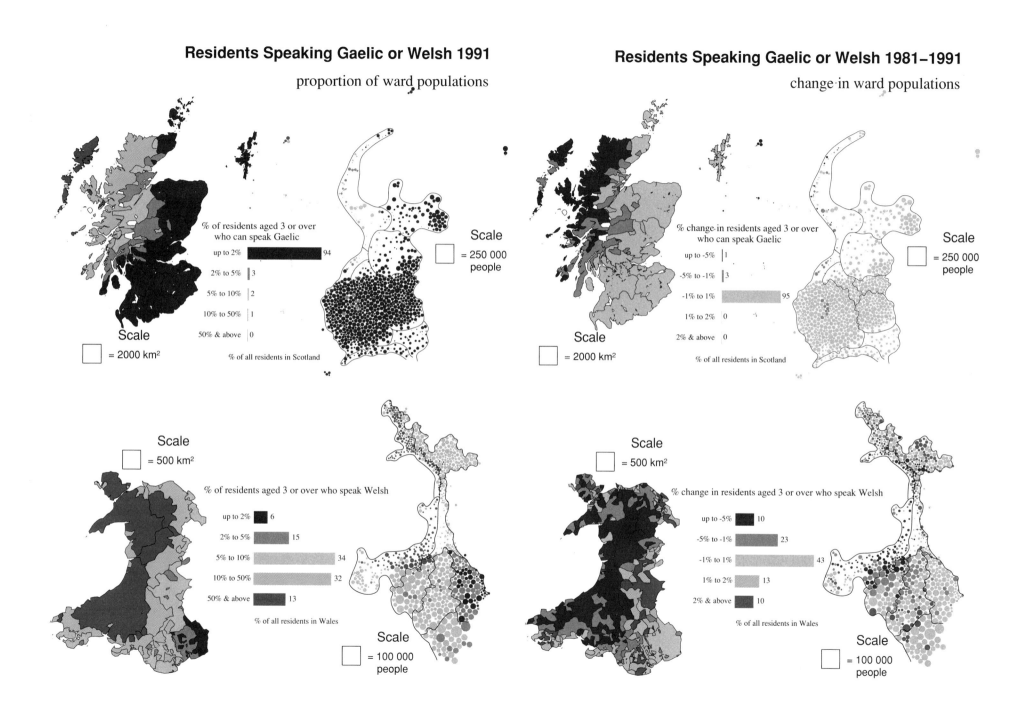

% of residents aged 3 or over who can speak Gaelic

up to 2%	94
2% to 5%	3
5% to 10%	2
10% to 50%	1
50% & above	0

% of all residents in Scotland

Scale = 250 000 people

Scale = 2000 km²

% change in residents aged 3 or over who can speak Gaelic

up to -5%	1
-5% to -1%	3
-1% to 1%	95
1% to 2%	0
2% & above	0

% of all residents in Scotland

Scale = 250 000 people

Scale = 2000 km²

Scale = 500 km²

% of residents aged 3 or over who speak Welsh

up to 2%	6
2% to 5%	15
5% to 10%	34
10% to 50%	32
50% & above	13

% of all residents in Wales

Scale = 100 000 people

Scale = 500 km²

% change in residents aged 3 or over who speak Welsh

up to -5%	10
-5% to -1%	23
-1% to 1%	43
1% to 2%	13
2% & above	10

% of all residents in Wales

Scale = 100 000 people

Conclusion: People in Britain

Who We Are

Demographic statistics concern some of the most basic facts about people: how old they are, how many children they have, their sex, marital status, birthplace, movement and so on. In Britain some of this information is seen as so important that it has been centrally collected since 1837, with many local records dating back to the Reformation of the 1530s. There has long been official concern over the growth, make-up and movement of the population, which has been particularly active regarding immigration and ethnic identity. However, only at the most recent census were all people in this country explicitly asked to state what they felt their ethnic group to be; before then it had been inferred from their birthplace. Who the people of Britain are, where they come from, whether they choose to marry, what languages they speak and how many children they have is of interest to social researchers as well as to government. For geographical studies it is necessary to know who makes up the population in each area in order to understand the effects of many changes which occur in particular localities and so impact disproportionately upon different groups of people. For example, to know if children are likely to grow up in areas of high unemployment, the distributions of both children and of adults out of work have to be mapped. Mapping demography shows how the chances and decisions of different groups in society are spatially constrained. To talk of the opportunities and problems faced by young adults growing up in Bangladeshi families is not possible without an appreciation of the places where most of those families live.

Mapping Minorities: Colour Print C

If a cartogram were drawn of the dominant ethnic group in each ward in Britain then 99.6% of the page would be coloured to represent white (on an equal area map over 99.9% of the page would be white). An interesting distribution is shown when the second largest group of residents is used to colour the cartogram — the largest minority. The same cartogram can also indicate differences within the mostly white category if country of birth divisions are also included. This has been done to paint the distributions of largest minorities shown in Colour Print C. Each ward is shaded one of fifteen colours depending on which national or ethnic group minority is largest within it. Thus, if a ward contained one hundred people, ninety of whom were white, seven were Indian, two Pakistani, one "Other Other" (see page 40), and eighty were born in England, ten in Scotland, one each in Wales, Ireland and somewhere else within the European Community, and seven elsewhere in the world, then that ward would be shaded to show that the largest minority were Scottish born. The ten Scottish born residents in the ward being a larger minority than the eight residents identifying with the Indian ethnic group;

the ethnic group and birthplace majorities being white and English born, respectively. This may appear to be a very arbitrary statistic, in that the presence of a single person can determine a ward's category, but it produces a simple pattern, as Colour Print C shows. However, it should be noted that amalgamating two groups will increase their overall representation dramatically (if they overlap at all spatially), while dividing a group could markedly reduce its total representation.

Just over a third of all wards are coloured blue, showing that in these places the largest minority is Scottish born. Scotland itself is not coloured blue because the Scottish born themselves are in the majority there. The second largest classification of wards are those where the largest minority was born in Ireland (mostly in Eire). Of the remaining 50% of wards, over half have English or Welsh born residents as their largest minority. The border between England and Wales is clearly shown by the group which is in the minority on each side. A further 3% of wards have people born in other European countries as the largest minority by this classification, most of these being in or around the capital. Less than a fifth of the population of Britain live in wards where the largest minority is from an ethnic rather than from a national group, and in half of these the largest minority are Indian as this is the most widely spread group to have been given a category. This group can also be seen to be spread out further from urban areas than most other ethnic minority groups. The next largest group of wards to be classified have Black Caribbean residents as their largest minority, mainly in north and south London. They are followed by the populations in wards in which the Pakistani ethnic minority is largest, mostly in West Yorkshire cities. All other ethnic groups are the largest minorities in areas containing less than 1% of the population. Black African and Bangladeshi residents are located mostly in central London. The clearest cluster of wards typified by Black Other residents are near American airforce bases in East Anglia. The wards shaded to show Chinese minorities are few and far between, while the Other Asian groups, which cover a similarly sized population, are clustered in south west London, and the smallest group of seven wards is typified by the "Other Other" miscellaneous minorities.

Age and Sex

Traditionally British censuses asked demographic questions partly to ensure that enough men of "fighting age" were being produced, just as questions on place of birth were asked to monitor the influx of predominantly Irish labour. More recent justifications for these questions are that appropriate educational, health and housing services should be provided in each part of the country but, under the veneer of social provision, issues of morality and nationalism still affect what is asked and shown in official statistics. This atlas reflects these debates. For instance, in 1991 the number of babies born to married mothers was at its lowest level in at least 150 years. The reciprocal increase has been in births registered by unmarried couples rather than by lone mothers. The combination of high numbers of young women and low rates of marriage in London mean that over a third of all children in most wards in the capital do not live with two married parents (see page 175). This is partly because children growing up in London and in other large cities tend to be young and will often have young parents who may have decided to delay marriage until they leave those cities (see page 31). The parts of these cities in which most young children are brought up also contain the most local authority housing (page 119) and so it is not surprising that many lone parent households are in this tenure. It is difficult to study these social changes in perspective without understanding the geographical changes that have occurred in patterns of marriage, child rearing, family structure and housing tenure, as well as appreciating the processes by which adults choose to have children, and by which housing is distributed. Similarly, an understanding of changes in the social structure of many inner city areas (see page 191), requires an understanding of dramatic demographic changes such as the influx of young adults into these areas caused by the growth of higher education (page 33). This in turn will affect family structures which are closely related to age (Figure 6.1).

Migration and Projection

Population movement through migration is the simplistic cause of most social change in Britain. When an area as small as a ward is compared over decades it is usually the characteristics of different groups of people which are being contrasted, due to the effects of in- and out-migration. The most dramatic localized changes to the social geography of Britain have been a result of people moving between countries. As English migrants settle in increasing numbers in the more rural regions and counties of Scotland and Wales they change the complexion of these places in many ways (see, for example, page 183 which shows the spread of graduates into these countries). Similarly, the destinations of migrants from the most recent periods of overseas immigration can be seen reflected in the family structure of changed communities (page 177). The changing preferences of pensioners, who no longer move in great numbers to the coast, alters the map of dependency in Britain (page 209). The maps in this atlas show the results of migration, rather than migration flows themselves, which are more difficult to draw (see Dorling 1995), and so it is necessary to remember that there is a great deal of population movement which "cancels itself out" in terms of social change (page 59). Although migration is the most important demographic influence on other social changes, other factors are also vital. The ageing of the population in-situ affects many patterns shown in the chapters which follow; the pattern of ill-heath in particular (page 137). Concern with the changing demographic structure of Britain is also a major reason for monitoring population change.

In 1991 one person in 27 in Britain was aged 80 or over. By 2031 this proportion will have almost doubled to one person in 15. Simultaneously, the proportion of people aged under 40 is projected to fall from 56% to 47% (OPCS 1995). Thus demographic change will change many other aspects of society. In the short term, projections have been made at the level of standard regions and metropolitan counties in England which show just how unevenly distributed these demographic changes could be (Population Trends 1994). In the Northern region, the West Midlands region and in Merseyside county an additional 1% of the population will be aged 75 and over by 2011. This represents relative rises in the size of that group of over 18%, 17% and 20%, respectively. Over the same period the number of people aged 75 and over is projected to fall by 11% in Greater London and to increase its share of the population by only 0.1% in the South East as a whole. The South West will continue to have the highest regional share of this group, rising from one resident in twelve to one in eleven being aged 75 years or older in only a few years time.

References

Brant, J., 1984, Patterns of migration from the 1981 census, *Population Trends*, 35:23–30.

Coleman, D. and Salt, J., 1992, *The British Population: Patterns, Trends, and Processes*, Oxford: Oxford University Press.

Craig, J. 1987, Changes in the population composition of England and Wales since 1841, *Population Trends*, 48:27–36.

CSO, 1995, *Social Trends 25*, London: HMSO.

Devis, T., 1983, People changing address: 1971 and 1981, *Population Trends*, 32:15–20.

Dorling, D., 1995, Visualizing the 1991 census, in S. Openshaw (ed.) *A Census Users' Handbook*, London: Longman.

GRO(S), 1983, *Mid-1991 Population Estimates*, Scotland, London: HMSO.

GRO(S), 1993, *Mid 1991 Population Estimates*, Scotland, London: HMSO.

Kennett, S.R., 1983, Migration within and between labour markets, in J.B.Goddard and A.G. Champion (eds) *The Urban and Regional Transformation of Britain*, London: Methuen.

King, R. and Shuttleworth, I., 1989, The Irish in Coventry: the social geography of a relic community, *Irish Geography*, 22/2:64–78.

OPCS, 1983, *Mid-1981 Population Estimates*, England and Wales, London: HMSO.

OPCS, 1987, *Birth Statistics, Historical Series of Statistics from Registrations of Birth in England and Wales*, Series FM 1 No.13, London: HMSO.

OPCS, 1990, *Marriage and Divorce Statistics, Historical Series of Statistics on Marriages and Divorces in England and Wales*, Series FM 2 No.16, London: HMSO.

OPCS, 1992, *1991 Census Definitions*, London: HMSO.

OPCS, 1993, *Mid-1991 Population Estimates*, England and Wales, London: HMSO.

Population Trends, 1977, Editorial: 126 years ago, *Population Trends*, 9:27.

Population Trends, 1994, Statistical Tables 2 and 3, *Population Trends*, 78:49–51.

3: Economic

The economic aspects of British society considered in this chapter concern the paid work in which people are engaged. The chapter begins by looking at what proportion of the population are employed in paid work, or say they would wish to be in such work if they could find it. This group of people is defined here as the *workforce* of Britain and much of the rest of the chapter concerns these people alone. Very little official information is available about unpaid work, or about the actual earnings of people. The census does not ask about income. Conversely, an enormous amount of information is available concerning people in receipt of unemployment benefit. This is because data from the computerised unemployment benefits register has been made available for research through the National Online Manpower Information System. This source is used extensively in this chapter, as is information from the Labour Force Survey.

A ten year perspective is taken to show many of the changes which have occurred in the spatial economic structure of Britain. This is because changes in the workforce can take place quite quickly as large numbers of people lose their jobs in some areas, while other groups who previously have rarely been in paid employment are now finding work. Economic changes occur so quickly that many of the graphs in this chapter show annual or even monthly changes, and some maps are of changes which occurred only in the year up to 1991. Within all this economic turmoil it is easy to miss gradual shifts, so maps showing these are also included (for instance maps of the changing proportion of the population in the workforce between 1971, 1981 and 1991). When looking at economic trends it is particularly important to remember that dates are imposed by the available data. Nevertheless, enough detailed information is available to see how the economic shape of Britain is changing at the level of the localities in which people live.

The workforce can be divided most simply into four groups: people employed full-time (more than thirty hours a week), part-time, self-employed, or unemployed, and the changing sizes of each of these groups can be measured. The workforce can also be categorised by the type of industry in which people work, and the economic fortunes of people working in each type of industry can be charted over time. Seven broad classifications of industry are used here, ranging from agriculture, forestry and fishing, to banking, finance and similar services. A third means of categorising the employment of people is by their occupation. Here nine broad groups are identified for mapping. With all these divisions the number of maps which could theoretically be drawn is large. To save space, and because some of these groups can include quite low numbers of people in certain parts of the country, a series of district level cartograms has been used in the middle of this chapter to illustrate the diversity of economic activity. Several of these cartograms can be fitted onto a single page. Similarly, the relationships between people's employment status, industry and occupation are explored with montages of small graphs. These also show the importance of age and sex in determining the likelihood of different types of employment; factors often more important than location.

In the case of people's occupation, differences between men and women are so relevant that it can make little sense to draw detailed maps without differentiating. This division between men and women has been used in this chapter to map the distributions of the modal occupation in each ward in 1991. It is also necessary to distinguish the sexes when comparing the number of hours worked in paid employment by people in different wards. This is because women, on average, are employed for ten hours fewer a week than men. A map of hours worked which did not separate men and women would simply highlight the wards where fewer women worked — as the average hours of all people in employment there would be higher. Other variables can only be compared over time for just one sex. Here the changing working hours of women with young children are mapped as they have altered since 1971. This can only be done for women. Conversely, the changing map of early retirement can only be drawn for men because women of any age were so often classified as housewives if they were not at work and were not unemployed before 1991 (Joshi and Owen 1987).

The hours people work provides only part of the story of how much time work consumes. How long it takes to travel to work is also important and this is affected by how far away each person's workplace is and by the means they use to get there and back each day. Most people in Britain travel to work by car and most people who travel by public transport use a bus for most of their journey. What means of transport you use depends critically on where you live and so the map of means of travel to work shows some very clear spatial patterns. The changes over the last ten and twenty years have also been dramatic, with an extra 10% of people travelling by car each decade.

This chapter ends by concentrating on those people in the workforce who are out of work. The censuses allow a measure of the changing size of this group to be made which is not affected by changes to the official government definition of unemployment (Employment Gazette 1994). A very clear pattern of twenty years of change is revealed at the ward level. The situation in 1991 is described in more detail by showing how many people became unemployed at any point in the year before the census or had been unemployed for more than a year by the time of the census. Non-census ward level data are used to show this. Finally, the relationship between a person's chance of being out of work, his/her ethnic group and his/her location is depicted for young people in Britain using data which are only available in detail from the census. Thus many cross-sections of the workforce are shown here from many sources, all attempting to produce a picture of the economic activity of people of working age in Britain today.

3.1: Employment Status of All Residents by Age and Sex in Britain 1991

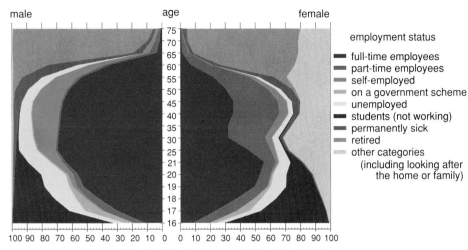

male   age   female

employment status

■ full-time employees
■ part-time employees
▨ self-employed
▨ on a government scheme
▨ unemployed
■ students (not working)
■ permanently sick
▨ retired
▨ other categories
(including looking after
the home or family)

% of residents aged over 16 in each category

3.2: Employment Status of Residents by Ethnic Group and Sex in Britain 1991

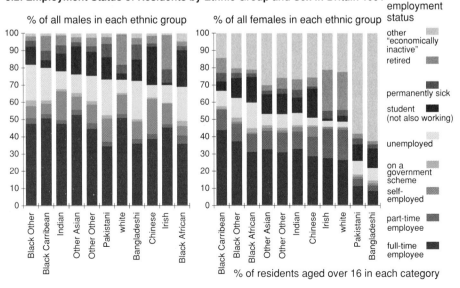

% of all males in each ethnic group   % of all females in each ethnic group

employment status

other
"economically
inactive"

retired

permanently sick

student
(not also working)

unemployed

on a
government
scheme

self-
employed

part-time
employee

full-time
employee

% of residents aged over 16 in each category

The Workforce

The workforce of Britain is made up of every resident aged 16 and over who is either in work, on a government scheme, or looking for work. Students who also have a part-time job are included in this definition of the workforce. The proportion of the population of an area which is in the workforce gives a very crude indication of how closely that area is tied in with the economy of the country as a whole and of how much money people in that area are, in aggregate, likely to have to spend. This is closely connected to the concept of the dependency ratio — the proportion of people in an area who are dependent on the earnings of people at work in that area. The map and cartogram opposite show how this ratio varies widely across the country. More than two fifths of the population live in wards where more than half of all residents aged over 16 are in the workforce. On the map it appears that very rural and coastal areas have the lowest proportions of people in the workforce and thus have the highest dependency ratios. On the cartogram it is apparent that the largest concentrations of people who are neither working, nor looking for work, are to be found inside large cities and across Wales.

People not included in the workforce are a disparate group. They are made up of over eight million pensioners who have retired, five million women who are looking after the home and family, almost two million people who cannot work because they are permanently sick (see Chapter 5) and over a million and a half students who do not also have part-time jobs. Sixteen and a half million people were in full-time employment in Britain in 1991, making up just over 60% of the workforce. In addition, almost four million women were in part-time employment, more than two million men described themselves as self-employed, while 2.8 million residents were unemployed or on a government scheme. Figure 3.1 shows how important a person's age and sex are in determining what they are likely to do — their *employment status*. The maps opposite partly reflect this age and sex profile as it is distributed across the country.

Many other factors are also important. Figure 3.2 shows how varied are the chances of people being of each employment status according to their ethnic group and their sex. The groups are sorted in descending order of *economic activity* — the rate of participation in the workforce. These graphs also reflect the age structure of each group; but in all cases men of any ethnic group are more likely to be in the workforce than women. Some of the most telling differences are to be found between men and women of the same ethnic group. For instance, for men the lowest participation rate is for Black Africans while for women it is for Bangladeshis, but Black African women have one of the highest rates of participation for women in the workforce.

The patterns of economic activity found across the country reflect the demographic structure of the country as much as the economic prosperity of each area. Prosperous areas may also attract young mobile people and so this explanation operates both ways.

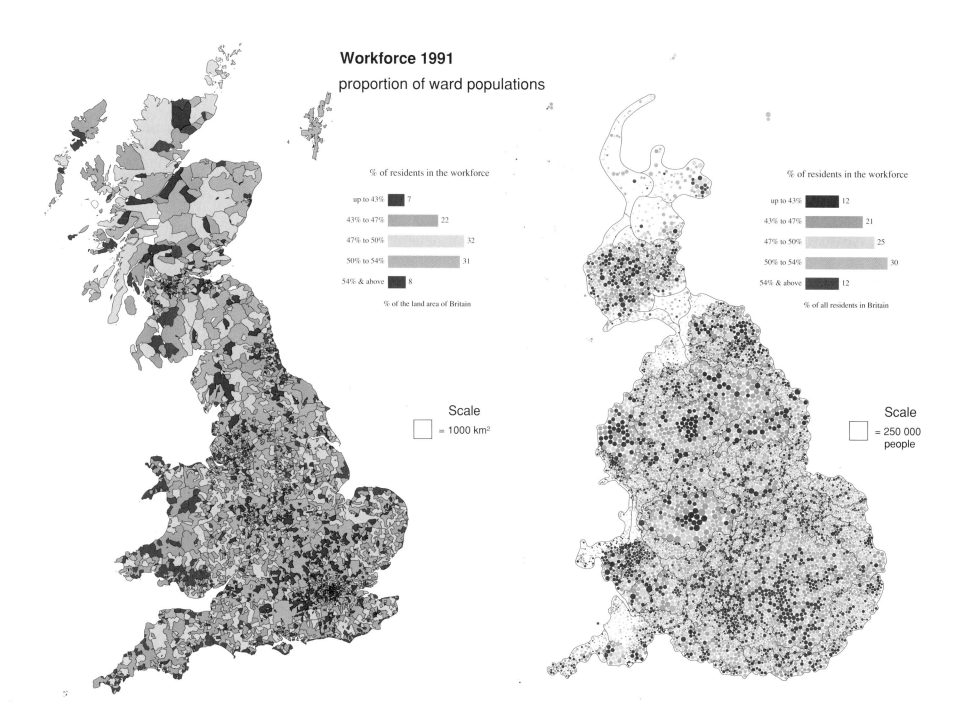

Workforce 1991

proportion of ward populations

% of residents in the workforce

up to 43%		7
43% to 47%		22
47% to 50%		32
50% to 54%		31
54% & above		8

% of the land area of Britain

% of residents in the workforce

up to 43%		12
43% to 47%		21
47% to 50%		25
50% to 54%		30
54% & above		12

% of all residents in Britain

Scale

☐ = 1000 km²

Scale

☐ = 250 000 people

3.3: Residents in the Workforce by Sex and Marital Status in Britain 1971, 1981 and 1991

% of residents who were classified as being in the workforce

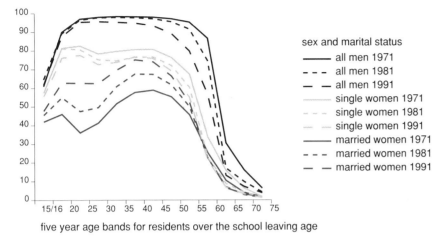

sex and marital status
— all men 1971
- - - all men 1981
— — all men 1991
— single women 1971
- - single women 1981
— - single women 1991
— married women 1971
- - - married women 1981
— — married women 1991

five year age bands for residents over the school leaving age

3.4: Absolute and Relative Change in Employment Status by Sex in Britain 1971–1981–1991

% change from the base level in each decade for each group

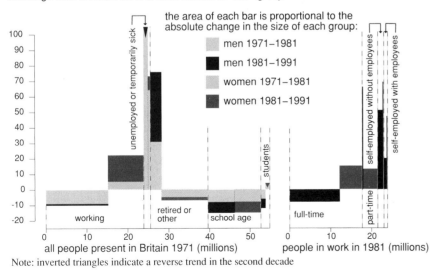

the area of each bar is proportional to the
absolute change in the size of each group:

men 1971–1981

men 1981–1991

women 1971–1981

women 1981–1991

Note: inverted triangles indicate a reverse trend in the second decade

Workforce Change

Over the last decade the proportion of people in the workforce increased in many areas. The map opposite shows how these increases were most apparent in the more rural areas of the south, and around Wandsworth in London. The workforce shrank in much of the rest of London and in the other major cities as more people living in these places said they were neither in work nor looking for a job.

The change over the last two decades shown on the far map illustrates how these changes are reinforcing a pattern which has been forming for over twenty years. In each period the average growth in workforce participation for Great Britain (GB on far map) has been roughly one additional person per hundred per decade. This has occurred despite the school leaving age being raised from 15 to 16 after the 1971 census was taken. A quarter of the population live in wards where the growth in participation has been below this level both in the 1970s and in the 1980s, and a third of the population live in areas where the growth has been above average across both periods. The areas in which economic activity slowed down only in the 1980s tend to be suburbs adjacent to the centres of large cities. These areas are shaded grey and include, for instance, most of Merseyside and most of Tyne & Wear.

The aggregate spatial changes shown here mask the detail of who by 1991 was (more or less) likely to be in the workforce. Figure 3.3 shows the participation rates for nine groups of people in thirteen age bands. Women have been separated into married and single, as in former years a woman's marital status greatly affected her likelihood of being in the workforce. Now, as the figure shows, after the age of 30, marital status gives little indication of whether a women is likely to be in the workforce or not. The biggest decreases in working rates have been for men aged over 50, while married women aged under 50 now constitute far more of the workforce. The position of single women has only altered slightly over the decades so that they are now slightly less likely (at all ages) to be in the workforce.

Figure 3.4 shows the nature of these changes in employment status in more detail. The left hand graph shows changes in the 1970s and the 1980s separately as well as differentiating between men and women. It shows how the net loss of well over a million male jobs occurred almost exclusively in the 1970s whereas most of the gain of almost two million jobs for women occurred in the 1980s. The increases in unemployment for both groups have been very sharp but still affect a relatively small proportion of the workforce. The increases in retirement for men and the decreases for women (mostly from being housewives) have affected much larger numbers of people. The school age population has dropped uniformly over both time periods. The censuses recorded an overall decrease in the number of students who do not also work (and were enumerated). The graph to the right shows in more detail the changes which occurred in the 1980s.

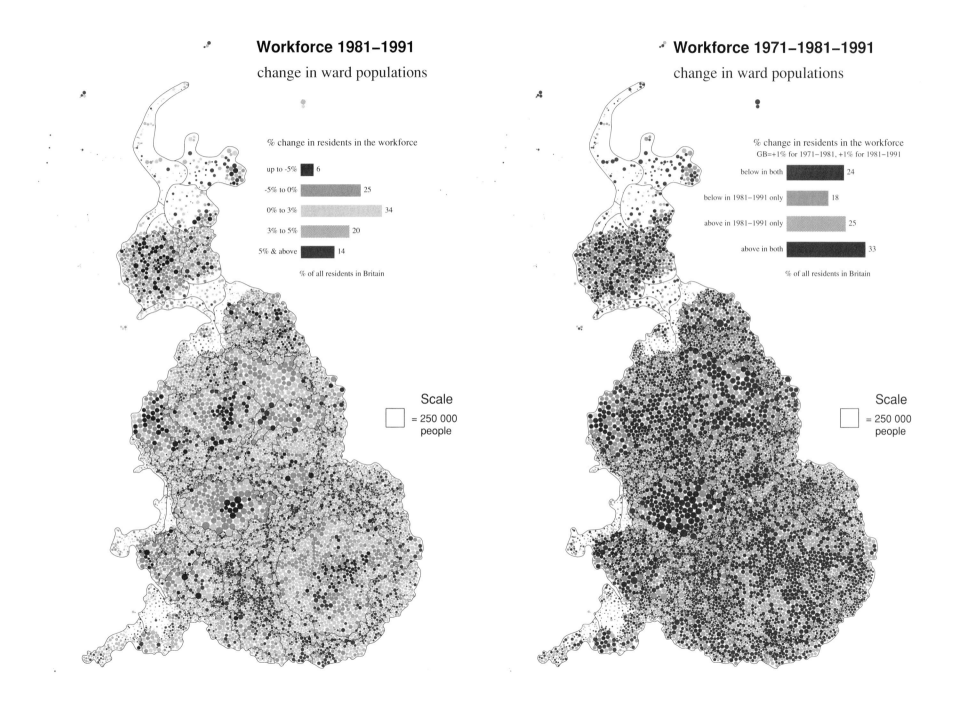

Workforce 1981–1991

change in ward populations

% change in residents in the workforce

up to -5% ▮ 6

-5% to 0% ▮ 25

0% to 3% ▮ 34

3% to 5% ▮ 20

5% & above ▮ 14

% of all residents in Britain

Scale
☐ = 250 000
people

Workforce 1971–1981–1991

change in ward populations

% change in residents in the workforce
GB=+1% for 1971–1981, +1% for 1981–1991

below in both ▮ 24

below in 1981–1991 only ▮ 18

above in 1981–1991 only ▮ 25

above in both ▮ 33

% of all residents in Britain

Scale
☐ = 250 000
people

3.5: Residents in the Workforce by Age, Sex and Employment Status 1991, 1981–1991

% of all residents in Britain who were
classified as economically active 1991

change in % for groups of residents who were
classified as economically active 1981–1991

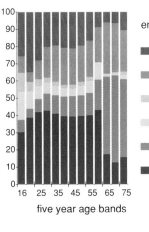

five year age bands

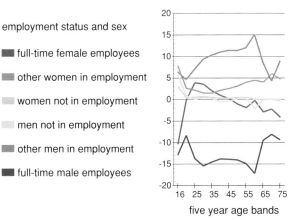

employment status and sex

■ full-time female employees

■ other women in employment

▨ women not in employment

▨ men not in employment

▨ other men in employment

■ full-time male employees

five year age bands

3.6: Workforce by Sex and Employment Status in Britain 1971–1991

% of workforce in employment plus claimant unemployed

employment status and sex

■ full-time female employees

■ part-time female employees

▨ self-employed women

▨ unemployed women

▨ unemployed men

▨ self-employed men

▨ part-time male employees

■ full-time male employees

seasonally adjusted figures for June of each year

Source: The Employment Gazette, June 1992.

Employment Status

Figure 3.4 demonstrated the relative importance to the size of the workforce in Britain of the changes in the numbers of people in each type of employment since 1981. On the map opposite the geographical distributions of those changes, and the patterns which they had formed by 1991, are shown at the level of local authority districts.

Full-time employees are defined as people who work more than thirty hours a week, *part-time employees* are people in employment who work fewer hours than this. *Self-employed people* are those who described themselves as such, while the *unemployment count* includes people who were temporarily sick in 1981 and people on government schemes in 1991 — for the comparison to be as fair as is possible. The geographical differences in the relative sizes of each of these four groups are quite simple at this scale. Full-time employment levels are highest west of London. Part-time employment is most common along the coast. Self-employed people are to be found mainly in the south of England and people are most likely to be unemployed if they live in metropolitan boroughs.

The patterns in the four lower maps, which show the net changes which have taken place since 1981, are almost as clear although perhaps not as expected. Full-time employment has fallen least in the Midlands. Part-time employment has fallen most in London while the rise in self-employment has been most dramatic in districts to the east of the capital. Unemployment levels have risen most starkly in and around London and across the Yorkshire coalfield, while there have been dramatic falls in the proportion of the workforce seeking work in the West Midlands, Wales, parts of the north of England and in Scotland. It should be born in mind, however, that here only two specific points in time are being compared. There are also many routes out of employment other than unemployment, some of which are discussed at the end of this chapter

Figure 3.5 shows how a person's employment status is likely to vary according to his/her age and sex in a similar manner to Figure 3.1, but now only for people in the workforce and for six categories of people for whom it is possible to chart changes since the 1981 census. The changes have been quite dramatic, with men in full-time employment losing the most jobs over the decade, especially men aged over 45. Conversely, the biggest relative rise in employment has been for men in part-time employment or for those who are self-employed, and again the group aged over 45 has seen the greatest change in ten years. Unemployment rates have risen most rapidly for people aged under 25.

Analysis of employment change between the censuses can give the impression that these changes have been gradual. Figure 3.6 shows how the changes have been spread over the last twenty years. The 1980s has been a far more turbulent time for employment change than the 1970s. The influence of the census dates on statistics is also apparent.

Employment Status 1981–1991

proportion of workforce and change (quintiles)

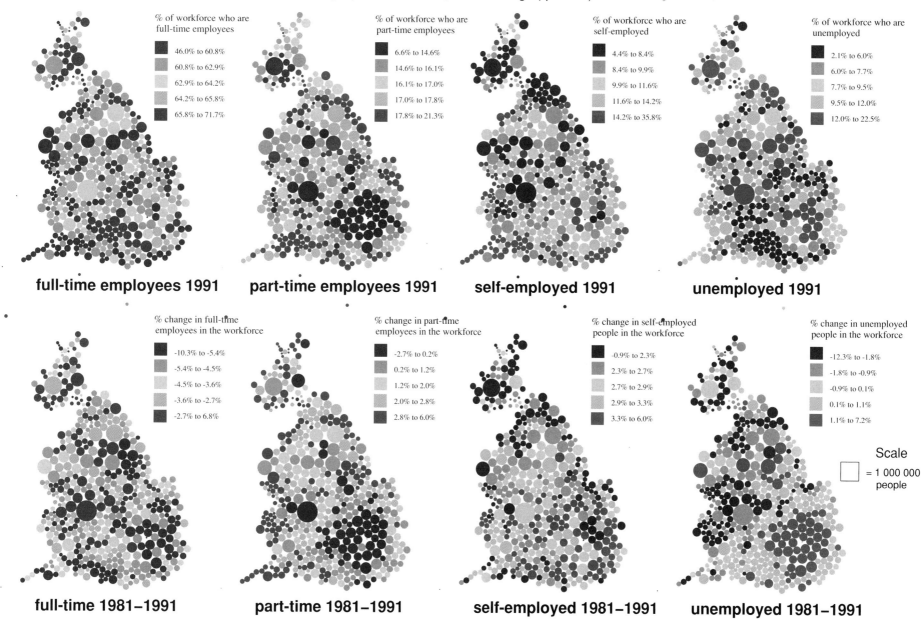

% of workforce who are
full-time employees

- 46.0% to 60.8%
- 60.8% to 62.9%
- 62.9% to 64.2%
- 64.2% to 65.8%
- 65.8% to 71.7%

% of workforce who are
part-time employees

- 6.6% to 14.6%
- 14.6% to 16.1%
- 16.1% to 17.0%
- 17.0% to 17.8%
- 17.8% to 21.3%

% of workforce who are
self-employed

- 4.4% to 8.4%
- 8.4% to 9.9%
- 9.9% to 11.6%
- 11.6% to 14.2%
- 14.2% to 35.8%

% of workforce who are
unemployed

- 2.1% to 6.0%
- 6.0% to 7.7%
- 7.7% to 9.5%
- 9.5% to 12.0%
- 12.0% to 22.5%

full-time employees 1991   **part-time employees 1991**   **self-employed 1991**   **unemployed 1991**

% change in full-time
employees in the workforce

- -10.3% to -5.4%
- -5.4% to -4.5%
- -4.5% to -3.6%
- -3.6% to -2.7%
- -2.7% to 6.8%

% change in part-time
employees in the workforce

- -2.7% to 0.2%
- 0.2% to 1.2%
- 1.2% to 2.0%
- 2.0% to 2.8%
- 2.8% to 6.0%

% change in self-employed
people in the workforce

- -0.9% to 2.3%
- 2.3% to 2.7%
- 2.7% to 2.9%
- 2.9% to 3.3%
- 3.3% to 6.0%

% change in unemployed
people in the workforce

- -12.3% to -1.8%
- -1.8% to -0.9%
- -0.9% to 0.1%
- 0.1% to 1.1%
- 1.1% to 7.2%

Scale

☐ = 1 000 000
people

full-time 1981–1991   **part-time 1981–1991**   **self-employed 1981–1991**   **unemployed 1981–1991**

3.7: Residents in Work in Britain by Industry, Employment Status and Sex 1991

area proportional to number of workers, GB=23.5 million

industrial group (% of total workforce)

male   female   not stated or outside UK (0.9%)

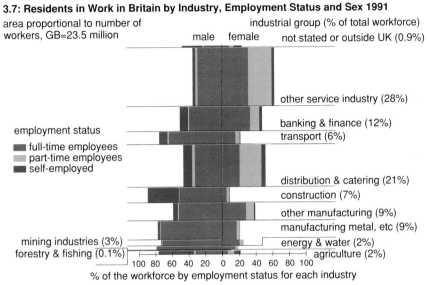

other service industry (28%)

banking & finance (12%)
transport (6%)

employment status

■ full-time employees
▨ part-time employees
■ self-employed

distribution & catering (21%)
construction (7%)
other manufacturing (9%)
manufacturing metal, etc (9%)

mining industries (3%)
forestry & fishing (0.1%)

energy & water (2%)
agriculture (2%)

100 80 60 40 20 0 20 40 60 80 100

% of the workforce by employment status for each industry

3.8: Residents in Work in Britain by Age and Sex for each Industrial Group 1991

area proportional to number of workers, GB=23.5 million

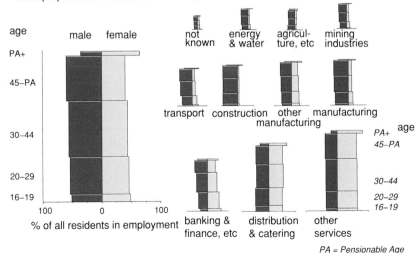

age

male   female

PA+

45–PA

30–44

20–29

16–19

100   0   100

% of all residents in employment

not known   energy & water   agricul-ture, etc   mining industries

transport   construction   other manufacturing   manufacturing

banking & finance, etc   distribution & catering   other services

age

PA+
45–PA
30–44
20–29
16–19

PA = Pensionable Age

Industrial Structure

The industrial geography of Britain provides part of the explanation for the patterns of different levels of economic activity found across the country. As Figure 3.7 shows, each industry employs very different proportions of men and women and of people in full-time employment, in part-time employment or in self-employed work. Wherever employment in the construction industry is buoyant, for instance, a high proportion of self-employed men is likely to be in the workforce. This figure also gives an impression of the relative importance of each industry: four people work in banking & finance for every one person working in the mining industries.

The maps opposite show how jobs in each type of industry are spread across the country, district by district. Broader categories of industry are used in these maps than are used in the figures for simplicity. The same shading categories are used in each map so that the relative importance of each industry can be seen for each place. People working in agriculture, forestry & fishing never constitute more than a fifth of a district's workforce and only number more than 5% in a few of the most rural areas. People working in industries associated with energy, water & mining constitute more than a fifth of the workforce in only two districts — Stoke-on-Trent (potteries) and Copeland (nuclear). In contrast, manufacturing industries employ between a fifth and a half of the workforce right across the midlands and in many districts further north. These areas are thus likely to have high numbers of men in full-time employment among their workforces. The construction industry in 1991 rarely employed more than 10%, or less than 5%, of a district's workforce, with the work being fairly evenly spread across the country.

Two thirds of the British workforce are employed in the last three types of industrial group as shown in the lower maps. Distribution & catering includes people working in shops and other retail establishments and shows a distinct geographical pattern. People working in transport & communication number more than a fifth of the workforce in only one district — Dover. It is, however, the final group of industries which employs the most significant group of people: banking, finance & other services. In no district in Britain are less than a fifth of the workforce engaged in this kind of employment and in most London boroughs these industries provide work for over half the employed population (as they also do in Edinburgh and Cardiff). Together these industries employ more women than men. Almost half of these women are working part-time.

Different industries tend not only to employ distinct numbers of people of different sexes and of different employment status categories, but also people of different ages. Figure 3.8 shows the age and sex pyramids for each type of industry. More older men tend to be employed and more younger women, but this is not true in the distribution & catering industries, although it is very much the case in banking and finance.

Industries 1991

share of people in employment

agriculture, forestry & fishing

energy, water & mining

manufacturing industries

construction

distribution & catering

transport & communication

banking, finance & other services

% of workforce in employment
working in each type of industry

- up to 5%
- 5% to 10%
- 10% to 20%
- 20% to 50%
- 50% & above

Scale

= 1 000 000
people

3.9: Change in the Total Numbers of People in Employment by Industry in Britain 1971–1991

% change in numbers of employees by industrial group (service industries shown in red)

1971 = 100 for each type of industry   industrial group (SIC number) % of 1971 level by 1991

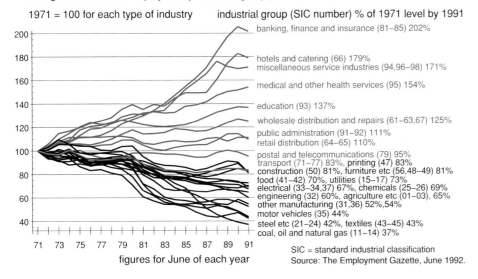

banking, finance and insurance (81–85) 202%

hotels and catering (66) 179%
miscellaneous service industries (94,96–98) 171%

medical and other health services (95) 154%

education (93) 137%

wholesale distribution and repairs (61–63,67) 125%
public administration (91–92) 111%
retail distribution (64–65) 110%

postal and telecommunications (79) 95%
transport (71–77) 83%, printing (47) 83%
construction (50) 81%, furniture etc (56,48–49) 81%
food (41–42) 70%, utilities (15–17) 73%
electrical (33–34,37) 67%, chemicals (25–26) 69%
engineering (32) 60%, agriculture etc (01–03) 65%
other manufacturing (31,36) 52%,54%
motor vehicles (35) 44%
steel etc (21–24) 42%, textiles (43–45) 43%
coal, oil and natural gas (11–14) 37%

figures for June of each year

SIC = standard industrial classification
Source: The Employment Gazette, June 1992.

3.10: Change in Employment for each Industrial Group by Age and Sex in Britain 1981–1991

Workforce Grouped by Sex and Age	Total Jobs Change (%) 1981 to 1991	Agriculture, Forestry & Fishing SIC number 01–03	Energy, Water & Mining 11–17	Manu-facturing Industries 21–49	Const-ruction Industry 50	Distribution & Catering Industries 61–67	Transport & Comm-unication 71–79	Other Service Industries 81–99
Total	2%	-11%	55%	-33%	8%	9%	-0%	22%
Male								
All 16+	-5%	-15%	39%	-34%	7%	8%	-4%	14%
16–29	-6%	-20%	20%	-32%	6%	17%	-8%	4%
30–44	4%	-10%	71%	-28%	5%	12%	6%	29%
45–64	-11%	-15%	23%	-39%	10%	-0%	-10%	8%
65+	-28%	-21%	197%	-47%	-28%	-39%	-18%	-15%
Female								
All 16+	13%	8%	165%	-30%	22%	10%	16%	28%
16–29	11%	-10%	149%	-27%	19%	24%	21%	18%
30–44	27%	10%	234%	-24%	21%	17%	43%	47%
45–64	4%	14%	118%	-37%	34%	-2%	-13%	23%
60+	-12%	21%	252%	-37%	1%	-22%	-22%	0%

Note: here change (%) is calculated as 100 × (jobs_in_1991 − jobs_in_1981) ÷ jobs_in_1981, rather than as the usual % point change.

Industrial Change

Just as the industrial structure of Britain helps to explain the patterns of employment across the country, so changes in that structure often lie behind geographical changes in the characteristics of those who are employed and how they are employed. Estimates of the share of people working in each type of industry from the last two censuses are compared here. Again, the same scale is used on all the maps so that the relative importance of the changes to the entire workforce of an area can be judged equitably.

The numbers of people working in agriculture, forestry & fishing could not fall much in many districts because they were already so low. The biggest falls in this sector were recorded in rural areas, whilst increases have only been seen in Lochaber, the Western Isles and the Shetland Isles. In aggregate, the energy, water & mining industries have seen employment grow over the 1980s although this has generally only occurred in the first two sectors of this group. The map emphasises those parts of the Welsh, Yorkshire and Northumberland coalfields which have seen falls of up to 10% of their total workforce from this sector alone. Losses of over 10% of the total workforce have not been unusual in many districts for manufacturing jobs. Only six small districts out of the 459 in Britain have seen rises in manufacturing employment of above one new job for every hundred in 1981. The picture for change in the construction industry shows a gradual evolution over the decade, with jobs moving out from the centre of the country.

The most significant increases in employment have been seen in the service industries. Employment in distribution & catering has increased almost everywhere apart from in large cities. The growth which has occurred in the transport & communications industries shows a very clustered pattern centred on Coventry whilst the traditional transport centres of London, Bristol, Liverpool, Edinburgh and Hull have experienced declining employment in this sector. The most significant increases in employment in almost every district in the country have come from jobs in banking, finance and other services. East London, Bristol, Liverpool and Glasgow have seen rises of more than ten new workers for every hundred workers (in employment) from these industries alone.

Again, the rate of change has been different at different times and for different industries over the last twenty years. Figure 3.9 illustrates these changes using a classification of employment by industry which allows comparisons to be made over three decades. What is most striking about this diagram is that every type of service industry has had more job growth than any of the manufacturing or primary sectors. The rate of change, and its direction, has also been different for different people working in each industry. The table in Figure 3.10 shows how much variation the total percentage change in employment statistics conceals about the changing nature of who is working in each type of industry. Percentages are shown in this table and so it is important to remember that some of the denominators for these fractions will be quite small.

Industries 1981–1991

share of people in employment

agriculture, forestry & fishing

energy, water & mining

manufacturing industries

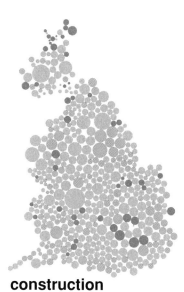

construction

distribution & catering

transport & communication

banking, finance & other services

% change in workforce in employment
working in each type of industry

- up to -10%
- -10% to -1%
- -1% to 1%
- 1% to 10%
- 10% & above

Scale

= 1 000 000
people

3.11: People in Employment by Industry and Occupation in Britain 1991

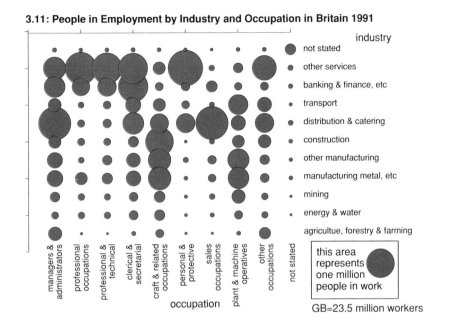

3.12: Residents in Work in Britain by Age and Sex for each Occupational Group 1991

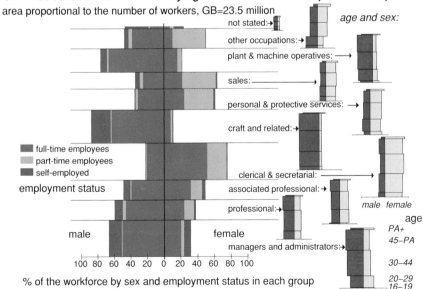

Occupational Structure

Knowing in which kind of industry a person is employed — what is made — reveals little about what kind of work he or she does. For instance, a cleaner working in a building firm is classified as being in the construction industry. It is the nature of work people do which is most important in determining what they earn, whether they are likely to live in a city and so on. The industries people work in and their occupations are certainly not unrelated, as Figure 3.11 shows. More clerical & secretarial staff work in banking & finance than in any other sector; but the relationship between people's industries and their occupations is sufficiently loose for very different geographical patterns to emerge. Within an industry, the managers are unlikely to live in the same neighbourhoods as the machine operators.

The maps opposite show the geographical distributions of the nine most highly aggregated classifications of occupations from the 1990 Standard Occupational Classification, which groups jobs involving similar tasks; see Figure 3.13 to find which particular occupations are assigned to each of these groups. The same scale has been used on each map so that the relative importance of each group can be contrasted between areas. People whose work involves managing, clerical, or craft & related work are in the largest groups, usually comprising over half the workforce of a district when combined. Professionals and "associated professionals" tend to live in similar areas, concentrated in the South East and in provincial centres such as Edinburgh. Personal & protective occupations include people working in security (such as the police) and care (such as retirement home staff), hence their concentration round the coast, looking after the elderly. People working in sales tend to be found in higher numbers in the more rural districts while machine operatives are clustered in the North, Wales and the Midlands. "Other occupations" include those jobs which are most difficult to classify; these are most commonly found in Glasgow, Liverpool, Manchester and in South Yorkshire.

The distribution of people of different ages and sexes among occupations is even more uneven than that found among industries. Figure 3.12 shows both the relationship between sex, employment status and occupation and, for each occupation, the age and sex profile of people employed in it. Each of the bars in each of the graphs has been scaled so that the area of the bar is proportional to the total number of people in the group being shown. Thus the bar and population pyramid for clerical and secretarial workers is largest, representing almost 3.8 million people, mostly women (about a third of whom work part-time). The population pyramid confirms just how unlikely it is that men are employed in clerical and secretarial occupations, particularly those aged 30–44. It also shows that unusually high numbers of people aged under 20 are in this occupational group. This contrasts with managers and administrators, where the 16–19 age bar is so thin that it is evident that almost no teenager works in these occupations.

Occupations 1991

share of people in employment

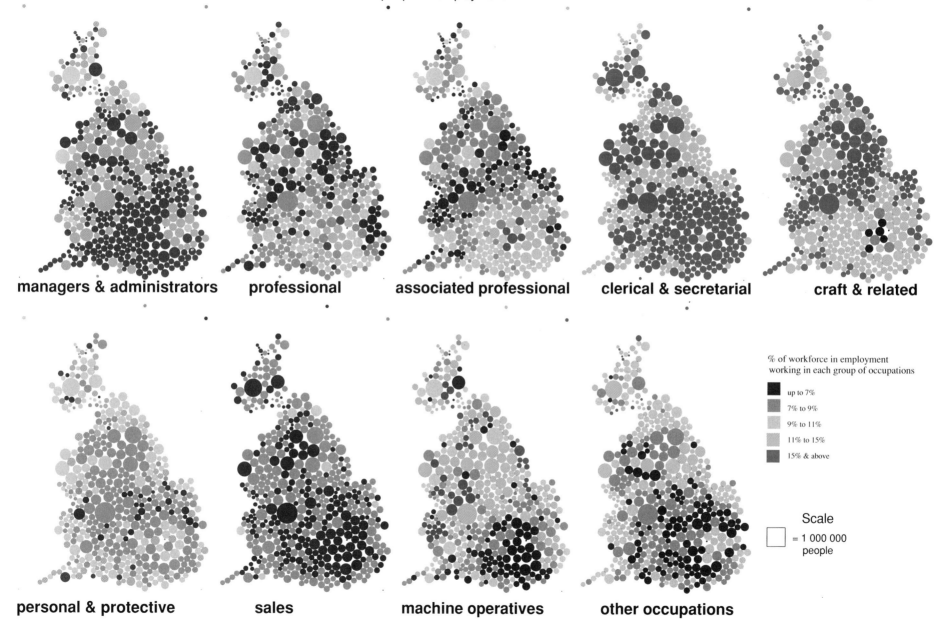

managers & administrators

professional

associated professional

clerical & secretarial

craft & related

personal & protective

sales

machine operatives

other occupations

% of workforce in employment
working in each group of occupations

up to 7%

7% to 9%

9% to 11%

11% to 15%

15% & above

Scale

= 1 000 000
people

3.13: Occupation of all Residents in Employment in Britain 1991

Standard Occupational Classification	%GB	%Female	District: highest proportion	%
ALL OCCUPATIONS	100.0	44		
1. managers and administrators				
a) corporate managers and administrators	9.6	29	Wokingham	18.9
10. government and large companies	0.5	39	Kingston upon Thames	1.6
11. production managers	2.6	10	South Bucks	5.3
12. specialist managers	2.8	35	Richmond Upon Thames	8.3
13. financial and office managers	1.9	47	City of London	6.2
14. in transport and storing	0.6	14	Spelthorne	1.6
15. in protective services	0.2	5	North Kesteven	2.3
19. not elsewhere categorised	0.9	41	City of Westminster	2.0
b) other managers/proprietors	6.3	36	Isles of Scilly	25.7
16. in agriculture and forestry	0.9	15	Carmarthen	11.7
17. in service industries	5.4	40	Isles of Scilly	18.6
2. professional occupations				
a) science and engineering professionals	2.3	10	Cambridge	6.6
20. natural scientists	0.5	29	Vale of White Horse	3.1
21. engineers and technologists	1.8	5	Hart	4.5
b) 22. Health professionals	0.7	33	Bearsden and Milngavie	2.5
c) 23. Teaching professionals	3.6	62	Bearsden and Milngavie	10.8
d) other professional occupations	2.1	32	City of London	15.0
24. legal professionals	0.3	28	City of London	8.4
25. business and financial	0.7	21	City of London	3.5
26. architects and surveyors	0.4	8	Kensington and Chelsea	1.5
27. librarians and related	0.1	64	Ceredigion	0.8
28. not elsewhere categorised	0.6	58	City of London	1.8
3. associated professional and technical				
a) science and engineering	2.3	20	Eastleigh	4.3
30. scientific technicians	1.2	24	Copeland	2.9
31. draughtpersons and surveyors	0.5	8	Barrow-in-Furness	1.4
32. computer analyst/programmers	0.6	21	Winchester	1.6
b) 34. health associate professions	2.6	89	City of London	10.6
c) other associate professional	3.8	41	Kensington and Chelsea	13.9
33. ship and aircraft officers	0.1	4	Orkney Islands	1.6
35. legal associate professionals	0.1	50	Epping Forest	0.3
36. business and finance associated	1.0	30	Kensington and Chelsea	4.0
37. social welfare associated	0.6	74	Argyll and Bute	1.4
38. literary, artistic and sports	1.3	37	Camden	8.5
39. not elsewhere categorised	0.7	39	South Bucks	1.3
4. clerical and secretarial occupations				
a) clerical occupations	11.5	69	Barking and Dagenham	17.6
40. civil service and local government	1.6	73	Wyre	6.0
41. numerical clerks and cashiers	4.3	73	Castle Point	8.6
42. filing and records clerks	1.1	72	Suffolk Coastal	2.5
43. clerks not otherwise specified	2.6	82	Corby	5.0
44. stores and dispatch clerks, storekeepers	1.3	19	Peterborough	3.0
49. clerical not otherwise specified	0.7	71	Stevenage	1.5
b) secretarial occupations	4.6	97	Redbridge	8.6
45. secretaries, personal assistants, typists	3.4	99	Bromley	6.8
46. receptionists, telephonists and related	1.2	92	Camden	2.0
5. craft and related occupations				
a) 50. skilled construction trades	2.6	1	North Cornwall	5.1
b) skilled engineering trades	4.4	2	Barrow-in-Furness	9.8
51. machining, fitting, instrument making	2.5	2	Nuneaton and Bedworth	6.2
52. electrical / electronic trades	1.9	3	Barrow-in-Furness	3.8

Standard Occupational Classification	%GB	%Female	District: highest proportion	%
c) other skilled trades	7.5	19	Roxburgh	19.8
53. metal forming, welding & related	1.6	3	Barrow-in-Furness	7.6
54. vehicle trades	1.1	3	North Shropshire	1.9
55. textiles, garments & related trades	1.2	70	Roxburgh	13.3
56. printing and related trades	0.6	31	Wansdyke	2.3
57. woodworking trades	1.4	2	Badenoch and Strathspey	4.3
58. food preparation trades	0.4	22	Isles of Scilly	2.6
59. not elsewhere classified	1.2	14	Stoke-on-Trent	11.9
6. personal and protective service				
a) protective service occupations	2.2	12	Richmondshire	17.9
60. armed forces (but not officers)	0.7	8	Richmondshire	16.9
61. security and protective services	1.5	14	Dumbarton	3.6
b) personal service occupations	7.0	78	Badenoch and Strathspey	14.2
62. catering occupations	2.0	66	Isles of Scilly	8.8
63. travel attendants and related	0.2	56	Crawley	1.7
64. health care and related	2.1	91	Blaenau Gwent	4.3
65. childcare and related	1.3	99	South Wight	2.3
66. hairdressers and related	0.4	92	Merthyr Tydfil	0.8
67. domestic staff and related	0.7	55	City of London	2.6
68. not elsewhere classified	0.3	39	Rhuddlan	1.1
7. sales occupations				
a) buyers, brokers and sales reps.	1.8	24	Eastwood	3.8
70. buyers, brokers and related agents	0.3	29	City of London	1.8
71. sales representatives	1.5	23	Eastwood	3.2
b) other sales occupations	5.3	78	Berwick-upon-Tweed	8.6
72. assistants & check-out operators	4.7	83	Berwick-upon-Tweed	8.0
73. market & door-to-door sales	0.4	22	Isles of Scilly	0.9
79. not elsewhere classified	0.3	81	Harlow	0.7
8. plant and machine operatives, assemblers				
a) stationary machine operatives	6.4	33	Corby	21.8
80. food, drink & tobacco processing	0.6	45	Great Grimsby	8.2
81. textiles and tannery processing	0.2	40	Clackmannan	2.5
82. chemicals, paper, plastics etc.	0.8	16	Copeland	5.4
83. metal making and treating	0.2	5	Scunthorpe	2.5
84. metal working processing	0.8	17	Sandwell	4.0
85. assemblers / lineworkers	0.7	52	Sedgefield	4.8
86. other routine process operatives	1.7	55	Corby	9.0
89. not elsewhere classified	1.5	12	Blaenau Gwent	4.3
b) Drivers, mobile machine operatives	3.9	4	Scunthorpe	8.0
87. road transport operatives	2.9	5	Eden	5.4
88. other transport and machinery	1.0	3	Scunthorpe	4.3
9. other occupations				
a) 90. agriculture, forestry and fishing	0.7	25	Berwickshire	11.6
b) other elementary occupations	7.9	53	Lochaber	15.4
91. in mining and manufacturing	0.7	13	Port Talbot (was Afan)	3.9
92. in construction	0.8	1	Sutherland	3.7
93. in transport	0.4	3	Crawley	1.9
94. in communication	0.8	16	Islington	3.0
95. in sales and services	4.9	81	Lochaber	10.0
99. not elsewhere classified	0.3	9	Isles of Scilly	1.8
not stated or inadequately described	1.0	38	Sutherland	4.1

This table shows for each major, sub-major and minor group of the Standard Classification of Occupations, the proportion of people in employment in Britain it includes, the percentage of those people who are women, the district containing the highest proportion of workers in that group, and then what that proportion is for all the workers in that district.

For example, 16.1% of the population work in clerical and secretarial occupations (major classification 4.), 4.6% work in just secretarial occupations (sub-major classification 4.b) of whom 97% are women. The borough of Redbridge contains the highest proportion of secretaries (by this definition) at 8.6% of it workforce.

Occupation and Sex

A most influential factor governing the kind of work a person in Britain is likely to be engaged in is his or her sex. Over half of all men in work are managers & administrators, machine operatives, or are employed in craft & related occupations. Over half of all women in work are in jobs which are clerical, secretarial, personal, protective or in sales. Figure 3.13 gives the proportion of women working in each "minor occupational group" and the size of that group. The local authority district which contains the highest proportion of people doing each kind of work is also listed. The table shows that, for instance, 99% of secretaries, personal assistants, typists and word processor operators (minor group 45) in Britain are women and that the district containing the highest proportion of all of these workers is Bromley, at 6.8% of that borough's workforce.

These enormous differences between the occupations of men and women mean that in looking at the type of work people do it is necessary to consider the sexes separately. The two maps opposite do this. They classify every ward in the country into five modal occupational types. A ward is classified into a type if proportionately more people are working in that type of occupation *above the national average proportion*, as compared to the number of people working in the other four types of occupation. The five groups used here amalgamate major occupational groups 3 and 4 to "clerical & technical", 5, 6 and 7 to "craft, personal & sales" and 8 and 9 to "operative & others". On average 38% of women in a ward will work in clerical and technical occupations and 8% will work in professional occupations. If, however, in a particular ward 10% of women are found to be working in the latter group and 39% in the former group, then that ward is classified as having an unusual number of women in professional occupations. If this approach were not taken almost all the wards in Britain would be seen to have a simple majority of women in clerical & technical jobs. By comparing the proportions of women who work in each group given in Figure 3.13 with the classification used in this map, it is evident that the majority of women in wards with unusual numbers of clerical & technical workers will be in secretarial occupations, whereas men in wards categorised as being over-represented by clerical & technical occupations are most probably technicians.

The increased complexity required to define the keys to these maps is rewarded by the clarity of the patterns which these classifications of wards produce. Shown opposite is a pattern which reflects many of the other differences across the country to be seen later in this atlas. Professional workers can be seen to cluster in a few dense groups of wards in particularly affluent parts of cities, similarly for men and women. In contrast, wards are far more likely to be classified as managerial on the basis of the men rather than women (as male managers and administrators tend to be less evenly spread across the country). It should be remembered that a classification of wards by where workers live is shown opposite, not the value of a single variable. The patterns are nevertheless striking.

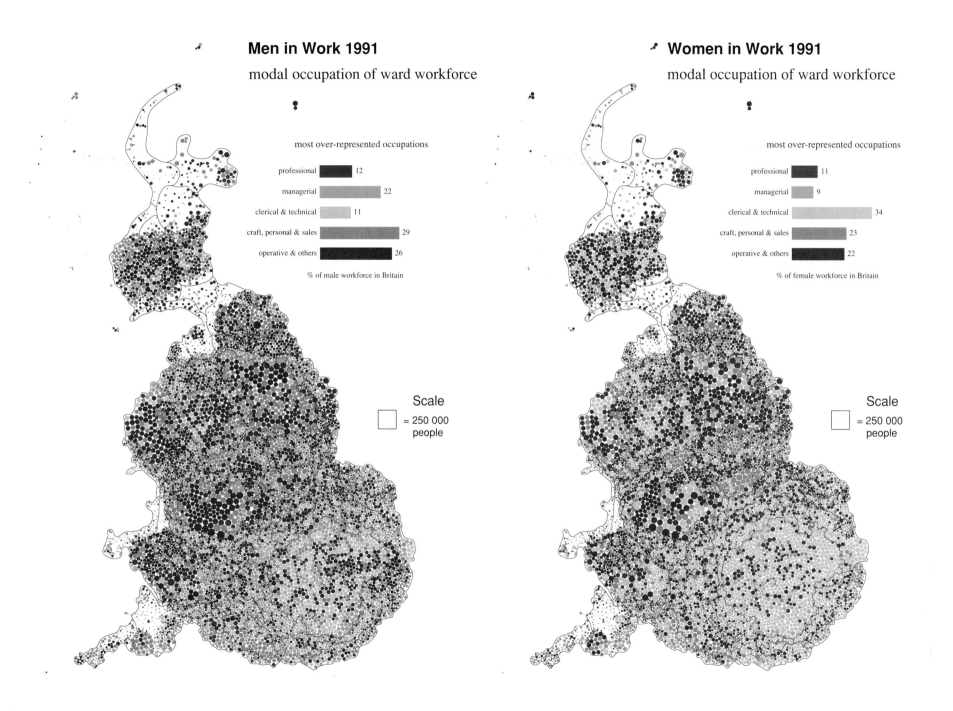

Men in Work 1991

modal occupation of ward workforce

most over-represented occupations

professional	12
managerial	22
clerical & technical	11
craft, personal & sales	29
operative & others	26

% of male workforce in Britain

Scale

☐ = 250 000 people

Women in Work 1991

modal occupation of ward workforce

most over-represented occupations

professional	11
managerial	9
clerical & technical	34
craft, personal & sales	23
operative & others	22

% of female workforce in Britain

Scale

☐ = 250 000 people

3.14: Means of Travel to Work for Selected Groups in the Workforce in Britain 1991

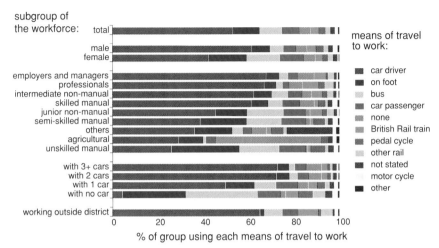

subgroup of
the workforce:

means of travel
to work:

- car driver
- on foot
- bus
- car passenger
- none
- British Rail train
- pedal cycle
- other rail
- not stated
- motor cycle
- other

% of group using each means of travel to work

3.15: Residents in Employment in Britain Working at Home 1991, 1981–1991

proportion of district populations

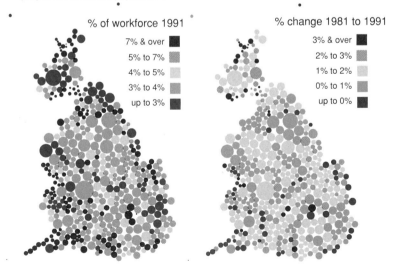

% of workforce 1991

- 7% & over
- 5% to 7%
- 4% to 5%
- 3% to 4%
- up to 3%

% change 1981 to 1991

- 3% & over
- 2% to 3%
- 1% to 2%
- 0% to 1%
- up to 0%

Travel to Work

Nowadays most people in employment in Britain travel to their workplace by car. The next most popular means is on foot, and then by bus. Figure 3.14 shows how the chances of people using any particular means to travel to work vary according to their sex, the kind of job they do, how many vehicles are available to be used by people in their household and by whether they work outside the district in which they live. Commuting to and from work takes up a large part of many people's lives. How people commute is largely determined by what they do, where they live, and the resources which are available to them.

The conventional map and cartogram opposite both show the same distribution of wards classified by which mode of transport is most over-represented when compared to the national average. This modal classification method is the same as that which has just been described in the previous section on occupation and sex. If this method were not used almost all of Britain would be classified as being typified by car drivers. What the maps show is that travel to work by rail is only significant in and just around London. To the east and south of London people rely on British Rail. "Other rail" includes the London Underground, dominant almost exclusively within the boundary of that city, and a few other light rail transit systems elsewhere. These can be seen in Tyne & Wear, for example, but their influence is not great at the national scale.

It is by bus that most public transport passengers travel. Buses dominate all the metropolitan centres other than London, and almost all of Scotland. The importance of public transport for getting to work is not at all apparent from the conventional map. Instead, that map highlights the fact that in almost three fifths of Britain's wards, by land area, people are disproportionately likely to be travelling to work by foot (or "other"; this category includes people who work at home — many of whom are farmers). The cartogram shows this category to dominate only a quarter of wards by population.

Between the city centres and the most rural areas the classic suburban means of travel is dominant. Car ownership comes with the kinds of jobs people in these areas tend to have, but it is also almost a prerequisite of living there. Britain is as divided by how people travel to work as it is by what they do when they get there.

Not everybody who works travels to work. One in twenty people in employment in Britain worked at home in 1991. In 1981 this figure was one in twenty seven. Figure 3.15 shows those areas where more people work at home than is usual, and the areas where this group of workers is growing most quickly. Rural areas dominate the first map, reflecting the likelihood of agricultural workers to live on a farm, but the London boroughs of Westminster, Kensington & Chelsea and Camden also feature strongly. Camden has seen one of the largest increases in home-based work, along with the more rural parts of Scotland, Wales, Buckinghamshire and Hampshire.

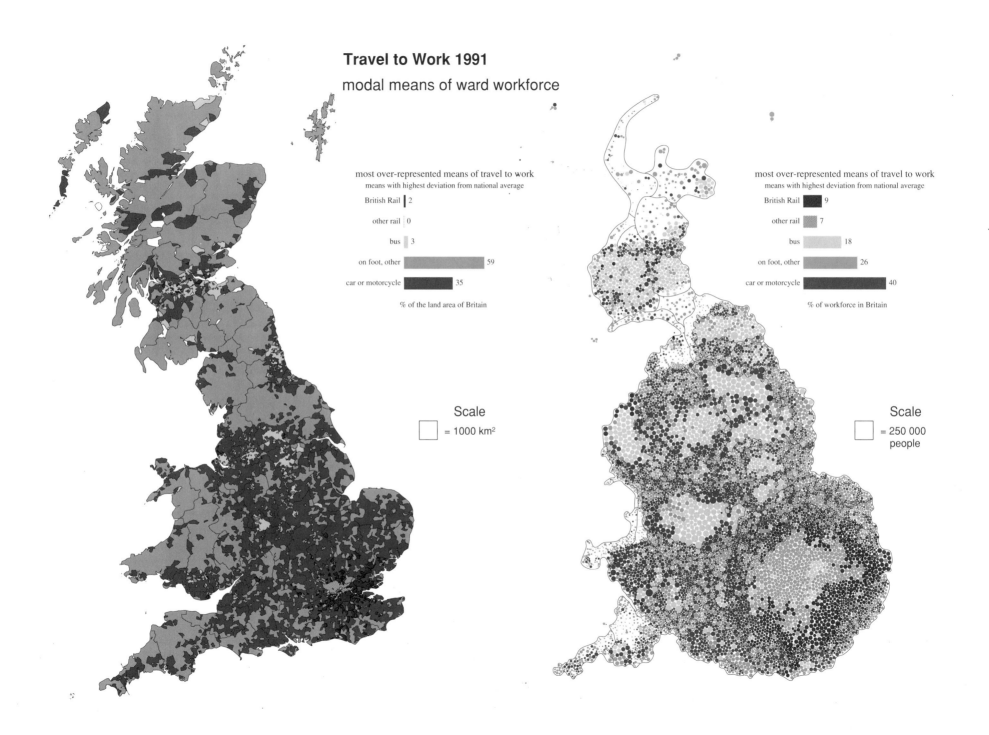

Travel to Work 1991

modal means of ward workforce

most over-represented means of travel to work
means with highest deviation from national average

British Rail | 2
other rail | 0
bus | 3
on foot, other | 59
car or motorcycle | 35

% of the land area of Britain

most over-represented means of travel to work
means with highest deviation from national average

British Rail | 9
other rail | 7
bus | 18
on foot, other | 26
car or motorcycle | 40

% of workforce in Britain

Scale

☐ = 1000 km²

Scale

☐ = 250 000 people

3.16: Change in Methods of Travel to Work by Socioeconomic Groups in Britain 1971–1991

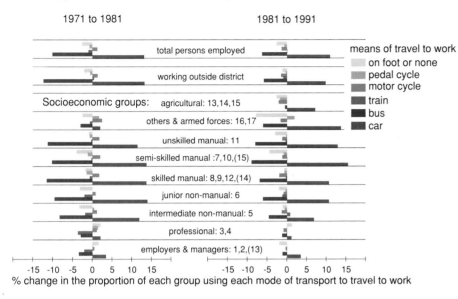

1971 to 1981   1981 to 1991

total persons employed

working outside district   means of travel to work

Socioeconomic groups: agricultural: 13,14,15   on foot or none
                                                                pedal cycle
others & armed forces: 16,17   motor cycle
                                                                train
unskilled manual: 11   bus
                                                                car
semi-skilled manual :7,10,(15)

skilled manual: 8,9,12,(14)

junior non-manual: 6

intermediate non-manual: 5

professional: 3,4

employers & managers: 1,2,(13)

-15 -10 -5   0   5 10 15   -15 -10 -5   0   5 10 15
% change in the proportion of each group using each mode of transport to travel to work

3.17: Travel to Work by Car in Britain 1971, 1981–1991 by Ward

% change in residents in employment travelling to work by car 1981–1991

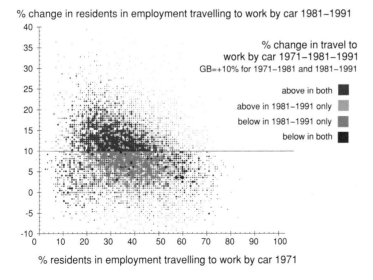

% change in travel to
work by car 1971–1981–1991
GB=+10% for 1971–1981 and 1981–1991

above in both
above in 1981–1991 only
below in 1981–1991 only
below in both

% residents in employment travelling to work by car 1971

Commuting Change

The creation of a "car culture" in Britain was just as much a feature of the 1970s as it was a caricature in the 1980s. Figure 3.16 shows that more people switched to travelling to work by car in the 1970s: an additional thirteen commuters in every hundred, compared to eleven extra in the 1980s. In both decades it was the buses which suffered most from these changes, while the motorcycle saw the increased popularity which it had won in the 1970s reversed during the next decade.

The 1980s were very much a catching up period in which many semi-skilled and unskilled workers gained access to cars for the first time. Over 70% of professional workers now travel to work by car, but they undertook a larger rise in walking to work as compared to commuting by car during the last decade. The only other case in which the car did not win outright in the 1980s was among members of the armed forces and other people without an easily categorised occupation, for whom the pedal cycle has seen a small revival. The definition of socioeconomic groups shown in this figure changes slightly between the first period and the second as indicated by the group numbers in brackets. These changes are unlikely to affect significantly any comparisons.

The cartograms opposite show these changes mapped out across space. District level maps are shown here for the changes which have occurred for travel by train, pedal cycle, bus and on foot. The two former means of travel did not suffer as badly as the two latter. Bus travel fell most in the cities where travel by pedal cycle became more popular. The only districts to see an increase of more than one person in every twenty travelling to work on foot were Reading, Worthing and Richmondshire in North Yorkshire.

Enough people travel to work by car for a ward map to be drawn of the pattern of change over twenty years. Wards have been classified by whether car travel rose by above or below 10% in each decade. It is largely the residents of cities in the north of England, the Midlands and Wales who have seen their levels of car travel rise faster than this level during both of the last two decades. Conversely, London contains almost all the wards in Britain where the rise in car travel has been below this level for both periods. London contains more people in those occupational groups more likely to have had a car in the first place, and also the most congested roads in Britain and the most extensive public transport system.

Figure 3.17 shows the relationship between the level of commuting to work in 1971 in each ward and the subsequent rise in this form of travel which took place between 1981 and 1991 in those same areas. Each ward is shaded using the same scheme as on the cartogram opposite. The largest increases in commuting by car were generally seen in those areas with fewer such commuters in the first place. Those wards shaded black on the map and in the figure which have seen the least growth, however, tended either to have very high, or very low, car commuting levels in 1971 — they have not changed.

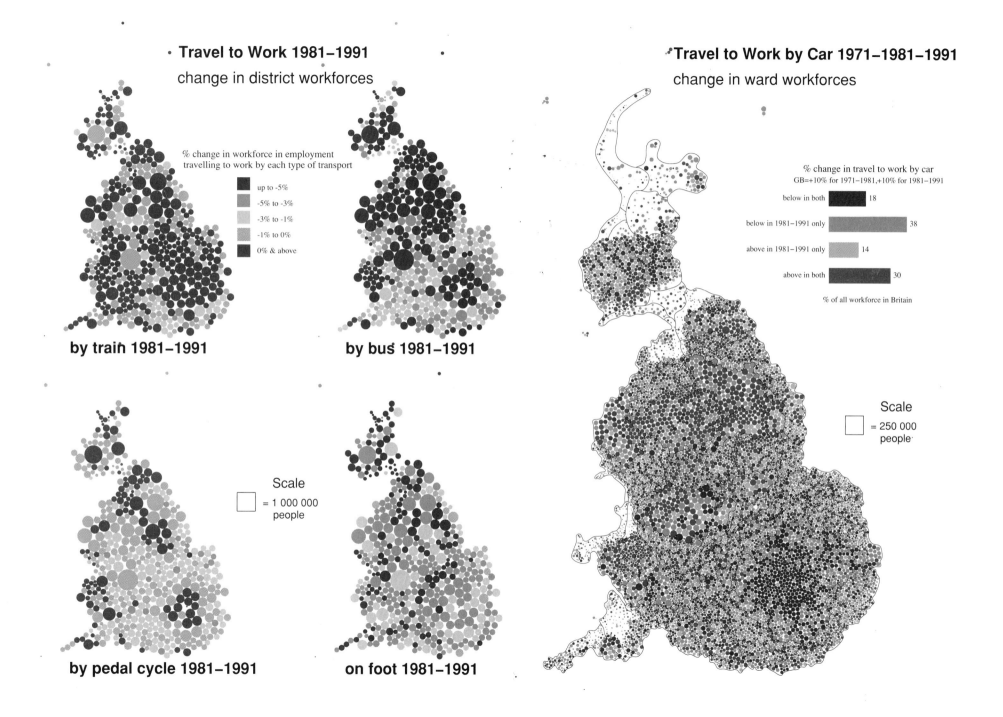

Travel to Work 1981–1991

change in district workforces

% change in workforce in employment
travelling to work by each type of transport

- up to -5%
- -5% to -3%
- -3% to -1%
- -1% to 0%
- 0% & above

by train 1981–1991

by bus 1981–1991

Scale

= 1 000 000
people

by pedal cycle 1981–1991

on foot 1981–1991

Travel to Work by Car 1971–1981–1991

change in ward workforces

% change in travel to work by car
GB=+10% for 1971–1981,+10% for 1981–1991

below in both — 18
below in 1981–1991 only — 38
above in 1981–1991 only — 14
above in both — 30

% of all workforce in Britain

Scale

= 250 000
people

3.18: Hours Worked of People in Employment by Age and Sex in Britain 1991

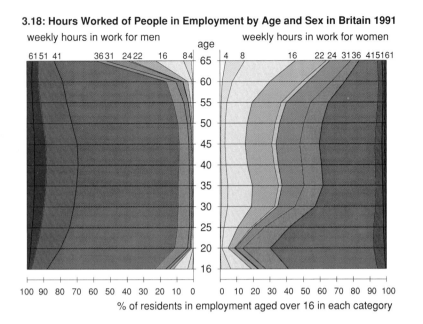

weekly hours in work for men   age   weekly hours in work for women

% of residents in employment aged over 16 in each category

3.19: Hours Worked for People In Employment by Occupation in Britain 1991

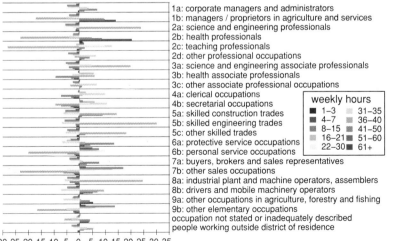

1a: corporate managers and administrators
1b: managers / proprietors in agriculture and services
2a: science and engineering professionals
2b: health professionals
2c: teaching professionals
2d: other professional occupations
3a: science and engineering associate professionals
3b: health associate professionals
3c: other associate professional occupations
4a: clerical occupations
4b: secretarial occupations
5a: skilled construction trades
5b: skilled engineering trades
5c: other skilled trades
6a: protective service occupations
6b: personal service occupations
7a: buyers, brokers and sales representatives
7b: other sales occupations
8a: industrial plant and machine operators, assemblers
8b: drivers and mobile machinery operators
9a: other occupations in agriculture, forestry and fishing
9b: other elementary occupations
occupation not stated or inadequately described
people working outside district of residence

weekly hours	
■ 1–3	31–35
■ 4–7	■ 36–40
■ 8–15	■ 41–50
16–21 ■	51–60
22–30 ■	61+

% difference from the national proportion of residents working these hours per week ˙ .

Working Hours

When combined with the time they spend commuting, one person in every sixteen in Britain spends over sixty hours a week working; one person in every six spends more than forty hours a week at work; while one person in every four works thirty hours or less a week. A person's age and sex give a good indication of how long he or she is likely to spend at work in his or her job, as Figure 3.18 demonstrates. Women, on average, work ten hours less a week in paid employment than men. The longest hours are spent by men aged between 40 and 45, very few of whom work less than thirty six hours a week.

The maps opposite differentiate between the experiences of men and women. If this were not done then the pattern would tell more about the rate of women's participation in the workforce of each area than about how working hours differ between people who live in different areas. The map for men has a strong similarity with the ward map showing the distribution of male occupations on page 79. Men living in areas where high numbers of people have management or professional jobs tend to spend less time in these areas and more time at work. Very rural areas are also characterised by long working hours for men. Of the total population of Britain, 12% of people live in wards where all the working men are at work for, on average, more than eight hours a day. The areas where men work the lowest hours coincide with areas where a low proportion of the workforce is employed to begin with (see page 67).

The picture for women is very different and is dominated by that quarter of the country in which it is usual for women to be in paid employment to work for more than thirty hours a week: London, Birmingham, Leicester, central Manchester, Edinburgh and Glasgow. These are areas where women in work tend to be younger but they are also areas where there are less restrictions on women working these hours. Women tend to work the lowest hours in north east England, Yorkshire and in parts of East Anglia. Cultural factors probably have as much influence as social and economic factors in determining this pattern, but above all it is the occupation that a person holds which affects how many hours he or she is likely to spend a week at work.

Figure 3.19 illustrates the detailed relationship between the different sub-major occupational groups and the hours usually worked in each type of job. Health professionals are more likely to be working more than sixty hours a week than people in any other group. Teaching professionals are unlikely to have paid working hours of longer than thirty six hours a week, whereas for many skilled and manual jobs thirty six to forty hours a week is very much the norm. The lowest hours worked are to be found in certain sales, personal service and "elementary" occupations where part-time work is usual. The figure shows the overall picture to be complex but, in general, the less prestigious a job is, the fewer hours of work a week it entails.

Hours Worked by Men 1991

average for ward workforce

average weekly hours of employed men

up to 37	6
37 to 38	28
38 to 39	35
39 to 40	19
40 & above	12

% of all residents in Britain

Scale

☐ = 250 000 people

Hours Worked by Women 1991

average for ward workforce

average weekly hours of employed women

up to 27	17
27 to 28	19
28 to 29	22
29 to 30	18
30 & above	25

% of all residents in Britain

Scale

☐ = 250 000 people

3.20: Hours Worked in Employment by Women by Age and Children in Britain 1971–1991

% of women in employment in each category by hours worked weekly

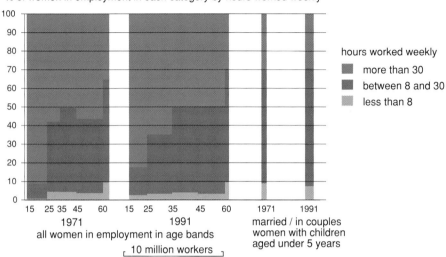

hours worked weekly

■ more than 30
■ between 8 and 30
▨ less than 8

1971 / 1991 all women in employment in age bands
[10 million workers]

married / in couples women with children aged under 5 years

3.21: Hours Worked by Men by their Family Type in Britain 1991

% of all men working these hours by type of family unit

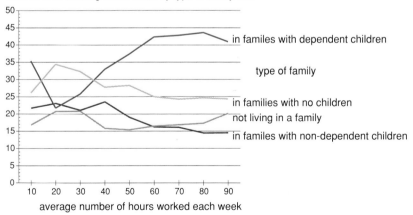

in familes with dependent children

type of family

in families with no children

not living in a family

in familes with non-dependent children

average number of hours worked each week

Mothers in Work

The working hours of women with young children was a topic in both the 1971 and 1991 censuses, so it is possible to measure how the hours of work for these women has changed over the last twenty years. Men were not asked their working hours then, and there was no question on working hours in 1981, so the only comparison which it is possible to make in looking for changes in the length of the working day is for women.

Figure 3.20 shows that the working hours of women in paid employment have changed very little over the last twenty years. The average length of time worked by women is now thirty one hours a week which is a few minutes less than the average number of hours worked by women in 1971. Many more women are now in paid employment and this is reflected in the figure through the width of the bars. The height of the bars shows the proportion of women of each age group working a certain number of hours. The most significant change has been that there is no longer a dip in the proportion of women who work full-time after the age of 45. More than half of all women aged over 35 now work full-time. For women with young children there has been almost no change in the number of hours worked although far more women with children now work. Women with children who are in employment now work on average twenty five hours a week, representing a very slight rise over their time spent in work in 1971.

The first map opposite shows what proportion of women in work with children aged under five worked full-time hours in 1991. The picture it presents is very similar to the pattern for the hours of all women, although the areas where less than a fifth of these mothers work full-time are more likely to be in the affluent rural parts of southern England than along the north east coast. The second map shows the pattern of change over the last twenty years. In places this map is based on very low numbers of women with children under five in work, particularly for 1971; where the numbers are too low the ward is not shaded at all (in 6% of wards). Even though the distribution is speckled, a faster rise within some of the larger cities is evident. It also tends to be the edges of cities and the more suburban wards, particularly in Yorkshire, which have seen falls in the proportion of women with children in full-time work. The comparison being made here is between married women in 1971 and married or cohabiting women in 1991.

As an aside, access to the Sample of Anonymised Records allows the work of men with children to be monitored comprehensively for the first time in 1991. Figure 3.21 shows that almost half of all men working more than sixty hours a week are likely to live in families with dependent young children of whom they are only likely to see much if they do not also work over the weekend. Most men working part-time live in families with no children. Men in families containing older non-dependent children tend to work less than forty hours a week, as do men who are not living in a family. The censuses cannot show whether fathers' working hours have increased over the last two decades.

Women in Work with Children 1991

proportion full-time workers by ward

% of employed women with children under 5
who are in full-time employment (more than 30 hours a week)

up to 20%	20
20% to 30%	23
30% to 40%	21
40% to 50%	14
50% & above	21

% of all residents in Britain

Scale

☐ = 250 000
people

Women in Work with Children 1971–1991

change in full-time workers by ward

% change in employed women with children under 5
who are in full-time employment (more than 30 hours a week)

up to -15%	18
-15% to 0%	16
0% to 15%	25
15% to 30%	19
30% & above	15

% of all residents in Britain (less 6% in 1971)

Scale

☐ = 250 000
people

3.22: Numbers of People Registered as Unemployed by Sex in Britain 1971–1993

'000s (seasonally adjusted and revised for "consistency")   claiments: ■ women ▨ men

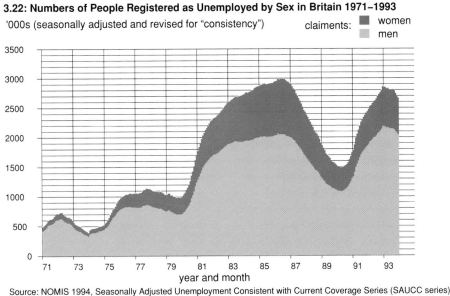

Source: NOMIS 1994, Seasonally Adjusted Unemployment Consistent with Current Coverage Series (SAUCC series)

3.23: Chance of Going On or Off the Unemployment Register by Sex in Britain 1983–1993

% of workforce registering as unemployed over the subsequent twelve months

% of workforce ceasing to be unemployed over the next month (three month average)

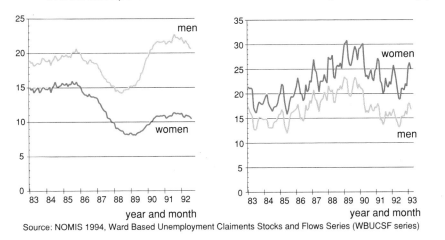

Source: NOMIS 1994, Ward Based Unemployment Claiments Stocks and Flows Series (WBUCSF series)

Unemployment Levels

Unemployment statistics are one of the most contested sets of facts in Britain. The endless changes which have been made to the definition used for the official series have generally led to a more restrictive definition of who is "out of work and looking for work" among the population (Gregg 1994). Figure 3.22 shows how the absolute numbers of people who are unemployed have varied over time according to the most recent official definition of unemployment. By 1993 male unemployment was higher than at any point since the 1930s depression, according even to this restrictive definition. The total number of people unemployed is lower now than the peak of three million people in August 1986. This is the peak of a seasonally adjusted and revised series which only includes people allowed to claim unemployment benefit who are 18 years old or older.

The censuses have an advantage over other official statistics in that they report how many people classed themselves as unemployed. In April 1991 this included 2.48 million people, almost half a million more people than were included in the statistics used to draw Figure 3.22 for that date (and making no allowance for the possibility that any of the "missing million" people are out of work). To find an unemployment statistic which is comparable across time it is now necessary to adjust even the census figure and include people who are on government schemes as unemployed. This definition brings the count of people in the workforce who were *out of work* in April 1991 to 2.83 million people or 10.5% of the workforce. The first map opposite shows how this proportion varied across the country. The degree of inequality of access to work in Britain is clear, with the most fortunate fifth of the population living in wards where they are more than two-and-a-half times less likely to be out of work than the worst off fifth in Britain.

More surprising perhaps are the geographical changes which have occurred over the last twenty years, as shown by the second map. As expected, the inner cities have seen rises in levels of unemployment above the national average over both decades, while affluent rural areas have seen the lowest rises. In the 1980s, however, the inner cities were joined by almost all the wards of Outer London and many small cities in the South East in experiencing rises in unemployment levels above the national average. In the north of England this change occurred mainly in the Yorkshire and Northumberland coalfields and affected far fewer people in total.

Unemployment levels are only a part of the statistical story that official data sets now make available. Figure 3.23 shows how a person's crude chance of entering or leaving the register has altered over the last ten years. The average male worker had more than a one in five chance of becoming unemployed during 1991. For women this was one in ten, but the gap between the chances of the sexes is widening. It is similarly so for a person's chance of leaving the register each month, which in 1991 for men was one in six, whereas women on the register had a one in four chance of leaving it each month.

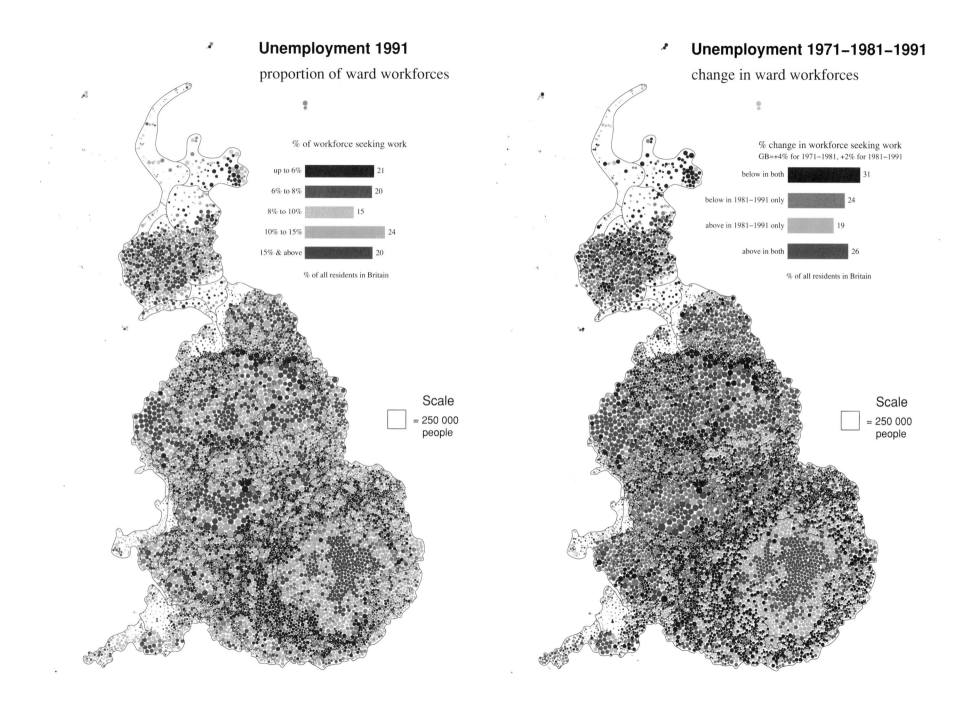

Unemployment 1991

proportion of ward workforces

% of workforce seeking work

up to 6%		21
6% to 8%		20
8% to 10%		15
10% to 15%		24
15% & above		20

% of all residents in Britain

Scale

☐ = 250 000 people

Unemployment 1971–1981–1991

change in ward workforces

% change in workforce seeking work
GB=+4% for 1971–1981, +2% for 1981–1991

below in both		31
below in 1981–1991 only		24
above in 1981–1991 only		19
above in both		26

% of all residents in Britain

Scale

☐ = 250 000 people

3.24: Duration on the Unemployment Register by Age and Sex in Britain 1991

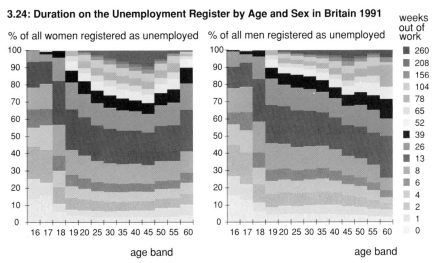

% of all women registered as unemployed   % of all men registered as unemployed

weeks out of work
- 260
- 208
- 156
- 104
- 78
- 65
- 52
- 39
- 26
- 13
- 8
- 6
- 4
- 2
- 1
- 0

age band   age band

Source: NOMIS 1994, Ward Based Unemployment - Computerised Claims by Age and Duration (WBUCCAD) Series

3.25: Duration on the Unemployment Register in Britain 1985–1993

% of all people registered as unemployed

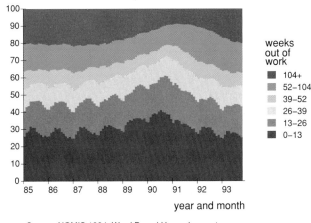

weeks out of work
- 104+
- 52–104
- 39–52
- 26–39
- 13–26
- 0–13

year and month

Source: NOMIS 1994, Ward Based Unemployment -
Computerised Claims by Age and Duration (WBUCCAD) Series

Unemployment Flows

The basic differences between men's and women's chances of becoming and remaining unemployed are shown in Figure 3.23. Here a more detailed survey is made of the information that is available on the flow of people on and off the unemployment register. Figure 3.24 shows the lengths of time men and women had been unemployed for those who were on the register in April 1991. Women's chances of finding work, or of leaving the register for another reason, tend to improve once they are aged over 50. For men, the older they are, the longer they are likely to have been out of work. It should be noted that, by definition, no 16 year old has been out of work for over a year. The median length of time for which most people who were claiming benefit in April 1991 had been claiming benefit was between three months and six months.

The first map opposite shows the likelihood of a person in Britain becoming unemployed according to the ward he or she lived in. More than two thirds of the population lived in areas where the average worker had at least a one in ten chance of losing his or her job and having to register for unemployment benefit in 1991. Although the geographical pattern of these flows is very similar to that for the static rates of unemployment, the suburbs can be seen to be even better off by this measure. People living there who were in work in 1991 were less likely to lose that work during the year.

The really clear differences between areas are to be found in the second map which shows what proportion of people on the register have been out of work for over a year and live in each ward. In the South East outside Inner London less than a tenth of people who were unemployed in April 1991 had been out of work this length of time. In the northern English and Scottish cities more than a quarter of unemployed people signing on for over twelve months is not unusual. This map, perhaps more than any of the others presented so far, shows how the economic space of Britain is divided between places where work is relatively bountiful, and is well rewarded (if requiring long hours and commuting), and places where there are very obviously not enough jobs to go round, or where you are likely to live if you are employed in work with little job security.

Again it must be stressed that April 1991 and the year leading up to that date is one particular time, the choice of which could well influence the patterns being described here. Figure 3.25 shows how the average durations of unemployment have altered over time and illustrates that unusually few people had been out of work for over a year in 1991. The severity of the recession since then is apparent. What is also striking from this figure is the pattern of lags between rises in the number of people who have been unemployed for less than three months, and rises in longer term unemployment which result directly from those increases. The rises in short term unemployment occur in August each year, as a new set of school and college leavers starts looking for work. By the summer of 1990 many had failed to find it, or could find only intermittent jobs.

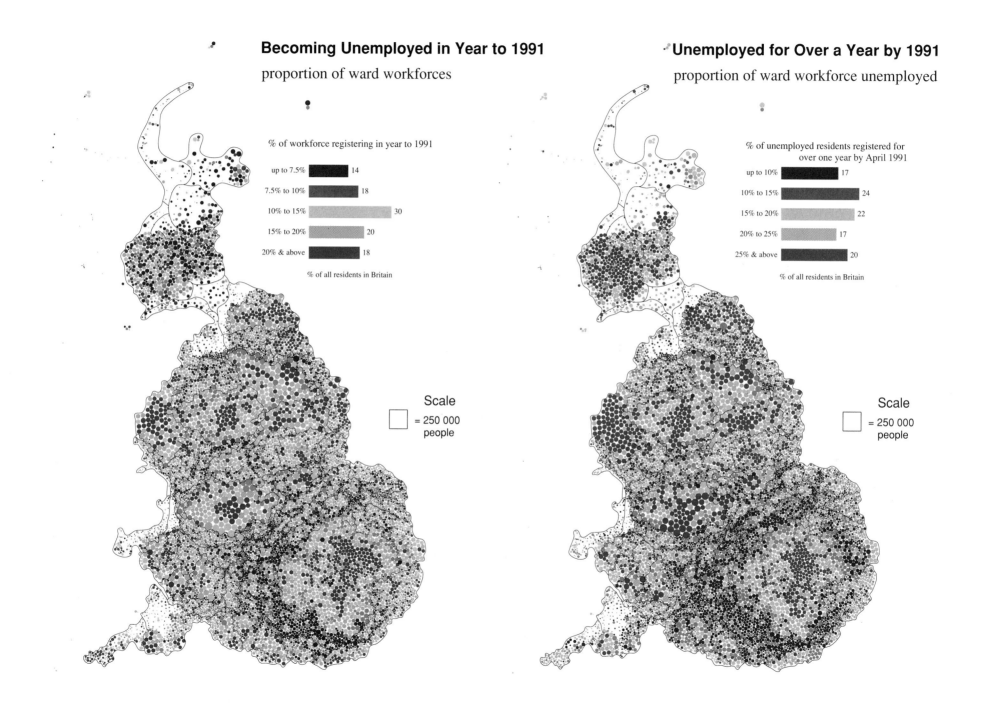

Becoming Unemployed in Year to 1991

proportion of ward workforces

% of workforce registering in year to 1991

up to 7.5%	14
7.5% to 10%	18
10% to 15%	30
15% to 20%	20
20% & above	18

% of all residents in Britain

Scale

☐ = 250 000 people

Unemployed for Over a Year by 1991

proportion of ward workforce unemployed

% of unemployed residents registered for over one year by April 1991

up to 10%	17
10% to 15%	24
15% to 20%	22
20% to 25%	17
25% & above	20

% of all residents in Britain

Scale

☐ = 250 000 people

3.26: Numbers of People Registered as Unemployed by Age in Britain 1984–1994

'000s of people registered in each age group

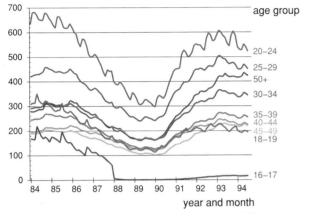

year and month

Source: NOMIS 1994, Ward Based Unemployment - Computerised Claims by Age and Duration (WBUCCAD) Series

3.27: Unemployment by Age, Sex and Ethnic Group in Britain 1991

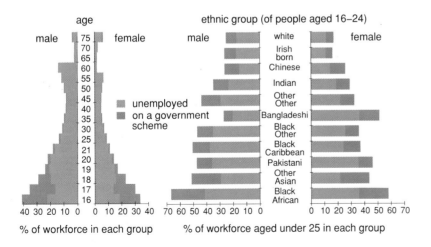

% of workforce in each group   % of workforce aged under 25 in each group

Unemployment and Age

Age is a most important correlate of unemployment. Figure 3.5 shows how young adults were far more likely to be out of work than any other group in 1991. It is difficult to tell how this situation is changing year by year because there is no simple way of estimating what proportion of each age group is in the workforce apart from using the censuses. Figure 3.26 shows the absolute numbers of people in each of nine age bands who have been registered as unemployed each month since June 1984. This figure illustrates one of the effects of the changes to the official definition of unemployment. In October 1988 almost all 16 and 17 year olds ceased to be classified as claimants. The graph implies that the younger a person is, the more likely he or she is to be out of work. Since 1991 more people aged over 50 are now out of work than are people aged between 30 and 34. However, the unemployment rate of the former will still be much lower because so many more of them are in work. The total number of people aged over 50 has also grown quickly since 1991 (as shown by Figure 2.4), just as the number of people aged 18 to 19 is falling — so unsurprisingly the number of people who are unemployed and aged 18 and 19 is falling. Factors such as these should be born in mind when studying this figure.

By including people on government schemes in 1991 in the count of people out of work it is possible to alleviate some of the problems of changing definitions. Figure 3.27 shows most clearly how unemployment rates are related to a person's age and sex. The figure also shows the influence of a third factor — ethnic group — having allowed for some of the effects of different age structures by concentrating only upon people aged under 25 years. This is necessary because people in all ethnic groups, other than those born in Ireland, tend to be younger than the white majority and so can be expected to experience higher rates of unemployment (see Figure 2.20). By concentrating only on young adults the differences which cannot be explained by age structure are exposed. Members of all ethnic groups are more likely to be out of work than whites in Britain. Chinese men alone do better than average, however, and Bangladeshi women are three times more likely to be unemployed than white women. The graph is sorted to show the ordering of the overall proportion of people who are unemployed for each ethnic group.

The geographical discrepancies from these headline figures are highlighted in the maps shown opposite. For all ethnic groups there are districts where the rate of unemployment for their young adults is more than 25% above that of all young adults in the district. There are also always a few districts where their rate of unemployment is at least 10% lower than that for the average 16 to 24 year old. These patterns are not particularly simple but it is evident that, when compared with the overall distribution of these groups (see page 45), the unemployment rates tend to be lower for people in ethnic minorities who live in predominantly white districts. The Irish born group does not fit neatly into this pattern, doing well for jobs in London but badly in Wales.

Unemployment by Ethnic Minority Group 1991

proportion of district workforces aged under 25

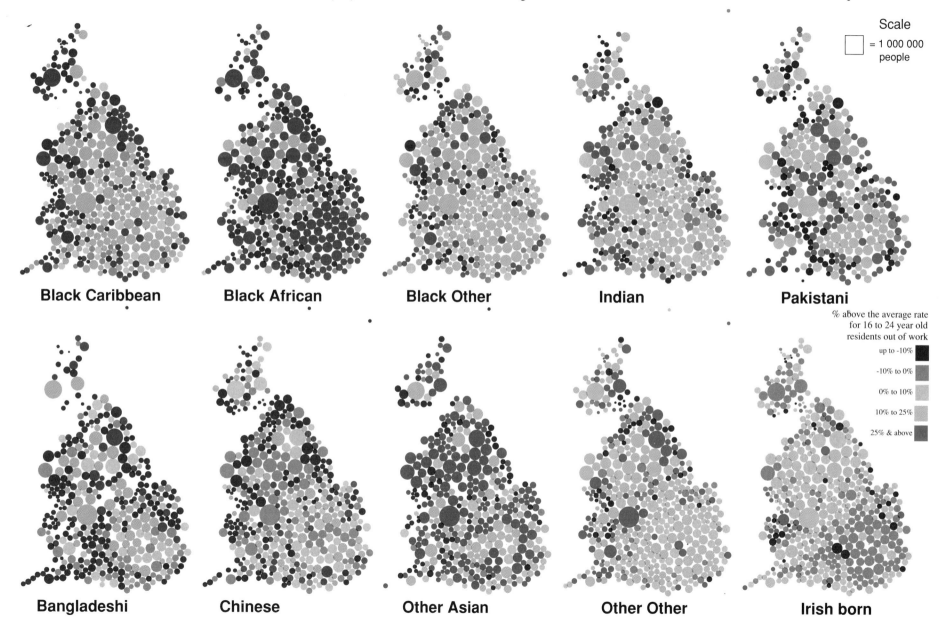

Scale

□ = 1 000 000 people

Black Caribbean **Black African** **Black Other** **Indian** **Pakistani**

Bangladeshi **Chinese** **Other Asian** **Other Other** **Irish born**

% above the average rate
for 16 to 24 year old
residents out of work

up to -10%

-10% to 0%

0% to 10%

10% to 25%

25% & above

3.28: Residents Out of Work by Industry, Occupation and Sex in Britain 1991

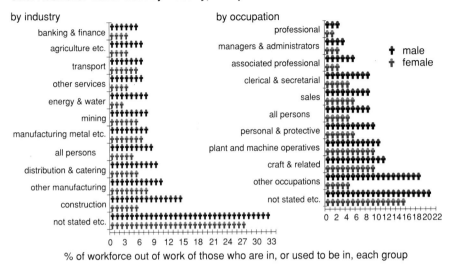

% of workforce out of work of those who are in, or used to be in, each group

3.29: Change in Economic Position of Residents by Age and Sex in Britain 1981–1991

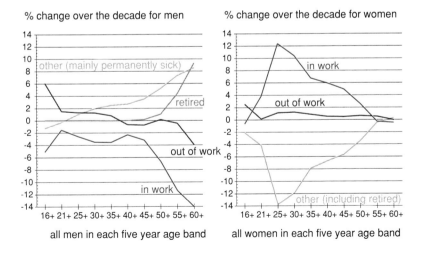

Early Retirement

Different industries and occupations are associated with different rates of unemployment as Figure 3.28 demonstrates. Each icon in the figure represents one person who is out of work for every one hundred of those who used to work, or do work, in that sector. In all cases men are more likely to be out of work than women. The highest rates are for people who did not state a former industry or occupation; most of these people are school or college leavers who had not found a job by April 1991. Some of the rates are surprisingly low. For example, only 8% of men in the mining industry were out of work. This is because many of the men who lost their jobs in that industry during the 1980s, and failed to gain alternative employment, are not now unemployed.

Unemployment is only one route out of work and employment is only one possibility after unemployment. Retirement before the official pensionable age of 60 for women and 65 for men is increasing rapidly, faster in some areas than others. It is difficult to estimate the increase for women because of the ambiguity between the categorisations of "housewife" and "retired". In 1981 1.79 million women said they were retired and 9.16 million said they were looking after the home (or something similar to that). By 1991 4.77 million women stated that they were retired and only 5.89 million claimed to be looking after the home. This change has more to do with how women's views of themselves have changed than with changing economic circumstances. Women's employment status has not been dealt with consistently by the census (see page 65).

Because of these problems the maps opposite concentrate on the situation for men, by showing the proportion of men aged above 34 who have retired and are not yet aged 65, and how that is changing. The coalfield areas of Wales, Nottinghamshire, Yorkshire, Durham and Northumberland stand out clearly as places where over 6% of the men of these ages are retired. If these people were added to the "out of work" category a very much more dramatic picture of economic waste would be drawn. There is no way of knowing from official figures what proportion of these men would choose to work if they could. The high numbers living along the south coast suggest that many may have wished to retire before they were 65, as does the fact that the proportions in this area have not been rising. The other places which have seen little increase are in the Home Counties north and west of London. Here, if men do retire early, they tend to leave.

The very different experiences of economic change for men and women are summarised in Figure 3.29 by age. Fewer men are in work and more are retired than ten years ago. Traditional unemployment has risen only for younger men, and more men may now be looking after the home or will be permanently sick (included in "other"). In general, the converse is true for women, although it is difficult to distinguish between those who are retired and other categories. Unemployment rates, however, have increased for all women apart from those aged between 21 and 24.

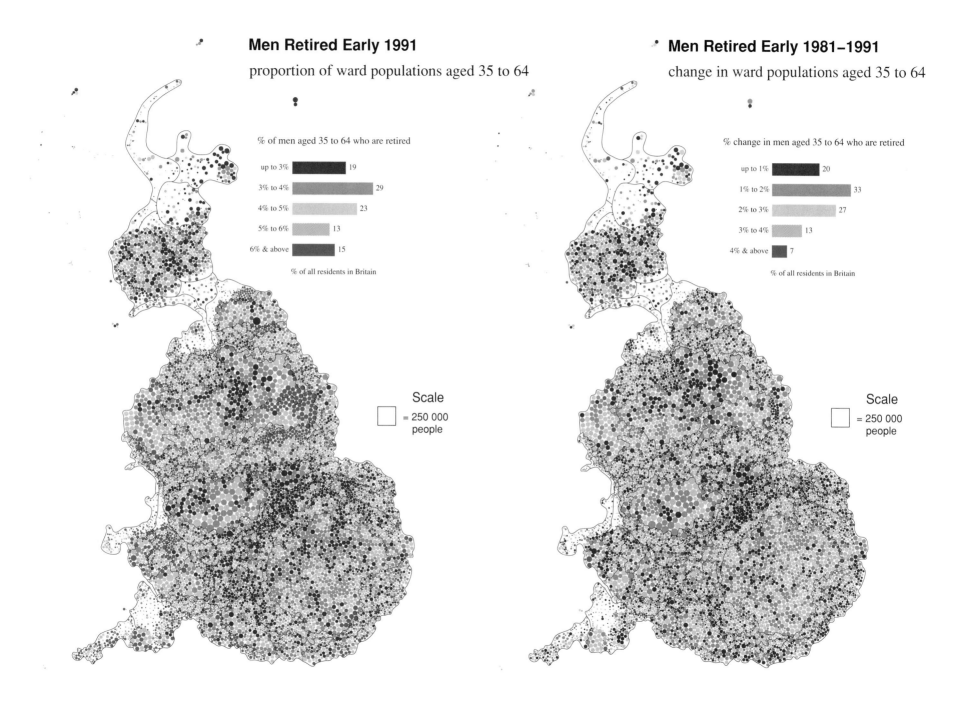

Men Retired Early 1991

proportion of ward populations aged 35 to 64

% of men aged 35 to 64 who are retired

up to 3%	19
3% to 4%	29
4% to 5%	23
5% to 6%	13
6% & above	15

% of all residents in Britain

Scale
☐ = 250 000
people

Men Retired Early 1981–1991

change in ward populations aged 35 to 64

% change in men aged 35 to 64 who are retired

up to 1%	20
1% to 2%	33
2% to 3%	27
3% to 4%	13
4% & above	7

% of all residents in Britain

Scale
☐ = 250 000
people

3.30: Official Adjusted Unemployed Rate by Region in Britain 1974–1993

% of workforce registered as unemployed in each region

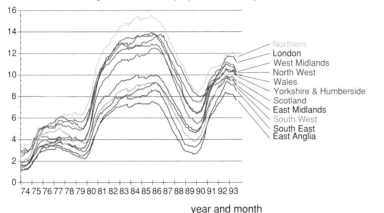

year and month

Source: NOMIS 1994, Seasonally Adjusted Unemployment Consistent with Current Coverage Series (SAUCC series)

3.31: Year and Rate of Highest Unemployment Levels in Britain 1979–1993

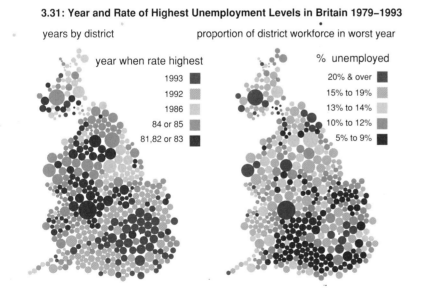

Unemployment Rates

This chapter ends by looking at the geography of the changing annual rate of unemployment among the workforce of Britain. Figure 3.30 shows the seasonally adjusted regional changes in this rate for each month since April 1974. The highest "official" level recorded was 15.6% in the Northern region in March 1986. The Northern region has had the highest rate since October 1977. The lowest rate shown is 1.1% for the South East at the beginning of the period. Southern and northern regions are coloured to differentiate them, with the two regions furthest from London shaded lighter so that their individual trajectories can be traced. Contrasting changes can be seen in the fortunes of the workforces of London and the South West region.

The fifteen maps opposite show the year by year fluctuations in unemployment rates by local authority district. The maps use unemployment counts (divided by an estimate of the size of the workforce for each district) to illustrate the change between the twelve month moving average rates of unemployment centred at the beginning and end of each year shown. The economic similarity of 1991 to 1981 should be evident, as most districts saw their levels of unemployment rise by around two percentage points during these census years. However, in the earlier year unemployment rose faster in the north, whereas a decade later it was rising the least in Scotland. Particular points as well as the general trends in employment history can be identified from these maps, such as the aftermath of the miners' strike in Yorkshire in 1985, or the dramatic reduction in unemployment in Glasgow which took place in the early 1990s.

The 1990s saw the emergence of some of the clearest spatial patterns in the changing geographical distribution of unemployment in Britain. The north–south divide in the latest recession is stark, as are the continued strong levels of job losses in the South East in 1992, compared with the falls in unemployment which were being experienced across the north in that year. Care should be taken when reading these graphs, bearing in mind the evidence of the last few pages, and knowing that many people who come off the unemployment register do not get a job, while many more who would have been counted as unemployed in the past are now dissuaded from joining the register. Nevertheless, the patterns shown here are indicative of the changes which have occurred in the real maps of redundancies and of new recruitment which should, ideally, be drawn.

Finally, Figure 3.31 attempts to summarise these patterns by showing the year for which unemployment rates were highest in each district during this period. The clustering of areas into such a small number of common regions in the first map is remarkable. The second map in the figure shows the level of unemployment for the year in which it was highest in each district. Recent years may have seen greater rises in the south than in the north, but what are now seen as bad levels for much of the south are barely half the worst levels experienced by people living in the north and in London.

Unemployment 1979–1993

change in district workforces

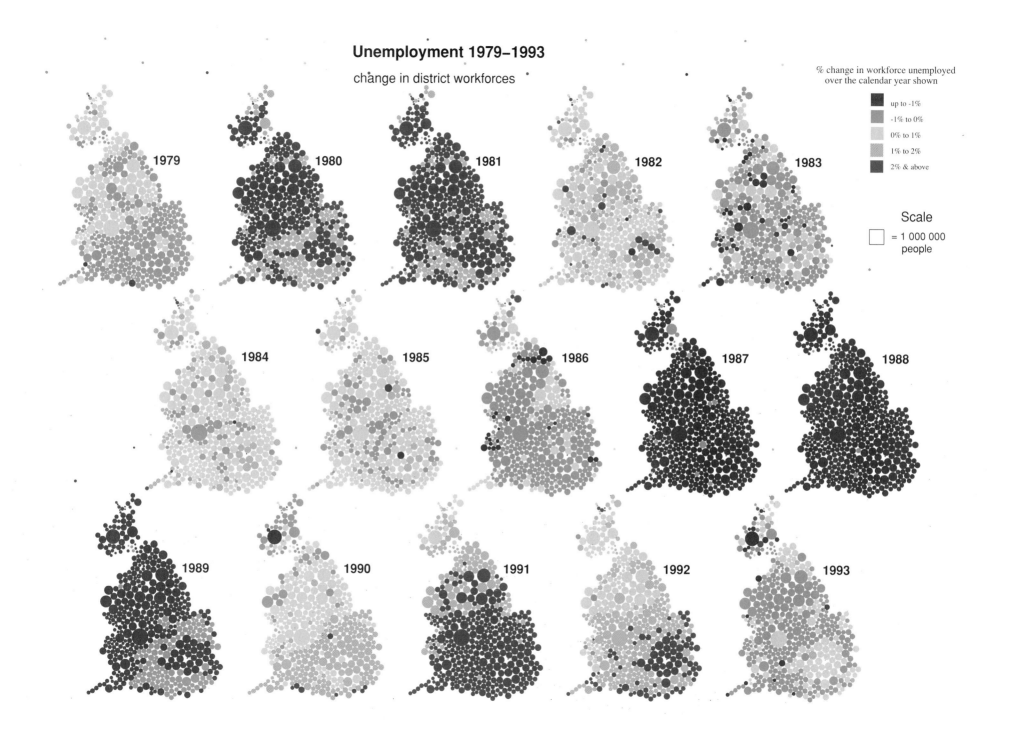

% change in workforce unemployed
over the calendar year shown

up to -1%
-1% to 0%
0% to 1%
1% to 2%
2% & above

Scale

= 1 000 000
people

Conclusion: Work and Unemployment

Economics and Society

The social status and standards of living of most people depend on the economic activity of adults in their household — on whether they work, what they do in their work, or why they are not in work. Social classes and socioeconomic groups are defined mainly by the type of work done by adults in work (page 184). The kind of work people do also determines how they are rewarded, the kind of home they can afford to live in, the lifestyle they can lead and the general level of affluence of local areas. During the 1980s the workforce living inside many large cities shrank, reducing the aggregate spending power in these places. Since 1971 employment levels have risen most strongly amongst adults living in wards in small towns and in the rural South East (page 69). These new jobs are in different occupations which involve very different working patterns and hours as well as commuting times. The type of work adults do affects how long they have to spend at home with their children. Just as some workers' commuting times have increased, in many areas, substantial numbers of people now work from home and hence alter the daytime social composition of their areas (Figure 3.15). It is important to understand the economic geography of employment in Britain in tandem with other distributions. For instance, for women by ethnic group, employment rates are highest amongst Black Caribbean residents (Figure 3.2). Given the age profile and location of most of this ethnic group (page 44) and the geography of the availability of full-time work for women (page 85), it is not surprising to find that these people are more likely than not to be in work.

Out of Work

For many people of working age it is not divisions within the workplace which most influence their lives, but lack of work (by which others often define them). Two and a half million people were counted as "unemployed" at the last census, almost half a million more than were included in the seasonally adjusted and revised official count of that month. A further third of a million adults were on "government schemes" in 1991. In addition to these people who are out of work, one and a half million adults of working age are "permanently sick" and another six hundred thousand adults have "retired early". In Britain, then, the census counted almost five million working-age adults as being out of work due to unemployment, retirement, sickness or from being on a scheme. This total still excludes working-age adults who are out of work but who ticked some other category on the census form and it will exclude many of the missing million who (given their age and location) are likely to be out of work. The people who are included above represent 15% of their age group. These are a very diverse group of residents whose

distribution and composition cannot easily be mapped with only two colours.

Over the 1980s adults were separating geographically into places where people were relatively more likely and less likely to have work (Figure 6.39). Different parts of the country came to rely to differing degrees on social security benefits (Figure 6.35). Sickness amongst people of working age rose most strongly in Wales, the Northern region, the North West and Scotland, and least in the South West, East Anglia and the South East (Figure 5.4). People who were not in work for long periods of time were most likely not to be living in a family (Figure 6.16), and were most often young and male (Figure 6.15), but were also much more likely to have a degree in 1991 as compared to 1971 (Figure 6.20). Long-term unemployment portrays one of the most stark of all geographical divides in Britain (page 91). Thus, the distribution of people who are out of work can be seen in many other distributions shown later in this atlas. Unemployment underlies many other problems and processes in society.

Mapping Mixes: Colour Print D

It would be wrong to treat adults who are out of work for officially very different reasons as a single group, although the geographical connections between the groups they are in are strong. One way to represent this complexity is through bivariate colour mapping where the relationship between two univariate geographical distributions is revealed. Colour Print D uses bivariate mapping to show the pattern between the locations of different groups of working-age adults who are not working. Here the two distributions being compared are working-age adults who are unemployed or on a government scheme and working-age adults who are retired or permanently sick. Shades of colour ranging from yellow to red are used to represent increasing rates of unemployment, while shades of colour ranging from yellow to blue show the proportion of adults retired early or permanently sick in each ward. Wards which contain few of either group remain yellow, or are shaded light green or orange to show which group is relatively more numerous. Wards which contain high proportions of both groups are coloured various darker shades of purple as the red and the blue mix, to coalesce eventually as black in those place where both high unemployment and high rates of retirement and sickness predominate. The numbers by the key boxes show what proportion of the population lives in each category of ward. Thus, 7.8% of people in Britain live in areas where more than a tenth of the working age population is in each of these out-of-work groups. Almost all these wards are in Wales, Scotland and the northern metropolitan countries, with none in Greater London or the West Midlands county. At the other extreme, 16.0% of the population live in areas with the lowest proportions of both groups. It is immediately evident that most wards have either high rates of both groups or low rates of both, but there are interesting exceptions to this generalization. These exceptions together form patterns in space that show how lack of employment in suburban London is different from the northern cities, affecting mainly younger people, and so colouring these wards red. The most unusual wards are those which have low unemployment but a high proportion of working-age people who have retired early or are permanently sick. On Colour Print D these wards are given shades of blue and can be seen in counties such as Lancashire, which has one of the most diverse socioeconomic landscapes in the country.

Who Makes What?

To understand how the current pattern of employment came about, the industrial structure of the economy has to be considered. The 1980s collapse of manufacturing employment in the north and the midlands, and the rise of jobs in services in the South East and in some regional capitals (page 75), underlie much of the change which has brought about the pattern just described. Almost without exception, all types of manufacturing industry have declined over the last two decades, and all service industries (other than transport) have seen rising employment (Figure 3.9). These changes have not only occurred in different places but also to different groups of people within those places. In the last decade employment rates have fallen for all broad age-groups of men except those aged between 30 and 44, and have risen for all groups of women below age 60 (Figure 3.10). Industrial changes also alters the compositions of people by occupation in each area. Most people employed in manufacturing are in craft and related occupations or are plant & machine operatives (Figure 3.11) and almost all of these people are male (Figure 3.12). Professional occupations have tended to be in the "other service industries" which have grown most strongly in recent years. The distinctive local geography of occupations is revealed by listing the districts which contain the most of each group. For instance, various types of professionals were most numerous in Cambridge, Vale of White Horse, Hart, Bearsden & Milngavie, the City of London, Kensington & Chelsea and Ceredigion (see Figure 3.13). The very different geographical patterns to men's and women's work is shown by mapping their most likely occupations in each ward (page 79).

Change in Work

Although the proportion of women in the workforce has risen steadily over the last two decades, a dramatic change in economic activity has also occurred between different groups of men in employment. The proportion of men in full-time employment fell sharply over the 1980s whilst the proportion who were self-employed rose by a slightly smaller amount. When differentiated by age, these two changes can be seen to mirror one another (Figure 3.5), and so it is reasonable to assume that many men who lost full-time work during the last decade stated that they were self-employed in 1991. It is almost impossible to know how many of their new businesses were successful. For women it is often forgotten that the rise in full-time work has been larger than the increase in part-time work, both in absolute and in relative terms (Figure 3.4). It is also interesting to see that full-time work suffered the lowest falls in recent years in parts of the midlands, the north and in Scotland (page 71). Employment growth in the south was largely attributable to increases in self-employment. Part-time employment increased around the coast, while unemployment rates appeared to fall in the Northern region and increased most strongly in the South East between the last two censuses. This was partly the result of the timing of these statistics, as the annual maps of unemployment change show (page 97; Dorling 1992), with London suffering particularly badly from 1990 onwards. More important, however, is the geography of the increases in early retirement and of increases in sickness amongst people of working-age (see Figures 3.29 and 5.4). Formerly working people have been encouraged to reclassify themselves as not seeking work, and only detailed analysis of sources such as the census can show what the effect of these changes has been over space. Simultaneously, men who are in work are now working longer hours than they used to, with the majority of men working more than sixty hours per week having families with young children (Figure 3.21). This increase has been due, in part, to the sharp rise in jobs in those managerial & professional occupations which involve long hours of work (Figure 3.19). Increasingly it appears that people who have work have too much work to do, while many other adults have too little work, and thus cannot afford what the majority are producing so earnestly.

References

Balls, E. and Gregg, P., 1993, *Work and Welfare: Tackling the Jobs Deficit*, London: IPPR.

Buck, N., 1990, *Social Polarisation, Economic Restructuring and Labour Market Change in London and New York*, Occasional Paper No.2, University of Essex: ESRC Research Centre on Micro-social Change.

Dorling, D. (1992) Visualizing people in space and time, *Environment and Planning B*, 19: 613–637.

Employment Gazette, 1992, Historical Supplement 3, Employment Statistics, *Employment Gazette*, 100/6: 11–17.

Employment Gazette, 1994, Economic activity results from the 1991 Labour Force Survey and Census of Population, *Employment Gazette*, 102/3: 87–96.

Gregg, P. 1994, Out for the count: a social scientist's analysis of unemployment statistics in the UK, *Journal of the Royal Statistical Society Series A*, 157/2: 253–270.

Joshi, H. and Owen, S., 1987, How long is a piece of elastic? The measurement of female activity rates in British censuses, 1951–1981, *Cambridge Journal of Economics*, 11: 55–74.

NOMIS, 1994, *National On-line Manpower Information System*, Department of Geography, The University, Durham.

4: Housing

Housing issues affect almost the entire population of Britain, as 98% of people live in households. Censuses are the principal source of information on the quantity and distribution of the nation's housing and on how the population is housed. There is, however, little good geographical information available on the quality, costs and availability of housing. In England, the quality of housing is monitored officially by a periodic survey (DoE 1993) which is too small to be relied upon even to produce accurate national statistics. The local costs of owner-occupied housing can be estimated from information provided by building societies and these data are used in this chapter. Housing availability is inferred from census estimates of the number of vacant dwellings and the number of households who appear to be unsatisfactorily housed.

Several new objects of analysis are used in this chapter, and are defined here. A group of people constitute a *household* when they live at the same address and share at least one meal a day or use a common living room. Many households thus consist of only one person. It is thus also possible for more than one household to live in the same dwelling. A *dwelling* is accommodation designed for one household. For each dwelling a count of the number of rooms it contained was made in the census. The count of *rooms* did not include bathrooms, toilets and kitchens less than two metres wide.

The physical stock of housing changes slowly as property is built to last and entails a long pay-back period due to its cost, so a twenty year perspective is used in many of the maps of change shown here. This is also done because dramatic changes in the provision of housing occurred in the 1970s. Although it takes a long time to change the supply of housing, the way in which housing is used can alter relatively quickly. For instance, the proportion of dwellings which are vacant and the proportion of households which are poorly housed can fluctuate year by year. This balance is influenced by changes in how property is held (tenure) and by changes in the market price of private housing and by rents. The propensity of different kinds of households to form in different places over time, the availability of the kind of housing they need, and their ability to afford it, also require consideration in understanding how people are housed.

This chapter begins by mapping the distribution of different types of dwellings across Britain, distinguishing between detached, semi-detached and terraced houses and between different types of flats. The spatial distribution and change in different kinds of household is then shown through a most basic statistic — average household size. Bringing these two factors together, the geography of the balance of dwellings to households is then shown. This balance is a measure of the excess of dwellings over households in each place and it can provide a rough indication of where housing demand is strongest and how that pattern is changing.

A second slightly more sophisticated measure of the pressure on housing is of overcrowding, indicated by the number of people per room exceeding some threshold. This measure has been used since housing statistics were first recorded. At the start of this century an average occupancy rate of more than four people per room was seen as unacceptable (Rowntree 1902). Now a rate of more than one person per room is judged to be too crowded (Audit Commission 1992).

Density of occupation is one measure of housing suitability; privacy and permanence are others. If the members of a household have to share parts of their accommodation with other households, for instance having to use a common stairway to visit the kitchen, that accommodation is described as *not self-contained*. Here, households living in "not self-contained" and temporary accommodation are combined to provides an indication of where there appears to be an overall shortage of suitable housing.

The map showing the distribution of vacant dwellings also demonstrates where part of the means to overcome housing shortages exists. A note of warning is included here as some of the dwellings which were thought to be vacant at the census were occupied by households who avoided being enumerated. Despite this, the pattern shown is intriguing and suggests that where there appears to be the greatest shortage of housing there is also often the highest proportion of vacant dwellings.

The most important factor in understanding the irony of there being most empty housing where there is most need for housing is tenure — the way in which housing in each area is owned. Each of the major forms of tenure is mapped separately along with the geography of its growth or decline over the last two decades. The ward level detail of the effect of 1980s "right-to-buy" legislation is reflected by the decline of council tenure and the increase in owner occupation. Changes in the proportions of households living in housing association or private rented accommodation are also shown.

The large owner occupier group is then split into those who owned outright and those who were still buying their houses with a mortgage. Then, the changing geography of house prices is shown at the district level for each year during the 1980s because these changes, to a large degree, determined local affordability. The geographical dimension of the housing market slump of the late 1980s is next explored through mapping the distribution of unsecured mortgage debt, where a household owes a mortgage lender more money than it could realise if it sold its home — this is known as having *negative equity*. Finally, issues of arrears and home possessions are addressed and the changing geography of homelessness is shown.

Despite all the improvements in housing provision over the last twenty years, housing problems look more complex than ever in the 1990s. Traditional problems of overcrowding, privacy, quality, affordability and under-use remain and new problems such as mass debt, mortgage and rent arrears and eviction have emerged.

4.1: Housing by Type, Households, People and Rooms in Britain 1991

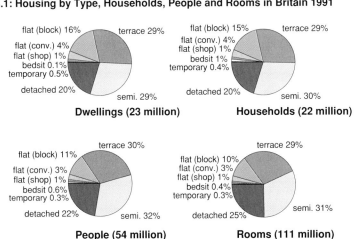

flat (block) 16%   terrace 29%
flat (conv.) 4%
flat (shop) 1%
bedsit 0.1%
temporary 0.5%
detached 20%
semi. 29%

Dwellings (23 million)

flat (block) 15%   terrace 29%
flat (conv.) 4%
flat (shop) 1%
bedsit 1%
temporary 0.4%
detached 20%
semi. 30%

Households (22 million)

terrace 30%
flat (block) 11%
flat (conv.) 3%
flat (shop) 1%
bedsit 0.6%
temporary 0.3%
detached 22%
semi. 32%

People (54 million)

terrace 29%
flat (block) 10%
flat (conv.) 3%
flat (shop) 1%
bedsit 0.4%
temporary 0.3%
detached 25%
semi. 31%

Rooms (111 million)

Note: bedsits are defined here as flats where the hall, landing or stairways are shared;
figures in brackets are the totals from the 1991 census (rounded to the nearest million).

4.2: Household Space (Rooms) by Dwelling Type in Britain 1991

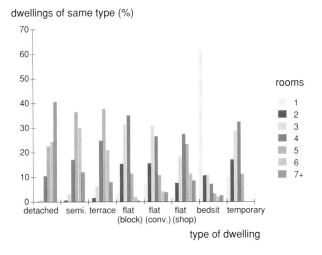

dwellings of same type (%)

rooms
1
2
3
4
5
6
7+

type of dwelling

Housing Type

The type of housing people live in is often a good guide to their general level of affluence due to the differentials in the costs of different types of dwelling. The most expensive dwellings are detached houses which, as Figure 4.1 illustrates, constituted one fifth of all dwellings and contained one fifth of all households, which included 22% of all residents who between them had access to one quarter of all the rooms in Britain in 1991. The (arithmetical) average price of detached houses in the United Kingdom was £111 000 at the time of the 1991 census. Semi-detached houses cost on average half this amount, while terraced houses were £10 000 cheaper than semi-detached (Halifax 1991); these types also each accommodate a higher proportion of people in fewer rooms.

Flats are not as simple to categorise as houses. A *flat* is a dwelling where all the rooms are on one floor and where the building in which the dwelling is contained consists of more than one floor. Most flats are purpose-built residential buildings, called "flat (*blocks*)" here. If the flat is in a commercial building, above a shop for example, it is categorised as "flat (*shop*)". If a flat is in a building which has been converted to flats it is labelled as "flat (*conv.*)", unless it is not self-contained (i.e. to move between rooms a passageway open to other households has to be used), in which case it is labelled here as a *bedsit*. Finally, dwellings can be classified as *temporary*, mobile homes for instance.

This eight-fold classification of dwelling types is used in Figure 4.2, which shows how many rooms each type of dwelling typically contains. Most detached houses have six or more rooms, whereas most bedsits consist of only one room. Semi-detached houses and terraced houses typically have five rooms — three bedrooms, a sitting room and a kitchen. Purpose-built flats and temporary accommodation usually contain four rooms, while flats in buildings which have been converted typically have three rooms. The figure also shows the degree of variation about these national averages.

The land area map and population cartogram opposite both show the same distribution: which type of dwelling is most common in each ward. All the types of flat other than those in purpose-built residential blocks are grouped. The land area map illustrates another important difference between the dwelling types — detached houses predominate in rural wards and so they dominate this image. The cartogram shows how most people live in wards where the predominant dwelling is either a semi-detached or a terraced house. Flats are only dominant in large numbers in London, Tyneside and Scotland. Flats in commercial or converted buildings and bedsits are only typical on the western side of London and along parts of the south coast.

The average price of a flat at the time of the census was £50 500. This was almost £1500 more than the average price of a terraced house. The reason for this is that so many flats are in London where prices are generally high. In any individual area flats are generally the cheapest form of accommodation.

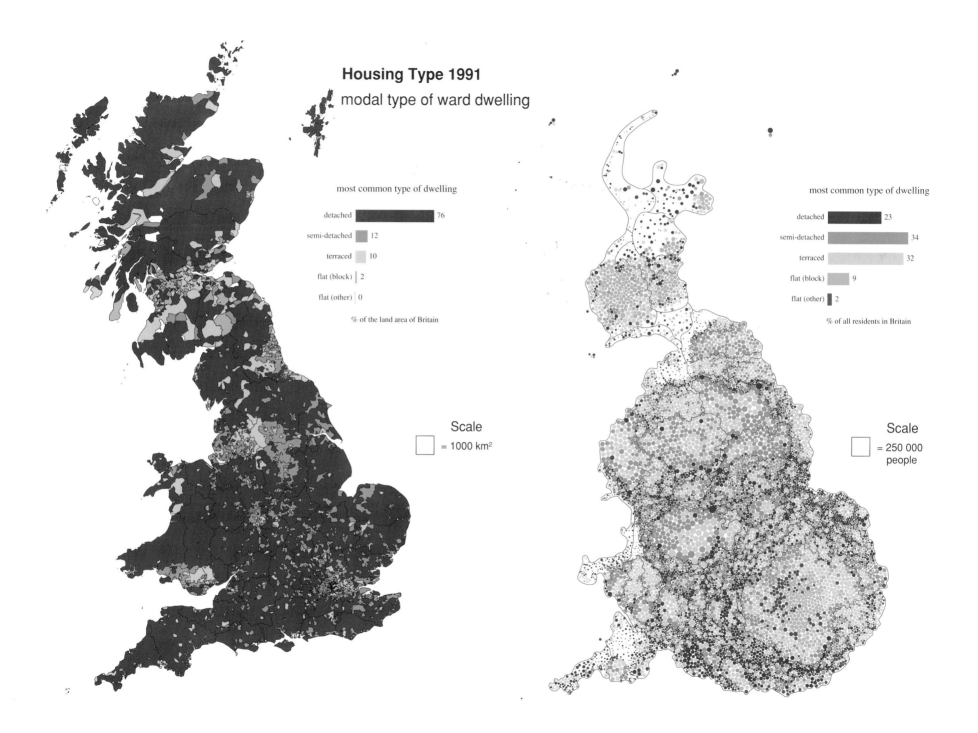

Housing Type 1991

modal type of ward dwelling

most common type of dwelling

detached		76
semi-detached		12
terraced		10
flat (block)		2
flat (other)		0

% of the land area of Britain

Scale

☐ = 1000 km²

most common type of dwelling

detached		23
semi-detached		34
terraced		32
flat (block)		9
flat (other)		2

% of all residents in Britain

Scale

☐ = 250 000 people

4.3: Average Household Size in Britain 1971–1990

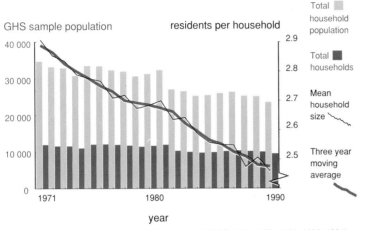

Source: General Household Survey estimates (OPCS 1973, 1975, 1986, 1989, 1991)

4.4: Households and Rooms by Household Size in Britain 1971, 1981, 1991

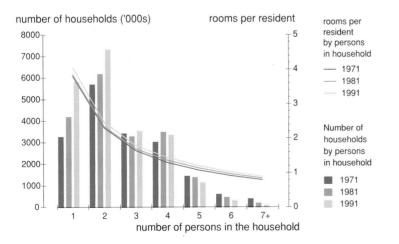

Household Size

The type of dwelling that is most suitable for a particular household depends primarily on the size of that household. Changes in average household size are also the most important influence on the changing need for housing. Between 1971 and 1991 the number of residents enumerated by the census increased by only 3%. The number of households these residents lived in rose by 18% over the same period. This is because the average size of a household fell from 2.9 to 2.5 people over this period.

Figure 4.3 shows the annual changes in average household size over the twenty years to 1990. Household size can be seen to have been falling quickly in the years between censuses, which has led to estimates of need based on past censuses often underestimating the changing demand for housing. However, the General Household Survey sample which is used to estimate this statistic is small, as the figure shows, and so for individual years it is difficult to estimate average household size and hence difficult to estimate the change in aggregate housing demand accurately.

The first map opposite shows the average household size recorded in each ward in Britain in 1991. Large cities contain many single person households and so these areas typically have the lowest average household sizes. The coast, where many older people live on their own, also tended to have smaller households. Suburban and rural areas tended to have larger households. These are the areas with most married couples and most teenage children (see pages 31 and 37). There are always exceptions, which is the reason for depicting the distribution in this detail. For instance, central Birmingham has some of the largest households in Britain.

The geography of the changes in this distribution since 1971 has been very variable across Britain. Average household size has fallen almost everywhere, but most dramatically in Scotland, the North East, Liverpool and the Home Counties, and least in London, the south coast, Manchester, Lancashire, Leeds and in central Birmingham. Where the population has risen fastest and average household size has fallen the most, the demand for new housing will have been greatest.

Figure 4.4 shows how the number of households of different sizes has changed between the censuses. The number of single person households has almost doubled since 1971 and two person households have also increased in number significantly. Three person households fell in number in the 1970s but increased again in the 1980s. The converse was true for four person households. All larger households have fallen in number. The largest (seven or more people) households have become three times less common than they were in 1971. The figure also shows how the average number of rooms available to each person in each size of household has increased over time. The typical one person household now occupies a dwelling with just over four rooms. This improvement has been less for the larger households.

Household Size 1991

average for ward households

people per household

up to 2.4	23
2.4 to 2.5	19
2.5 to 2.6	24
2.6 to 2.7	18
2.7 & above	16

% of all residents in Britain

Scale

☐ = 250 000 people

Household Size 1971–1991

change in average for ward households

change in people per household

up to -0.5	25
-0.5 to -0.4	16
-0.4 to -0.3	20
-0.3 to -0.2	17
-0.2 & above	22

% of all residents in Britain

Scale

☐ = 250 000 people

4.5: Balance of Dwellings over Households in Britain 1971–1991

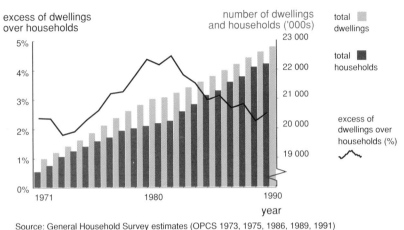

Source: General Household Survey estimates (OPCS 1973, 1975, 1986, 1989, 1991)
and Housing and Construction Statistics (DoE 1982, 1990, 1991).

4.6: Estimates of Dwellings, Households and the Housing Balance in England 1991, 1992

Estimates for England	Raw Census 1991	DoE figures 1991	Updated 1992	Notes
Dwellings ('000s)	19 671	19 700	19 860	1
Households ('000s)	18 766	19 111	19 338	4
Private Household Population ('000s)	46 337	48 100	48 269	2
Excess Dwellings ('000s)	1092	639	572	5
Average Household Size	2.47	2.52	2.50	3
Excess of Dwellings over Households	5.55%	3.24%	2.88%	6

Source: 1991 Census Small Area Statistics, DoE (1993) and see notes below:

Notes:

1. JRF Housing finance review 1993 p.51, from Housing and Construction Statistics (DoE).
2. Mid-1992 population estimates for England and Wales OPCS monitor PP1 93/3, resident population multiplied by same ratio as DoE used to remove institutional population in 1991.
3. Average household size assumed to have changed by the same amount as the General Household Survey three year moving average has from 1989–1991 to 1990–1992 (-0.8%) (the 1992 General Household average size was 2.45, dramatically below the figure used here).
4. The result of dividing private household population estimate (2) by average household size (3).
5. The results of subtracting households from dwellings assuming the same proportion of households are sharing as the DoE estimated there to be sharing a dwelling in 1991.
6. Just before this atlas was printed revised official statistics were released which added roughly 100 000 more households to the 1991 England figure, reducing the 1992 "excess" to under 2.5%, half the census figure (DoE, 1995, Projections of Households in England to 2016, London: HMSO).

Housing Demand

Demand for housing is shown here in the most simple way possible — through the relationship between numbers of dwellings and households. As a dwelling is accommodation designed for one household, an idealised view of housing is that each household should live in one dwelling, and thus the proportion of dwellings which remain unassigned provides an indication of the demand for housing in an area. Because dwellings are empty when households move between them, and because many are unfit to live in, or in the wrong place, or are second homes, there is usually an excess of dwellings to households. However, as Figure 4.5 shows, the excess has fluctuated greatly over time, with the lowest excess and therefore the greatest crude demand for housing in recent years being in 1973 and 1989.

The excess of dwellings over households has also varied greatly over space as the map opposite illustrates. Excesses of one in ten more dwellings than households are not unusual in central city areas, while less than one in fifty excess dwellings can be found in 11% of wards (by population). In three quarters of the wards the excess has increased since 1971. In one fifth of the country this amounts to one "surplus" dwelling for every twenty existing dwellings. This fifth includes almost all of London and most of Bristol, the West Midlands, Liverpool, Manchester and many other urban areas. Crude housing demand in the more affluent areas, the areas which are dominated by detached houses (page 103) and increasing employment (page 69) has risen since 1971.

A note of caution is required at this point. Just as the 1991 census failed to enumerate many people (see Figure 1.13), it also missed many households. At the time of writing there is little agreement as to how many households were missed, with different parts of government publishing different figures (Simpson and Dorling 1994). Figure 4.6 shows just how big those data discrepancies are and how serious they are for estimating even crude housing demand. Compared with Department of the Environment estimates for 1991, the census statistics omit 1.76 million residents of private households and 345 000 households in England alone. The result of this is that when the "surplus" of dwellings over households is compared, the census figure is 70% higher!

The census figures must therefore be viewed with some scepticism. Unfortunately, at the local level they are the only statistics which can be used. Thus when reading the map opposite, it must not be assumed that more than 7% of the dwellings in central Manchester are surplus to requirements. All that can be said is that the census enumerators found 7% more dwellings than households, but that it is easier to count dwellings than households. Nevertheless comparisons across the map can be made, and where the level of imputation was low (page 11) and the excess of dwellings was high, for instance in north Wales, it is quite likely that a large proportion of buildings were empty in 1991.

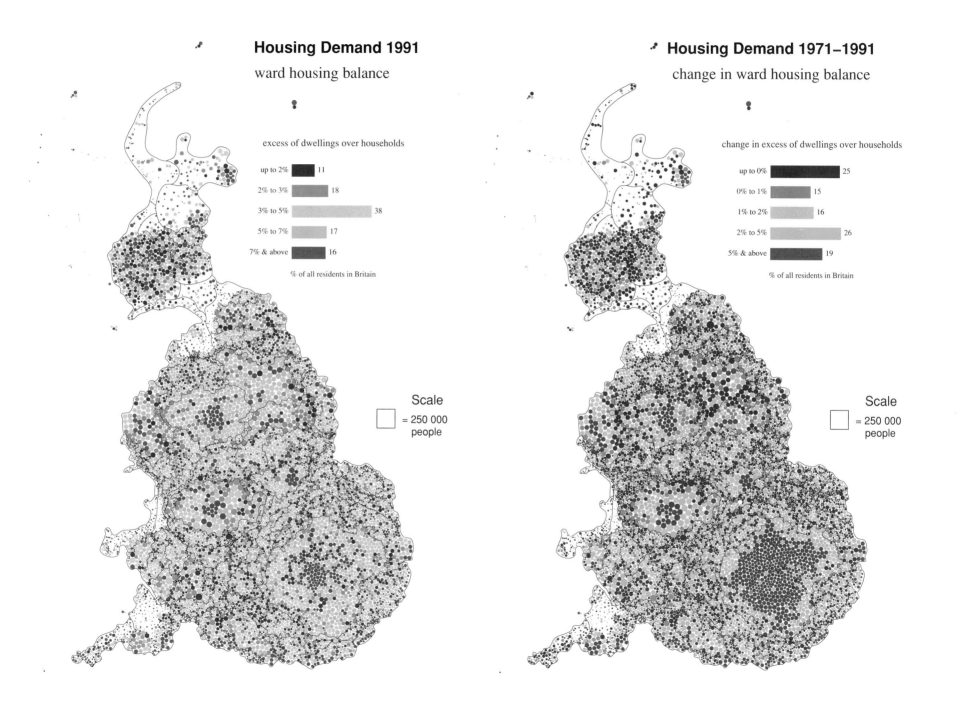

Housing Demand 1991

ward housing balance

excess of dwellings over households

up to 2%		11
2% to 3%		18
3% to 5%		38
5% to 7%		17
7% & above		16

% of all residents in Britain

Scale

☐ = 250 000 people

Housing Demand 1971–1991

change in ward housing balance

change in excess of dwellings over households

up to 0%		25
0% to 1%		15
1% to 2%		16
2% to 5%		26
5% & above		19

% of all residents in Britain

Scale

☐ = 250 000 people

Overcrowding

There are better ways of trying to assess where there is greater housing demand than dividing the total number of dwellings by households. These better measures include comparing how densely dwellings are occupied. Measures of overcrowding have been derived from the British census since 1901, when rooms were first counted (Dale and Marsh 1993). Living at densities of more than one person per room is the definition of overcrowding used here. A household consisting of two adults and three children living in a two bedroom house with an average sized kitchen and one living room would be considered overcrowded. On the other hand the same dwelling occupied by only one person, thus at a density of less than 0.5 people per room, could be considered under-occupancy. Nationally, 64% of dwellings are under-occupied by this measure, while only 2% are overcrowded.

Figure 4.7 shows the difference between the proportion of households which live at these densities for each type of dwelling as compared to the overall proportions. Households living in bedsits or in temporary accommodation are more than four times more likely to be overcrowded than is usual. Households living in detached houses are almost five times less likely to be overcrowded, and 12% more likely to be under-occupying, when compared to the typical household in Britain.

The map opposite, of overcrowding in 1991, shows stark differences in the proportion of households living in dwellings with more than one person per room. More than 4% of households are typically overcrowded in London and in Scottish wards. In wards comprising 60% of the population, less than 2% of households are overcrowded. This geographical pattern exists despite the large falls that have taken place in overcrowding since 1971. These falls have been strongest in Scotland, the North East and London as the second map shows. These changes are due to both falling average household sizes and increasing numbers of rooms in dwellings (through the addition of extensions and the building of larger property). Slum clearance has also been a factor. It is noteworthy that densities of occupation have not fallen much in Outer London.

Studying the simple ratio of persons to rooms simplifies the changes which have taken place in the way in which people occupy their homes and in how those homes are changing. Figure 4.8 shows the changes for each combination of household size and dwelling size from 1971 to 1991. What is most striking about this graphic is that all the combinations which have seen large increases are on the back margins of the matrix. This shows that the two major changes to have occurred have been the huge increases in the number of single person households and in the number of households who live in dwellings with seven or more rooms. In fact, over one million households in Britain in 1991 (4.6% of all households) consisted of a single person living in a dwelling with six or more rooms to him or herself.

4.7: Persons per Room by Dwelling Type in Britain 1991

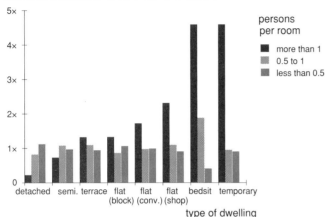

4.8: Persons and Rooms per Household in Britain 1971–1991

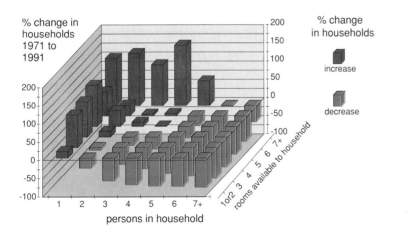

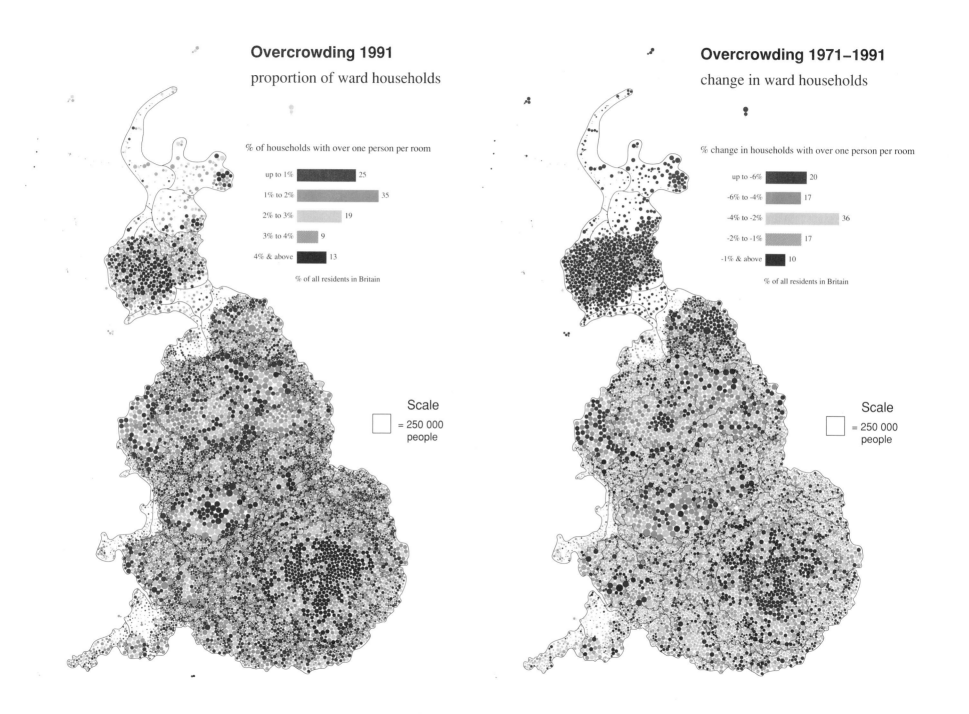

Overcrowding 1991

proportion of ward households

% of households with over one person per room

up to 1%	25
1% to 2%	35
2% to 3%	19
3% to 4%	9
4% & above	13

% of all residents in Britain

Scale

☐ = 250 000 people

Overcrowding 1971–1991

change in ward households

% change in households with over one person per room

up to -6%	20
-6% to -4%	17
-4% to -2%	36
-2% to -1%	17
-1% & above	10

% of all residents in Britain

Scale

☐ = 250 000 people

4.9: Indicators of Housing Shortage in Britain 1991, 1981–1991

Shortage of:	Privacy		Permanence		Preference	
Type of household, people or family:	Having to share parts of their home with other households:		Households living in non-permanent accommodation:		People living in a household with two or more families:	
	1991 total	1991% (1981%)	1991 total	1991% (1981%)	1991 total	1991% (1981%)
All households (in the census)	220 000	1.0% (1.3%)	94 000	0.43% (0.41%)	199 000	0.93% (0.87%)
All residents in households	312 000	0.6% (0.7%)	180 000	0.333% (0.326%)	1 081 000	2.0% (1.9%)
Children aged under 16	29 000	0.26% (0.36%)	25 000	0.23% (0.26%)	285 000*	2.4% (2.2%)
Lone parent households	8100	0.88% (0.92%)	2700	0.3% (0.4%)	148 000	7.2% (6.6%)
Households with children	20 000	0.3% (0.4%)	14 000	0.2% (0.3%)		
Pensioner only households	31 000	0.6% (1.3%)	28 000	0.5% (0.4%)		
Families**	403 000	2.6% (2.4%)			*(figures shown in red when rising)*	

* estimates of children in two plus family households include those aged 16 to 18 years old who are still at school (for comparability).
** the number of families living in households which contain two or more families and hence share parts of the home with another family.

Source: 1991 and 1981 Census Small Area Statistics

Note:
A family is a group of people within a household who are related and span two generations. If a woman lives with her parents and her child, altogether they form a two family household. In 1991 cohabiting couples were identified as families whereas in 1981 they were not. This change of definition should reduce the number of two or more family households. Despite this change in definition, the number of separate families sharing the use of a living room in their dwelling with another family, or having at least one group meal a day, has increased over the decade.

4.10: Residents in Two or More Family Households in Britain 1991, 1981–1991

proportion of district populations

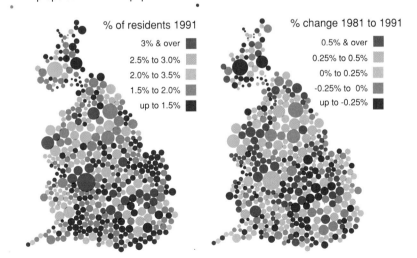

% of residents 1991
- 3% & over
- 2.5% to 3.0%
- 2.0% to 3.5%
- 1.5% to 2.0%
- up to 1.5%

% change 1981 to 1991
- 0.5% & over
- 0.25% to 0.5%
- 0% to 0.25%
- -0.25% to 0%
- up to -0.25%

Housing Shortage

Given the recent improvement in overcrowding and the general excess of dwellings over households, it may appear contradictory to talk of a housing shortage. Indeed, the situation in 1991 was vastly different from that in 1971, when 653 000 households shared a dwelling and 3.2 million households did not have exclusive access to amenities such as an inside toilet, a bath or hot water. However, there are many households who still do not have the privacy of exclusive use of their own home, or are housed in accommodation which was designed to be temporary. There are also many families who share a home with another family. Many of these families may prefer to live separately but cannot. This is one form of homelessness. More acute measures of housing shortage are discussed at the end of this chapter (see page 130).

Figure 4.9 presents estimates of the shortages of privacy, permanence or preference and shows how these statistics have changed over the 1980s. Caution is again needed in interpreting these figures as many of the households missing from the 1991 census statistics may be living in dwellings which would be classified as having two families or to be lacking privacy, had they been recorded. The number of lone parent households may also be inflated through one parent being omitted from the enumeration. However, an increase to over a million can be seen in the number of people living in households containing two or more families. In general, fewer people are having to live in households where they share parts of their homes with other households (although 29 000 children still live in this situation). There has been a fall in the use of non-permanent accommodation among all groups other than pensioners.

The maps opposite show the proportion of households who lack privacy or permanence and how this has changed geographically during the 1980s. London has experienced the most significant improvement but, by this measure, it is still the area of Britain with the most acute housing shortage. The situation can be seen from the map to have deteriorated most quickly in towns such as Leeds, Bristol, Coventry, Lancaster and Liverpool. These maps are, however, difficult to interpret because some households may like temporary accommodation, just as some families might want to live in households with other families. However, it is unlikely that most are happy with this (Niner 1989).

Figure 4.10 shows that the highest proportions of families sharing accommodation are found in London boroughs such as Brent, Ealing, Newham and Tower Hamlets, and in districts like Slough, Leicester, Wolverhampton, Knowsley and Birmingham; these are the same sorts of areas as those which contain the highest proportion of households in temporary accommodation or sharing dwellings. The geography of the changes in this statistic are also similar to those shown opposite. This exercise suggests that all these measures do provide complementary indications of the areas where there may be the greater shortages of housing.

Housing Shortage 1991

proportion of ward households

% of households not in permanent
or self-contained accommodation

up to 0.1%	21
0.1% to 0.5%	29
0.5% to 1%	15
1% to 2%	14
2% & above	21

% of all residents in Britain

Scale

☐ = 250 000
people

Housing Shortage 1981–1991

change in ward households

% change in households not in permanent
or self-contained accommodation

up to -0.5%	20
-0.5% to -0.1%	23
-0.1% to 0%	13
0% to 0.1%	32
1% & above	13

% of all residents in Britain

Scale

☐ = 250 000
people

4.11: Empty Dwellings by Reason to be Vacant and Type in Britain 1991

proportion of all dwellings (%)

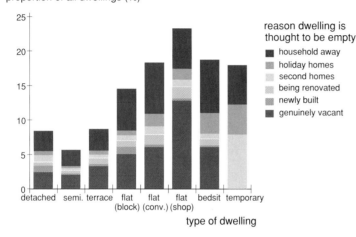

reason dwelling is
thought to be empty

- household away
- holiday homes
- second homes
- being renovated
- newly built
- genuinely vacant

type of dwelling

4.12: Empty Household Spaces and Rooms by Reason in Britain 1981, 1991

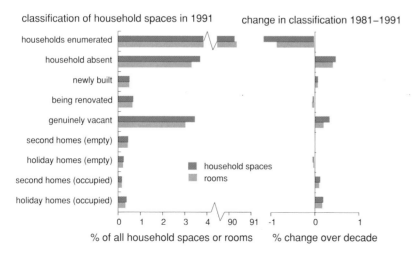

classification of household spaces in 1991   change in classification 1981–1991

% of all household spaces or rooms   % change over decade

Vacant Housing

The housing shortage in Britain is not a shortage of buildings but a shortage of access to suitable, affordable accommodation where households need it. The numbers of vacant dwellings in Britain and their location strongly imply this. The first map opposite shows the locations of the one million dwellings which the census enumerators thought were vacant in 1991. These are generally concentrated in the same areas as have the most obvious housing shortages. Despite the more probable number of vacant dwellings being closer to half this number (see Figure 4.6), the basic pattern to the geographical distribution shown here may well hold true.

Although dwellings were not enumerated by the 1981 census, which is one reason why many of the maps here show change since 1971, it is possible to deduce the numbers of vacant dwellings from the estimates of the numbers of rooms found in vacant *household spaces* (which were defined as the accommodation available for a household, and therefore can include subdivisions of dwellings). The map of change in vacant housing is, in fact, a map of the changing proportions of rooms in a ward which were vacant between 1981 and 1991. Inner London, Birmingham, Liverpool and Glasgow can all be seen to have fewer vacant rooms, while the numbers have increased in the suburban parts of cities and along the south coast.

Most vacant dwellings are unlikely to be suitable for the kinds of households most needing housing, or the dwellings may not actually be available to buy or rent. Figure 4.11 shows how it is flats, particularly those above shops, which are most likely to be genuinely vacant when they are found to be empty. Semi-detached houses, which are often most suitable for households needing housing, are least likely to be vacant. Temporary accommodation, by definition, cannot be vacant — or every empty caravan in Britain could be classified as a potential empty home!

Figure 4.12 shows how the numbers of household spaces and rooms in Britain have altered since 1981, according to their form of occupancy. Again, this figure should be read with caution as many of the homes found to be vacant in 1991 may have been housing some of the one million residents unaccounted for by the census. Over 1% fewer household spaces were found to contain households on census night 1991 than in 1981. Just over half of these empty homes were thought to contain households who were away on census night, the other half were estimated to be actual vacant accommodation. The number of household spaces which were second or holiday homes is also recorded as having risen. The changes in the proportions of rooms falling into each of these classifications have been lower, suggesting that it is most likely to be flats which are becoming vacant in larger numbers. However, if a flat is above the ground floor, and the neighbours do not know who lives there, establishing that the address is vacant (when nobody answers the door) can involve little more than an educated guess.

Vacant Housing 1991

proportion of ward dwellings

% of dwellings enumerated as vacant

up to 3%	25
3% to 4%	25
4% to 5%	19
5% to 6%	12
6% & above	19

% of all residents in Britain

Scale

□ = 250 000 people

Vacant Housing 1981–1991

change in ward rooms

% change in rooms enumerated as vacant

up to -1%	19
-1% to 0%	21
0% to 1%	30
1% to 2%	18
2% & above	11

% of all residents in Britain

Scale

□ = 250 000 people

4.13: Change in Tenure of Households in Britain 1971–1991

annual change in number of households ('000s)

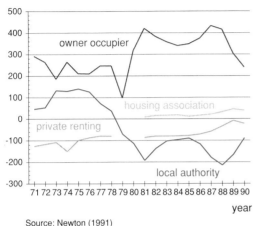

Source: Newton (1991)

Note: private renting comparisons between 1979 and 1981 are unreliable

4.14: Dwelling Type by Tenure in Britain 1991

households (%)

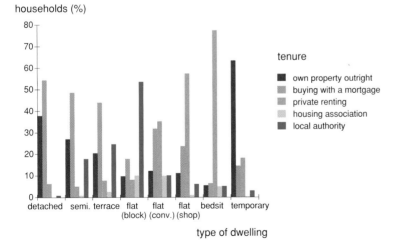

Housing Tenure

The nature of the *tenure*, the form of title under which property is occupied or held, may be one of the reasons why so many homes are vacant. Most vacant accommodation is not available for rent (JRF 1991). Unfortunately, the census could not collect information on the ownership of vacant property because, by definition, there was nobody there to ask. Of all households in occupied dwellings in Britain in 1991, 66% owned their home or were buying it, 12% rented privately or with a housing association and 21% rented from a local authority (including New Towns or Scottish Homes). Figure 4.13 shows graphically the changes which have taken place year by year in the absolute numbers of households in each form of tenure. Most striking has been the rise in owner occupation, which in the peak years of 1981 and 1987 increased by almost half a million households annually. These rises were mirrored by falls in the number of households renting from local authorities as a result of "tenure transfer", notably following the extension of right to buy legislation during the 1980s. The next largest form of tenure, private renting, can be seen to have been slowly recovering over the twenty year period to reach a point, in 1989, where, for one year, it was no longer reducing in size. The number of households in housing association tenure has been steadily rising since that category was distinguished in official statistics in 1981. However, it is important to remember that this tenure only houses 2.45% of the population (see page 122).

The maps opposite show which tenure of household in each ward is furthest above the national average proportion for that tenure, and which is furthest below that proportion. Households in local authority tenure — council housing — are most distinctly concentrated, being above average in many wards in almost all metropolitan counties, Durham, Cleveland and across Scotland. Houses are being bought in high proportions in the Home Counties and in much of the remainder of the metropolitan counties. They are usually owned outright in many parts of Wales, in Lancashire, Cumbria and along the coast. Only in London is a large area dominated by private renting, while housing association tenure stands out above the others only in a few wards, most notably in Merseyside and the West Midlands. The map showing the tenure most under-represented in each ward largely mirrors this picture and so is dominated by the distinct lack of local authority housing in wards in which almost half the population of Britain live.

Type of dwelling is a good indicator of its tenure. Figure 4.14 shows that 92% of detached houses are occupied by their owners, while the majority of flats in blocks are owned by local authorities and over three quarters of bedsits are privately rented. Tenure reflects the financial resources of people in an area — whether they can afford to rent privately, or tend to hold property worth many thousands of pounds. Increasingly tenure also reflects the quality of housing in an area, as much of the better local authority stock was transferred to owner occupation through right to buy legislation.

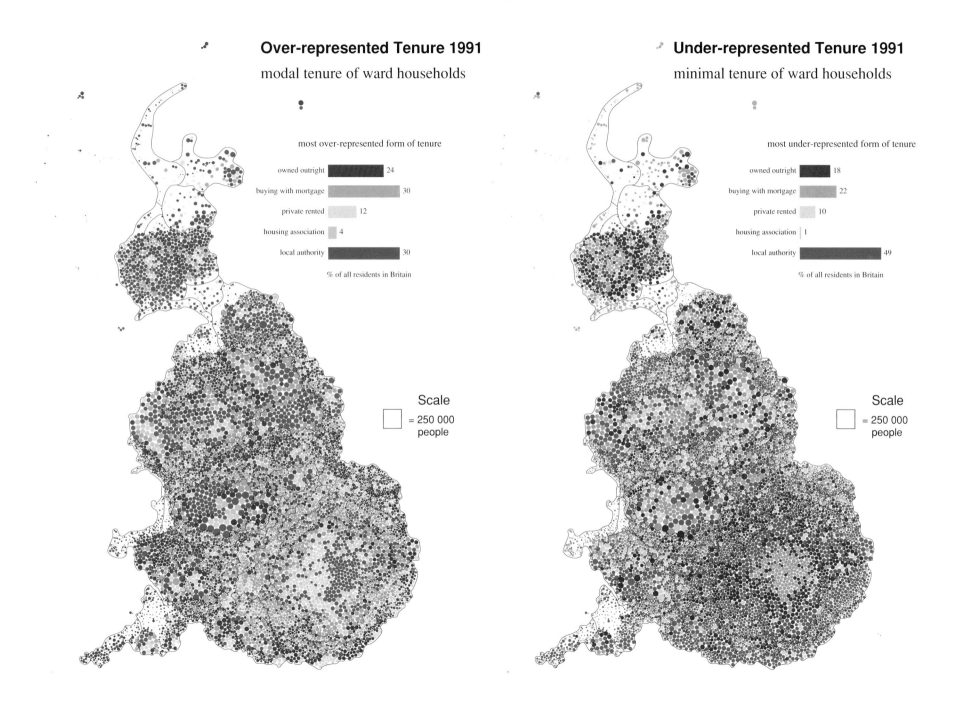

Over-represented Tenure 1991

modal tenure of ward households

most over-represented form of tenure

owned outright	24
buying with mortgage	30
private rented	12
housing association	4
local authority	30

% of all residents in Britain

Scale

☐ = 250 000 people

Under-represented Tenure 1991

minimal tenure of ward households

most under-represented form of tenure

owned outright	18
buying with mortgage	22
private rented	10
housing association	1
local authority	49

% of all residents in Britain

Scale

☐ = 250 000 people

4.15: Size of Home by Tenure in Britain 1971, 1981, 1991

% of households of each tenure

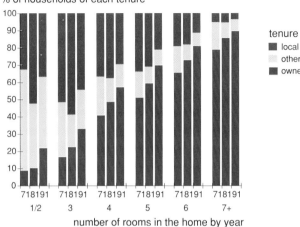

tenure

■ local authority
□ other renting
■ owner occupiers

number of rooms in the home by year

4.16: Overcrowded Households by Tenure in Britain 1971, 1981, 1991

% of all households

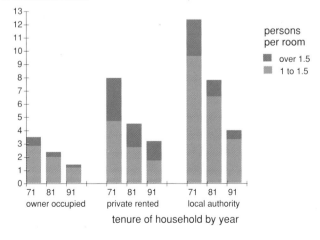

persons
per room

■ over 1.5
■ 1 to 1.5

tenure of household by year

Owner Occupiers

Owner occupation is a deceptive term as most housing in this tenure is, in fact, owned by the bank or building society with whom the *home-buyer* has a mortgage. On page 124 the geographical differences between home owners who own their homes outright, and those who are buying them, are explored. Here, however, both groups are treated as a single tenure, not least because this is how they were treated in the past, from which comparisons are drawn. As the first map opposite shows, owner occupation is now the dominant tenure in Britain, with half the population living in wards in which over 70% of households "owned" their home in 1991. Only in the centres of the seven metropolitan counties and in Scotland are groups of wards to be found where less than half the households own or are buying the homes that they occupy.

In 1971 less than half of all households were owner occupiers. During the 1970s an further 7.5 households in every hundred joined this tenure, which rose by an additional 10.7% in the 1980s. The second map opposite shows those areas which exceeded growth rates of 10% in both decades. Areas of West London, South Yorkshire and parts of towns such as Plymouth feature prominently. The areas with the lowest growth rates tended to have either quite high or quite low levels of owner occupation in 1971, and not to have changed greatly. The revealing contrasts are between those areas which exceeded this growth rate only in the 1970s, and those which exceeded it only in the 1980s.

It is important to remember that just as the proportions of households changed over time, the nature of dwellings in each type of tenure altered over the decades. Figure 4.15 illustrates how a larger proportion of all sizes of home became owner occupied. Even the smallest two and three room homes were transferred in significant numbers from local authority tenure, reversing the trend of the 1970s (when many of these homes, which were probably flats, had been built). After one or two room homes, the largest proportional increase in owner occupation was in large houses of seven or more rooms. These increased in number by 60% in the 1970s, and by 47% in the 1980s. Most of this increase was due to the building of new larger homes for sale.

Figure 4.16 shows how the building of larger homes in recent years, and the reduction of average household size, has led to a decline in overcrowding in each tenure group. In 1971, one household out of every eight in local authority tenure was overcrowded. By 1991 this had fallen to only one in every twenty five. This is still higher, however, than was the case for owner occupied housing in 1971. Now, only one owner occupied household in every seventy is overcrowded and one in over four hundred is living at a density of over 1.5 people per room. Densities as high as this are usually only found in private rented accommodation, as the figure shows. Overcrowding has fallen most significantly for households in owner occupation because these households have bought the largest available dwellings while having themselves fallen in size most quickly.

Owner Occupiers 1991

proportion of ward households

% of households in owner occupation

up to 50%		17
50% to 60%		14
60% to 70%		19
70% to 80%		25
80% & above		25

% of all residents in Britain

Scale

☐ = 250 000
people

Owner Occupiers 1971–1981–1991

change in ward households

% change in households in owner occupation
GB=+10% for 1971–1981, +10% for 1981–1991

below in both		38
below in 1981–1991 only		19
above in 1981–1991 only		28
above in both		16

% of all residents in Britain

Scale

☐ = 250 000
people

4.17: Tenure by Type of Home in England and Wales 1981-1991

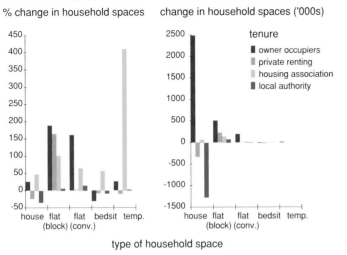

type of household space

4.18: Tenure by Type of Home in Scotland 1981-1991

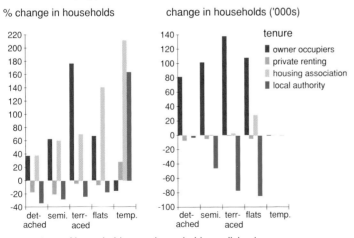

type of household space households are living in

Council Housing

One third of households in Britain rent and most of these rent from their local authority or council. The map of council housing is distinctive and can be seen to be reflected in many of the other distributions shown here. Because households renting from Scottish Homes are included in this tenure almost the whole of Scotland appears to be made up of wards where over 30% of the households rent from a "local authority".

The proportion of households living in council accommodation fell from 31% in both 1971 and 1981, to 22% in 1991. The second map shown opposite is shaded to highlight which areas have seen sustained falls, and in which decades the relatively larger falls occurred. Most of London and the centres of other cities, such as Glasgow and Edinburgh, can be seen to have had above average falls in both decades. Falls have been low in most of Scotland and some English districts such as St Helens and South Tyneside. Central London, South Yorkshire and Wolverhampton saw above average falls in the number of households in this tenure during the 1970s. It tended to be the more suburban or rural wards which saw the greatest falls in this tenure during the 1980s.

This pattern is reflected in the type of accommodation which was being transferred from council housing to owner occupation and the type which was not being built as council housing during the 1980s. For England and Wales census figures in 1981 distinguished different types of flats but not houses (and then presented only numbers of household spaces). Nevertheless, using this information, Figure 4.17 shows that the largest relative and absolute falls in tenure were for houses which used to be owned by the local authority, of which there were 1.27 million less by 1991 compared with a rise of 2.49 million in the number of owner occupied houses. The number of household spaces in flats owned by local authorities actually increased by 92 000 over this period, but this figure should be compared with a rise of 693 000 in the number of household spaces enumerated as flats which were owner occupied. Private renting and housing association renting also saw large relative rises amongst flats. The biggest relative rise can be seen to have been in the amount of temporary accommodation held by housing associations which rose by 411%; however, this was an absolute increase from 81 to just 414 household spaces for the whole of Britain in tenure of this type.

The picture for Scotland given in Figure 4.18 is very similar. In Scotland different types of houses were differentiated in 1981 and so it is possible to compare their rates of transfer. In relative terms, local authorities lost detached houses most, but they had very few to lose in absolute terms. Local authority terraced houses and flats have been depleted in greatest numbers. By both measures, terraced housing has seen the greatest increases in owner occupation. Housing association tenure has increased most in flats, while private renting has fallen for every category of housing except for temporary accommodation, in contrast to the rise in privately rented flats in England and Wales.

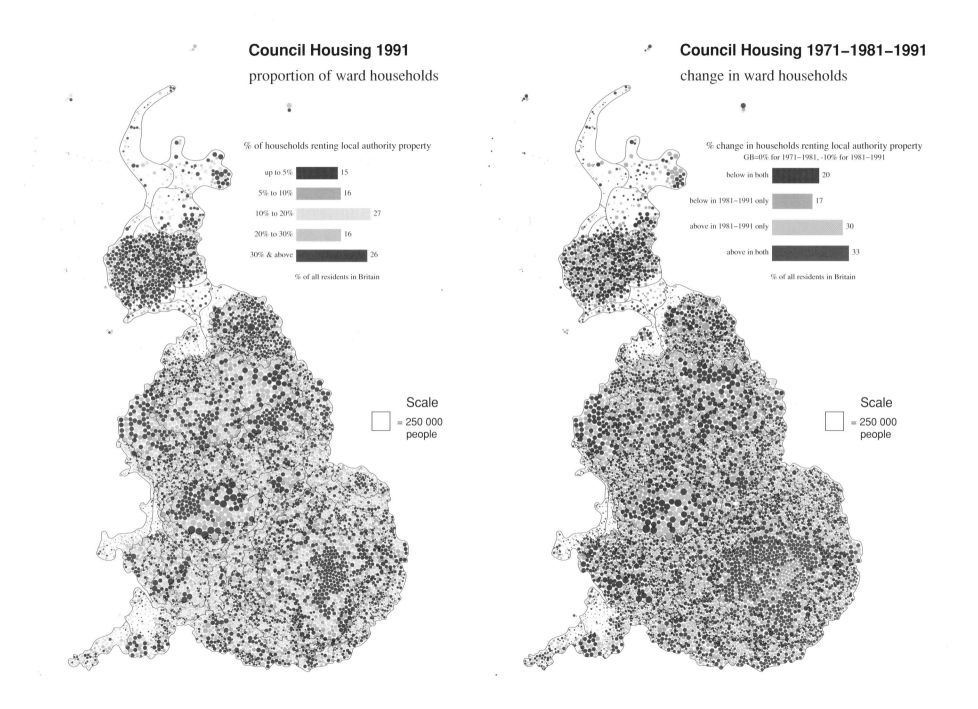

Council Housing 1991

proportion of ward households

% of households renting local authority property

up to 5%	15
5% to 10%	16
10% to 20%	27
20% to 30%	16
30% & above	26

% of all residents in Britain

Scale

☐ = 250 000
people

Council Housing 1971–1981–1991

change in ward households

% change in households renting local authority property
GB=0% for 1971–1981, -10% for 1981–1991

below in both	20
below in 1981–1991 only	17
above in 1981–1991 only	30
above in both	33

% of all residents in Britain

Scale

☐ = 250 000
people

4.19: Ethnic and Socioeconmic Group by Tenure in Britain 1991

% of households of each tenure for each group of households

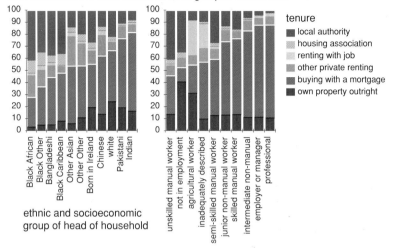

tenure
- local authority
- housing association
- renting with job
- other private renting
- buying with a mortgage
- own property outright

ethnic and socioeconomic
group of head of household

4.20: Age and Sex of Residents by Tenure in Britain 1991

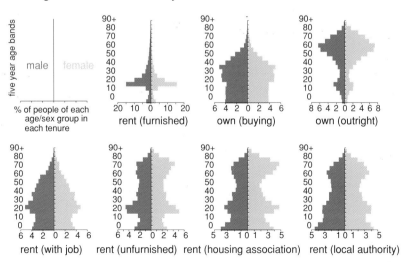

Private Renting

After those households who own or are buying their home and those who are renting from a local authority, the next largest group are people who are renting from private landlords. In 1971 this group, which then included housing associations, constituted 19% of all households. By 1981 this proportion had fallen to 13% and when (for statistical reasons) just under half a million housing association tenancies were excluded it fell to 11%. By 1991 only 7% of all households were renting privately. However, in recent years the proportion of households renting privately may have stabilised, although very up to date tenure figures are particularly unreliable (given the number of households missed by the last census for whom tenure is not known, see Figure 4.6).

The geographical distribution of these households can be seen to cluster in just a few locations on the first map opposite, notably London, around the coast and in Birmingham, Liverpool, Manchester and other towns with large numbers of students. In Scotland the divide between those areas where more than one in eight households rent privately and those where less than one in thirty do is very clear.

The pattern of change over the last ten years, the longest period for which comparisons of private renting excluding housing associations can be made, is less clear. London, Liverpool, Leeds and distinct parts of Scotland — which tend to have the highest levels of private renting — have seen some of the strongest falls. Growth in private renting can be seen in the suburbs. Part of this growth may be due to home owners renting out property which they could not sell in 1991. This question is addressed again later.

For particular ethnic and socioeconomic groups, private renting is more important than for the population as a whole. Figure 4.19 shows the share of tenure among the census classifications of these groups, ordered by the proportion living in owner occupation. In this diagram private renting is subdivided into households whose home comes with their job or business and all other forms of private renting. Households headed by agricultural workers were most likely to rent privately in 1991 (37%). Those households least likely to rent privately were headed by skilled manual workers (6%). Only households headed by members of Black Caribbean and Indian ethnic groups are less likely than whites to rent privately. Between a fifth and a third of all households in mixed groups, or of Chinese ethnic origin, rented privately in 1991.

One of the reasons for the imbalances between the tenures which different ethnic groups hold, apart from their differing geographical and social positions, is their different age structures (see Figure 2.20). Figure 4.20 shows the age and sex profiles for each different type of tenure. In this figure private renting is divided into three groups, so that the distinct profile of people renting furnished accommodation is shown. People renting privately tend to be younger than the population as a whole, while people in households which own their home outright are, on average, 56 years old.

Private Renting 1991

proportion of ward households

% of households renting private property

up to 3%		13
3% to 6%		33
6% to 9%		19
9% to 12%		12
12% & above		23

% of all residents in Britain

Scale

☐ = 250 000
people

Private Renting 1981–1991

change in ward households

% change in households renting private property

up to -3%		24
-3% to -1%		27
-1% to 0%		20
0% to 1%		17
1% & above		12

% of all residents in Britain

Scale

☐ = 250 000
people

4.21: Tenure by Size of Household in Britain 1981–1991

% change in the number of households of each size and tenure

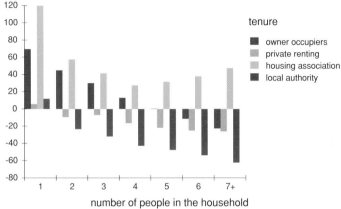

number of people in the household

4.22: Some Characteristics of People and Households by Tenure in Britain 1991, 1981–1991

Category:	Distribution *down* list of characteristics		Distribution of people or households included in each category *across* tenures							
			owner occupiers		private renting		housing association		local authority	
	1991	change	1991	change	1991	change	1991	change	1991	change
All census household residents:	53.86 million	(2%)	70%	(11%)	8%	(-1%)	2%	(1%)	20%	(-11%)
aged under 5 years	7%	(1%)	63%	(4%)	8%	(0%)	3%	(1%)	27%	(-5%)
aged 5 to 15	14%	(-3%)	69%	(10%)	6%	(-1%)	2%	(1%)	23%	(-10%)
aged 16 to pensionable age	61%	(1%)	73%	(13%)	9%	(-1%)	2%	(0%)	17%	(-13%)
pensionable age to 74	12%	(-0%)	65%	(13%)	6%	(-5%)	3%	(1%)	26%	(-9%)
aged 75 or more	6%	(1%)	58%	(6%)	9%	(-4%)	6%	(3%)	28%	(-5%)
All types of household:	21.89 million	(13%)	66%	(10%)	9%	(-2%)	3%	(1%)	21%	(-10%)
one pensioner living alone	15%	(1%)	49%	(7%)	9%	(-5%)	7%	(3%)	35%	(-5%)
one adult (not pensioner) alone	12%	(4%)	55%	(12%)	19%	(-6%)	5%	(1%)	21%	(-8%)
two or more adults living together	43%	(-1%)	74%	(15%)	8%	(-2%)	2%	(0%)	16%	(-13%)
one adult living with child(ren)	4%	(2%)	31%	(2%)	9%	(2%)	7%	(2%)	53%	(-6%)
Two or more adults with child(ren)	26%	(-6%)	75%	(13%)	6%	(-1%)	2%	(0%)	17%	(-12%)
Households by number of families:										
members of household not related	30%	(3%)	52%	(9%)	13%	()	6%	()	28%	(-6%)
household contains one family	69%	(-3%)	73%	(13%)	4%	()	2%	()	19%	(-12%)
household contains two+ families	1%	(0%)	68%	(11%)	3%	()	2%	()	25%	(-10%)
Households by head's occupation:										
employer or manager	20%	(4%)	88%	(7%)	8%	()	1%	()	3%	(-5%)
professional worker	7%	(2%)	88%	(2%)	10%	()	1%	()	2%	(-2%)
intermediate non-manual worker	12%	(3%)	83%	(8%)	10%	()	2%	()	6%	(-6%)
junior non-manual worker	12%	(-0%)	74%	(10%)	11%	()	2%	()	13%	(-8%)
skilled manual worker	28%	(-3%)	77%	(22%)	6%	()	2%	()	15%	(-20%)
semi-skilled manual worker	13%	(-3%)	60%	(19%)	11%	()	3%	()	27%	(-19%)
unskilled manual worker	4%	(-1%)	46%	(17%)	10%	()	4%	()	40%	(-18%)
agricultural worker	2%	(-1%)	55%	(7%)	37%	()	1%	()	8%	(-5%)
inadequately described	2%	(-1%)	57%	(22%)	32%	()	2%	()	9%	(-26%)

Figures in red show proportions or changes which are above the national average rate

Housing Associations

The smallest tenure group identified in this analysis is made up of households who rent from housing associations. This group is identified separately because housing associations are unique institutions, being neither in the public sector nor profit-making, and because this group is growing in size. Figure 4.21 shows how housing associations are also unique in that they are renting to increasing numbers of households of all sizes. While only 3.13% of households and only 2.45% of people live in this tenure, they are not a typical group of people. They are disproportionately female and older, as Figure 4.20 showed. Households headed by someone belonging to one of the three black ethnic groups were three or four times more likely to be renting from a housing association than was the population in general (while Indian or Pakistani headed households were 25% less likely to be in this tenure, see Figure 4.19). In fact, housing association property is more often found in the places where these groups of people are more likely to be found. This is shown on the first map opposite which highlights a very similar set of places to those with high proportions of people in local authority tenure, except that housing association properties can also be found in significant numbers in the Home Counties. This is partly due to the complete transfer of local authority stock in some districts. The map showing increases in the number of households in this tenure is also similar to the map showing the number of households in the tenure, indicating that much of the present pattern was created during the 1980s and that associations tended to expand most where they were already present in a ward.

Traditionally, some housing associations have tried to cater for types of households which would otherwise find securing a home difficult. Figure 4.22 illustrates this showing that, for instance, 6% of very old people live in this tenure, as opposed to 2% of the population in general, and that this number has doubled over the last ten years as more and more housing association property is taken up by elderly people. Similarly, this tenure accommodated more single adults with children, more households within which people were not related, more unskilled workers and more children under five than would be expected from an even distribution. Many other facts for different tenures and groups of households and people can be extracted from this table. For example, households made up of one adult with one or more children (4% of all households) are the only group that is more likely to be living in private rented accommodation than it was ten years ago. The highest rates of increase in owner occupation have been for skilled, semi-skilled and unskilled manual workers and those whose occupations were "inadequately described". These groups also saw the greatest rates of decrease in their proportions in local authority tenure. Changes in households' socioeconomic and family compositions for housing association and private rented tenures could not be distinguished in the 1981 statistics.

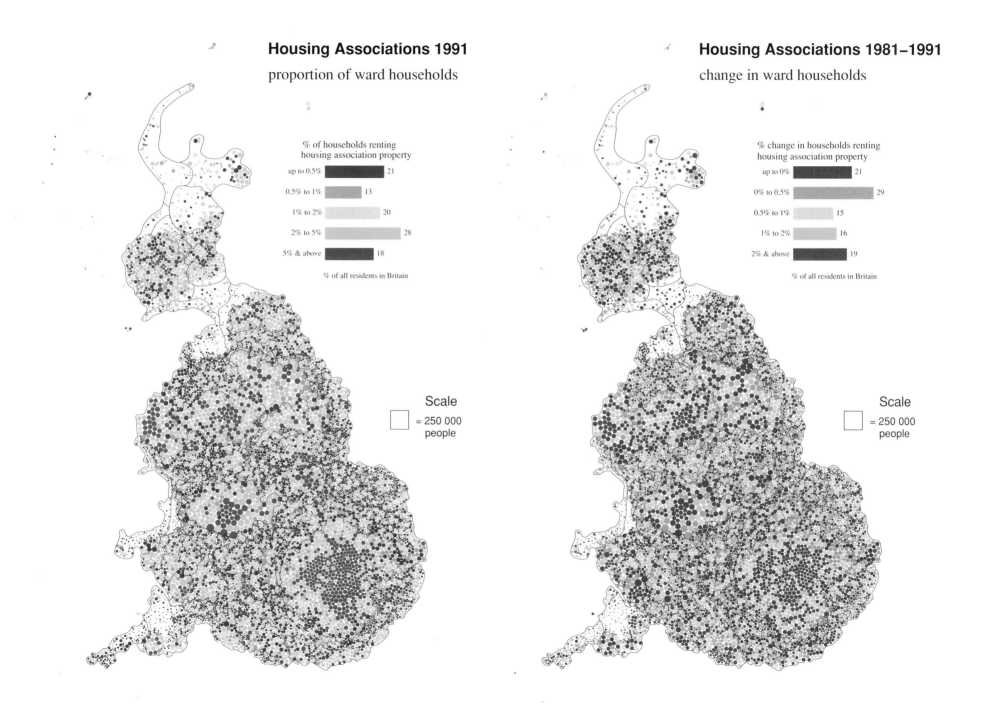

Housing Associations 1991

proportion of ward households

% of households renting
housing association property

up to 0.5%	21
0.5% to 1%	13
1% to 2%	20
2% to 5%	28
5% & above	18

% of all residents in Britain

Scale

☐ = 250 000
people

Housing Associations 1981–1991

change in ward households

% change in households renting
housing association property

up to 0%	21
0% to 0.5%	29
0.5% to 1%	15
1% to 2%	16
2% & above	19

% of all residents in Britain

Scale

☐ = 250 000
people

4.23: House Prices by Type of House and Region in Britain 1991

% premium on average prices given type of house and region

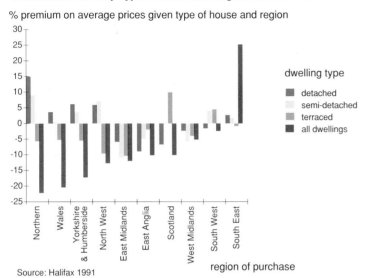

dwelling type

- detached
- semi-detached
- terraced
- all dwellings

region of purchase

Source: Halifax 1991

4.24: First-time Buyer Deposits by Region in Britain 1981, 1991

average £s deposited towards first property purchases by buyers

year of purchase
- 1981
- 1991

region of purchase

Source: unadjusted unpublished Building Society Mortgage Records

House Buying

The increase in owner occupation means that more households now have a mortgage than ever before in Britain. Figure 4.22 showed how most of this increased borrowing could be attributed to households made up of at least two adults or single working age adults without children. Manual workers also made up a significant component of the additional buyers of the 1980s. The first map opposite shows where the highest proportions of owner occupiers were buying their properties in 1991. Buyers are in the majority in almost every ward. In wards containing over half the population at least two thirds of owner occupied property is actually owned by the mortgage lender.

The second map opposite shows the average prices which buyers were paying to own property in each ward by 1991. These prices are estimated by using sale records from a building society and calculating a weighted average price for all the "market sales" in the ward over ten years. The weights applied allow for national inflation so that the prices shown here relate to the prices for which property was selling in 1991. This method produces robust estimates based on large samples, but the estimates will not be very sensitive to local price changes in the years immediately prior to 1991.

Figure 4.23 shows the premium that buyers can expect to pay for wishing to live in particular types of housing or in particular regions. In 1991 property prices in the South East were 25% above the national average. Within the South East, detached houses attracted a further premium of 3%. Semi-detached houses attracted a premium in all regions other than the midlands and East Anglia. Terraced houses attracted premiums only in Scotland and the South West. The map of average prices reflects the property in greatest demand as well as the areas in which people are prepared to pay the most to live.

Figure 4.24 shows the average deposits first-time buyers needing a mortgage were raising in each region in 1981 and 1991, calculated from the same source as the local property prices. *First-time buyers* are all purchasers who were not recorded as selling or owning an owner-occupied property at the time that they applied for their mortgage. The very different levels broadly reflect the differences in average property prices between regions and how these have changed. Within this pattern, however, there are differences. First-time buyers in East Anglia and the East and West Midlands were putting down average deposits of over 13% of the purchase price of their property in 1991. In contrast, buyers in the South West and North West were putting down average deposits of less than 11% of their purchase price. The biggest relative rises in deposits have not been in the regions which have experienced the largest increases in property prices over the period but in the East Midlands, Yorkshire & Humberside and the Northern Region. The largest absolute increase has been in the South East, however, where the average first-time buyer put down £11 500 towards the purchase of his or her new home in 1991.

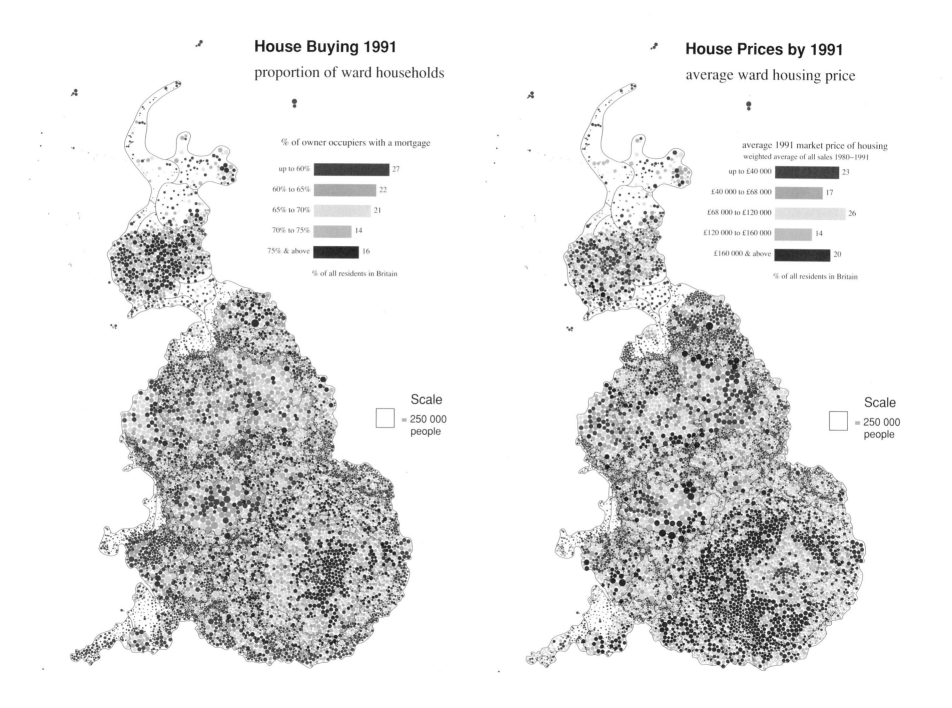

House Buying 1991

proportion of ward households

% of owner occupiers with a mortgage

up to 60%	27
60% to 65%	22
65% to 70%	21
70% to 75%	14
75% & above	16

% of all residents in Britain

Scale

☐ = 250 000 people

House Prices by 1991

average ward housing price

average 1991 market price of housing
weighted average of all sales 1980–1991

up to £40 000	23
£40 000 to £68 000	17
£68 000 to £120 000	26
£120 000 to £160 000	14
£160 000 & above	20

% of all residents in Britain

Scale

☐ = 250 000 people

4.25: House Prices by Type of House in Britain 1980–1991

£ 000s average prices by quarter showing 95% confidence limits

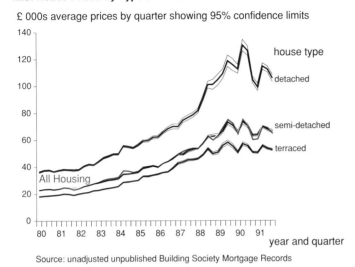

year and quarter

Source: unadjusted unpublished Building Society Mortgage Records

4.26: Unemployment and House Prices in Britain 1981–1991 Shaded by Years

annual increase in housing prices in district (%)

year of change

1990 & 1991
1988 & 1989
1986 & 1987
1984 & 1985
1981, 1982 & 1983

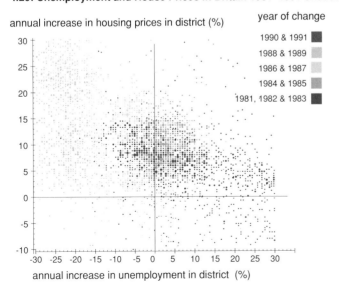

annual increase in unemployment in district (%)

House Prices

The changes in house prices over time are of importance not only to home owners and potential home owners, but also to the economy in general as they affect how wealthy people feel themselves to be and thus how much they spend on things other than housing. Figure 4.25 shows the average price for different types of housing for each quarter in each year since 1980, along with confidence limits on these prices. Prices rose steadily in the early 1980s and then accelerated between 1988 and 1989 before collapsing in a series of erratic false recoveries which disguise the general downward movement since 1990. When the market collapsed, the number of sales diminished greatly, and so the confidence with which prices could be estimated also fell.

To estimate the changing price of housing in an area, weighted averages of all market sales at specific periods need to be taken to allow for changes in the mix of dwellings being sold at any particular time. If this is not done then the sale of a large number of flats in an area one year, followed by the sale of many detached houses the next year, will appear as a price rise — even when prices are falling. The maps opposite show the changes at district level between mix-adjusted annual average property prices. These prices are referred to as *housing prices*, and relate to a hypothetical average dwelling.

The eleven maps show the geography of how the housing market moved from slump to boom and then bust. In some central London boroughs (and in a few other districts) prices were actually falling slightly at the start of the 1980s. After 1982 rapid inflation began to occur which was particularly strong in districts in the south east of England, but even during this period prices were not rising in some remote rural districts in the north and in Wales. Between 1985 and 1986 inflation in central London boroughs exceeded 20%. The following year this rate spread throughout southern England and then across all England. By 1989, however, the ripple had passed out of the South East and in the following year price falls there were widespread. By the summer of 1991 the price falls had spread across the whole country.

An impression of the relationship between the housing market and the wider economy (in the form of the labour market) is given in Figure 4.26. Here the correlation between the annual changes in the rate of unemployment in each district (taken from page 97) and the annual change in housing prices is presented visually. Each dot shows the rates of change of both statistics for a district in a given year, the colour of the dots indicates the year. The correlation is negative: rising unemployment implies falling house prices and vice versa. In the period up to 1987 the relationship is not particularly strong, but it has strengthened since, with the boom of 1988–1989 and the bust of 1990–1991 involving particularly rapid changes in the levels of both housing prices and unemployment. The advantage of the graphic, however, is in showing the extent to which this statement generalises a much more complex situation.

House Prices 1980–1991

change in district average prices

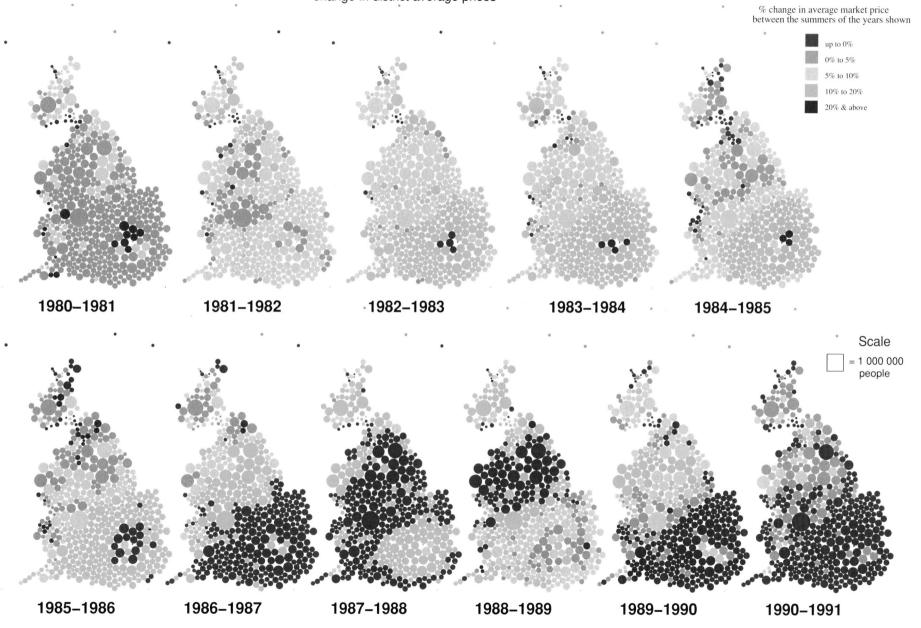

% change in average market price
between the summers of the years shown

- up to 0%
- 0% to 5%
- 5% to 10%
- 10% to 20%
- 20% & above

1980–1981   1981–1982   1982–1983   1983–1984   1984–1985

Scale

☐ = 1 000 000 people

1985–1986   1986–1987   1987–1988   1988–1989   1989–1990   1990–1991

4.27: Negative and Low Equity by Region and Purchase Year in Britain 1993

% of households who bought 1988–1991 by equity level in 1993

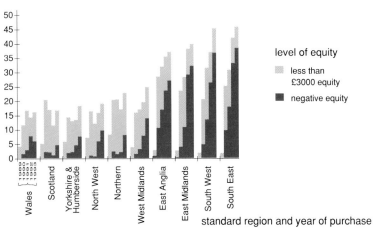

level of equity

░ less than
£3000 equity

▓ negative equity

standard region and year of purchase

Source: unadjusted unpublished Building Society Mortgage Records

4.28: Households Holding Negative Equity in Britain 1993

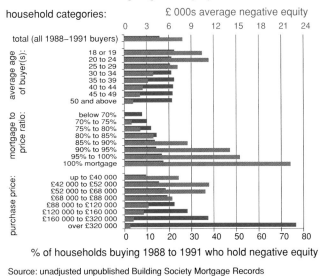

% of households buying 1988 to 1991 who hold negative equity

Source: unadjusted unpublished Building Society Mortgage Records

Negative Equity

Falling house prices at the end of the 1980s resulted in the widespread emergence of a housing problem which had rarely been experienced before in Britain — households holding negative equity. When the market price of a property is less than the mortgage secured upon that property the difference is the amount of *negative equity* held by the household living there. This is additional money which that household is liable for if it sells its home, and having to find this money prevented many households from being able to move home in the early 1990s. The emergence of negative equity also tended to reduce spending and confidence in the local economies where it struck most deeply.

For the figures presented here, the building society records which were used to estimate local housing prices and first-time buyers' deposits have been employed to calculate the proportion of households who bought their home between 1988 and 1991 and who held negative equity in 1993. This group of buyers is concentrated on because they hold almost all negative equity and because their exposure to this problem can be estimated with confidence. Price changes monitored by the Halifax Building Society are also used in these calculations. Figure 4.27 shows how the levels of negative equity and low equity rose across the country at the regional level between 1988 and 1993. Having low levels of equity can also deter households from moving home, particularly when the move would be to a more expensive property for which they would need to raise a larger mortgage than they currently hold.

The maps opposite show how in 1993 a line divided Britain in half between those recent buyers who were likely to hold negative equity (living in the south) and those who were unlikely to have mortgages worth more than their property (who were living in the north or in Wales). The first map shows the proportion of recent buyers holding negative equity, the second map shows, for each ward, the average amounts of negative equity recent buyers held. Nationally, these figures were 26% and £4800, respectively. Local discrepancies in the national pattern are found both sides of the dividing line because exposure to negative equity is a function of both local house price changes and the average size of deposits in each area. The proportion of the purchase price which home owners tend to borrow fluctuates greatly between local areas as people living in less affluent wards tend to need to borrow larger amounts of money and hence are more likely to suffer from even slight falls in local housing prices. Young buyers and buyers of the cheaper kinds of property are also more likely to have taken out relatively larger mortgages and so their chances of holding negative equity are higher, as Figure 4.28 illustrates. However, they are unlikely to have been allowed to take out particularly large mortgages in absolute terms and so the average amounts of negative equity they hold will be lower. This figure also shows the closeness of the relationship between the size of deposit and the chance of a buyer holding negative equity.

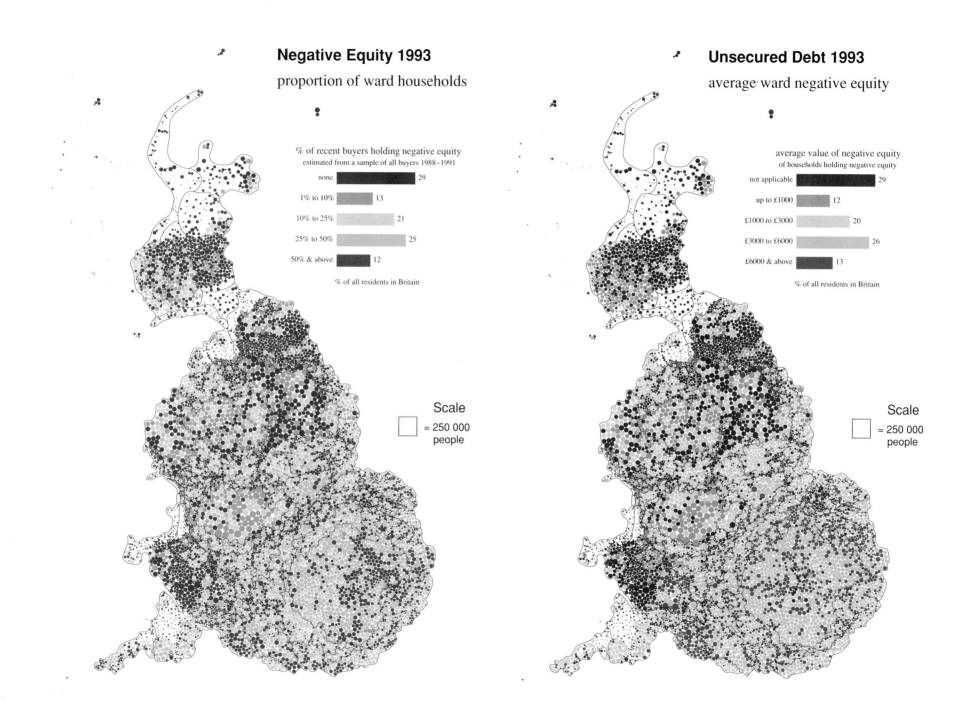

Negative Equity 1993

proportion of ward households

% of recent buyers holding negative equity
estimated from a sample of all buyers 1988–1991

none	29
1% to 10%	13
10% to 25%	21
25% to 50%	25
50% & above	12

% of all residents in Britain

Scale

☐ = 250 000
people

Unsecured Debt 1993

average ward negative equity

average value of negative equity
of households holding negative equity

not applicable	29
up to £1000	12
£1000 to £3000	20
£3000 to £6000	26
£6000 & above	13

% of all residents in Britain

Scale

☐ = 250 000
people

4.29: Homelessness and Temporary Accommodation in Britain and England 1981–1991

households which local authorities accepted as homeless each year in Britain ('000s)

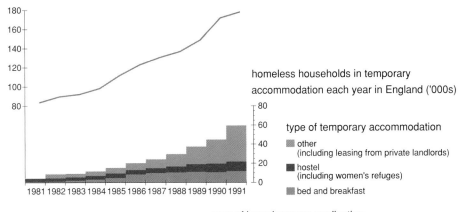

homeless households in temporary accommodation each year in England ('000s)

type of temporary accommodation

■ other
(including leasing from private landlords)

■ hostel
(including women's refuges)

■ bed and breakfast

year of homelessness application

Source: Wilcox (1993) tables 70 and 71

4.30: Mortgage Possessions and Arrears in Britain 1981–1991

% of all households with a mortgage in each category

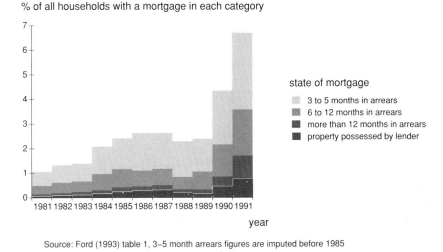

state of mortgage

▨ 3 to 5 months in arrears
▨ 6 to 12 months in arrears
■ more than 12 months in arrears
■ property possessed by lender

year

Source: Ford (1993) table 1, 3–5 month arrears figures are imputed before 1985

Homelessness

Homelessness means different things to different people. Reliable figures are available only for the numbers of households who applied to local authorities to be housed under the homelessness legislation. Thus those households which applied and were accepted by local authorities as homeless are reported here. This definition excludes homeless single people and other groups who did not qualify and about whom very little is known.

The first map opposite is shaded according to the proportion of households who were accepted as homeless by each local authority in 1991. In total 178 000 households were accepted; this number represents 0.8% of all households. In Scotland 7600 households assessed as potentially homeless are also included. The highest proportion of households who applied and were accepted as homeless in 1991 was 4.5% in Manchester. The map also shows the actual number of households accepted in each district in 1991. The highest figure is 7812 in Birmingham (which is also the most populous district).

The second map opposite shows how the pattern of homelessness has changed over the last decade. The districts are shaded according to the percentage point change in the proportion of households accepted to be homeless by local authorities. In districts containing a fifth of the population the incidence of homelessness has fallen, but in most districts it has risen. The sharpest rise over the decade was of 3.9% additional households being accepted as homeless in Manchester, followed by 2.6% in Dumbarton and 2.3% in Southwark. In relative terms these rises are much more dramatic, being 802%, 215% and 400% for these three areas, respectively. These figures are shown in each district. The national average rise in the numbers of households homeless was 115% over the decade.

Figure 4.29 shows how the numbers of households accepted as homeless rose over the 1980s. The figure also shows how some of those households were dealt with after the local authorities had accepted them. An accelerating number were placed in temporary accommodation, and a rapidly growing number of these households were placed in private rented accommodation which had been leased on their behalf.

Most households became homeless because relatives or friends were no longer willing to accommodate them. However, by the end of the period an increasing proportion of households was becoming homeless due to mortgage arrears (12% of all households accepted in 1991). Figure 4.30 shows how the proportions of households in arrears with their mortgage rose to unprecedented levels by 1991. In that year the homes of 75 500 households were possessed by mortgage lenders because of arrears in repayment. Having negative equity made it difficult for some borrowers in arrears to sell (page 128).

Finally, given that the last census missed over a million people who were thought to be resident in dwellings in 1991, the official counts made of the numbers of people "sleeping rough" are likely to be gross underestimates. Nevertheless, for the record, 2395 men and 457 women were recorded as living on the streets of Britain in 1991.

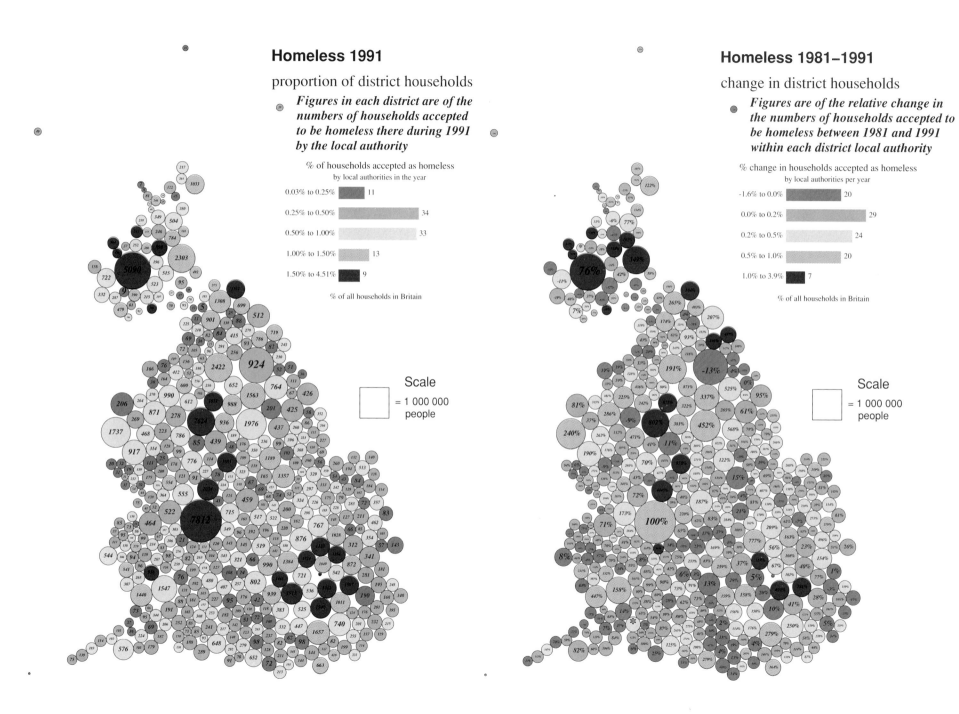

Homeless 1991

proportion of district households

Figures in each district are of the numbers of households accepted to be homeless there during 1991 by the local authority

% of households accepted as homeless
by local authorities in the year

0.03% to 0.25%	11
0.25% to 0.50%	34
0.50% to 1.00%	33
1.00% to 1.50%	13
1.50% to 4.51%	9

% of all households in Britain

Scale
= 1 000 000 people

Homeless 1981–1991

change in district households

Figures are of the relative change in the numbers of households accepted to be homeless between 1981 and 1991 within each district local authority

% change in households accepted as homeless
by local authorities per year

-1.6% to 0.0%	20
0.0% to 0.2%	29
0.2% to 0.5%	24
0.5% to 1.0%	20
1.0% to 3.9%	7

% of all households in Britain

Scale
= 1 000 000 people

Conclusion: Housing and Wealth

The Housing Census

The decennial census, upon which so much of our knowledge of society is based, is a census of housing as well as of population. It provides the basic counts of how households are housed and how many dwellings are standing in each area. Only the census gives a national picture of the distribution of dwelling types, sizes, occupancy and ownership, and these measures reflect other aspects of housing which it does not count, such as price and quality. This chapter has shown how all these characteristics of housing provision are related to one another, as well as to some of the living conditions of their inhabitants. For instance, people living in non-permanent accommodation are twenty times more likely to be overcrowded than residents of detached houses (Figure 4.7). The largest differences, however, are not to be found between households living in different types of housing, but in different tenures. The maps of tenure distribution (pages 114–123) reflect both the economic and demographic geography of Britain shown previously (see Figures 4.19 and 4.20) and other social and political patterns which are drawn in later chapters. The geography of the transfer to private ownership of a quarter of the 1979 stock of local authority housing has sharpened the divides between people with different forms of tenure. The transfer to home ownership has been most prevalent amongst households with families of two adults of working age, where the main breadwinner was most likely to be a skilled manual worker; while the only group more likely to be living in private rented accommodation by 1991 were lone parent families (Figure 4.22). Particularly telling is the fact that in almost every district in Britain the level of car ownership amongst households in local authority tenure has fallen over the 1980s (Figure 6.27). The census also allows some aspects of housing quality to be compared with the composition of families living in each dwelling. Households where all adults are ill and at least one is aged 85 or over are least likely to have central heating; as are children living in the north and west of Britain (Figures 5.7 and 5.8). Housing amenities and quality are considered in more detail in the following chapter on health.

Social Housing

The census asks questions about housing because government has a traditional commitment to provide a decent home for every family (Audit Commission 1992). In crude terms the requirement for new social housing is as high now as it was twenty years ago (Figure 4.5). Measures such as rates of overcrowding, lack of privacy and the requirement for temporary accommodation show that this need is still strongest in large cities (pages 108–111), but these are also the places where the largest numbers of homes are empty and which already have the largest rented sectors. However, as the census

missed over a million people, estimates of vacant housing cannot be reliable, particularly as most people were missing where more homes were thought to be empty (page 217). The census also fails to record information such as household income and property rent, so a clear picture of where rented housing is affordable is very difficult to draw. Alternative detailed information is available on the home ownership market which is discussed below. What the census did suggest is that the property least likely to be vacant was that defined as semi-detached houses (suitable for most families), whereas small flats and bedsits were most likely to be vacant (Figure 4.11). The tenure of vacant property can only be implied from the census, but independent estimates have shown that local authority housing is most unlikely to be vacant (Newton, 1991: 52). The imbalance of the supply of housing of different tenures to the need for housing in each area appears to underlie housing shortages. The strongest evidence for this argument is provided by official homelessness figures which show where households accepted as homeless are most likely to live and how that pattern has changed over the last decade (page 131). Again the same city centres are highlighted as those areas that showed all the other indications of housing shortage and supply imbalance. New social housing has to be built in the right places, to be rented at the right prices, and must be of the right quality, if the additional need which has developed over the last decade is to be met.

Housing Market

The converse problem to the lack of affordable rented accommodation in Britain is the over-supply and under-use of expensive privately owned property, which over 40% of all households were buying in Britain in 1991, while less than a quarter of all households owned their home outright. The price paid (and hence the mortgage borrowed) by different buyers varies more by the area they live in than by the type of property they buy (Figure 4.23). House buying is currently most prevalent in central London, the outer South East and in Scotland (page 125), but each of these groups are paying very different prices for their homes and have had very different experiences of the housing market in recent years. The collapse of property prices in 1989 was as clearly differentiated geographically as was the rise in the early 1980s (page 127). Price falls have yet to affect Scotland significantly and so the increase in house buying there, which resulted from the introduction of the right-to-buy council housing, has not been reflected in increased housing debt in that country. However, owner occupation levels are still below 50% in most of Scotland. The same is true of Inner London, but there prices have fallen severely so that the greatest numbers of people now living in homes worth less than their mortgage are to be found in the south and east of that city. The map of negative equity shows how a clear divide cut across the country by 1993, separating the south — where unsecured debt is most commonly held — from Wales and the north, where households have been able to borrow less and where these lower prices have held up more strongly (page 129). However, households in peripheral regions have the lowest levels of positive equity, so even small falls in prices in these regions could put large numbers of households into this form of housing debt (Figure 4.27). A more serious form of debt occurs when households fall into arrears with the monthly payments on their mortgage. Mortgage arrears and property possession rose to unprecedented levels by 1991 (Figure 4.30) following a period of high interest rates, rising unemployment and the collapse of the housing market, which together made it very difficult for mortgaged households in difficulties to cut their losses and sell.

It is important to remember that this situation is only economically tolerable because 60% of all households in Britain still have positive equity in their homes and only 34% rent. At the end of 1993 only 6% of all households had negative equity (this proportion fell in early 1994 but then rose again, so that 1.3 million households were still holding negative equity by the start of 1995: Dorling and Cornford 1995). Thus most people who bought homes between 1987 and 1991 still have tens of thousands of pounds worth of positive equity held in them, despite the market slump (see Figure 6.28). Our current system of allocating and financing housing is accepted politically because a majority of households still fare well from the process and a minority have made a profit from it (page 199). Two fifths of households live in increasingly expensive rented accommodation or now owe more to a mortgage lender than they could raise if they could sell their home, while the wealthy "invest" their savings in old bricks and mortar rather than in enterprises which create jobs and goods. This division underlies the geographical distribution of wealth in Britain.

Mapping Wealth: Colour Print E

If life assurance and pension funds are excluded from the equation, then half of all personal wealth in Britain is held in housing (Figure 6.30). This can be mapped. To estimate this wealth in each ward, the average price of housing (page 125) is multiplied by the number of households who own their homes outright and then the average positive equity of home buyers (page 199) is multiplied by the number of buyers who do not have negative equity (page 129). From these two figures an estimate of total positive equity is made, from which the total value of negative equity in each ward can be subtracted. When this total net housing equity is divided by the total number of households living in each ward an estimate of local housing wealth is produced, and hence an indication of total wealth in each small area. The resulting map, combining census and building society data, is shown in Colour Print E which divides the wards of Britain into thirteen groups at intervals of thousands or tens of thousands of pounds. This is only an estimate of housing wealth because it under-values both the positive equity of all buyers (see page 198) and the extent to which households may have borrowed additional money secured on the value of their property. These two effects work in opposite directions and so there is no reason to presume that this map of wealth is biased in any particular direction. The map key illustrates just how divided Britain is in terms of wealth. The richest 8% of the population live in wards where the average housing wealth is at least £75 000 per household, while the poorest 8% of people live in areas with negligible housing wealth, averaging less than £5000.

References

Audit Commission, 1992, *Developing Local Authority Housing Strategies*, London: HMSO.

Dale, A. and Marsh, C., 1993, *The 1991 Census User's Guide*, London: HMSO.

DoE, 1982, *Housing and Construction Statistics 1971–1981*, London: HMSO.

DoE, 1982, *Local Housing Statistics*, No. 62, London: HMSO.

DoE, 1984, *Local Housing Statistics*, No. 68, London: HMSO.

DoE, 1990, *Housing and Construction Statistics 1979–1989*, London: HMSO.

DoE, 1991, *Housing and Construction Statistics* Parts 1 and 2, No. 45, London: HMSO.

DoE, 1992, *Local Housing Statistics*, No. 102, London: HMSO.

DoE, 1993, *English House Condition Survey: 1991*, London: HMSO.

Dorling, D. and Cornford, J., 1995, Who has negative equity? *Housing Studies*, 10/2: 151–178

Ford, J., 1993, Mortgage possession, *Housing Studies*, 8/4: 227–240.

Halifax, 1991, *Regional House Price Bulletin*: First Quarter 1991, Halifax: Halifax Building Society.

JRF, 1991, *Inquiry into British Housing, Second Report*, York: Joseph Rowntree Foundation.

Newton, J., 1991, *All in One Place: the British Housing Story 1971–1990*, London: Catholic Housing Aid Society.

Niner, P., 1989, *Housing Needs in the 1990s*, National Housing Forum, London: National Federation of Housing Associations.

OPCS, 1973, *General Household Survey 1971*, London: HMSO.

OPCS, 1975, *General Household Survey 1972*, London: HMSO.

OPCS, 1986, *General Household Survey 1984*, London: HMSO.

OPCS, 1989, *General Household Survey 1986*, London: HMSO.

OPCS, 1991, *General Household Survey: preliminary results for 1990*, Monitor SS 91/1 London: HMSO.

Rowntree, B.S., 1902, *Poverty: a Study of Town Life*, London: Macmillan.

Scottish Development Department, 1983, *Scottish Housing Statistics*, No. 19, 3rd Quarter 1982, London: HMSO.

Scottish Office, 1992, *Statistical Bulletin, Housing Series*, HSG/1992/5, London: HMSO.

Simpson, S. and Dorling, D., 1994, Those missing millions: implications for social statistics of undercount in the 1991 census, *Journal of Social Policy*, 23/4: 543–567.

Wilcox, S., 1993, *Housing Finance Review*, York: Joseph Rowntree Foundation.

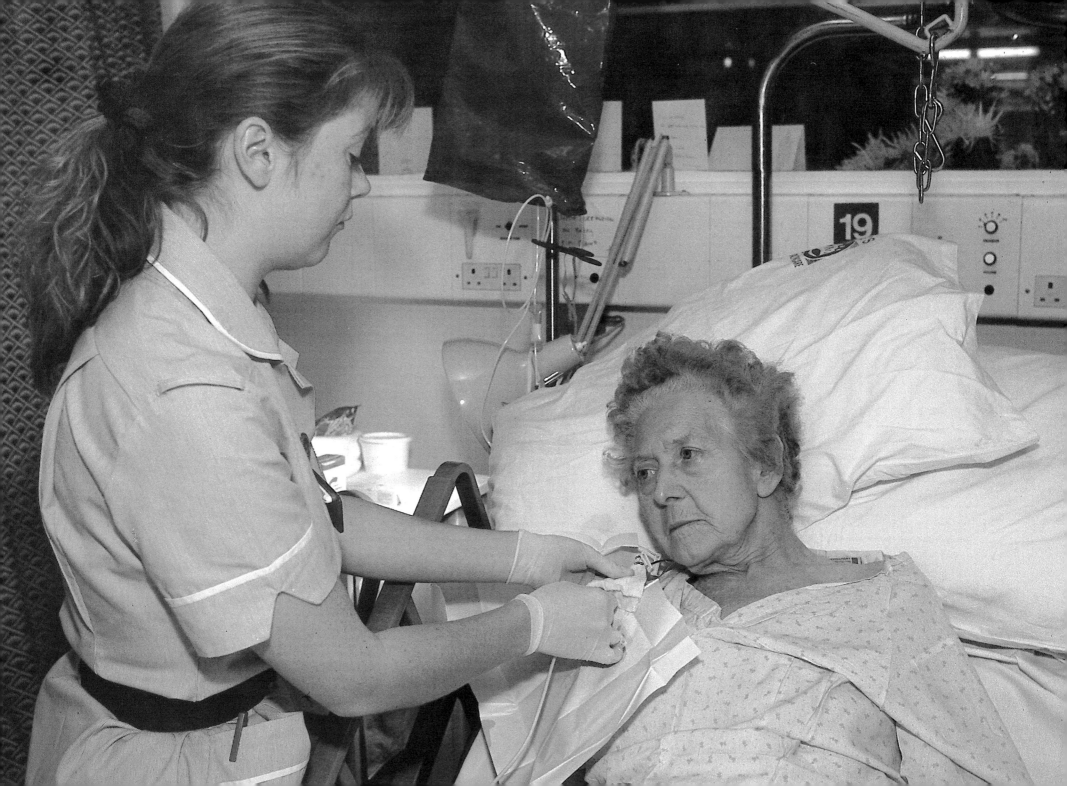

5: Health

There is as strong a geographical pattern to inequalities of health as there is to almost any other topic which concerns people's well-being. This suggests that your health is just as strongly influenced by where you live as are other life chances. Such an argument does not necessarily suggest that living in certain places causes good or bad health, more that people in good or bad health tend to end up living in different places. This may largely be because issues of health are so closely connected with other social topics which geographically differentiate the population, and which are discussed in this atlas. Some of these connections are described below.

There is very little information published about the health of groups of people for local areas. However, two recent innovations have improved this situation. The first is that the 1991 census asked all residents in Britain whether they were suffering from a "long-term illness, health problem or handicap", defined as a condition which limits daily activities or work. Earlier censuses had only been concerned with illness which prevented economic activity, although questions on infirmity (deafness and blindness etc.) were asked in British censuses between 1851 and 1911 (Norris and Mounsey 1983). The second improvement in information on British medical geography arose from the postcoding of mortality records which has been routine in England and Wales since 1981. It is now possible to see what people are dying of at particular ages for very local areas. This information is used extensively here because it is indicative of the general health of the population.

Several concepts need to be introduced in this chapter. *Sickness*, *illness* and *handicap* are words which have all been used in censuses to elicit answers about ill heath. Here these words are used to indicate what people feel about the state of their own health. A section on amenities has also been included in this chapter because the presence or absence of these may be linked to people's state of health. *Amenities* means here something conducive to comfort or convenience, and the examples presented later are hospitals, and home washing and heating facilities. The final set of concepts concerns *disease* and *mortality*, words which are used to indicate what medical assessors thought to be the case in defining types of diseases and causes of death. The ninth standard classification of the World Health Organisation is used in these cases (WHO 1977).

The chapter begins by looking at the current distribution of ill health across the country as measured by people's own conception of their health. The distribution is then shown in former years for those groups who were asked (in past censuses) whether they were permanently or temporarily sick. In 1971 only people "intending to seek work" were asked if they were sick. Illness has always been a major reason why some people do not work and in recent years, when more people have not been able to find work, rates

of sickness have increased. Particular occupations, for example mining, have also been linked with causing ill health. The economic implications of ill health are important, as are the implications of social and economic circumstances on health.

Having considered what is known of illness for small communities, the chapter then considers some basic factors which can be linked to health. These primarily concern housing amenities. Whether homes can be centrally heated can be determined from the 1991 census (although it is not possible to discover which households can always afford to heat their homes). In past censuses more simple comforts were of issue such as whether a household had access to its own sink or stove. Washing facilities are also a good indicator of the general quality of housing in an area. If households do not have their own baths or showers it is likely that the general quality of their housing is poor and this lack of amenities could be correlated with ill health.

The spatial distribution of hospitals is shown next as hospitals are both an amenity and an indication of where people who are very ill are likely to be located. As with all health care facilities, hospitals follow the distribution of the population and so the patterns shown in the first chapter of this book need to be appreciated if the pattern of hospital provision is to be understood. Demographic factors, principally the ageing of the population, are important in determining the hospitalized population, as are medical decisions over how long patients should stay in hospitals and political factors such as who should run hospitals. Some of the effects of these decisions are shown here.

The last section of this chapter concentrates on life expectancy, mortality rates, causes of death and how these have been changing geographically over the last decade and over the last century. Demographic factors are important here, but it is also evident that social differences in standards of living are reflected by the causes and likelihood of dying. Here the individual postcoded mortality data have been used in different ways to show where different causes of death are most prevalent and how life expectancies are related to illness and other factors geographically (Cliff and Haggett 1988). Unfortunately, the mortality data available for this study do not cover Scotland. The section ends by comparing the current geography of life chances with that of previous periods going back to before the Second World War. The political implications of inequalities in health are stressed at the end of the chapter. How governments choose to organize health provision and to regulate society has an influence which extends quite clearly to how and where and when we are most likely to die.

This chapter demonstrates how issues of health are linked to the geographies of population, demography, economics, housing, society and politics. These in turn are affected by, and have an impact upon the health of the nation (Whitehead, 1987; Townsend *et al.* 1988; Black and Whitehead 1992). When considering these maps, however, it must be remembered that it is not places which are well or ill — but people.

5.1: Residents with Long Term Illness by Age and Location in Britain 1991

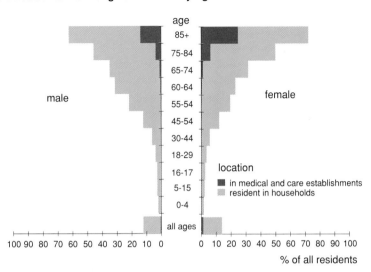

male   female

location
■ in medical and care establishments
▨ resident in households

100 90 80 70 60 50 40 30 20 10 0   0 10 20 30 40 50 60 70 80 90 100

% of all residents

age: 85+, 75-84, 65-74, 60-64, 55-54, 45-54, 30-44, 18-29, 16-17, 5-15, 0-4, all ages

5.2: Ill Residents, by Employment, Amenities and Socioeconomic Group in Britain 1991

Proportion of people in each socioeconomic group with long term illness, who are unemployed, have no central heating or lack/share a bath

Socioeconomic Group	With Illness	Unemployed	No Central Heating	Lack or Share Bath
16 Members of armed forces (all ranks and occupations)	2.3%	4.0%	9.6%	0.2%
4 Professional workers (eg solicitor) - employees	2.5%	3.2%	7.3%	0.5%
1 Employers and managers in large establishments	2.5%	1.6%	7.1%	0.2%
2.2 Managers in small establishments	3.0%	7.0%	9.2%	0.3%
5.2 Foremen and supervisors - non-manual (clerk)	3.1%	3.8%	13.5%	0.4%
6 Junior non-manual workers (check-out operator)	3.3%	5.2%	13.2%	0.4%
5.1 Ancillary workers & artists (teacher , nurse)	3.3%	3.4%	10.3%	0.5%
3 Professional workers (architect) self-employed	3.4%	0.7%	3.6%	0.1%
7 Personal service workers (chef , waiter/ess)	3.5%	7.3%	17.9%	0.8%
15 Agricultural workers (forester , fishing worker)	3.8%	9.1%	30.8%	1.3%
9 Skilled manual workers (builder , baker, driver)	4.0%	11.3%	19.6%	0.5%
2.1 Employers in small establishments	4.1%	0.1%	8.3%	0.2%
8 Foremen and supervisors - manual (eg storekeeper)	4.2%	5.7%	16.2%	0.4%
12 Self-employed non-professionals without employees	4.4%	5.7%	15.7%	0.6%
10 Semi-skilled manual workers (care assistant)	5.2%	11.4%	22.0%	0.7%
– Economically active, but not worked in last ten years	5.6%	31.4%	17.7%	1.0%
13 Farmers - employers and managers (who own/rent)	5.8%	1.4%	17.9%	0.1%
17 Inadequately described and not stated occupations	6.1%	14.7%	18.6%	0.8%
11 Unskilled manual workers (road sweeper)	6.4%	13.2%	24.7%	0.8%
14 Farmers - own account (has only family employees)	6.8%	0.5%	30.4%	1.5%
Economically inactive (eg retired, looking after home)	23.0%		18.6%	0.6%
Total households with residents in Britain	13.1%	5.7%	16.8%	0.6%

figures shown in red are above the overall average

Illness

Illness is not easily defined. Because of this, illness is not a variable which is often seen in official statistics. Illness is, however, a condition which affects the lives of over seven million people in Britain so badly that they agreed it was having "a long term limiting effect on their daily activities". This response was raised from a question on illness asked by the last census. The distribution of these *ill people* in Britain across wards is shown on the map and cartogram opposite (which both use the same shading categories).

The map emphasizes the coalfields of Wales, Yorkshire and the North East of England where high rates of illness in relatively sparsely populated areas prevail. The population cartogram shows a much sharper divide along very different lines. The high rates of illness in the coalfields are important, but are only part of a pattern which is dominated by the cities of the north and Scotland, within which over one person in six or even five is suffering from a long term illness. In the south high rates of illness are confined to the coast and central London, reflecting the distribution of pensioners in those parts of the country (see page 39).

The importance of age on a person's likelihood of suffering from a long term illness is demonstrated by Figure 5.1. Over half of all the people who said they were ill under the census definition were aged over 65. Over two thirds of people aged over 85 were suffering from a long term illness in 1991. At all ages up to 74 men are more likely to consider themselves ill. Thereafter women are more likely to consider themselves ill than are men and, because of the larger numbers of women who survive to old age, women in total are more likely to be ill than are men and ill women occupy more than twice as many places in medical and care establishments as do ill men.

Age and sex are not the only obvious correlates with illness. Figure 5.2 emphasises one social connection where people in certain occupations are less likely to be ill than are people doing other forms of work. The connections run both ways: illness may make getting or holding certain jobs harder, while certain jobs, or the life-styles associated with them, are more likely to lead to higher rates of illness. Demographic factors are still important here, for instance the figure shows that the lowest rates of illness are to be found in the armed forces where youth dominates and fitness is a requirement for getting the job.

Figure 5.2 shows that people in work, regardless of their occupation, are less likely to be ill than are the population as a whole. The figure also shows the likelihood of all people in each group being unemployed, lacking central heating or exclusive access to a bath or shower. These measures are generally higher for occupations in which illness is more common. Farmers with no employees (own account), for instance, have some of the poorest rates of access to amenities and the highest rate of illness of any occupational group — despite being unlikely to be unemployed.

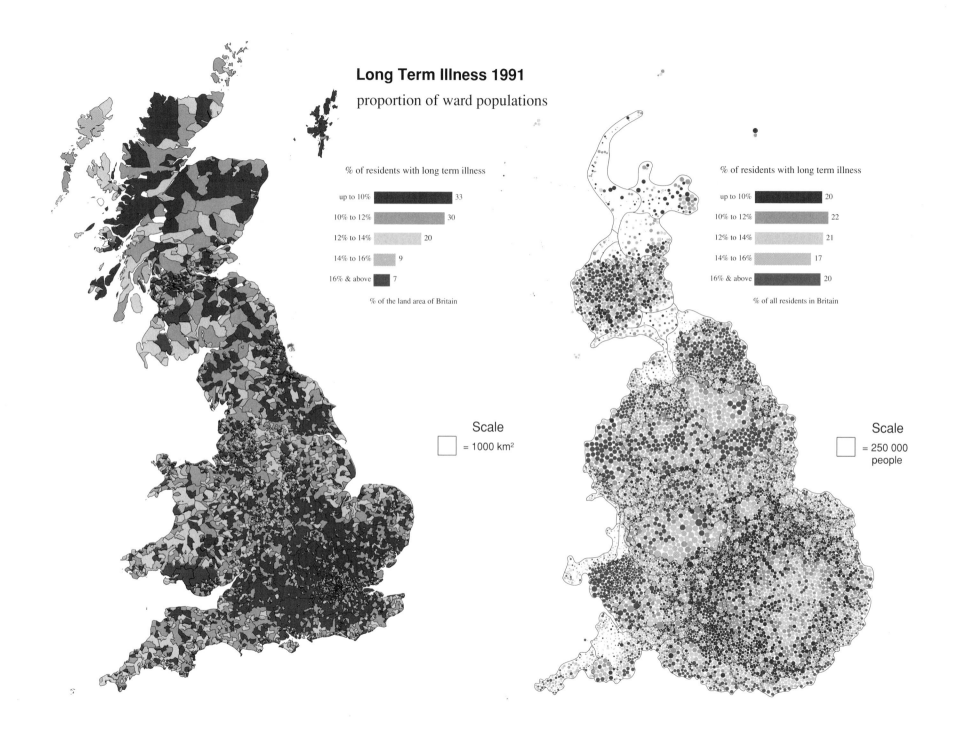

Long Term Illness 1991

proportion of ward populations

% of residents with long term illness

up to 10%		33
10% to 12%		30
12% to 14%		20
14% to 16%		9
16% & above		7

% of the land area of Britain

% of residents with long term illness

up to 10%		20
10% to 12%		22
12% to 14%		21
14% to 16%		17
16% & above		20

% of all residents in Britain

Scale

☐ = 1000 km²

Scale

☐ = 250 000 people

5.3: Temporary Sickness by Marital Status and Region in Britain 1971–1981

% change in each category for temporarily sick workers

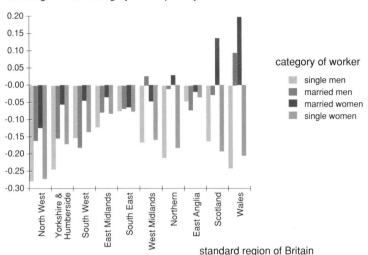

category of worker

- single men
- married men
- married women
- single women

standard region of Britain

5.4: Permanent Sickness by Sex and Region in Britain 1981, 1991

% of residents aged 16 and over who are permanently sick

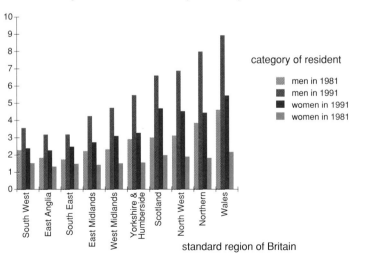

category of resident

- men in 1981
- men in 1991
- women in 1991
- women in 1981

standard region of Britain

Sickness

Sickness is a narrower concept than illness and usually refers to the inability to work due to ill health. In 1971 the census tables only distinguished people who were *temporarily sick* meaning sickness that was temporarily preventing them from working. The first map opposite shows where these people tended to live. The pattern is remarkably similar to that of long term illness in 1991, given how different the question, applicable group and the times were. The 1981 census categorized people as either temporarily sick (but in the workforce) or "permanently sick or disabled" and thus not in the workforce. It was not possible to be retired and disabled by this categorization and so the definition of sickness used at that time differed from both those which preceded it and those which came later. Nevertheless, when the geography of permanent sickness is plotted, as it is in the map on the far right, the pattern can again be seen to be very similar to that of previous and future censuses. One notable change between the patterns of 1971 and 1981 is the fall in the proportion of people sick just to the west of central London.

A question on temporary sickness was asked in both the 1971 and 1981 censuses and so a comparison can be made, bearing in mind the problems outlined above. This is done in Figure 5.3 which shows how temporary sickness fell in each region in Britain. In Britain as a whole the proportion of residents aged over 15 who were temporarily sick fell from 0.7% to 0.6% over the decade. This may partly reflect many people choosing to define themselves as permanently sick in 1981, but also the very different economic climate of that time. Intriguingly, the falls in sickness were generally higher for single men and women and lowest for married women (who also accounted for most of the rare rises in temporary sickness which occurred in a minority of regions). The regions in the figure are ordered according to the overall fall in temporary sickness which was lowest in Wales and highest in the North West.

A question on permanent sickness was asked in both 1981 and 1991 although, again, the different questions in each census and the changing times may have influenced their comparability. The absolute rates of permanent sickness for both women and men at both times are shown for each region in Figure 5.4. Again the regions are sorted from that which has seen the lowest rise, the South West, to that which has seen the highest, Wales. Across all of Britain the proportion of men aged over 15 who defined themselves as permanently sick between 1981 and 1991 rose from 2.5% to 5.0% while the proportion of women rose from 1.6% to 3.3%. Thus permanent sickness was seen to double, despite the availability of an alternative census question which allowed people to categorize themselves as ill but otherwise occupied in 1991. Figure 5.4 shows how in only three regions was permanent sickness in men below 4% in 1991, and how only in Wales was it above this level in 1981. This graph should be compared with Figures 3.29 and 3.30 on early retirement and unemployment change during the 1980s.

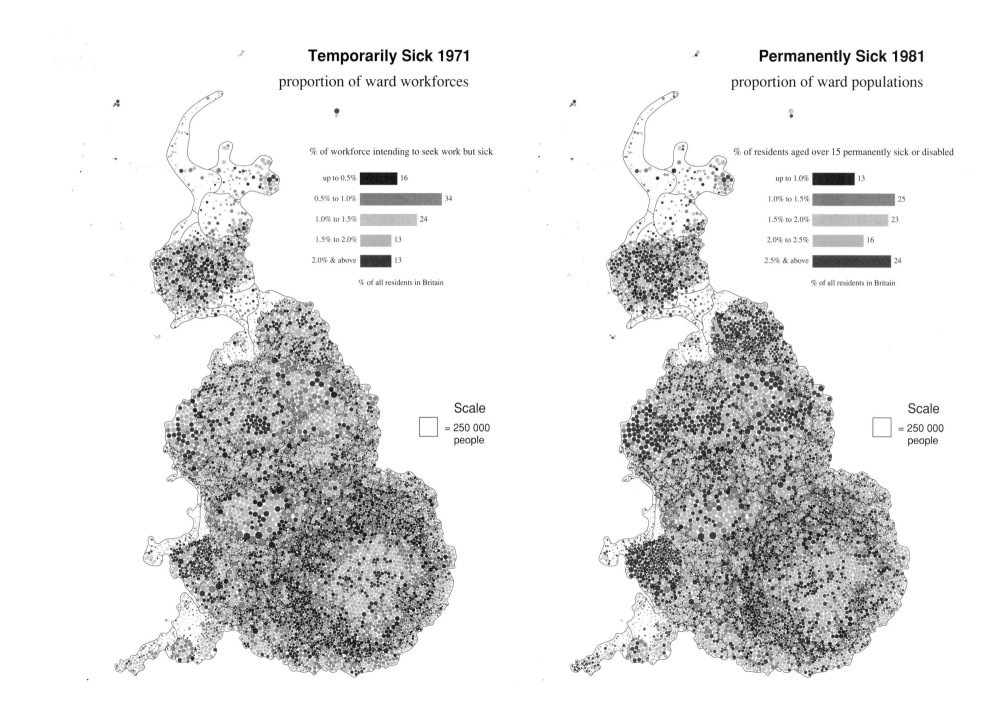

Temporarily Sick 1971

proportion of ward workforces

% of workforce intending to seek work but sick

up to 0.5%	16
0.5% to 1.0%	34
1.0% to 1.5%	24
1.5% to 2.0%	13
2.0% & above	13

% of all residents in Britain

Scale

☐ = 250 000 people

Permanently Sick 1981

proportion of ward populations

% of residents aged over 15 permanently sick or disabled

up to 1.0%	13
1.0% to 1.5%	25
1.5% to 2.0%	23
2.0% to 2.5%	16
2.5% & above	24

% of all residents in Britain

Scale

☐ = 250 000 people

5.5: Residents with Illness by Age, Sex and Household Employment in Britain 1991

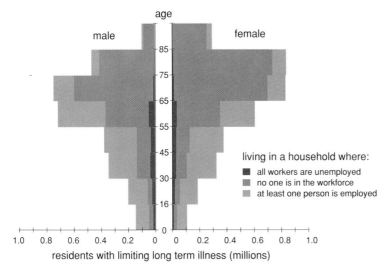

living in a household where:

■ all workers are unemployed
▨ no one is in the workforce
▨ at least one person is employed

residents with limiting long term illness (millions)

5.6: Pensioners with Illness by Age, Tenure and Household Composition in Britain 1991

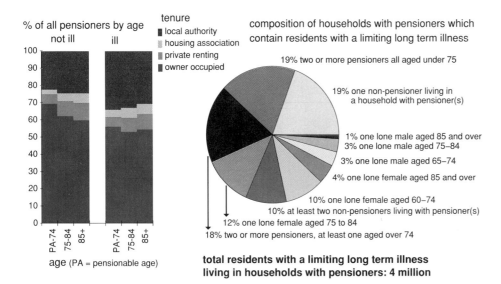

% of all pensioners by age
not ill   ill

tenure
■ local authority
▨ housing association
▨ private renting
■ owner occupied

age (PA = pensionable age)

composition of households with pensioners which contain residents with a limiting long term illness

19% two or more pensioners all aged under 75

19% one non-pensioner living in a household with pensioner(s)

1% one lone male aged 85 and over
3% one lone male aged 75–84

3% one lone male aged 65–74

4% one lone female aged 85 and over

10% one lone female aged 60–74

10% at least two non-pensioners living with pensioner(s)

12% one lone female aged 75 to 84

18% two or more pensioners, at least one aged over 74

total residents with a limiting long term illness living in households with pensioners: 4 million

Illness and Age

The brief treatment of illness here ends with two maps illustrating the different geographies of ill health amongst the elderly and the young. Although the overall rates of long term illness for these two groups are very different, as the keys to the two maps opposite illustrate, the importance of factors associated with place in influencing the likelihood of illness are quite similar. Given this, the most striking difference between the two maps is that, although children are more likely to be ill in London than is usual, elderly London residents are relatively unlikely to be ill. Similar examples can be seen for other parts of the country, in Merseyside for instance.

Figure 5.5 gives the absolute numbers of people who were suffering from a long term illness by age and sex in 1991. The figure shows how the two groups which the maps opposite contrast are of a similar size, despite representing very different proportions of their respective age groups. However, the very elderly who are ill are much more likely to be women and probably live in a household in which no one is in the workforce. Most ill children live in households where at least one person is in employment.

The living conditions of the long term ill are explored further in Figure 5.6 which concentrates on the housing and household circumstances of ill pensioners. The bar charts in this figure show that, whereas pensioners who are not ill are increasingly likely to be housed by the public sector as they get older, pensioners who are ill are less likely to have been owner occupiers in the first place. By the time they are aged over 84 the tenure profiles of pensioners are similar regardless of illness. The pie chart in Figure 5.6 shows how a third of pensioners who were ill in 1991 were pensioners living on their own. Only one in five of these pensioners was male. Male pensioners, because they tend to die earlier, are far more likely to be living in households with their partners or other relatives when they are ill. Only 29% of ill residents in households which contain an ill pensioner also contain someone who is not a pensioner. More old ill people live alone than are cared for by people of working age.

With a better understanding of the probable housing circumstances of the old and young who are ill, it is worth returning to the two maps shown opposite. In almost a quarter of the country (by population) over 70% of pensioners aged over 84 are ill. Two thirds of these ill pensioners do not live in medical and care establishments. These are the pensioners who are shown opposite, three quarters of them are women. Of these — three hundred thousand ill women aged over 84 living in the community — almost two in three live alone. The map opposite also includes one hundred thousand men who are ill and aged over 84. Forty percent of these men are living on their own. Thus, whereas the first map of children is of ill people who are almost certainly living in a household with adults of working age at least one of whom is in work, the elderly who are ill are most probably living alone and otherwise rarely with someone in work.

Ill Children 1991

proportion of ward populations

% of residents under 16 with long term illness

up to 1.5%	19
1.5% to 2.0%	21
2.0% to 2.5%	22
2.5% to 3.0%	17
3.0% & above	21

% of all residents in Britain

Scale

= 250 000 people

Ill Residents Aged Over 84 1991

proportion of ward populations

% of residents aged over 84 with long term illness

up to 55%	18
55% to 60%	17
60% to 65%	23
65% to 70%	19
70% & above	23

% of all residents in Britain

Scale

= 250 000 people

5.7: Availability of Central Heating by Household Type in Britain 1991

selected households categorized by size, carers, dependants and age

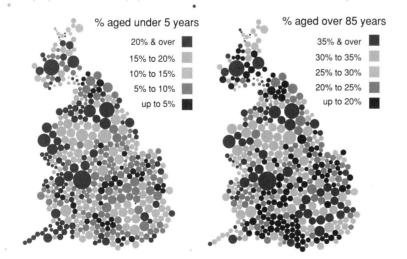

households most likely to have central heating

two plus carers with dependants aged 5–15 and 16–PA (12%)
two plus carers with dependant(s) aged 5–15 (12%)
two plus carers with dependant(s) aged 0–4 (15%)
two plus carers with dependants aged 0–4 and 5–15 (16%)
two plus carers with dependant(s) aged 16–PA (15%)
two plus carers with dependants aged 5–15 and PA plus (14%)
one male carer with dependant(s) aged 0–4 (15%)
one male carer with dependants aged 5–15 and 16–PA (23%)
two plus carers with dependants aged 16–PA and PA plus (21%)

households with no dependants (33%)

two plus dependants one aged PA–74 one aged 75–84 (59%)
two plus dependants one aged below PA one aged PA–74 (51%)
one male carer with dependants aged 0–4 and PA plus (35%)
one male carer with dependant(s) aged 0–4 (50%)
one female carer with dependants aged 0–4 and 5–15 (77%)
one lone female dependant aged 75–84 (95%)
two plus dependants all aged 75–84 (66%)
one female carer with dependant(s) aged 0–4 (78%)
one male carer with dependant(s) PA plus (38%)
one lone female dependant aged below PA (81%)
two plus dependants one aged 75–84 one aged 85 plus (78%)
one male carer with dependants aged 16–PA and PA plus (39%)
one female carer with dependants aged 0–4 and PA plus (58%)
one lone male dependant aged PA–74 (68%)
one lone female dependant aged 85 plus (98%)
one lone male dependant aged 75–84 (77%)
two plus dependants all aged 85 plus (85%)
two plus dependants one aged below PA one aged 75–84 (68%)
one lone male dependant aged 85 plus (89%)
one lone male dependant aged below PA (74%)
two plus dependants one aged below PA one aged 85 plus (63%)

households least likely to have central heating

(proportion of households in each group with no access to a car in brackets)

Note: a dependant is either a child aged under 16 or aged 16–18 never married in full-time education or a person who has a limiting long term illness and whose economic position is either permanently sick or retired. A carer is a non-dependent person in a household with a least one dependant.

PA = pensionable age.

0   10   20   30   40

% of households with no central heating in each category

5.8: Young and Old Residents with no Central Heating in Britain 1991

proportion of district populations in households with no central heating

% aged under 5 years

20% & over
15% to 20%
10% to 15%
5% to 10%
up to 5%

% aged over 85 years

35% & over
30% to 35%
25% to 30%
20% to 25%
up to 20%

Heating

Household amenities have been linked to patterns of ill health since studies of the geographical distribution of poverty and its consequences began in Britain. The amenities considered essential have changed over time as living standards have improved. The 1971 census recorded how many households did not have exclusive access to a stove or sink, for instance — amenities which would now be assumed to be available to practically everyone. The first map opposite shows where these facilities were in shortest supply at that time. The high proportion of residents lacking or having to share a stove or sink in London was due to the housing shortage in that place at that time (see page 107). Nowadays the absence of central heating in a home is seen as an indication of poor housing quality. Not having central heating may contribute to ill health, but even more importantly, for people who are ill and spend a lot of time at home it is obviously particularly undesirable not to have central heating.

The second map opposite shows those areas where central heating is least common. Large numbers of households without central heating can be seen to dominate most of the West Midlands, Merseyside and West Yorkshire. Few residents lack central heating in the South East and North East of England, reflecting both general affluence and the policy of some local authorities to ensure that as many homes as possible are fully heated. Lack of central heating was considered to be an important variable by a recent "Health of the Nation" study on the health of elderly people, which used figures from the General Household Survey to show that of four types of household, those consisting of a single elderly person were least likely to have central heating (CHMU 1992: 7).

Figure 5.7 identifies thirty two types of households (based on the criteria of dependency) and shows that the nine types of household more likely than the average to have central heating are those containing at least two people who are not dependants or at least one male non-dependant. Households which contain only dependants, one of whom is aged over 84 and another of whom is not a pensioner (but is suffering from a long term illness and is not working) are least likely to have central heating. Thus the types of household which might be thought to be most in need of central heating are least likely to have it. The figure also shows what proportion of these households have access to a car. All the households which are least likely to have central heating are also least likely to have this access to transport and so may spend more time in homes which are less likely to be fully heated than households with many non-dependent adults.

The geographical differences in the availability of central heating for very young and very old residents are shown by two maps in Figure 5.8. For both groups availability of central heating is common in the ring around London, although there are differences in other parts of the country. It is important to remember that just because a household has central heating does not imply that its members can always afford to use it.

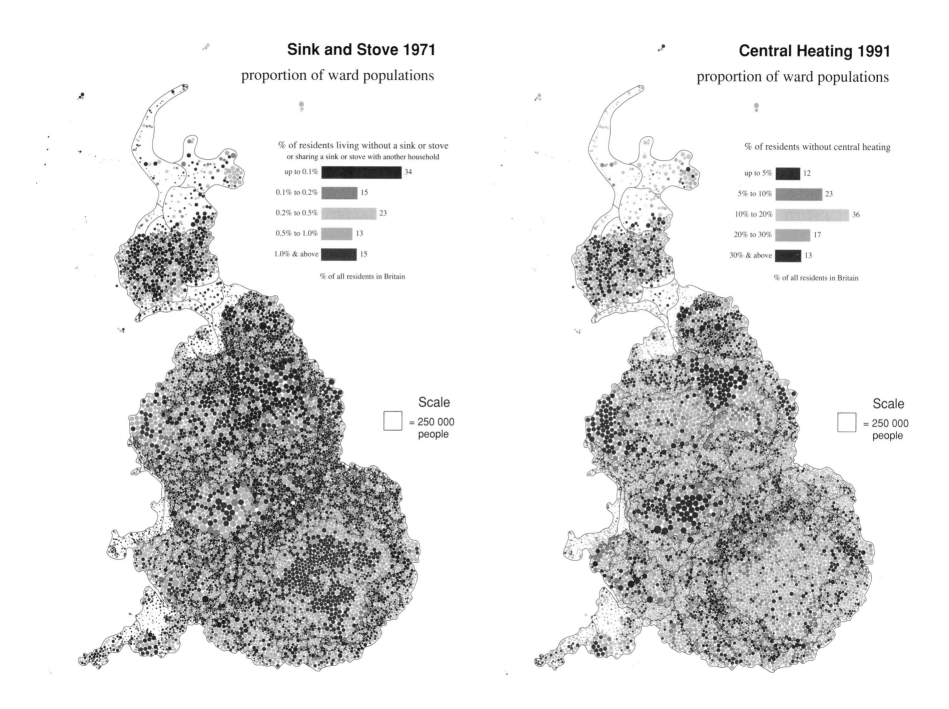

Sink and Stove 1971

proportion of ward populations

% of residents living without a sink or stove
or sharing a sink or stove with another household

up to 0.1% | 34
0.1% to 0.2% | 15
0.2% to 0.5% | 23
0.5% to 1.0% | 13
1.0% & above | 15

% of all residents in Britain

Scale

☐ = 250 000 people

Central Heating 1991

proportion of ward populations

% of residents without central heating

up to 5% | 12
5% to 10% | 23
10% to 20% | 36
20% to 30% | 17
30% & above | 13

% of all residents in Britain

Scale

☐ = 250 000 people

5.9: Households Lacking or Sharing Washing Facilities in Britain 1971, 1981, 1991

% of all households (log scale)

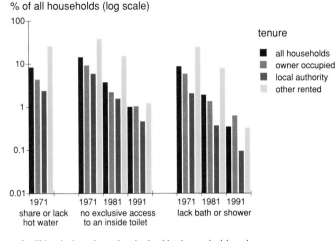

tenure

- ■ all households
- ■ owner occupied
- ■ local authority
- ▨ other rented

facilities being shared or lacked by household and year

5.10: Pensioners Lacking or Sharing Washing and Heating Facilities in Britain 1981, 1991

% of all pensioner residents in each category

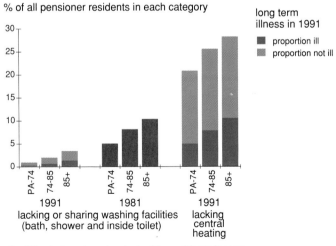

long term
illness in 1991

- ■ proportion ill
- ▨ proportion not ill

facilities being shared or lacked by residents by age

Washing

Questions concerning washing facilities have been asked at each of the last three censuses. The maps drawn here illustrate the geographical distribution of lack of exclusive access to a bath or shower. In 1971 one household in twelve did not have this facility; by 1981 that proportion had fallen to one household in fifty and by 1991 it was only one household in every three hundred. Nevertheless, the geographical pattern taken from the last census is interesting, identifying particular areas where decent washing facilities are still not universally available.

The general improvement in washing facilities has been so great that a log scale is needed to show it in Figure 5.9. This figure illustrates how access has improved for households living in different tenures in different years, and also shows the proportion of households which lacked exclusive access to hot water in 1971 (the last year in which that question was asked) and exclusive access to an inside toilet at each census. The improvement has been remarkable even across each tenure at each period; this trend is broken only by owner occupied households during the 1980s which did not experience the same rate of increase in access to toilets as did the other tenures. Similarly, owner occupied housing experienced a slower improvement in access to washing facilities during the last decade so that it became the worse served tenure by 1991.

The map of the improvement in washing facilities shown on the far right is dominated by two colours because the same areas which saw the most rapid improvements in the 1970s generally experienced them in the 1980s: suburban and rural areas. Urban areas in the north saw significant improvements in the last decade whereas suburban areas in the south underwent most improvement in the 1970s. New home building as well as the renovation of old accommodation was important in influencing these changes.

Part of the relationship between ill health, old age and amenities is shown in Figure 5.10. The proportion of pensioners of various ages lacking washing and heating facilities are shown subdivided by illness. Older pensioners are more likely to lack heating and washing facilities and the proportions who are ill rise similarly. A quarter of all ill pensioners (856 000 ill old people) lived in homes without central heating in 1991. Pensioners who were not ill were more likely to be living in homes with central heating. Of this group of ill pensioners 63 000 also lacked exclusive access to a bath or shower. Ill pensioners were 25% more likely to be in this position than pensioners who were not ill. It is not possible to say from the census whether lack of amenities led to a greater chance of illness, but what the census does show is that people who are ill are less likely than their healthy counterparts to be living with these facilities, facilities which become even more of a necessity with illness. It is the very oldest group who are least likely to have these facilities and who are also most likely to be ill. Of ill people aged over 84, 3.5% had neither central heating nor exclusive washing facilities in 1991.

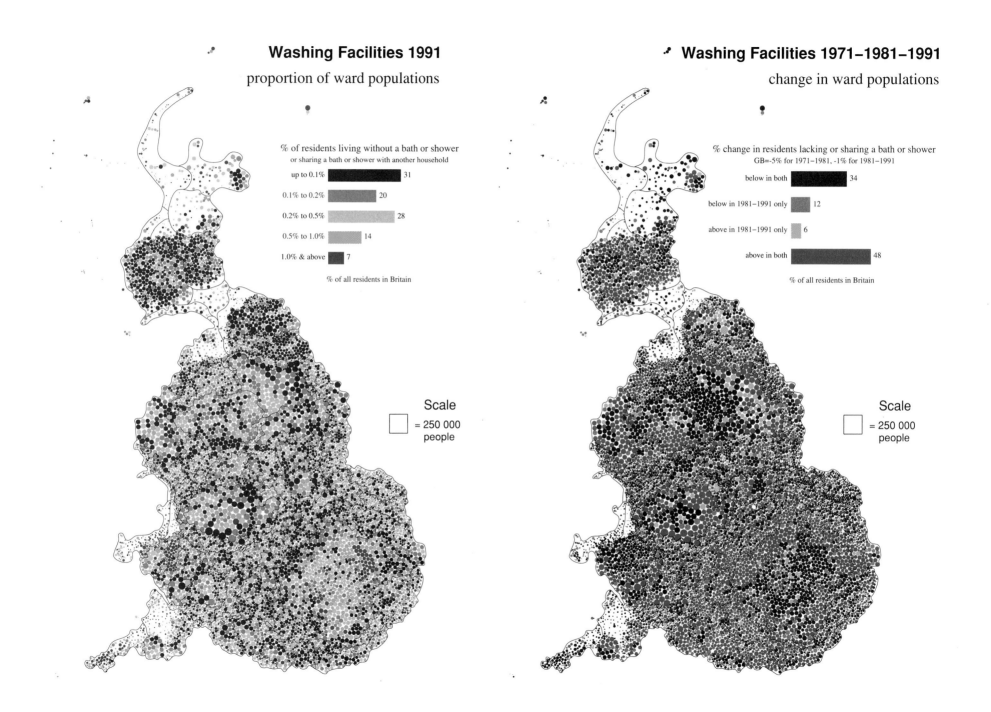

Washing Facilities 1991

proportion of ward populations

% of residents living without a bath or shower
or sharing a bath or shower with another household

up to 0.1%	31
0.1% to 0.2%	20
0.2% to 0.5%	28
0.5% to 1.0%	14
1.0% & above	7

% of all residents in Britain

Scale

☐ = 250 000
people

Washing Facilities 1971–1981–1991

change in ward populations

% change in residents lacking or sharing a bath or shower
GB=-5% for 1971–1981, -1% for 1981–1991

below in both	34
below in 1981–1991 only	12
above in 1981–1991 only	6
above in both	48

% of all residents in Britain

Scale

☐ = 250 000
people

5.11: Residents in Hospitals by Type and District Type in Britain 1981, 1991

type of districts and year:

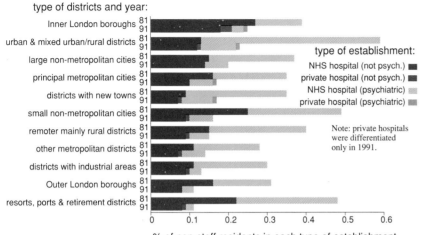

type of establishment:

NHS hospital (not psych.) ■
private hospital (not psych.) ■
NHS hospital (psychiatric) ▨
private hospital (psychiatric) ▨

Note: private hospitals
were differentiated
only in 1991.

% of non-staff residents in each type of establishment

5.12: Pensioners in Hospital by Sex in Britain 1991

proportion of district populations resident in hospitals

% men aged 65 or over

1.0% & over
0.5% to 1.0%
0.2% to 0.5%
0.1% to 0.2%
up to 0.1%

% women aged 60 or over

1.0% & over
0.5% to 1.0%
0.2% to 0.5%
0.1% to 0.2%
up to 0.1%

Hospitals

Hospitals provide facilities for people who are seriously ill and are the geographical locations where many people will die from illness. The first map opposite shows where all the 58 000 residents of medical facilities which were not psychiatric hospitals were staying on census night 1991. By plotting this distribution at the ward scale individual hospitals can be identified and by shading the wards according to the proportions of residents in hospital, the relative sizes of each establishment are shown (see page 13 for the district level). Hospitals can be seen to be very evenly spread across the night-time population. Areas with relatively high proportions of their residents in hospital can be seen in Inner London, south Birmingham and parts of Scotland. The second map opposite shows the distribution of residents in psychiatric hospitals. These can be seen to be even more evenly spread over the population as a whole. Only the wards in two counties did not contain any institutions large enough to be identified on this map.

The patterns shown opposite follow a period of falling numbers of patients being allowed to stay long term in hospitals during the 1980s. Figure 5.11 shows the proportion of residents in different types of hospital at two points in time for eleven types of district. The figure also shows where private hospitals are most likely to be found (as these were separately identified in 1991). The biggest falls have been in the proportion of people who were resident in psychiatric hospitals in resorts, ports & retirement districts and in Outer London. Inner London has experienced the slowest fall in the proportion of its residents who are in hospital. Figure 1.12 showed how these changes differed for men and women nationally and compared their experiences to changes for other groups of people living in communal establishments. In 1971 there were 171 000 patients resident in psychiatric hospitals; by 1981 this had fallen by 22% to 133 000; and by 1991 this number had fallen in a decade by 75% to stand at just 33 000 patients.

Most patients in hospital are elderly. Figure 5.12 shows what proportion of pensioners, by sex, were residents in a hospital in each district in 1991. A most striking feature of this figure is that elderly residents of Scotland appear much more likely to be in hospital than are residents of districts in England and Wales. This figure includes the residents of psychiatric hospitals. One reason for these differences may be the different way the changes to the health service have operated in different parts of Britain. In England between 1981 and 1991 the number of beds available in hospitals per day has fallen from 7.5 to 5 per thousand residents, while the number of "cases treated" has risen by 31% and the number of "day cases" has risen by 111% (Department of Health 1994: 37). Thus fewer people are staying in hospitals although more are being treated. There has been an 81% increase in the number of geriatric cases treated — the biggest rise of any group. However, all these figures should be interpreted with caution, particularly as one person can be counted as being treated many times if he or she is sent home between treatments.

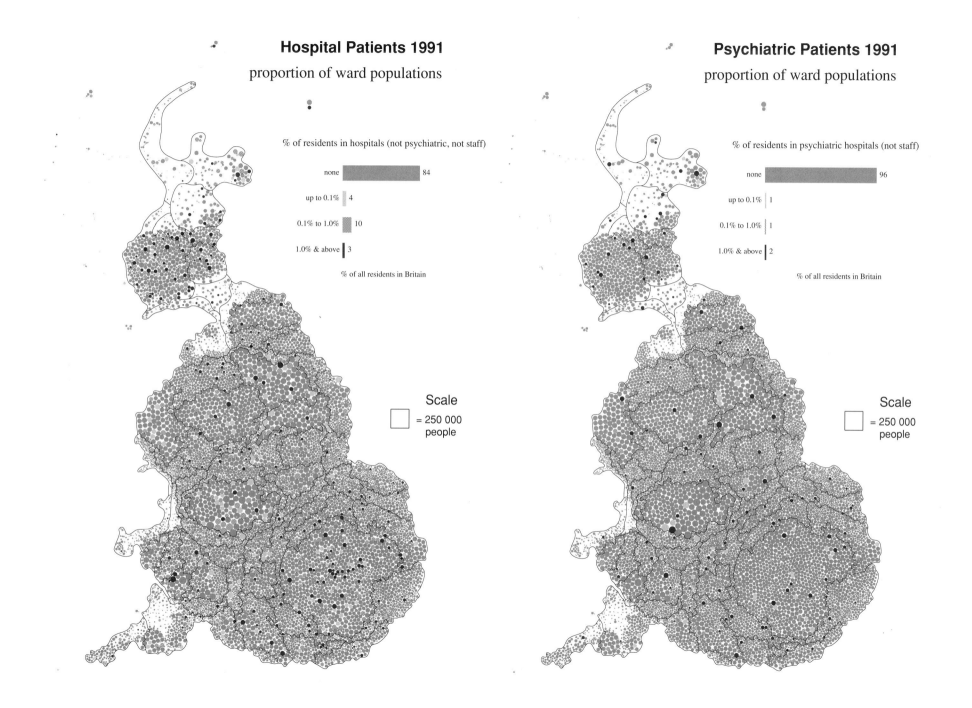

Hospital Patients 1991

proportion of ward populations

% of residents in hospitals (not psychiatric, not staff)

none		84
up to 0.1%		4
0.1% to 1.0%		10
1.0% & above		3

% of all residents in Britain

Scale

☐ = 250 000
people

Psychiatric Patients 1991

proportion of ward populations

% of residents in psychiatric hospitals (not staff)

none		96
up to 0.1%		1
0.1% to 1.0%		1
1.0% & above		2

% of all residents in Britain

Scale

☐ = 250 000
people

5.13: Life Expectancy by Sex and Age in England and Wales 1841–1990

expected years of life left

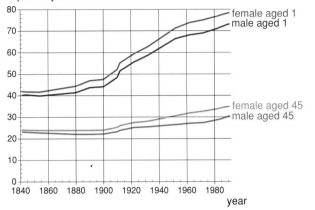

Source: Mortality Statistics Serial Tables, series DH1, no.26,
Review of the Registrar General on deaths in England and Wales 1991

5.14: Increase in Life Expectancy by Sex in England and Wales 1981–1985 to 1986–1989

average additional months of life

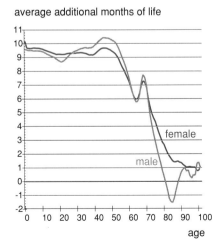

age

5.15: Month of Death in England and Wales 1981–1989

month of death 1981–1989

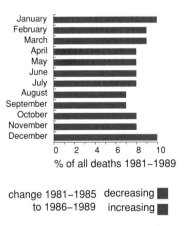

% of all deaths 1981–1989

change 1981–1985   decreasing ■
to 1986–1989   increasing ■

Life Expectancy

One of the most basic ways in which quality of life and health can be measured is through how long people can expect to live. The first map drawn opposite shows the *crude mortality rate* in each ward in England and Wales. This is the proportion of residents who died in each place over a given period of time. This measure largely reflects the areas where more older people live (see page 39) and so does not provide a great deal of information about the relative health of different groups of people, although it does show where there is most demand for certain types of health service. Scotland is not shaded because detailed mortality data for Scotland were not available to the author at the time of writing.

The second map opposite shows a more sophisticated method of illustrating the pattern of mortality. Instead of showing how many people died in each place, the average ages of people who died in each place are shown. This provides an estimate of the life expectancy of people living in each ward which varies from just under 70 years to just over 75 years. This may not seem a great difference, but is seen as a wide margin by demographers, and the geographical patterns of life expectancy shown are consistent with many of the other patterns drawn in this atlas. In strict terms the pattern shown for these wards is the mean age of death which, for all of England and Wales in 1991, was 71.4 years for men and 77.6 years for women. The general difference between men and women is thus greater than that found between very different local areas.

More exact calculations of life expectancy are standardized for the age structure of the local population. For the 1989–1991 period life expectancy in England and Wales was calculated by the government actuaries to be 73.2 years for men and 78.7 years for women. Figure 5.13 shows how life expectancy from age 1 has risen over the last century and a half for each sex and that life expectancy from age 45 has risen less dramatically. Figure 5.14 examines the changes which took place for people by single years of age during the 1980s. For people aged under 50 there was, on average, an improvement in life expectancy of ten months. Improvements around retirement age were much less dramatic, but for people who then lived to age 70 improvements of between seven and eight months were common. The experiences of men and women then differed dramatically, with men aged between 80 and 90 in the latter half of the 1980s living for two months less, on average, than their counterparts in the early 1980s. The group dying earlier were the men who survived the First World War but had had their health damaged by it or had been too unfit to be enlisted. Thus those who suffered but survived that war were less healthy than the generation born a few years before them.

Figure 5.15 shows how death rates vary with time of year. An unusually harsh winter or flu epidemic can increase death rates temporarily. Thus aggregate figures covering deaths over several years are used here.

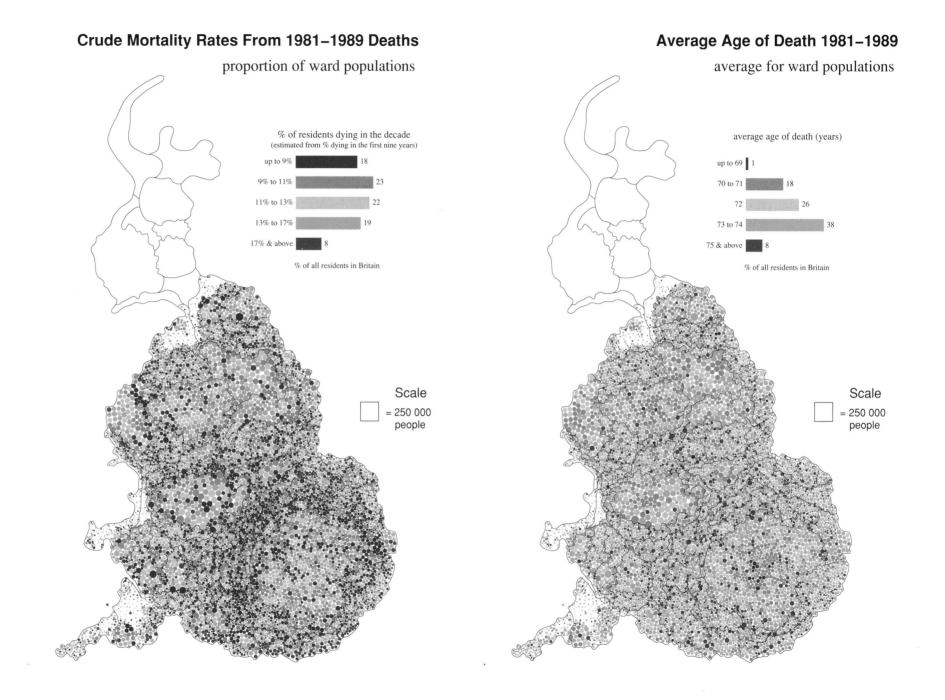

Crude Mortality Rates From 1981–1989 Deaths

proportion of ward populations

% of residents dying in the decade
(estimated from % dying in the first nine years)

up to 9%	18
9% to 11%	23
11% to 13%	22
13% to 17%	19
17% & above	8

% of all residents in Britain

Scale

☐ = 250 000
people

Average Age of Death 1981–1989

average for ward populations

average age of death (years)

up to 69	1
70 to 71	18
72	26
73 to 74	38
75 & above	8

% of all residents in Britain

Scale

☐ = 250 000
people

Standardized Mortality

The usual way in which death rates are expressed is in terms of *standardized mortality ratios* (SMRs). This is the ratio between the number of deaths which occur in an area and the number which could be expected to occur given the age and sex profile of that area and the national rates of mortality for the particular time period. Here the ratio is multiplied by one hundred. Thus, if there were twelve deaths in a ward where six deaths would have been expected (given the ages and sexes of the inhabitants of that ward) then the SMR of that ward would be two hundred. People living there are twice as likely to die as is usual for this country (taking into account the ages and sexes of those people).

The first map opposite shows the distribution of SMRs across all the wards of England and Wales. In the centres of many northern towns, in Wales and in London, one more person in every five dies per year than would be expected. Conversely, in the south outside London and in other affluent areas, one person less in every five dies a year than would be expected. Seventy percent of the population live in areas between these two extremes as the key to the map shows (and 10% of the population live in Scotland for which no figures are reported here). Figure 5.16 uses the chances of an individual dying each year according to their age and sex to illustrate why SMRs for areas need to be calculated; it also shows for which groups mortality rates were rising in the 1980s. The mortality rates were calculated using the final mid-year estimates of the numbers of people in each age group made for 1981 and 1991. The "hour-glass" shape produced reflects the physiology of human beings as well as the tendency of young men to be much more accident prone than young women.

The second map opposite shows how SMRs have changed over the 1980s. Inner cities show up clearly as experiencing the sharpest rises (Phillimore *et al.* 1994). It should be remembered that population profiles from the 1991 census had to be used to calculate the number of deaths which would be expected in the latter half of the 1980s. Because of under-enumeration in the last census the rise in SMRs may be over-emphasized in some urban areas. However, the calculation of the number of expected deaths is most reliant on estimates of the number of old people and these were relatively reliable (see page 10), so the estimates produced here should not be too misleading.

Standardized mortality ratios have fallen dramatically over the last 150 years and the rate for women has fallen faster than that for men. The figure here uses the mortality rates recorded around 1951 to calculate expected rates for every other period so that the different age profiles of different times have no effect on the statistics, thus both lines pass through 100 at this time. Since then women appeared to improve their relative situation even more, although in recent years this improvement has slowed down. The figure also includes a major cause of the rapid fall in mortality over time — the collapse in infant mortality rates which began at the turn of this century.

5.16: Mortality Rates by Sex and Age in England and Wales 1981–1989

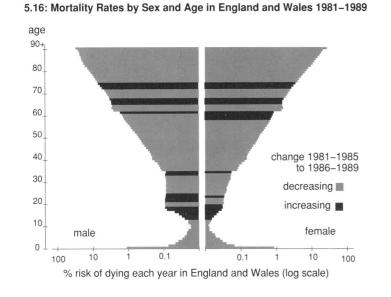

5.17: Mortality Rates by Sex and Age in England and Wales 1841–1990

standardized mortality ratios (SMRs 1950–1952=100)

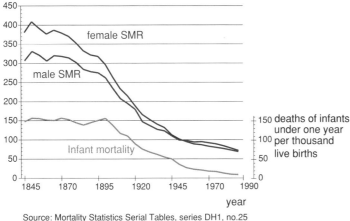

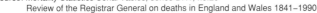

Source: Mortality Statistics Serial Tables, series DH1, no.25
Review of the Registrar General on deaths in England and Wales 1841–1990

Mortality from All Causes Between 1981 and 1989

relative risks for ward populations

standardized mortality ratios (E&W=100)

up to 80		12
80 to 95		27
95 to 105		19
105 to 125		24
125 & above		8

% of all residents in Britain

Scale

□ = 250 000 people

Mortality from All Causes 1981–1985 to 1986–1989

change in risk for ward populations

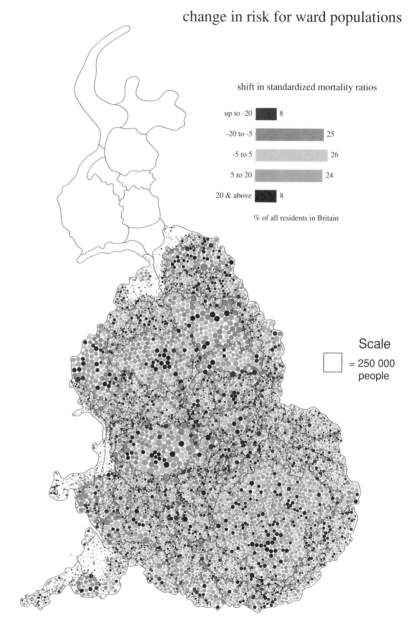

shift in standardized mortality ratios

up to -20		8
-20 to -5		25
-5 to 5		26
5 to 20		24
20 & above		8

% of all residents in Britain

Scale

□ = 250 000 people

5.18: Cause of Death by Age Group and Sex in England and Wales 1981–1989

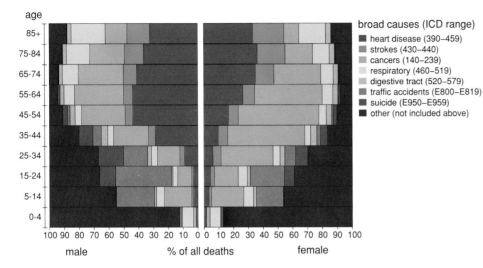

age

broad causes (ICD range)

- ■ heart disease (390–459)
- ▨ strokes (430–440)
- ▨ cancers (140–239)
- ▨ respiratory (460–519)
- ▨ digestive tract (520–579)
- ■ traffic accidents (E800–E819)
- ■ suicide (E950–E959)
- ■ other (not included above)

85+
75-84
65-74
55-64
45-54
35-44
25-34
15-24
5-14
0-4

100 90 80 70 60 50 40 30 20 10 0   0 10 20 30 40 50 60 70 80 90 100

male % of all deaths female

5.19: Cause of Death by District Type in England and Wales 1986–1989

standardized mortality ratio less 100 (England & Wales = 0 for each broad cause)

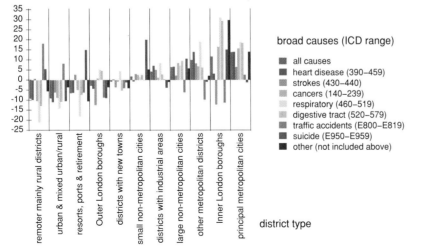

35
30
25
20
15
10
5
0
-5
-10
-15
-20
-25

broad causes (ICD range)

- ▨ all causes
- ■ heart disease (390–459)
- ▨ strokes (430–440)
- ▨ cancers (140–239)
- ▨ respiratory (460–519)
- ▨ digestive tract (520–579)
- ▨ traffic accidents (E800–E819)
- ▨ suicide (E950–E959)
- ■ other (not included above)

remoter mainly rural districts
urban & mixed urban/rural
resorts, ports & retirement
Outer London boroughs
districts with new towns
small non-metropolitan cities
districts with industrial areas
large non-metropolitan cities
other metropolitan districts
Inner London boroughs
principal metropolitan cities

district type

Main Causes of Death

To understand why people in different parts of the country die at different ages it is necessary to consider what people are dying of. Cause of death is also often indicative of life-style and, in aggregate, causes of death are informative about the standards of living of communities. Figure 5.18 shows how eight groups of causes of death account for different proportions of deaths for people by age and sex. Everyday terms have been used to describe the causes, and the precise definitions are indicated by the International Classification of Disease (ICD) numbers in the key to the figure (WHO 1977). Deaths in infancy are both rare and can be due to many obscure causes, whereas well known causes such as heart disease and cancers account for the majority of deaths of older people and thus for the majority of all deaths. There are important differences between the most probable causes of death for men and women, which the figure illustrates.

Because these eight sets of causes of death are each more prevalent in particular age and sex groups it is necessary to use standardized mortality ratios in mapping these causes if the maps are not merely to reflect the age and sex structure of the residents of each place. The nine maps opposite show which districts have particularly low and high rates of mortality from each group of causes and for all causes. The map of all causes is dominated by the north/south division of the country (to which central London is the main exception). Only five districts have standardized mortality ratios above 125 for this time period based on the 1991 census age–sex profiles, these are: Castle Morpeth, Manchester, Blackburn, Liverpool and Merthyr Tydfil. Similarly, only six districts had SMRs below 80: the City of London, East Dorset (which was Wimborne), Christchurch, Wealdon, Tewkesbury and the Vale of the White Horse. The differences between areas are much more dramatic for groups of causes of death partly because the numbers of deaths involved are less and so the sensitivity of the ratio statistic is increased.

In summary, the maps show how mortality from heart diseases, strokes, cancers and respiratory diseases is higher in the north and in cities, each set of causes accounting for the majority of the national pattern in different ways. Mortality from digestive diseases is highest in a band running along the Thames in London, whilst traffic accidents are unusually common in small rural districts in the Home Counties. Suicide rates are high in central London and around the coast, while other causes account for a high number of deaths in Inner London and Birmingham. Figure 5.19 provides the same information but using the eleven fold typology of districts to illustrate which causes of death are most prevalent in which types of place after having standardized for age and sex. The district types are ordered from those with the lowest overall rates of mortality to those with the highest. Within this general pattern particular causes can be seen to be over- and under-represented in particular types of places. Fewer strokes or traffic accidents occur in Inner London, for instance, than would be expected given the age and sex of its residents.

Causes of Mortality 1986–1989

relative risks for district populations

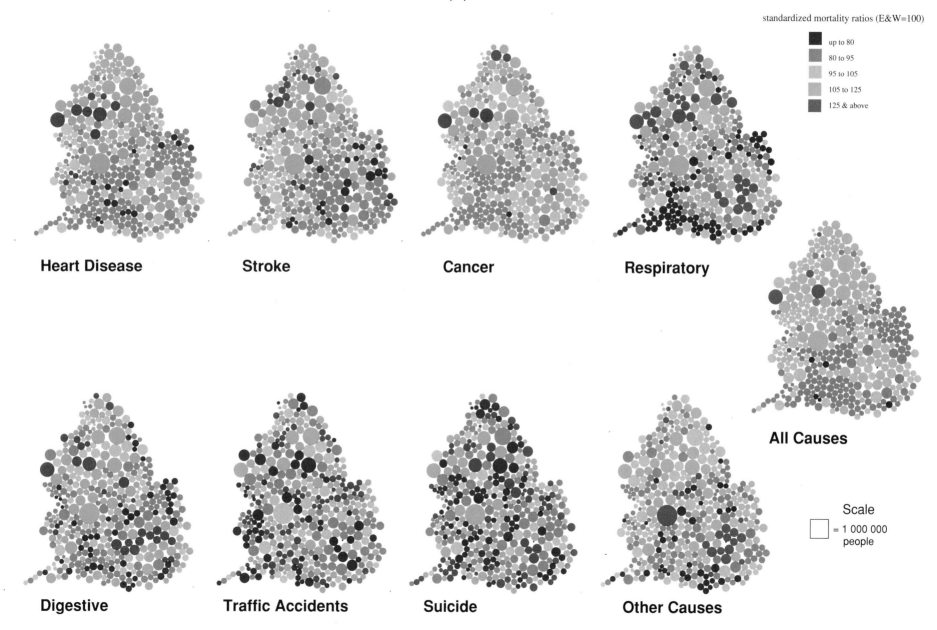

standardized mortality ratios (E&W=100)

- up to 80
- 80 to 95
- 95 to 105
- 105 to 125
- 125 & above

Heart Disease

Stroke

Cancer

Respiratory

All Causes

Digestive

Traffic Accidents

Suicide

Other Causes

Scale

☐ = 1 000 000 people

5.20: Change in Cause of Death by District Type in England and Wales 1981–1985 to 1986–1989

change in standardized mortality ratio (England & Wales = 0 for each broad cause)

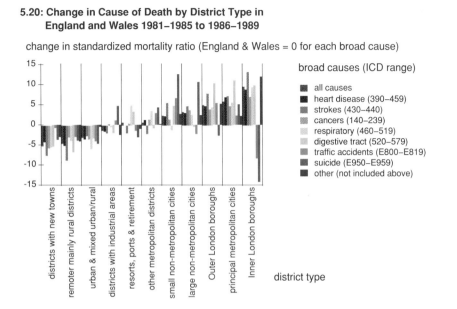

broad causes (ICD range)

- all causes
- heart disease (390–459)
- strokes (430–440)
- cancers (140–239)
- respiratory (460–519)
- digestive tract (520–579)
- traffic accidents (E800–E819)
- suicide (E950–E959)
- other (not included above)

district type

5.21: Change in Chance of Dying by Cause of Death in England and Wales 1851–1990

chance of an individual dying per year from each cause (log scale)

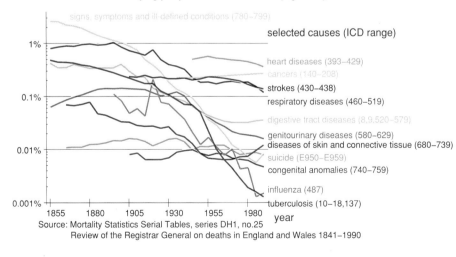

selected causes (ICD range)

signs, symptoms and ill-defined conditions (780–799)

heart diseases (393–429)
cancers (140–208)
strokes (430–438)
respiratory diseases (460–519)
digestive tract diseases (8,9,520–579)
genitourinary diseases (580–629)
diseases of skin and connective tissue (680–739)
suicide (E950–E959)
congenital anomalies (740–759)
influenza (487)
tuberculosis (10–18,137)

year

Source: Mortality Statistics Serial Tables, series DH1, no.25
Review of the Registrar General on deaths in England and Wales 1841–1990

Changing Causes of Death

The eight broad groups of cause of death selected and mapped at the district level on the previous page are used here to show the patterns of change over the last decade. Standardized mortality ratios are rising in some places and falling in others. Each of the nine maps opposite shows the difference between the SMR calculated for deaths in the 1986 to 1989 period (based on the 1991 census age and sex profiles) and for deaths in the 1981 to 1985 period (which use the 1981 census denominators). The usual caveats concerning the reliability of information from the 1991 census should be born in mind.

For all causes of death the most obvious increase has been in London, but many northern cities and Bristol have seen rises of between 5 and 20 percentage points, as have a string of southern coastal towns. Rates have fallen by a similar amount in the midlands, coastal Wales and in other rural areas. Changes in heart diseases and cancers have been the main cause of this trend. Strokes have followed a similar pattern although they have risen more sharply in central London (from a low base) and fallen sharply in mid and north Wales (from a high base). Respiratory diseases have seen a more complex pattern of change with rates rising in London and around Manchester quite sharply. The high rates of death through digestive tract diseases in London were mostly the products of a rise in the 1980s which also saw falls in East Anglia and around the principal cities. Traffic accidents, suicides and other less common causes of death do not show any simple geographical trend over this period.

Figure 5.20 shows district aggregate changes in the causes of death in Britain over the 1980s. Again the districts are ordered according to the overall trend, from largest improvement, worsening to the biggest relative deterioration, so that changes in rates which are particularly unusual for particular places stand out. Suicides can be seen to have increased out of line in industrial areas and non-metropolitan cities, and to have decreased dramatically in Inner London, where traffic accidents also fell significantly. Falls in strokes can be seen to be most outstanding in new towns and districts which are mainly rural. Strokes caused increasing numbers of deaths in London.

These recent changes are put in context by Figure 5.21, which shows how an individual's chances of dying each year from each of twelve causes of death have changed since 1855. Some groups of causes were not specified until later and so are not shown for the earlier periods, and a log scale has to be used because of the huge variation in chances over time and between causes. The figure reflects changes in the incidence and effective treatment of different diseases due to public health, medical advances and social change. The falls of influenza and tuberculosis from being major killers in the 1920s to rare causes of death today are striking. So too is the rise of cancer, digestive diseases and diseases of the skin in more recent years. Only heart disease kills more people than cancer, but the gap between these two major groups of causes is narrowing.

Causes of Mortality 1981–1985 to 1986–1989

change in risk for district populations

change in standardized mortality ratios (E&W=0)

up to -20
-20 to -5
-5 to 5
5 to 20
20 & above

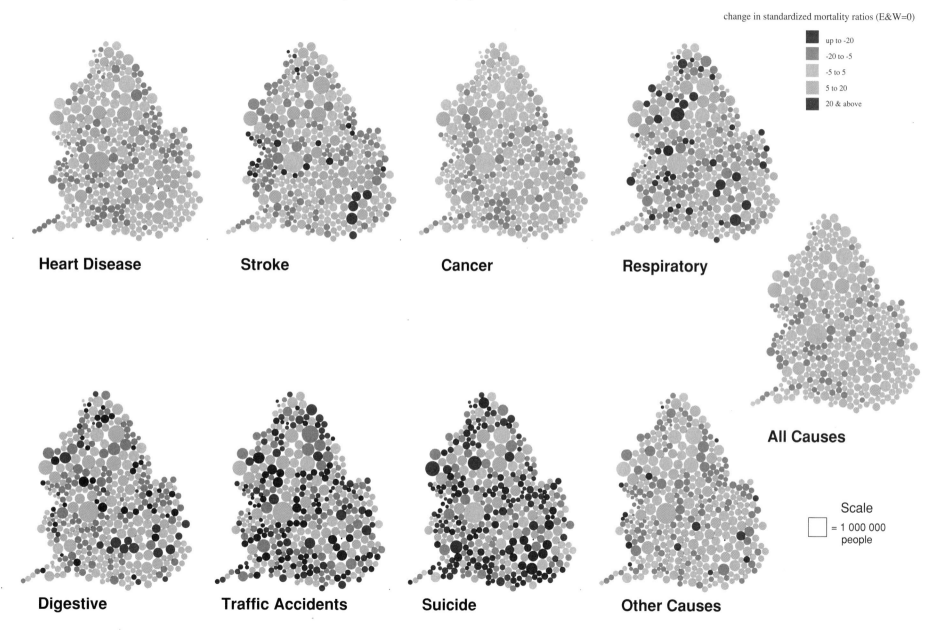

Heart Disease

Stroke

Cancer

Respiratory

All Causes

Digestive

Traffic Accidents

Suicide

Other Causes

Scale

= 1 000 000 people

5.22: Top Fifty Individual Causes of Death in England and Wales, 1981–1989

Rank	ICD Code	Cause of Death Description	Annual Rate per Million People	Proportion Female	Mean Age at Death	Change in Mean Age in Months*
–	All	all causes of death	11 521	50%	73	10
1	410	heart attacks (acute myocardial infarction)	2040	43%	73	15
2	414	other forms of chronic ischaemic heart disease	1042	46%	75	6
3	162	lung cancer (including trachea and bronchus)	698	28%	70	13
4	485	bronchopneumonia (organism unspecified)	647	63%	83	30
5	174	breast cancer (women)	265	100%	67	15
6	434	thrombotic stroke (occlusion of cerebral arteries)	253	63%	80	6
7	153	cancer of the colon	217	56%	73	10
8	491	chronic bronchitis	216	29%	76	12
9	151	stomach cancer	197	40%	72	11
10	441	aneurism of the aortic artery	147	36%	75	10
11	290	dementia (senile organic psychotic conditions)	146	69%	83	12
12	250	diabetes (mellitus)	130	57%	75	21
13	431	haemorrhage stroke (intracerebral haemorrhage)	130	60%	74	-2
14	185	cancer of the prostrate	129	0%	76	8
15	440	hardening of the arteries (atherosclerosis)	121	67%	84	8
16	157	cancer of the pancreas	117	50%	71	10
17	154	cancer of the rectum	117	45%	72	8
18	188	cancer of the bladder	91	31%	74	13
19	150	cancer of the oesophagus	89	41%	71	8
20	183	cancer of the of the ovaries	75	100%	66	11
21	332	Parkinson's disease	65	48%	79	16
22	402	heart disease from high blood pressure (hypertensive)	65	56%	75	7
23	430	brain haemorrhage (subarachnoid haemorrhage)	60	66%	61	5
24	571	chronic liver disease (including cirrhosis of the liver)	49	47%	61	-1
25	481	pneumonia (due to pneumoccus bacteria)	47	50%	76	11
26	191	brain tumour (malignant neoplasm of the brain)	46	43%	57	12
27	585	chronic kidney failure	43	53%	78	6
28	532	duodenal ulcer	43	49%	76	15
29	189	cancer of the kidney	42	38%	67	15
30	415	right-side heart failure (acute pulmonary heart disease)	41	60%	75	18
31	205	leukaemia (myeloid type)	38	49%	64	22
32	180	cancer of the cervix	38	100%	61	-7
33	492	emphysema of the lungs	38	25%	73	12
34	493	asthma	36	58%	62	28
35	E888	accidental fall (unspecified location and injury)	35	69%	80	-12
36	E812	motor vehicle collision (vehicle occupant)	34	26%	37	11
37	E814	motor vehicle collision (pedestrian)	32	41%	52	15
38	394	diseases of mitral heart valve	32	76%	71	24
39	531	stomach ulcer	32	58%	76	11
40	797	old age (senility without mention of psychosis)	31	82%	90	8
41	798	sudden death of unknown cause	29	38%	6	-16
42	486	pneumonia (organism not stated)	27	53%	74	37
43	562	diverticular disease of the bowel	27	75%	78	13
44	557	ischaemia of the bowel	27	61%	76	12
45	714	rheumatoid arthritis	27	79%	75	22
46	733	bone disease (osteochondropathies)	26	80%	84	4
47	342	stroke, cause not stated (hemiplegia)	25	59%	80	12
48	E953	suicide by hanging or suffocation	24	25%	51	-30
49	204	leukaemia (lymphoid type)	24	43%	65	33
50	155	cancer of the liver	23	41%	68	12
		all other causes of death not included above	3548	55%	71	18

Note: change is the increase, in months, in the average age of death from each cause between 1981–1985 and 1986–1989.

Common Fatal Diseases

All deaths in this country are classified using the International Classification of Diseases (ICD) codes. Figure 5.22 shows the fifty most common codes used. This is not the same as the fifty most common fatal diseases. Some diseases are subdivided into several codes while some codes include more than one disease. Some codes are less precise definitions of conditions often allocated to other codes. Because of factors such as these, 30% of all deaths are assigned to categories not in the most common fifty — not because many people are dying from rare diseases, but often because their deaths are being assigned to less commonly used categories. For instance "old age" may not be a popular cause of death to record with relatives (the deaths of women are four times more likely than those of men to be assigned to this category — see Figure 5.22). As diagnostic skills change, so too do death rates. The falling mean age of people suffering "sudden death of unknown cause" is due to better diagnosis of these deaths for adults rather than an increase in the incidence of cot deaths. Other illnesses with a falling mean age of death are haemorrhagic stroke, liver disease, cancer of the cervix, accidental falls and suicides by hanging, but only liver disease saw an increase in annual rates of death. The mean age of people dying from suicide by hanging in the 1980s fell by 30 months in effectively five years due mainly to an increase in young men killing themselves in this way.

The incidence of over twenty of the fifty categories shown in Figure 5.22 is known to be increased by smoking. Importantly the most common three causes of death — heart attacks, other heart diseases and lung cancer — which together account for a third of all deaths, have been clearly shown to be hastened by smoking. Changing smoking habits is the single public health measure which, it is thought, would have the greatest impact on mortality rates. Standardized mortality ratios for deaths attributable to all heart diseases (ICD 390 to 459) and cancers (ICD 140 to 239) have been mapped at the ward level opposite. The north/south pattern in heart disease is particularly clear, even at this spatial resolution. Only a very small minority of wards in the north have SMRs for heart disease below the national average whilst very few wards in the south of the country have above average rates for mortality attributed to heart diseases.

The distribution of deaths by cancers shows a different pattern in which northern towns and London dominate. Liverpool, central Manchester, Leeds and the banks of the Tyne, the Tees and the Thames contain most of the wards in which people are 25% more likely to die of cancer, and hence to die younger, than average. Rates of deaths from cancers are low in rural areas, particularly in the south of England. It is not possible to know (from the information which has been used here) whether people are likely to move to or remain in these areas when they get cancer, or whether people are more likely to get cancer if they live in these areas. All that can be discerned from death certificates is that if you die of cancer, these are the places in which you are more likely to last live.

Mortality from Heart Diseases Between 1981 and 1989

relative risks for ward populations

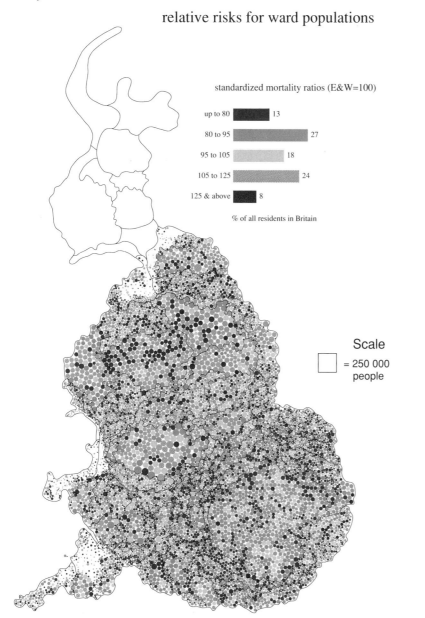

standardized mortality ratios (E&W=100)

up to 80	13
80 to 95	27
95 to 105	18
105 to 125	24
125 & above	8

% of all residents in Britain

Scale

☐ = 250 000 people

Mortality from Cancers Between 1981 and 1989

relative risks for ward populations

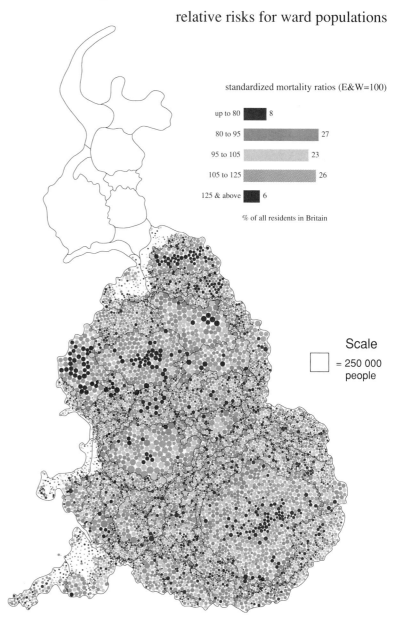

standardized mortality ratios (E&W=100)

up to 80	8
80 to 95	27
95 to 105	23
105 to 125	26
125 & above	6

% of all residents in Britain

Scale

☐ = 250 000 people

5.23: Mortality from Heart Diseases by Age and Sex in England and Wales 1981–1989

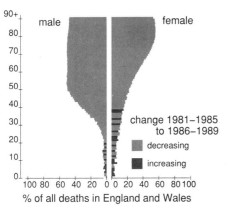

age

change 1981–1985 to 1986–1989
decreasing
increasing

% of all deaths in England and Wales

5.24: Mortality from Cancers by Age and Sex in England and Wales 1981–1989

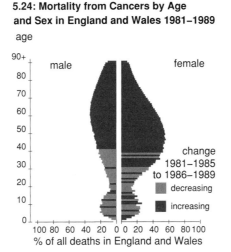

age

change 1981–1985 to 1986–1989
decreasing
increasing

% of all deaths in England and Wales

5.25: Mortality from Traffic Accidents by Age and Sex in England and Wales 1981–1989

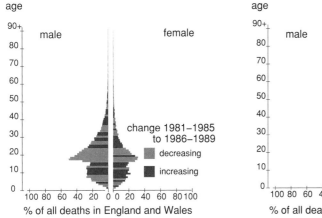

age

change 1981–1985 to 1986–1989
decreasing
increasing

% of all deaths in England and Wales

5.26: Mortality from Suicide by Age and Sex in England and Wales 1981–1989

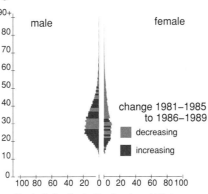

age

change 1981–1985 to 1986–1989
decreasing
increasing

% of all deaths in England and Wales

Avoidable Deaths

There are other forms of death which are even more obviously avoidable than smoking related diseases and which can be seen to be relatively important because of the young ages at which most people die from them. The two which have been selected here are deaths from traffic accidents (ICD E800 to E819) and suicides (ICD E950 to E959). The two most common individual causes of death from these groups of causes can be seen, from Figure 5.22, to lead to death at an average age of 51 for suicides by hanging and 37 for motor vehicle collisions with other vehicles. Among the top fifty causes shown in that figure, only sudden deaths of unknown cause (which are mainly cot deaths) account for people dying at average ages lower than these (see Figure 5.28). Most people who die of heart diseases or cancers still live to be 70.

The age and sex profiles of the causes of death which have been mapped at the ward level on this page and the last are shown in Figures 5.23 to 5.26. Heart disease can be seen to kill men earlier than women but appears to be decreasing for most age groups. Cancers, on the other hand, affect more women earlier in life than men and are increasing as a cause of death for most age and sex groups. Traffic accidents affect far fewer people but tend to do so at a much younger age and are much more likely to occur to men than to women. The peak year of death for men from traffic accidents is seventeen, the earliest year in which a provisional driving licence can be granted. Rates of death from traffic accidents are declining for men aged between 16 and 23 and rising for boys aged between 9 and 15. A similar picture is shown for women. Suicide, conversely, is almost unheard of for people aged below 15, but is increasing for men aged between 16 and 26 and for women aged between 18 and 22. Suicide is also an increasingly important cause of death amongst older men. Of all age and sex groups, 24 year old men are the most likely to die from suicide.

The first map opposite shows the geography of deaths attributable to traffic accidents. It is important to bear in mind that this map is based on quite low numbers of deaths in particular wards, so only where a group of wards exhibits the same pattern is there likely to be a reliable trend. However, this map does show a more precise geography to the urban/rural divide described earlier. It also shows that in certain parts of some major cities mortality rates are particularly high from traffic accidents while in some rural areas they are low. Note that the keys use a wider scale than has been used before.

The second map is of the geography of suicide. A large cluster of wards in Inner London, inner Manchester, in the centres of Leicester and Birmingham and strung along the coast show much higher rates than are normal, while in areas like South Yorkshire and the North East suicide rates tend to be unusually low. It is impossible to speculate on the causes of this pattern given only cross-sectional data, but it can be shown that if you take your own life you are more likely to do so when living in certain places.

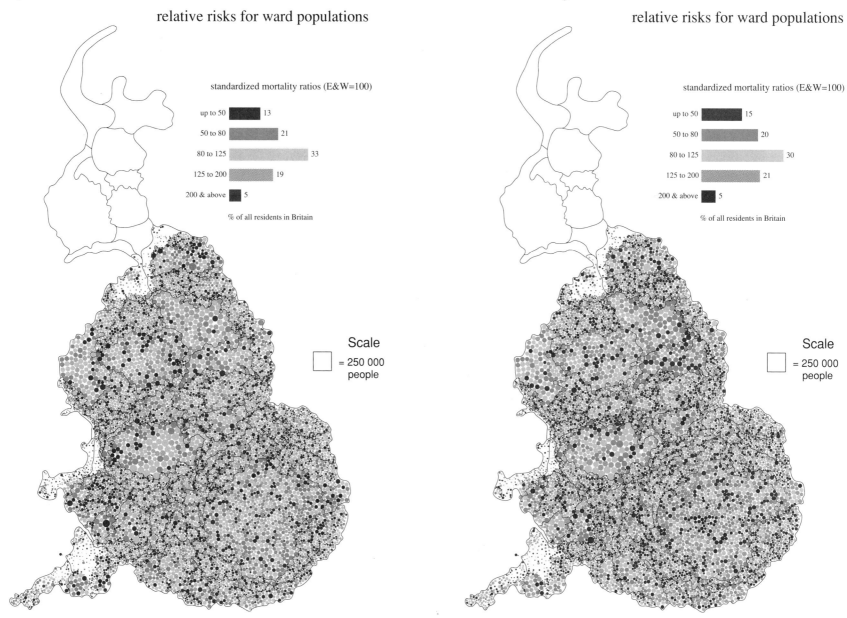

Mortality from Traffic Accidents Between 1981 and 1989

relative risks for ward populations

standardized mortality ratios (E&W=100)

up to 50	13
50 to 80	21
80 to 125	33
125 to 200	19
200 & above	5

% of all residents in Britain

Scale
= 250 000
people

Mortality from Suicide Between 1981 and 1989

relative risks for ward populations

standardized mortality ratios (E&W=100)

up to 50	15
50 to 80	20
80 to 125	30
125 to 200	21
200 & above	5

% of all residents in Britain

Scale
= 250 000
people

Premature Deaths

Everyone will die sometime and so the study of mortality from many common causes concentrates mostly on the deaths of the elderly. Most of these people, if their deaths had been prevented or preventable, would have died of something else within a few years, or may only be dying of their recorded causes because of such intervention. From the point of view of health policy, mortality of people below a certain age can provide a clearer picture of where particular causes are resulting in many *premature* deaths.

Figure 5.27 shows what proportions of deaths in people aged below 65 are attributable to eighteen sets of causes. This age limit is an arbitrary one and has been used here because it is the official retirement age for men and also because it is an age to which people can reasonably expect to live regardless of their sex, location or occupation. The eighteen groups of causes have been chosen to include some of the most topical as well as some of the most common causes. Despite this, a third of all people who died aged below 65 during the 1980s died of "other" causes. A quarter died of heart attacks and a quarter died from one of the six types of cancers shown. Strokes accounted for as many deaths as road traffic accidents and suicides combined. Homicide is much less common than might be assumed from watching the news or reading British newspapers. Between 1981 and 1989 a person aged under 65 was seventeen times more likely to kill themselves than to be killed maliciously.

The eighteen maps drawn opposite show the geographical distributions of most of these causes for deaths to people aged under 65. The distributions of stomach cancer, lung cancer, heart attacks and strokes have a similar national pattern. The other cancers exhibit less uniform patterns, perhaps because they are less closely associated with smoking, while the less common forms of death all have their own geographies. Liver disease and accidental falls are particularly acute in London and other major cities, traffic accidents clearly cluster in rural areas. Interestingly, drowning is much more likely to happen to people living in the centre of the country while murders are largely confined to the capital. Districts with no cases of death from a cause are shaded white.

Some of the apparently clearest patterning is seen for the set of causes labelled as "cot deaths", with high rates in London and around the coast and very low rates in some other areas. This category in fact includes all unexplained sudden deaths, 93% of which occur to children aged under two (the stricter definition used here-on). However, the maps opposite are standardized using only fourteen age and sex groups of the population. Because of how narrow the age band of the population at risk from cot death is, more accurate SMRs for the stricter definition of cot deaths are shown in Figure 5.28 for two periods using just the population aged under 2 as the denominator. The basic pattern remains, but it appears to be more volatile than the simple map would suggest. Different areas can show very different mortality ratios at different times.

5.27: Selected Causes of Death of People Aged Under 65 in England and Wales 1981–1989

% of deaths of people aged under 65 attributable to each cause

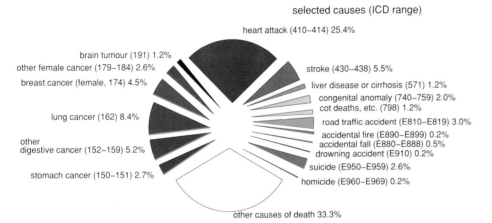

selected causes (ICD range)

heart attack (410–414) 25.4%

brain tumour (191) 1.2%
other female cancer (179–184) 2.6%
breast cancer (female, 174) 4.5%

stroke (430–438) 5.5%
liver disease or cirrhosis (571) 1.2%
congenital anomaly (740–759) 2.0%
cot deaths, etc. (798) 1.2%

lung cancer (162) 8.4%

road traffic accident (E810–E819) 3.0%
accidental fire (E890–E899) 0.2%
accidental fall (E880–E888) 0.5%
drowning accident (E910) 0.2%

other
digestive cancer (152–159) 5.2%

stomach cancer (150–151) 2.7%

suicide (E950–E959) 2.6%

homicide (E960–E969) 0.2%

other causes of death 33.3%

5.28: Cot Deaths in England and Wales 1981–1985 and 1986–1989

standardized mortality ratios for children aged under two years
who died suddenly of unkown cause

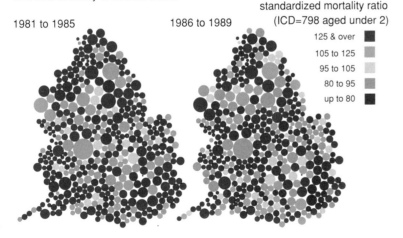

1981 to 1985   1986 to 1989

standardized mortality ratio
(ICD=798 aged under 2)

125 & over
105 to 125
95 to 105
80 to 95
up to 80

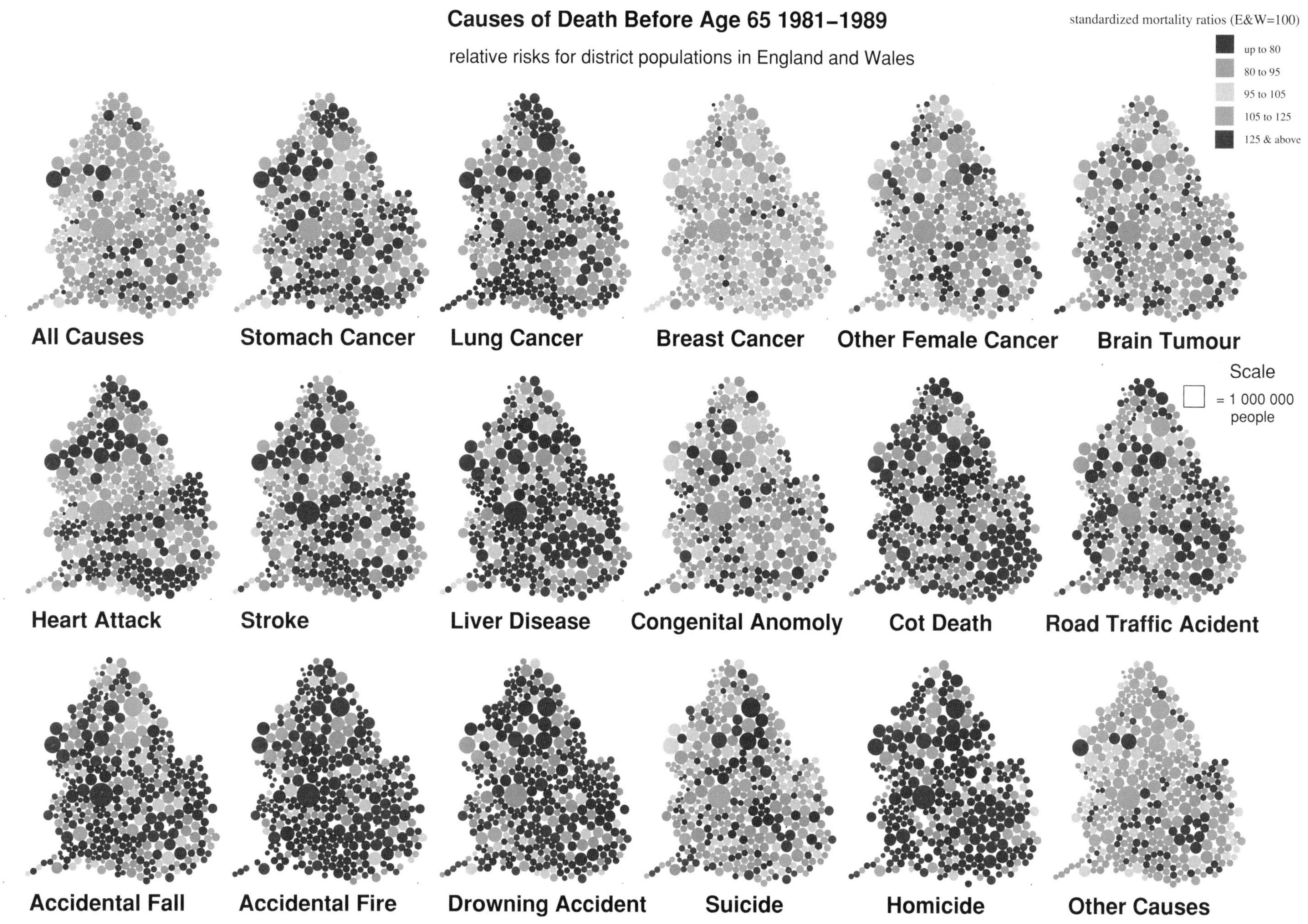

Causes of Death Before Age 65 1981–1989

relative risks for district populations in England and Wales

standardized mortality ratios (E&W=100)

- up to 80
- 80 to 95
- 95 to 105
- 105 to 125
- 125 & above

All Causes

Stomach Cancer

Lung Cancer

Breast Cancer

Other Female Cancer

Brain Tumour

Scale

☐ = 1 000 000 people

Heart Attack

Stroke

Liver Disease

Congenital Anomoly

Cot Death

Road Traffic Acident

Accidental Fall

Accidental Fire

Drowning Accident

Suicide

Homicide

Other Causes

5.29: Years of Life lost and Chance of Life Lost by Cause of Death and Sex in England and Wales 1991

% contribution of each cause of death to each measure of mortality

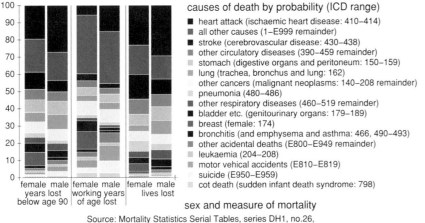

causes of death by probability (ICD range)

- heart attack (ischaemic heart disease: 410–414)
- all other causes (1–E999 remainder)
- stroke (cerebrovascular disease: 430–438)
- other circulatory diseases (390–459 remainder)
- stomach (digestive organs and peritoneum: 150–159)
- lung (trachea, bronchus and lung: 162)
- other cancers (malignant neoplasms: 140–208 remainder)
- pneumonia (480–486)
- other respiratory diseases (460–519 remainder)
- bladder etc. (genitourinary organs: 179–189)
- breast (female: 174)
- bronchitis (and emphysema and asthma: 466, 490–493)
- other acidental deaths (E800–E949 remainder)
- leukaemia (204–208)
- motor vehical accidents (E810–E819)
- suicide (E950–E959)
- cot death (sudden infant death syndrome: 798)

sex and measure of mortality

Source: Mortality Statistics Serial Tables, series DH1, no.26,
Review of the Registrar General on deaths in England and Wales 1991

5.30: Childhood Illness and Years of Life Lost by 1991 Shaded by Expectancy

average years of working life lost in ward 1981–1989

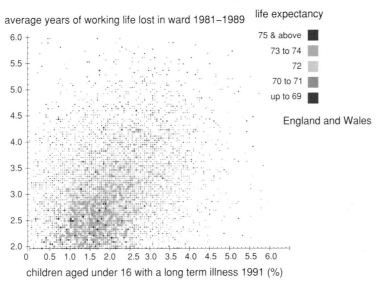

life expectancy

75 & above
73 to 74
72
70 to 71
up to 69

England and Wales

children aged under 16 with a long term illness 1991 (%)

Years of Life Lost

Examining only deaths below a certain age is quite a crude method of assessing the premature deaths in an area. A more sophisticated measure is to weight each death by the number of years of life for which that person could have been expected to have lived or, more commonly, for which the government is most concerned that they live. By these definitions individual cot deaths are more important than individual deaths from lung cancers because more potential years of life are lost. Again, however, an arbitrary decision needs to be made — this time concerning how many years of life people might expect to have. Here two measures used in official publications have been adopted: the number of years lost below age 90 and the number of working years of life lost.

Figure 5.29 illustrates how important the choice of definition of years lost is for various causes of death. On the right the relative importance of different causes of death is shown when each death is weighted equally. By this measure, motor vehicle accidents were only responsible for 0.9% of male and female deaths in England and Wales between 1981 and 1989. When deaths are weighted by the years up to age 90 which are lost by them, as is shown on the left of the figure, motor vehicle accidents account for 3.1% of male mortality and 1.4% of female mortality. Finally, when only years of life lost between ages 15 and 65 are considered, as in the central two bars of the figure, traffic accidents cause 9.0% of male mortality and 4.5% of female mortality. How important different causes of deaths are depends on how life is valued at different ages.

The two maps drawn opposite show the geographical distributions of years of life lost by these two measures. Both produce more stark patterns than do measures of standardized mortality (see page 150). The key to the maps is in terms of the average number of years lost by mortality to each resident in each ward. In England and Wales nationally, in 1991, the chance of a man dying was 1.1%; men on average lost 18.9 years of life to age 90 and 2.9 years of life to age 65. The comparable figures for women were 1.1%, 13.1 years and 1.7 years, respectively. However, as the maps show, there is a great deal of variation about these figures; more than the usual standardized measure of mortality shows. Untimely deaths were most common in central cities in the 1980s.

Years of life lost is also a useful measure of mortality to compare with measures such as long term illness among children. Figure 5.30 does this and shows how a positive relationship exists at the ward level between areas where a high proportion of children are ill and where people tend to die young. The figure also shows how these two measures are related to life expectancy at the ward level. The relationships are not simple, but a general pattern does appear to prevail. The groups of wards where (13% live and) each person, on average, loses at least four years of working life due to early mortality are the areas where the population as a whole can often not expect to live to age 70 and where a higher proportion of children will also be chronically ill.

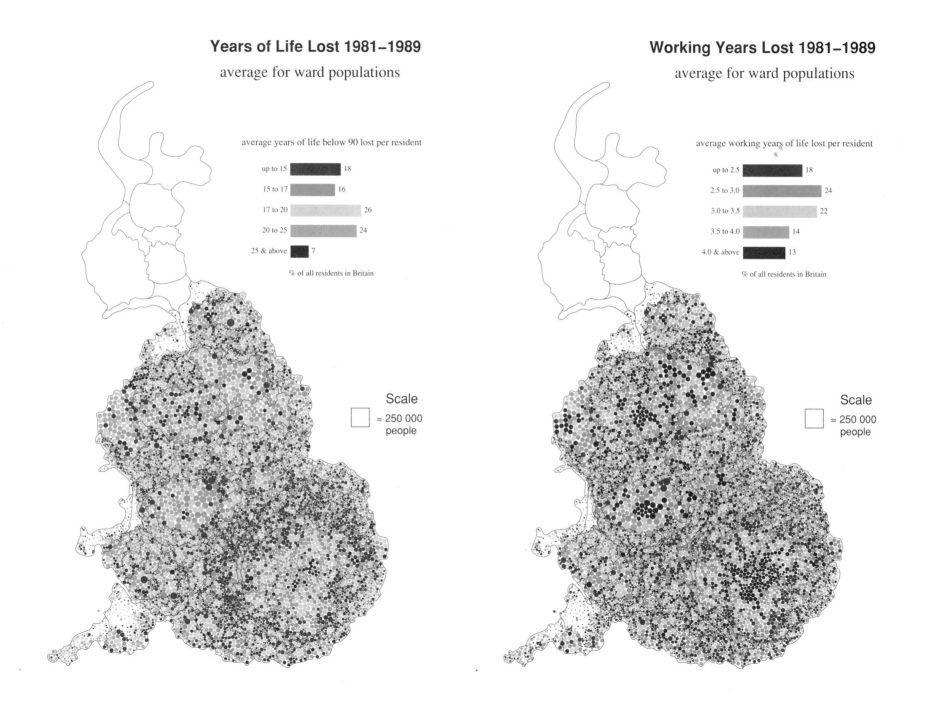

Years of Life Lost 1981–1989

average for ward populations

average years of life below 90 lost per resident

up to 15	18
15 to 17	16
17 to 20	26
20 to 25	24
25 & above	7

% of all residents in Britain

Scale

☐ = 250 000 people

Working Years Lost 1981–1989

average for ward populations

average working years of life lost per resident

up to 2.5	18
2.5 to 3.0	24
3.0 to 3.5	22
3.5 to 4.0	14
4.0 & above	13

% of all residents in Britain

Scale

☐ = 250 000 people

5.31: Standardized Mortality Ratios by Population in England and Wales 1939–1989

population living in old local authority areas (%, smoothed by SMR bands)

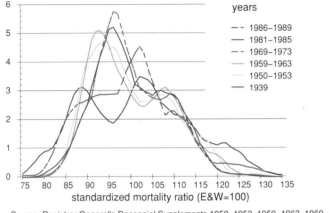

years

- -- 1986–1989
- —— 1981–1985
- -- 1969–1973
- ——— 1959–1963
- ——— 1950–1953
- —— 1939

Source: Registrar General's Decennial Supplements 1950–1953, 1959–1963, 1969–1973 and the Registrar General's Statistical Review 1939

5.32: Top 22 Highest Standardized Mortality Ratios by Old Local Authority Areas 1939–1989

County Borough	SMR rank for the period of all County Boroughs and Amalgamated Areas in England and Wales (n=234)					
	1986 to 1989	1981 to 1985	1969 to 1973	1959 to 1963	1950 to 1953	1939
Salford	1	2	2	1	4	1
Oldham	2	5	4	9	1	2
Blackburn	3	9	5	4	21	17
Gateshead	4	13	19	21	12	6
Manchester	5	15	15	8	7	15
St. Helens	6	4	8	18	33	39
Liverpool	7	27	16	14	8	5
Warrington	8	17	11	16	37	63
Merthyr Tydfil	9	10	14	7	2	12
Halifax	10	18	10	12	19	19
Burnley	11	3	6	2	6	9
Wigan	16	22	9	20	3	11
Stoke-on-Trent	20	6	17	13	9	14
Wakefield	22	1	1	19	98	45
Bootle	23	19	7	11	23	8
Bolton	24	38	41	29	10	7
Sunderland	26	28	26	73	29	4
Middlesbrough	35	21	23	10	11	3
Dewsbury	37	7	3	3	14	57
Rochdale	38	31	18	6	5	30
Bury	71	43	13	5	32	10
Cardiganshire (Urban Area)	95	8	65	64	54	68

ranks for years in which areas had one of the ten highest standardized mortality rates are shown in red

Mortality Over Time

It is important to remember in concluding this chapter that mortality rates and the severity of illness for most of the population today are much lower than they were just a few decades ago, while the levels of basic household amenities associated with good health and of health services have increased immensely. Figures 5.13 and 5.17 made some of these points. Despite this, what is often important to policy and politics is not whether the general measures have improved but whether the differences between areas have widened or narrowed: how equitable is the country in terms of good health?

Mortality measures are often the only way in which standards of health can be consistently compared across many areas over time because other records of ill health made in the past are not reliably comparable. One problem with comparing area mortality rates over long periods of time is that different collating areas were often used in the past. It is possible, however, to calculate current SMRs for former administrative areas and this has been done to make the comparison shown on the two maps drawn opposite, which contrast SMRs for the two four-year periods 1986–1989 and 1950–1953 across 234 aggregates of old local authority areas. Conventional maps rather than cartograms have been drawn as these areas may be unfamiliar to the reader. It is thus necessary to bear in mind the visual bias in these depictions (also note that London boroughs are not differentiated on these maps or in Figure 5.32).

The basic spatial pattern to mortality in England and Wales has remained relatively unaltered over at least the last forty years. The north (particularly northern cities) and Wales have had over-average rates of mortality and the south (excluding some urban areas and ignoring some rural northern areas such as North Yorkshire) has had under-average rates of mortality. In the 1950s, however, none of these areas exhibited SMRs of over 125, whereas, by 1989, 3% of the population were living in areas where they were 25% more likely to die each year than the "average" person in the country.

Figure 5.31 shows how this situation has evolved since 1939 when the geographical pattern of mortality was highly polarized, as can be seen from the bimodal structure of the the population distribution by SMR in that year. By 1953 the distribution had become more equal and, although it was still slightly bimodal, nobody lived in an area with an SMR above 125. This remained the case for the early periods of the next three decades, with mortality rates becoming less and less polarized at each period. Then, in the latest period, the distribution was seen to begin to revert back towards that seen at the end of the 1930s. The geographical similarities are even stronger, as Figure 5.32 demonstrates. The two former local authority areas with the highest SMRs in 1939 had the highest two ratios in 1989. It must be noted that the latest figures are susceptible to errors from the latest census, although these do not significantly alter the result: It does appear that where you live is becoming more critical in determining when you are most likely to die.

Mortality from All Causes Between 1950 and 1953

relative risks for old local authority populations

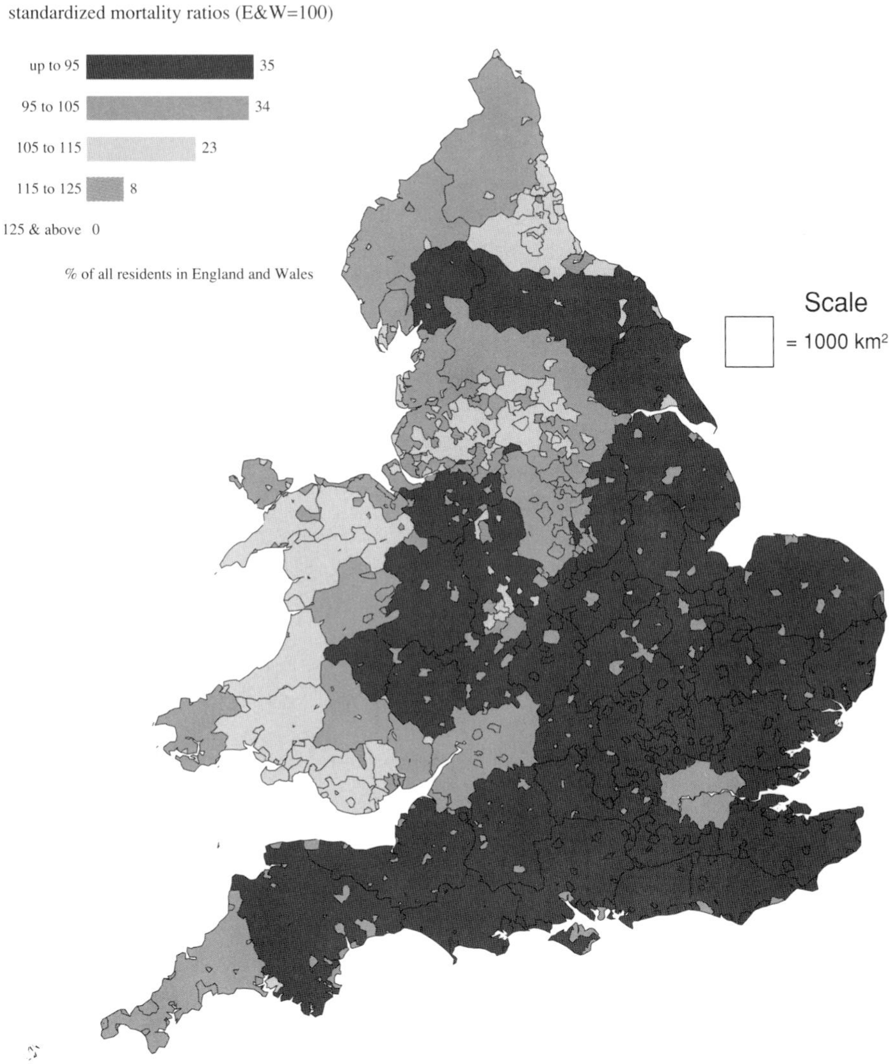

standardized mortality ratios (E&W=100)

	%
up to 95	35
95 to 105	34
105 to 115	23
115 to 125	8
125 & above	0

% of all residents in England and Wales

Scale

☐ = 1000 km²

Mortality from All Causes Between 1986 and 1989

relative risks for old local authority populations

standardized mortality ratios (E&W=100)

	%
up to 95	33
95 to 105	37
105 to 115	22
115 to 125	4
125 & above	3

% of all residents in England and Wales

Scale

☐ = 1000 km²

Conclusion: Sickness and Health

Sick and Ill

Having good health is often considered more important than having a good job or a good home, although all three may, to an extent, be related to each other, as this chapter has indicated. Of course, by far the most important correlate of good health is age, rather than employment or housing status. Self-reported rates of illness are highest amongst the most elderly (Figure 5.1) who have been growing in numbers rapidly (Figure 2.6), and growing most quickly in large northern cities (Figure 2.15). However, the map of illness rates (page 137) is still a poor reflection of the distribution of the elderly (page 39) and so other associations have to be found if illness is to be put in the general context of the social geography of Britain. If workforce sickness rates from previous censuses are compared with the self-reported illness rates which are now available, the patterns look remarkably similar (page 139). Levels of permanent sickness have risen most strongly in the northern regions and in Wales over the last decade (Figure 5.4). It is difficult to distinguish geographically this rise from that seen for early retirement over the same period (page 95). Both of these changes are due to increasing rates of illness in certain areas (see below) as well as to incentives not to register for unemployment benefit (page 98). Perhaps the strongest evidence that levels of illness are strongly correlated with the social geography of an area (and with levels of affluence in particular) is given by plotting the distribution of illness amongst children, which was monitored nationally for the first time in 1991 (page 141). If this map is compared even to a simple social distribution, such as the unemployment rate for adults in 1991 (page 89), the similarity is remarkable. Where adults are least likely to find work, children are most likely to be ill. However, it should not be forgotten that the vast majority of people suffering from illness are pensioners, and that the majority of ill residents aged 85 and over live on their own (Figure 5.6). How the ill are treated *by* our society is as important a question as is asking how many people are "unnecessarily" ill *in* our society.

Health and the Nation: Colour Print F

Because the census provides counts by age and sex of the number of people found to be suffering from a "limiting long term illness" in each ward it is possible to calculate a standardized illness ratio for each area which shows how the proportion of people found to be ill in that place compares with the proportion who could be expected to be ill given the local population profile. Thirteen levels of this ratio are plotted in Colour Print F which shows the detailed variation of levels of health across the country. The illness rate bands used to categorize the wards are reciprocally symmetrical: the high rate of 125 is comparable to the low rate of 80 (as $100 \div 80 = 125 \div 100$). The majority of people in

Britain live in wards with rates between these two levels, in areas where the prevalence of illness is similar to that found in the nation as a whole, having allowed for age and sex structure. A quarter of the population live in wards where their chance of being ill is at least 20% lower than average and a quarter of these people live in parts of these areas where more than a third fewer people are ill than would be expected. If Colour Print F is compared with Colour Print E it is evident that the people who are least likely to be ill are those who have the highest housing wealth. The most healthy quarter of the population overlaps strongly with the quarter who live in wards where the average household holds more than £45 000 of housing equity. Health and wealth go hand in hand as the advantages of avoiding sickness are reflected in the acquisition of material goods and lifestyles which themselves make ill health less probable (including such basic necessities as good heating, food and holidays). The reverse process, that people in ill health are more likely to get poor (if any) employment and thus cannot afford expensive housing also strengthens the association. One fifth of the population lives in parts of Britain where people are 25% more likely to be ill than the average, irrespective of age. A third of these people are 50% more likely to be ill. These people are most often found in the metropolitan cities and across the coalfields, with the highest rates of illness found in the Welsh valleys, in Strathclyde, County Durham, and South Yorkshire. Although these are similar places to the locations of the wards in which the average household wealth falls below £10 000, the overlap is not so strong. This is particularly true in central London where the housing market crash has significantly reduced levels of personal wealth. Also, households tend to be younger in central London and the estimates of wealth used in Colour Print E are not standardized for age or sex. There are other important reasons for some of these differences, which are related to the kinds of illness people tend to suffer from in different parts of the country, and ultimately in how they die. Because little geographical information is available on the way in which people tend to be ill, disease and death have to be mapped to investigate further (Dorling 1994).

Morbidity and Mortality

Only sixty years ago one baby in every twenty five was stillborn (Figure 2.1) and a further 6% died in the first year of life (Figure 5.17). Chances of not surviving to age one have halved for children of each of the three following generations, so that now less than 1% of infants die in the first year of life and less than 0.5% are stillborn. Over the same period, for those who reached age one, life expectancy has risen by fifteen years. To generalize, between 1935 and 1995, every school-child could expect his or her life to last three months longer than the average life of those children in the year above him or her (Figure 5.13). It is not hard to see how we may have come to view death as relatively unlikely and unimportant, despite its certainty. For the purposes of this atlas, death certificates provide the detailed national information available on the incidence of potentially fatal diseases. Thus more general patterns of morbidity have to be inferred from seeing how, when and where people die.

The crude mortality rate in Britain reflects the distribution of pensioners, as would be expected — mortality being more closely connected to age than illness. Ninety percent of people live in wards where the average age of death lies between 70 and 74 years (page 149). However, once mortality rates are standardized for age and sex, they can be seen to reflect the standardized distribution of illness shown in Colour Print F. The change in mortality ratios over the last decade (page 151) reflects the regional polarization seen in indicators such as permanent sickness. When the geographical differences between the standardized prevalence of different causes of death is drawn, the importance of heart disease and strokes in the north is emphasized, coupled with above-average rates of lung cancers and respiratory diseases in the cities. Deaths from traffic accidents are highest in remoter mainly rural districts where respiratory diseases are least common. Deaths from respiratory diseases are most concentrated in Inner London boroughs where diseases of the digestive tract are also more likely (Figure 5.19). In terms of geographical change over the 1980s, the biggest falls have been in suicides and traffic accidents in Inner London which has also experienced increases in deaths from strokes and heart disease (which are making the pattern of mortality in the capital more like that found in the north). Nationally, the most remarkable rise for any one cause has been the increased rate and decreasing average age of suicide (Figure 5.22). Suicide, however, still accounts for only one premature death in forty, while a heart attacks is the cause of the death of a quarter of all people who die aged under 65; murder accounting for less than one in six hundred (Figure 5.27). If working years of life are considered, rather than standardized ratios, then for men cot deaths, traffic accidents and suicides are seen as more important than respiratory diseases, strokes and genitourinary disease. For women, breast cancer also becomes more significant while pneumonia and heart attacks become less important because they are unlikely to strike women at an early age.

Health and Society

It is partly the age of incidence and the unpredictability with which different diseases occur, as well as their general prevalence, that dictates the importance with which they are viewed by society. In a similar way, the recent growing unevenness of the distribution of mortality rates across the country is viewed with concern as, for over forty years, standardized mortality rates had been becoming more equal between areas (Figure 5.31). Only in the last ten years have the differences between areas reverted towards the bimodal distribution last seen before the Second World War, with the same parts of the same northern cities faring worst (Figure 5.32). Inclusion of estimates of where people were missing from the census does alter the pattern slightly, but not the overall message (page 217). The geographical distributions of employment (page 67), earnings (page 205), and wealth (page 201) each highlight the same areas within which people are losing out from the growing inequality in the distribution of good health in Britain. Increasingly, people who become ill have had to take up less skilled work if they can work, and ill professionals who keep their jobs are now a very rare phenomenon (Figure 6.19). Ill children are concentrated most in the wards in which adults die youngest (Figure 5.30), while mortality rates are increasing for teenagers (Figure 5.16). The ill are least likely to have adequately heated homes or to have access to a car (Figure 5.7), and most ill people live in households where no one is earning. Far from being indicators of social well-being more appropriate for measuring quality of life in the nineteenth century, morbidity and mortality rates reflect the changing condition of life in Britain today more closely than many more "modern" statistics. In an age where the health of the average person is improving so markedly (Figure 5.21), the current growing divisions in health are an indictment of the extent to which one group in society cares about another. If the cartograms on page 229 are compared with the distribution of working years of life lost (page 163), then the political map of Britain can be seen to be as closely interwoven with health as it is with almost any other aspect of our lives.

References

Black, D. and Whitehead, M., 1992, *Inequalities in Health: the Black Report*, new edition, London: Penguin.

CHMU, 1992, *The Health of Elderly People: an Epidemiological Overview*, London: HMSO.

Cliff, A.D. and Haggett, P., 1988, *Atlas of Disease Distributions: analytic approaches to epidemiological data*, Oxford: Basil Blackwell Ltd.

Department of Health, 1994, *Health and Personal Social Service Statistics for England*, 1993 edition, London: HMSO.

Dorling, D. (1994) Visualizing the geography of the population with the 1991 Census, *Population Trends*, 76: 29–39.

Norris, P. and Mounsey, H., 1983, Analysing change through time, in D. Rhind (ed.) *A Census User's Handbook*, London: Methuen, 265–286.

Phillimore, P., Beattie, A. and Townsend, P., 1994, Widening inequalities of health in northern England, 1981–91, *British Medical Journal*, 308: 1125–1128.

Townsend, P., Davidson, N., Black, D. and Whitehead, M., 1988, *Inequalities in Health: the Black Report*, London: Penguin.

Whitehead, M., 1987, *The Health Divide: Inequalities in Health in the 1980s*, London: Health Education Council.

WHO, 1977, *Manual of the International Statistical Classification of Diseases, Injuries, and Causes of Death*, London: HMSO.

6: Society

Matters of traditional concern to social scientists are the focus of this chapter — the structure of society and the inequalities between social groups in Britain. The family, childhood, education, qualifications, occupations, segregation, mobility, wealth, income and dependency are the major issues which are addressed. These issues are brought together because they are closely linked both socially and spatially. The advantages a child has in growing up in a home with money are often reflected through educational achievement and then in the settlement patterns of university graduates. The geography of qualifications underlies the patterns of occupational segregation which are clear across Britain and which, in turn, create patterns of income differences and the unequal accumulation of wealth in different parts of the country. Higher-income households increasingly tend to reside in places where fewer pensioners or unemployed adults live and so a geographical divide has grown between areas where affluence amasses and the places where earnings are much lower. This divide is reinforced partly through the inheritance of wealth but more through the advantages the wealthy give their children: going to schools from which they will be more likely to succeed and living in areas in which they have the best chances of finding employment. These processes are thus self-reinforcing across generations and the maps of population, demography, economics, housing and health, shown in earlier chapters, have often betrayed facets of the social structure of this country which also help to sustain these patterns.

Because social issues are not the responsibility of a single government ministry and because they are often seen as personal matters with which the government (and private industry) should not be concerned, there is a paucity of information concerning institutional and financial inequalities in society. However, more light can be shed as government releases more of the information it does hold and private industries allow researchers access to their data. In this chapter information from the 1991 census Sample of Anonymised Records, the Department for Education, a building society and a data consultancy are brought together with other census information so that a broad spectrum of social issues can be covered. Here, though, it is necessary to draw attention to data that are not available. The census does not include questions on income and wealth, and the Inland Revenue are instructed not to release information below the level of national boundaries. Surrogate data from less comprehensive sources is often required. Issues such as crime, recreation and religion are omitted from this chapter because of the paucity of geographically disaggregated information on these and other subjects.

The first issue which is addressed here is the family, for which census data are used. In the census a *family* is a group of people living in one household who are related either through marriage or cohabitation to each other or through parentage. If, within one household, there is a lodger and the daughter of the married couple living there has a child herself, then that household is said to contain one "married couple family", one "lone parent family" and one "no family person" (OPCS 1992). From this example it is obvious that studying the family unit is inherently more complex than is studying the individual (see Chapter 1). Analysis of the census family question allows the geographical pattern of people's relationships to be mapped at a local level and also for family structure to be cross-tabulated against other social variables.

Educational achievement is also measured in the census, but only through qualifications obtained by adults. Thus it is possible to measure from the census the propensity of university graduates to be in a variety of relationships (which is done here), but it is not possible to see how many of the unemployed have no qualifications at all. The Department for Education and the Welsh Office do release information in an easily accessible form on the proportion of pupils who pass school examinations and, by knowing where the schools are, that information can be (crudely) linked to the census. Thus the picture presented in Chapter 2, on where school leavers and students live, can be embellished by what they achieve in terms of exam results.

After children leave school and students graduate, they enter a differentiated employment market as Chapter 3 illustrated. It is, however, possible to simplify the occupational hierarchies through an occupation's *socioeconomic group* (SEG) which "brings together people with jobs of similar social and economic status" (OPCS 1992: 41). Substantially the same seventeen main socioeconomic group classifications have been used since the 1971 census. Here, for mapping purposes, these seventeen have been amalgamated to four major *social groups* which combine occupations receiving similar remuneration (Dorling 1995). Between their geographies, these groups illustrate the changing spatial patterns to the social divisions of class in Britain.

The different remuneration of different social groups is reflected in measures of the wealth of local populations. Three measures of wealth are used in this chapter. The first is the number of cars which are available to a household. This is the only indicator of wealth collected by the census. The second measure is wealth held in the form of housing using the data from a building society which was described in Chapter 4. This source is also used to estimate income for a subset of the population — mortgage holders. The third measure of wealth employed here concerns share ownership, for which geographically disaggregated information from a data consultancy company was used. Together these very different measures of affluence produce a picture of where the financial resources of the population are concentrated and where they are lacking — a pattern which is then, for instance, reflected through the geography of health (Chapter 5). Thus, through the following maps, the social structure of Britain can be seen to underpin and reflect many other facets of the human geography of this country.

6.1: Type of Family Residents Belong to by Resident's Age and Sex in Britain 1991

single year age bands

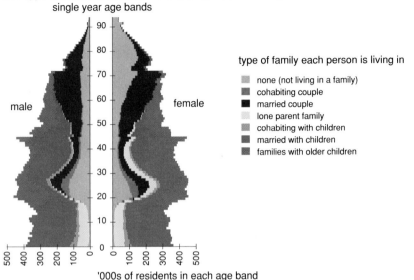

male

female

type of family each person is living in

none (not living in a family)
cohabiting couple
married couple
lone parent family
cohabiting with children
married with children
families with older children

'000s of residents in each age band

6.2: Residents Not in Families by Age, Sex and Employment Status in Britain 1991

single year age bands

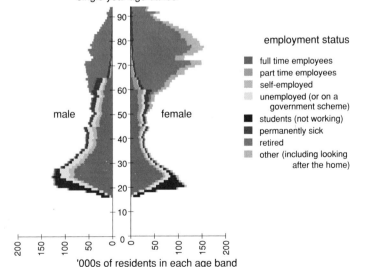

male

female

employment status

full time employees
part time employees
self-employed
unemployed (or on a government scheme)
students (not working)
permanently sick
retired
other (including looking after the home)

'000s of residents in each age band

Households and Families

People who live with relatives are classed as living in a family (see page 169). In 1981 one person in seven did not live in a family. Under the same definition of family this proportion rose to one in five of the population by 1991. However, by 1991 concepts of what was a family were changed to include three million people who stated that they were "living together as a couple". This change of definition has kept the number of people the census reports not to be living in a family relatively static at over seven million individuals. Their geographical distribution is shown using the same shading scheme for the equal area map and population cartogram opposite. The map, as always, highlights rural areas, showing that in the retirement districts of Scotland and Wales high proportions of residents do not live in families. The cartogram shows a clear urban/rural divide to the pattern. Almost all city centres stand out clearly as areas in which over a fifth of the population do not live in families. In the most rural areas, often at the boundaries between counties, over 90% of the population is living in a family.

Important correlates of whether individuals live in a family, and in what kind of family they live, are their age and sex. Figure 6.1 shows the population pyramid of Britain subdivided by the type of family in which each individual lives. A seven-fold classification of family types is used. First there are people who are not in families; second there are people who are living as a couple but have no children; and third there are people who are married and have no children. Fourth are people in lone parent families — this includes the parent and the children they live with; next are cohabiting and married couples with their children; and seventh are families where the youngest child is no longer dependent (as defined in Figure 5.7). This final group can include families in which the parent is elderly and is being looked after by a grown-up child. Figure 6.1, however, shows how few elderly people are in this type of family. The figure also contains information such as the likely ages of mothers in lone parent families and how few adult men look after children on their own.

Almost all people start life in a family but from their late teens onwards increasing numbers leave these families, most not starting or joining new families until their 30s, which then themselves dissolve in later years as Figure 6.1 illustrates. Figure 6.2 gives more detail on the group not living in families showing their employment status. Only a very small minority are students. The majority are either retired or in full-time employment. Living outside a family is most common for men in their 20s and for women in their 80s, but different people who live alone (or with people not in their family) often live in the same areas, principally inside cities such as London. Residents not living in families are roughly twice as likely to be students, unemployed, permanently sick or retired than the population in general, although this distinction could not be made if they were compared to people in families of their age living in their areas.

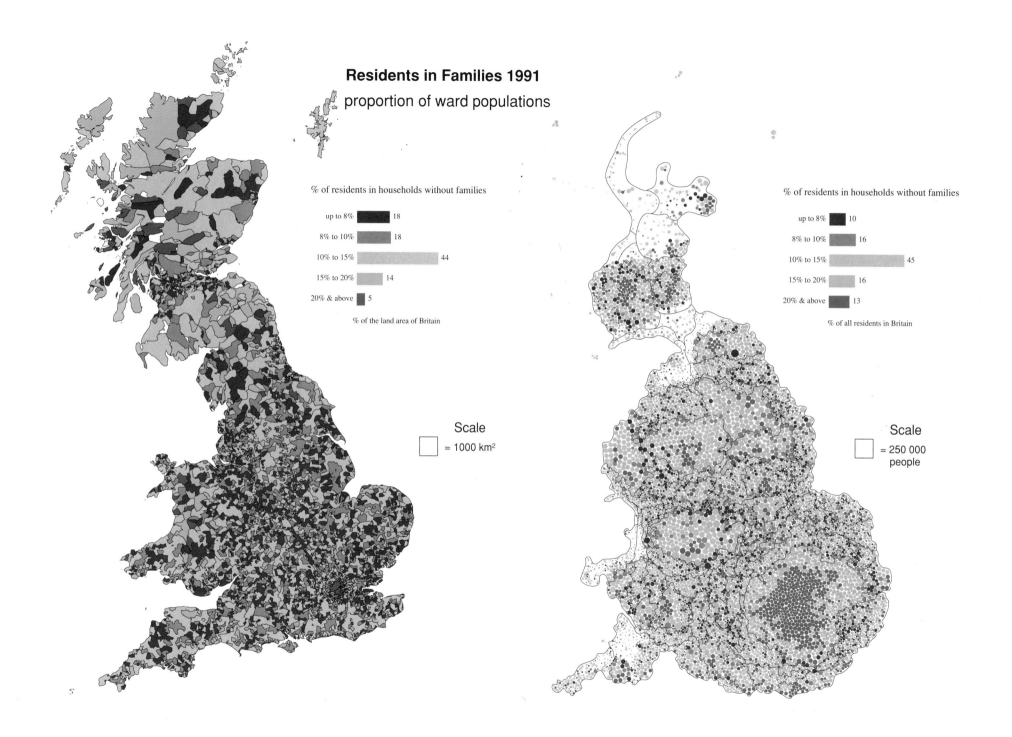

Residents in Families 1991

proportion of ward populations

% of residents in households without families

up to 8%		18
8% to 10%		18
10% to 15%		44
15% to 20%		14
20% & above		5

% of the land area of Britain

% of residents in households without families

up to 8%		10
8% to 10%		16
10% to 15%		45
15% to 20%		16
20% & above		13

% of all residents in Britain

Scale

☐ = 1000 km²

Scale

☐ = 250 000 people

6.3: People, Households, Children and Migrants by Family Type in Britain 1991

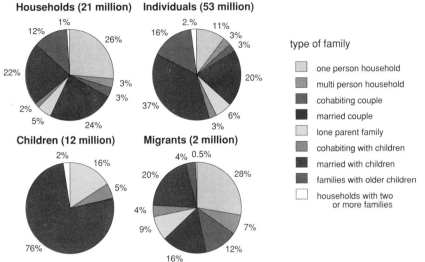

Households (21 million)   Individuals (53 million)

type of family

☐ one person household

■ multi person household

■ cohabiting couple

■ married couple

☐ lone parent family

■ cohabiting with children

■ married with children

■ families with older children

☐ households with two or more families

Children (12 million)   Migrants (2 million)

Note: only people who were residents — and households with residents — are included above; figures in brackets are the totals from the 1991 census (rounded to the nearest million).

6.4: Housing Tenure and Family Type in Britain 1991

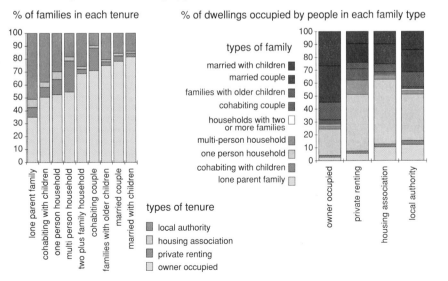

% of families in each tenure

% of dwellings occupied by people in each family type

types of family

married with children ■
married couple ■
families with older children ■
cohabiting couple ■
households with two ☐ or more families
multi-person household ■
one person household ■
cohabiting with children ■
lone parent family ☐

types of tenure

■ local authority
☐ housing association
■ private renting
☐ owner occupied

Family Type

What types of family are most common? The answer to this question depends on how you count families. As Figure 6.3 shows, the most common type of "family" (in one-family households) is a single person living alone, while the least common type of household is one which contains more than one family. The seven-fold categorization of family types has been extended to nine here by identifying separately multi-family households and multi-person-no-family households. Most people in Britain live in married couple families either with or without children. However, one in six children were living in lone parent families in 1991, and a further one in twenty lived with unmarried parents. Figure 6.3 also shows how different subsets of the population tend to have very different family profiles. For instance, migrants (those moving home between 1990 and 1991) were twice as likely to be in lone parent families as they were to be in families with older children.

Opposite are shown the geographical distributions of eight of the nine family types using the same shading scheme so that their relative importance can be appreciated (the geography of two-family households is shown in Figure 4.10). The major Scottish cities, Inner London boroughs, four south coast districts and Cambridge are the only districts where more than 15% of the population live alone. Multi-person-no-family households have a similar geography, as to an extent do cohabiting couple families, although these are very rare in the celtic fringes where it is more common for residents to live with older children or elderly parents. Married couples without children are more common around the coast, while in Britain as a whole, other than in a few districts in Inner London, more than one in four people live in married couple families with children.

Family type is a strong correlate of many other social variables, of which the most obvious are age and sex, which partly influence other relationships. For example, the housing tenure of an individual is closely linked with his/her family type. As the first bar chart in Figure 6.4 shows, people in lone parent families are least likely to own or to be buying their home, whereas married couples with children are most likely to be in this tenure. Multi-person households, followed by cohabiting couples without children, are most likely to be renting privately. Housing associations disproportionately let to lone parent families but also to one person households. The allocation policies of local authorities are clearly reflected by this figure, as families with children who cannot afford owner-occupation are given the highest priority. The second bar chart in the figure illustrates how these different priorities and opportunities result in very different family profiles for each of the four main tenure types. The geography of the availability and affordability of different forms of housing is one of the patterns which underlies the distributions of family types shown opposite; lone parent families (usually having the lowest income and least wealth) are unlikely to live in districts with expensive housing.

Types of Family 1991

proportions of district families

% of people in each type of family

- up to 2%
- 2% to 5%
- 5% to 15%
- 15% to 25%
- 25% & above

One person household

Multi-person household

Cohabiting couple family

Married couple family

Lone parent family

Cohabiting with children

Married with children

Families with older children

Scale

= 1 000 000 people

6.5: Children in Married Couple Families and Population Density in Britain 1991

% of dependent children in married couple families in each ward

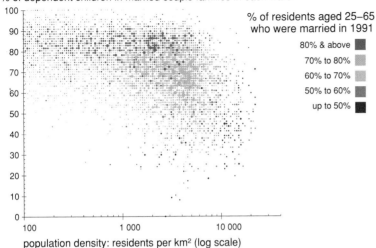

% of residents aged 25–65 who were married in 1991

80% & above
70% to 80%
60% to 70%
50% to 60%
up to 50%

population density: residents per km² (log scale)

6.6: Type of Family Children Belong to by District Type in Britain 1971, 1981, 1991

% of dependent children in selected types of family

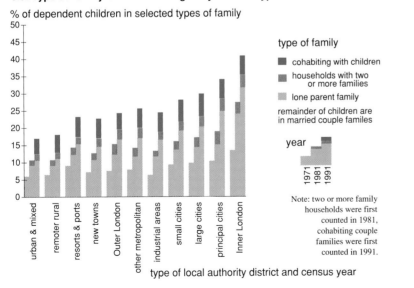

type of family

cohabiting with children
households with two or more families
lone parent family
remainder of children are in married couple familes

year

1971
1981
1991

Note: two or more family households were first counted in 1981, cohabiting couple families were first counted in 1991.

type of local authority district and census year

Married Families

There are significant differences between children who grow up in married couple families and children who are brought up by one parent (or by two parents who are unmarried) in terms of where they are likely to live, in the age and the earnings of their parents, in their housing tenure, employment opportunities and general life chances. It would be wrong to compare these different groups of children without appreciating the differences between the areas in which many of them grow up. Because previous censuses did not ask about relationships outside marriage (and because of the differing ways in which they treated *de-facto* marriage) only the changing geography of children in married family households can be compared over time — the "traditional" family. In 1971 92% of all children in Britain were in this type of family, by 1981 this proportion had fallen to 87% and by 1991 it was standing at 76%. Part of this fall was due to the increased social acceptability of not being in a married family at successive censuses, although the latest figure may well be deflated by men avoiding enumeration. Almost a quarter of all children in Britain were not in married couple families in 1991. The first map opposite shows where there are few and many of these children.

Interestingly it is the places where adults are unlikely to be in families at all that contain the highest proportions of children in lone parent or cohabiting couple families. These are the places where marriage has become less common (page 37) and in which high proportions of very young children live (page 31). As people migrate out of these places (page 59) they are more likely to marry, so living with unmarried parents may be a transitory state for many children. Figure 6.5 shows how children are most likely not to be living in married couple families in areas with more than one thousand people per square kilometre and only then where marriage itself is uncommon. The chances of a person being married and the chances of a child living with married parents is very much a function of where he/she lives, although the kind of family a person lives in, whether it contains two people earning for instance, strongly affects where his/her family can live.

The second map opposite shows how this pattern has built up over time, generally strengthening the existing divisions between town and country. But in some parts of some cities, south west London for instance, the decline in the propensity for children to be brought up outside marriage has been less acute than the national average fall, particularly in recent years. The eleven district types which have been used throughout this atlas are shown in Figure 6.6 sorted by the size of the increase over twenty years in the proportion of children not living in married couple families. For later years it is possible to show what proportion of these children lived in two or more family households or in cohabiting couple families. Outer London can be seen to be moving in a different direction to Inner London. The rise has been greatest in the most densely populated areas, thus principal cities and Inner London have seen the faster increases.

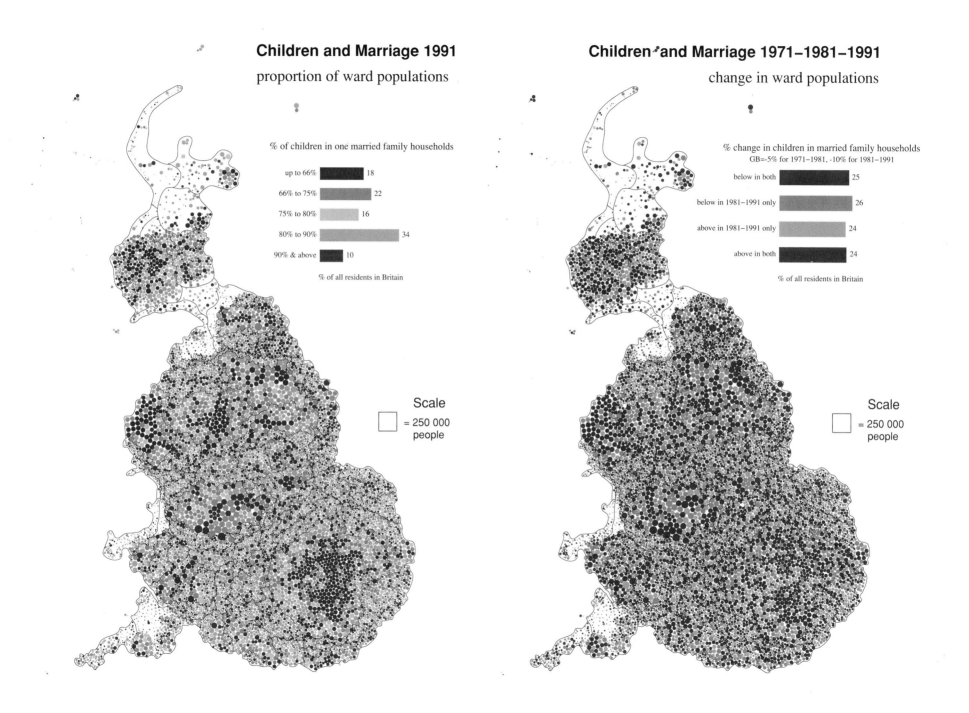

Children and Marriage 1991

proportion of ward populations

% of children in one married family households

up to 66%	18
66% to 75%	22
75% to 80%	16
80% to 90%	34
90% & above	10

% of all residents in Britain

Scale

☐ = 250 000
people

Children and Marriage 1971–1981–1991

change in ward populations

% change in children in married family households
GB=-5% for 1971–1981, -10% for 1981–1991

below in both	25
below in 1981–1991 only	26
above in 1981–1991 only	24
above in both	24

% of all residents in Britain

Scale

☐ = 250 000
people

6.7: Children and Household Composition by Ethnic Group in Britain in 1991

% of households of each type by ethnic group of the household head

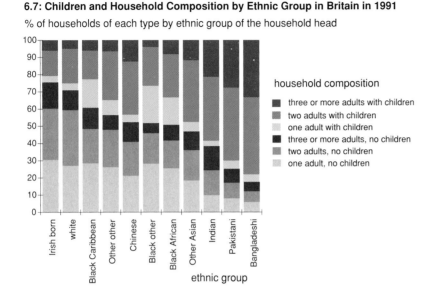

household composition

- ■ three or more adults with children
- ■ two adults with children
- □ one adult with children
- ■ three or more adults, no children
- ■ two adults, no children
- ▪ one adult, no children

ethnic group

6.8: Change in Number of Children in Households by District Type in Britain 1981–1991

% change in the share of all households with children of each size

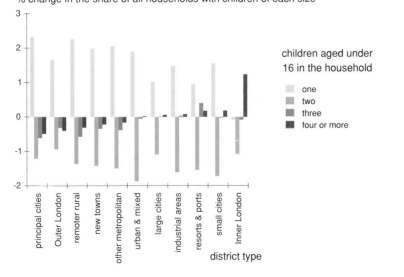

children aged under
16 in the household

- □ one
- ▨ two
- ▨ three
- ■ four or more

district type

Family Size

To children, the number of brothers and sisters they grow up with may be more important than whether their parents are married. Large and small families have advantages and disadvantages and their geographical location will reflect the migration patterns of families as they grow and shrink as well as the choices of people to have different numbers of children. In this page (and the next) the concepts of family and household are combined, as information on numbers of children is only available for the latter. As there are few families with children which are not also whole households this is unlikely to matter here. In 1981 a third of households contained children; by 1991 this proportion had fallen to 28%. Almost a quarter of all children in 1991 were the only child in a household. This proportion had risen from 23% in 1981. The first map opposite shows where children were most and least likely to be growing up in one child households in 1991. Roughly a third of all children living in central London and Glasgow were in one child families, whereas less than a fifth of children in central Birmingham and parts of east London lived in these small families.

One reason for different family sizes and compositions in different parts of the country is the uneven spread of ethnic minority groups. Figure 6.7 shows how different the household composition of different groups can be, with Bangladeshi household heads being five times less likely to be lone parents than household heads in the Black Other category. Combined with cultural differences are the differing age, tenure and locational positions of members of different ethnic minorities. The choices and pressures for different groups of people to live in different ways are clearly reflected through the maps of family structure shown here (compare the distribution of residents in the South-Asian ethnic groups given on page 43 with these maps for an example).

In 1991 just under a half of all children lived in households with one other child, one child in ten lived in households with two other children and one child in ten lived in households with three or more other children. All these types of family are becoming less common. The areas where the largest families tend to live are almost the opposite of where the smallest families are most commonly found, although in some places (north London for instance), both large and small families are unusually common. The second map drawn opposite shows these static patterns in detail. The changing geography of family size is presented in Figure 6.8. Most clearly, in every type of district, the most rapid decline has been in the number of households with two children. The "traditional family" is in decline. In every type of district, other than the Inner London boroughs, the fastest growth has been in households with only one child. In Inner London households with four or more children have been increasing the fastest (and it is by this measure that the areas are sorted). This trend could soon reverse as it may be peculiar to the immigration of the early 1980s which brought in many expanding young families.

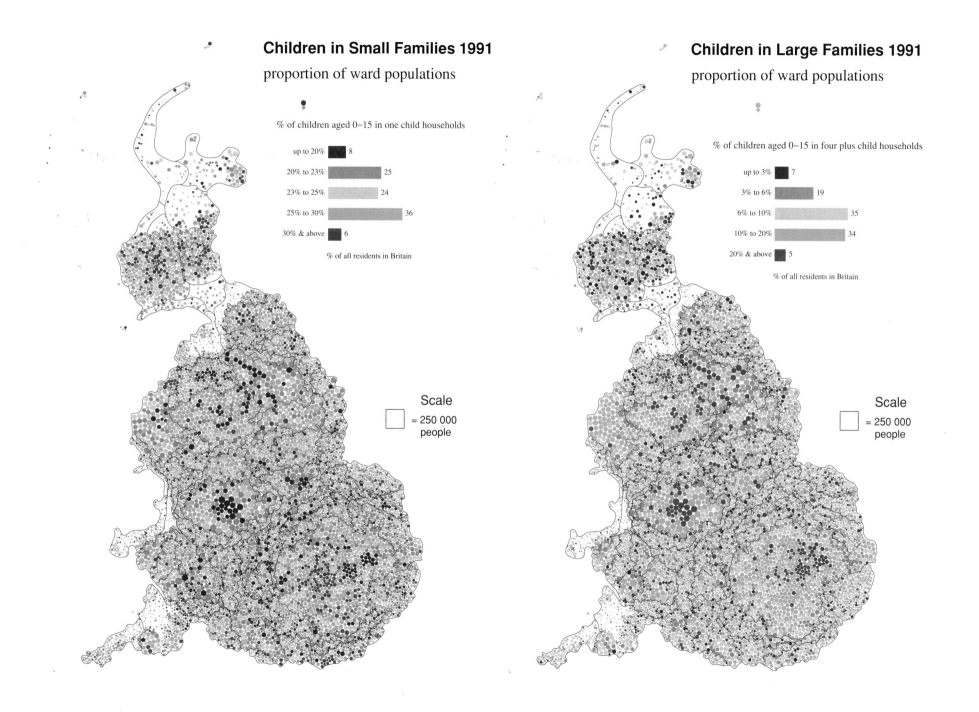

Children in Small Families 1991

proportion of ward populations

% of children aged 0–15 in one child households

up to 20%	8
20% to 23%	25
23% to 25%	24
25% to 30%	36
30% & above	6

% of all residents in Britain

Scale

☐ = 250 000
people

Children in Large Families 1991

proportion of ward populations

% of children aged 0–15 in four plus child households

up to 3%	7
3% to 6%	19
6% to 10%	35
10% to 20%	34
20% & above	5

% of all residents in Britain

Scale

☐ = 250 000
people

6.9: Household Composition by the Age of the Youngest Child in Britain 1991

age of youngest child in household

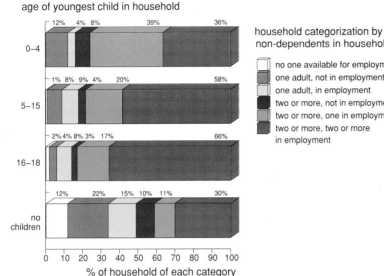

household categorization by
non-dependents in household

- no one available for employment
- one adult, not in employment
- one adult, in employment
- two or more, not in employment
- two or more, one in employment
- two or more, two or more in employment

% of household of each category

6.10: Change in Households by Potential Earners and Number of Children in Britain 1981–1991

	Total households		With no children		With one child		With two children		Three or more children	
Levels	**1981**	**1991**	**1981**	**1991**	**1981**	**1991**	**1981**	**1991**	**1981**	**1991**
1981 and 1991										
All households ('000s)	19 491	21 897	12 929	15 323	2728	2757	2717	2672	1117	1146
One adult not in workforce	15%	19%	22%	23%	3%	8%	3%	7%	4%	10%
One adult in the workforce	9%	12%	11%	15%	4%	8%	3%	5%	2%	4%
Two+ adults not in workforce	11%	12%	16%	16%	1%	2%	1%	2%	1%	3%
Two+ adults, one in workforce	25%	17%	16%	12%	34%	23%	45%	31%	51%	41%
Two+ adults, two+ in workforce	40%	40%	35%	33%	57%	59%	49%	56%	41%	43%
Change (absolute and relative)	**'000s**	**factor(×)**	**'000s**	**factor(×)**	**'000s**	**factor(×)**	**'000s**	**factor(×)**	**'000s**	**factor(×)**
1981 to 1991										
All households ('000s)	2406	1.12	2394	1.19	29	1.00	-46	0.98	29	1.03
One adult not in workforce	1075	1.36	761	1.27	138	2.70	108	2.52	67	2.60
One adult in the workforce	1050	1.63	864	1.60	105	1.91	63	1.78	18	1.76
Two+ adults not in workforce	530	1.25	467	1.23	20	1.53	20	1.91	22	2.43
Two+ adults, one in workforce	-1061	0.78	-255	0.88	-296	0.68	-402	0.67	-108	0.81
Two+ adults, two+ in workforce	807	1.10	556	1.12	58	1.04	164	1.12	29	1.06

Figures shown in red are below the national average proportions

Families Earning

Of great importance to the material well-being of children today is whether or not there is an adult in their household who is earning money. In 1991 one child in every ten lived in a household in which no adult was in paid employment. Thus the families of at least one million children in Britain were reliant on social security benefits to bring them up. The first map opposite shows where these children most often live and also where children are most likely to live in households in which someone is earning. Figure 6.9 shows how a child's chances of living in a non-earning household decreases as the child gets older. Children aged under five are most likely to be in this situation and also most unlikely to be in a household receiving two wages.

The second map drawn opposite shows how this pattern has been reinforced over the 1980s. The 1981 census did not differentiate between adults who were unemployed and those who were employed in households by number of children, so this map shows the change in the proportion of children living in households in which no adult is available for work, let alone has a wage. In a small minority of wards (containing 4% of the population of Britain) the situation has improved, while in almost half of Britain it has worsened slightly. But in areas in which a fifth of the population live, more than one additional child in every ten now lives in a household without earners, and these households are increasingly concentrated in particular parts of some cities.

A more detailed national breakdown of these changes by the number of children and adults in the household is given in Figure 6.10. The statistics in this figure show another facet to the decline of the "traditional family": the fall in the proportion of households consisting of two adults of which only one is in work. All other types of household are more numerous than they used to be and the fastest overall rise (of 1.63 times) has been experienced by single adult households in work. By numbers of children, the largest rise has been of households with no children which have increased proportionately by almost a fifth, and their share of all household types by almost 5%. These figures also show how, in absolute terms, the increases in households with one child or three or more children outstrip the decline (of 46 000) in the number of households with two children in Britain between 1981 and 1991. The biggest relative and absolute fall is seen to have occurred in households with one adult in work and two children, which have decreased in number by a third over ten years. The largest relative increase (of 2.7 times more households in ten years) has been in households with one child and only one adult, who is not in work; while the largest absolute increase of families with children has been of an additional 164 000 households which contain two children and in which at least two adults are earning a wage. Thus this single table reflects many of the changing employment opportunities, lifestyle choices, family structures and domestic constraints which affect bringing up children in Britain today.

Children With No Earners 1991

proportion of children in households

% of children with no earners in their households

up to 5%	34
5% to 10%	31
10% to 15%	17
15% to 20%	10
20% & above	7

% of all residents in Britain

Scale

☐ = 250 000 people

Children With No Earners 1981–1991

change in proportion of children in households

% increase in children in households with no "economically active" adults

up to 0%	4
0% to 5%	49
5% to 10%	28
10% to 15%	12
15% & above	7

% of all residents in Britain

Scale

☐ = 250 000 people

6.11: School Leavers with No Qualifications by Sex and Region in Britain 1991

% of school leavers with no graded GCSE, SCE, "O" level or standard level results

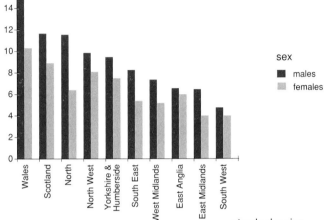

sex
■ males
■ females

standard region

Source: CSO, 1994, Social Trends 24, page 51, London: HMSO.

6.12: School Leavers' Qualifications in 1993 by Children in Households Without Earners 1991 by Ward in England and Wales

% of 15 year old children passing five or more GCSE exams at grades A to C in 1993

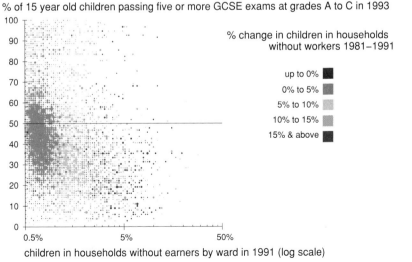

% change in children in households without workers 1981–1991

up to 0% ■
0% to 5% ■
5% to 10% ■
10% to 15% ■
15% & above ■

children in households without earners by ward in 1991 (log scale)

School Leavers

So far the concern of this chapter has been with families and, in particular, with the position of children in those families. As children grow older, other institutions grow in importance in their socialization, primarily schools.

Before children reach the statutory school leaving age, society puts them through a number of tests which categorize them and partially determine their choices later in life. How well a child performs in these tests is influenced by where they live and the school they attend. Thousands of parents pay for their children to attend private schools partly because of these differences in chances. Figure 6.11 shows how even at the regional level there can be a three-fold difference between a child's chances of not gaining any nationally recognized qualifications and, although girls perform better than boys in every region, regional location is more important than sex in influencing these life chances.

The school exam results of individual children are not available for research, but the government does publish results for the proportion of pupils in each school who attain certain grades and makes these statistics easily available for schools in England and Wales. Statistics for Scotland are more difficult to collate and the different examination system there means that they are not directly comparable with results from England and Wales, so they have been excluded from this analysis. Also excluded from the analysis are the results from special schools, although most private secondary schools are included. To analyse exam results, the pupils of each school were allocated to the ward in which their school lay (using the school's postcode). The first map drawn opposite shows the wards which contain secondary schools shaded according to the proportion of children who passed five or more GCSE examinations at grades A to C. This is the usual measure of success at this stage, and is also a requirement for many jobs. Of all school-leavers, 41% were awarded these grades in 1993. The map is correct but misleading, as each ward is not drawn in proportion to the number of pupils sitting examinations in the schools in that ward. The second map drawn opposite assumes that children attended their nearest school and, on this assumption, gives children's average chance in every ward of passing these examinations. Because most children actually do go to local schools this procedure should not produce an unrealistic picture. The result fills in a patchwork quilt of opportunity and constraint. Within each county there are clearly areas in which children are more likely to pass these tests and other wards where their chances are very low. One advantage of redistributing children to their likely home wards is that school leaver qualifications can then be compared with other social statistics. An example of the relationship between the financial welfare of children growing up in families without earners and exam results is illustrated by Figure 6.12. Children growing up in wards where more than one in twenty of them lived in families without earners are likely to go to schools from which few will pass many examinations.

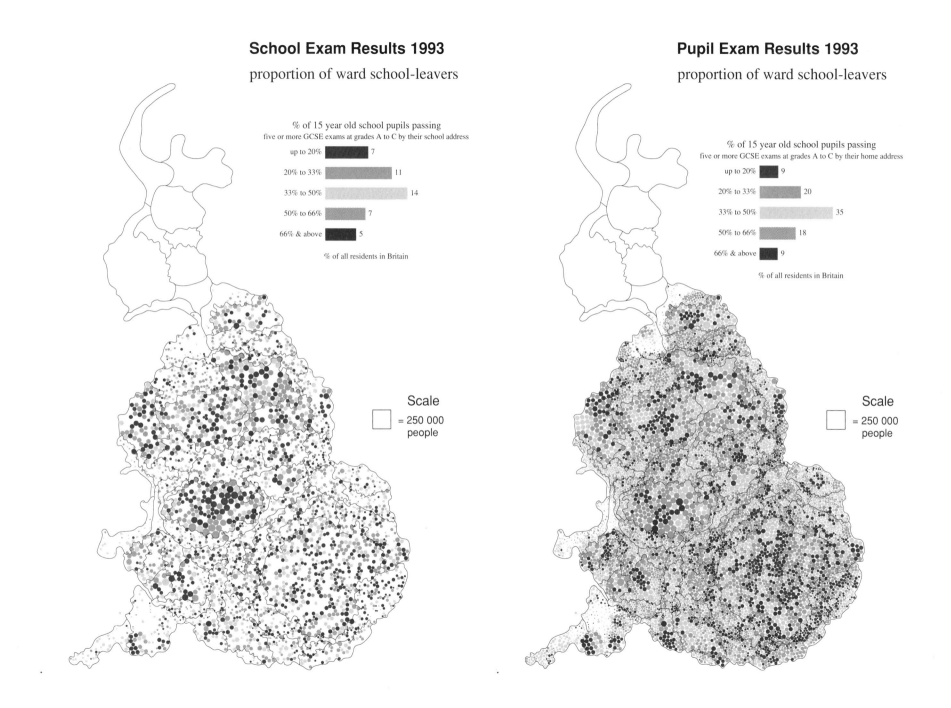

School Exam Results 1993

proportion of ward school-leavers

% of 15 year old school pupils passing
five or more GCSE exams at grades A to C by their school address

up to 20%	7
20% to 33%	11
33% to 50%	14
50% to 66%	7
66% & above	5

% of all residents in Britain

Scale

☐ = 250 000
people

Pupil Exam Results 1993

proportion of ward school-leavers

% of 15 year old school pupils passing
five or more GCSE exams at grades A to C by their home address

up to 20%	9
20% to 33%	20
33% to 50%	35
50% to 66%	18
66% & above	9

% of all residents in Britain

Scale

☐ = 250 000
people

6.13: Distribution of Graduates by Degree Subject and Family Type in Britain in 1991

Subject of highest degree level qualification	Not in a family (at usual address) rank (%)	Cohabiting couple (no children) rank (%)	Married couple (no children) rank (%)	Lone parent family (with children) rank (%)	Cohabiting couple (with children) rank (%)	Married couple (with children) rank (%)	Living with parents (or old children) rank (%)
Accountancy	32 (18%)	33 (3%)	3 (30%)	30 (1%)	32 (1%)	4 (35%)	9 (13%)
Agriculture / Forestry / Veterinary	22 (25%)	22 (4%)	17 (23%)	17 (1%)	22 (1%)	15 (31%)	7 (14%)
Architecture	15 (28%)	15 (5%)	10 (25%)	23 (1%)	29 (1%)	31 (27%)	11 (12%)
Art and design	3 (33%)	1 (9%)	35 (15%)	3 (3%)	1 (2%)	34 (25%)	14 (12%)
Art / Design / Music	1 (38%)	21 (5%)	26 (21%)	14 (2%)	14 (1%)	35 (23%)	29 (10%)
Biological sciences	16 (28%)	2 (8%)	29 (19%)	21 (1%)	10 (1%)	11 (33%)	33 (10%)
Chemical engineering	29 (21%)	20 (5%)	5 (29%)	32 (0%)	33 (1%)	6 (34%)	32 (10%)
Chemistry	23 (25%)	23 (4%)	18 (23%)	25 (1%)	30 (1%)	8 (34%)	12 (12%)
Civil engineering	33 (16%)	24 (4%)	11 (25%)	28 (1%)	11 (1%)	1 (38%)	3 (15%)
Classical studies	2 (34%)	10 (6%)	27 (21%)	8 (2%)	19 (1%)	33 (26%)	31 (10%)
Clinical (e.g. Medicine)	20 (25%)	34 (3%)	7 (26%)	20 (1%)	34 (1%)	2 (36%)	35 (7%)
Combined social studies	4 (33%)	4 (7%)	34 (18%)	5 (3%)	9 (1%)	32 (27%)	22 (11%)
Economics / Geography	10 (30%)	3 (7%)	32 (18%)	15 (2%)	24 (1%)	18 (31%)	26 (11%)
Education	28 (22%)	35 (2%)	8 (26%)	4 (3%)	28 (1%)	5 (35%)	13 (12%)
Electrical engineering	30 (21%)	19 (5%)	9 (26%)	29 (1%)	17 (1%)	19 (31%)	1 (16%)
English	5 (33%)	11 (6%)	28 (20%)	10 (2%)	6 (1%)	26 (28%)	34 (9%)
Environmental science	11 (29%)	14 (6%)	23 (22%)	12 (2%)	25 (1%)	27 (28%)	15 (12%)
General / Other engineering	25 (24%)	16 (5%)	16 (23%)	33 (0%)	16 (1%)	17 (31%)	5 (14%)
General arts	8 (31%)	31 (3%)	24 (22%)	11 (2%)	4 (2%)	28 (28%)	18 (12%)
Government / Law	18 (27%)	12 (6%)	20 (22%)	18 (1%)	18 (1%)	13 (32%)	25 (11%)
History / Archaeology	7 (32%)	18 (5%)	19 (22%)	19 (1%)	3 (2%)	30 (27%)	28 (10%)
Language subjects	6 (32%)	17 (5%)	30 (19%)	6 (2%)	5 (1%)	24 (29%)	19 (12%)
Management studies	27 (23%)	13 (6%)	15 (24%)	13 (2%)	15 (1%)	14 (31%)	8 (14%)
Maths / Computing / Statistics	9 (31%)	6 (7%)	33 (18%)	22 (1%)	20 (1%)	21 (30%)	16 (12%)
Mechanical engineering	34 (16%)	27 (4%)	1 (31%)	34 (0%)	23 (1%)	10 (34%)	4 (15%)
Medical / Health	24 (24%)	28 (4%)	12 (24%)	9 (2%)	26 (1%)	9 (34%)	23 (11%)
Mining / Metallurgy	35 (15%)	25 (4%)	4 (30%)	35 (0%)	27 (1%)	7 (34%)	2 (16%)
Nursing	21 (25%)	30 (4%)	21 (22%)	1 (4%)	13 (1%)	12 (32%)	17 (12%)
Pharmacy / Pharmacology	26 (24%)	32 (3%)	2 (30%)	31 (1%)	35 (0%)	16 (31%)	24 (11%)
Physics	13 (28%)	26 (4%)	13 (24%)	27 (1%)	21 (1%)	20 (31%)	20 (11%)
Psychology/ Sociology/ Anthropology	12 (29%)	5 (7%)	31 (18%)	2 (3%)	2 (2%)	22 (30%)	27 (11%)
Surveying	31 (19%)	29 (4%)	6 (27%)	26 (1%)	31 (1%)	3 (35%)	10 (13%)
Technology / Manufacture	19 (27%)	8 (6%)	25 (22%)	24 (1%)	7 (1%)	25 (29%)	6 (14%)
Vocational studies (e.g. Librarianship)	17 (28%)	9 (6%)	14 (24%)	16 (1%)	12 (1%)	29 (28%)	21 (11%)
West European studies	14 (28%)	7 (7%)	22 (22%)	7 (2%)	8 (1%)	23 (29%)	30 (10%)

Subjects for which each family type is least and most common have their ranks printed in red

Graduates

From school a minority of children gain sufficient qualifications to be able to choose to go to university, where almost everyone who enters is awarded a degree. The kind of degree which they gain has a strong influence on the kind of work they are likely to find later on in life (see page 190). However, gaining a degree of any kind separates graduates from other adults in terms of their opportunities in life. Most simply, graduates are able to make different choices over the places where they live as can be seen from the first map drawn opposite. *Graduates* are defined here as adults who have been awarded a degree level qualification or other professional qualification generally obtained in adulthood, such as a Higher National Diploma. From the map it can be seen that the places in which graduates tended to live in 1991 were a mix between the places where many of them lived as students (page 33) and the places where they were most likely to later obtain professional employment (page 77). These areas tend, however, to include the most affluent of places, reflecting how a degree has acted as a passport to wealth.

As higher proportions of young adults graduate from universities, the category of graduate becomes less exclusive. The second map opposite shows how the locations of graduates have changed over ten years. The increase in the numbers of students studying in London is reflected by an increase in graduates living there. Other university cities have seen an increase in graduates which reflects the high output of people with degree level qualifications from these places in recent years. Nationally, the number of graduates living in Britain rose from under four million in 1981 to over five and a half million by 1991. Despite this rise many parts of the country have seen a fall, or almost no rise, in the proportion of their populations who have these qualifications. Graduates, whilst growing in absolute numbers, have become more concentrated geographically.

The type of qualification a graduate has can be used to infer more than just his or her relative likelihood of holding particular jobs. Figure 6.13, for example, shows the probability of a graduate living in each of the seven family types which were defined at the start of this chapter. Thus an accountancy graduate is most likely to be married and living with young children and is very unlikely to be in a cohabiting couple household. Alternatively, graduates of architecture are most likely not to be living in families, but if they are, then they are roughly twice as likely to be cohabiting as are accountants. Obviously the different age and sex profiles of each group of graduates explains part of these differences, but by no means all. The figure also shows how each subject ranks among the 35 in terms of the chances of alumni in that subject living in each family type. Art and design graduates are thus most likely to be cohabiting (with or without children), nursing graduates are most likely to be lone parents, civil engineering graduates are most likely to be married with children whilst graduates of electrical engineering are most likely to be living with their parents or with their grown-up children.

Graduates 1991

proportion of ward populations

% of adult residents who are qualified
with a professional or degree level qualification

up to 5%	13
5% to 10%	28
10% to 15%	23
15% to 20%	17
20% & above	19

% of all residents in Britain

Scale

☐ = 250 000
people

Graduates 1981–1991

change in ward populations

% change in all residents who are qualified
with a professional or degree level qualification

up to 0%	9
0% to 2%	34
2% to 3%	16
3% to 5%	20
5% & above	21

% of all residents in Britain

Scale

☐ = 250 000
people

6.14: Proportion of Adults by Sex in each Socioeconomic Group in Britain 1971–1981–1991

% of men and women aged over 15/16 in each socioeconomic group

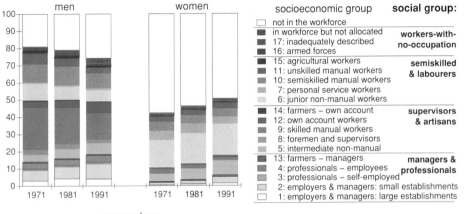

year and sex

6.15: Workforce by Age, Sex and Social Group in Britain 1991

% of workforce in each social group by age and sex

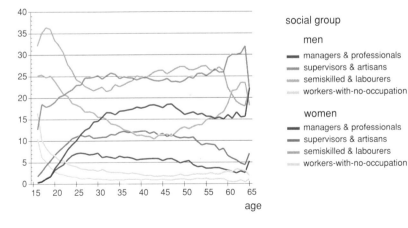

Workers-with-no-Occupation

Having left school or college, young adults who look for work enter a labour market in which their efforts are rewarded unequally depending on the kind of job they do. From this their status in society is largely derived. The categorization of people into different social classes based on their occupations has been a significant component of the census since 1911, and a detailed socioeconomic group classification has subsequently been developed which, since 1971, has categorized people into seventeen groups based on the "social and economic status" of their occupations and ignoring short term unemployment. Figure 6.14 shows how the number of adults in these groups has changed over time for both men and women. Over twenty years the basic social structure changes slowly, so the most common socioeconomic group for men has remained skilled manual workers (group nine), whereas women are still most likely to be junior non-manual workers (group six) if they are in work. For adults in the workforce, the 17 socioeconomic groups have been amalgamated into four social groups, the constitution of which is also shown in Figure 6.14. Here we are concerned with the miscellaneous group "workers-with-no-occupation" composed, in 1991, of just under a million and a half adults: 14% in the armed forces, 18% with inadequately described or unstated occupations and 68% who had never worked (or not worked for ten years) and wished to work and so could not be assigned a specific occupation. These three groups are combined by default, but their members do also share many things in common. Studies have found, for example, that former members of the armed forces and people who have never worked have similar high chances of ending up sleeping rough (JRF 1993).

The geographical distribution of workers-with-no-occupation is shown opposite. Not surprisingly it reflects the distribution of long term unemployment (page 91), although towns and villages with large army, navy or airforce bases also stand out in counties like North Yorkshire, Hampshire and Norfolk. In 1981 4.8% of the workforce were assigned to this social group, and by 1991 this proportion had risen to 5.7%, but the rise was far from evenly spread across the country. The second map opposite shows how the changes which took place in the 1980s reinforced this picture of growing urban/rural divides. This growth was also concentrated amongst younger people, especially men, while for both sexes the numbers of people within this group who were in the armed forces fell. Figure 6.15 contrasts the age and sex profiles for each of the four social groups which are discussed in detail here and in the following pages. Workers-with-no-occupation are predominantly aged under 25 and men are roughly twice as likely to be in this group as are women. Most women in work are in semiskilled & labouring occupations, and this is true regardless of their age. Men, however, by the age of 23 are more likely to be supervisors & artisans than to be semiskilled & labourers and by the age of 31 more men are professionals & managers than fall within the semiskilled & labourer category.

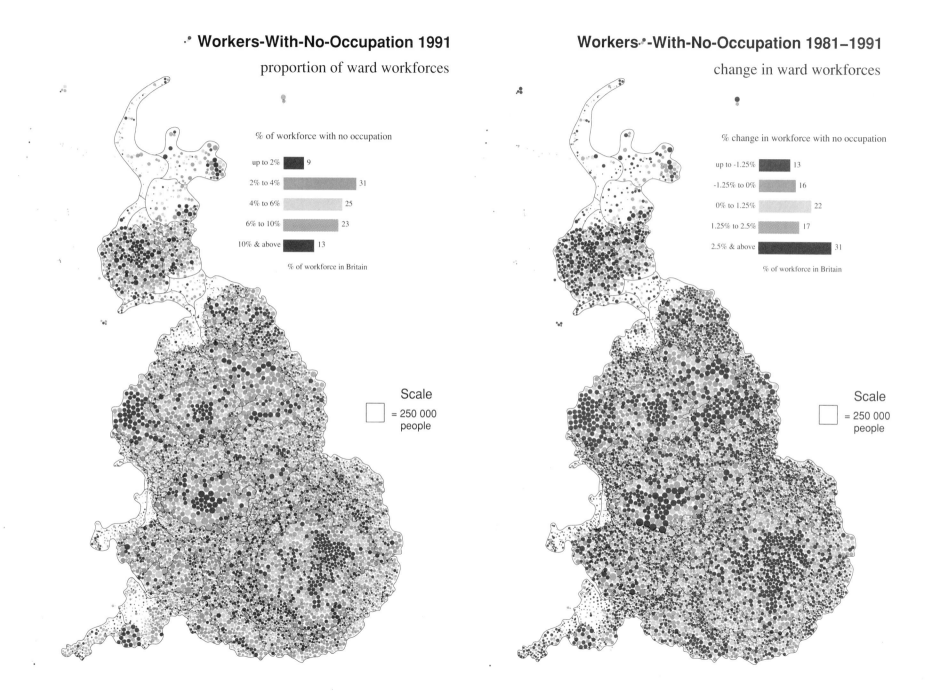

Workers-With-No-Occupation 1991

proportion of ward workforces

% of workforce with no occupation

up to 2%	9
2% to 4%	31
4% to 6%	25
6% to 10%	23
10% & above	13

% of workforce in Britain

Scale

☐ = 250 000 people

Workers-With-No-Occupation 1981–1991

change in ward workforces

% change in workforce with no occupation

up to -1.25%	13
-1.25% to 0%	16
0% to 1.25%	22
1.25% to 2.5%	17
2.5% & above	31

% of workforce in Britain

Scale

☐ = 250 000 people

6.16: Distribution of the Workforce Across Social Groups and Family Types in Britain 1991

circles show the absolute difference between the observed number of economically active residents in each family type and the number which could be expected if all social groups had similar family compositions

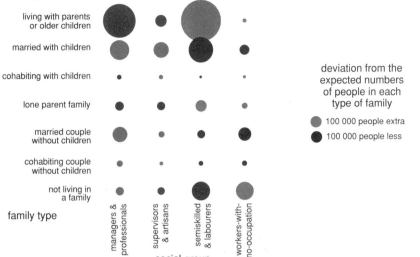

6.17: Residents in Employment by Social and Ethnic Group in Britain 1991

% of people in employment

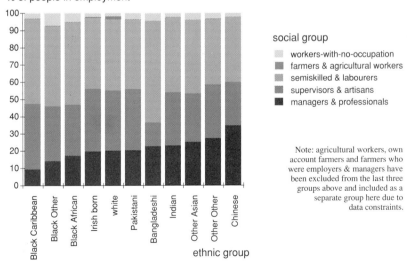

social group

- workers-with-no-occupation
- farmers & agricultural workers
- semiskilled & labourers
- supervisors & artisans
- managers & professionals

Note: agricultural workers, own account farmers and farmers who were employers & managers have been excluded from the last three groups above and included as a separate group here due to data constraints.

Semiskilled & Labourers

The largest of the four social groups studied here have occupations classed as "semiskilled & labouring" and included 48% of the workforce in 1971, 45% in 1981 and 41% in 1991. Most women in this group are employed in junior clerical or secretarial jobs whilst most men are employed as semiskilled or unskilled manual workers. What all the people in this group have in common is that they are the most lowly paid of employees and are also in jobs where they are likely to have little control over their work. Over time the proportion of this group made up of women has increased from 54% in 1971 to 62% by 1991.

The geographical distribution of workers in these occupations is shown opposite. In 1991 three quarters of the population of Britain lived in wards where between a third and a half of the workforce were semiskilled & labourers. Their work is obviously required everywhere, so that areas where there are relatively few people in this social group are often abutted by areas with over-average proportions: Richmond and Hounslow for example. However, the second map drawn opposite shows how this situation may be changing. Over three quarters of the population of Britain live in wards which have experienced falls in the size of this group since 1981, and a fifth of the population have seen falls of over 8%. Predominantly London but also Birmingham, Liverpool, Manchester and Glasgow have sustained the bulk of this decline. If this map is compared with the map of change in workers-with-no-occupation (page 185) it becomes evident that where there has been the greatest decrease in the proportion of workers who were semiskilled or labourers there have also been the largest increases in workers-with-no-occupation. One hypothesis for this change is that, as they grew up during the 1980s, many of the children of people in this social group were unable to find any work which, because of where they lived, would have probably been in semiskilled & labouring occupations. But, to explain all of the aggregate decline which has occurred in the number of workers in this social group, others of those children and some of the workers in this group must now be in higher status occupations.

Social groups can be caricatured in many ways. Figure 6.16 shows how workers in semiskilled & labouring occupations are much more likely to be looking after elderly parents or not leaving home when they reach adulthood (as opposed to managers & professionals). Members of different ethnic groups also have very different social group profiles as Figure 6.17 shows. These are partly influenced by their differing age and sex distributions and the geographical locations of each group (see page 44). Also, within each group there are differences which should be remembered when considering other aspects such as family type. For instance, Bangladeshi workers are more likely to be professionals & managers than are Pakistanis or whites, but are also more likely to be semiskilled & labourers than are the members of any other ethnic group.

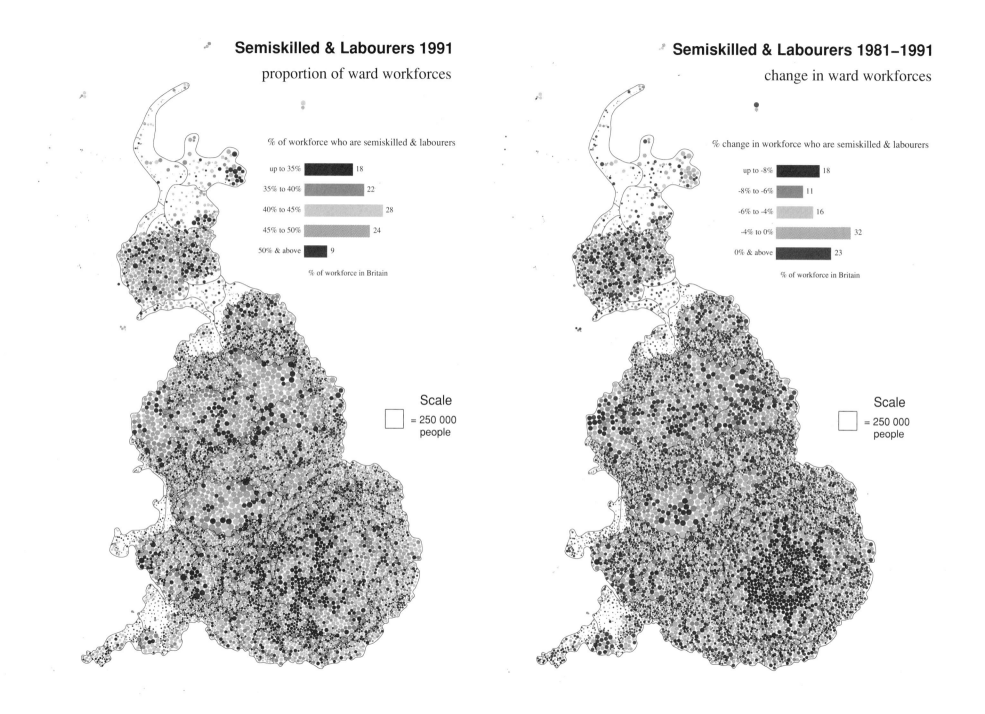

Semiskilled & Labourers 1991

proportion of ward workforces

% of workforce who are semiskilled & labourers

up to 35%	18
35% to 40%	22
40% to 45%	28
45% to 50%	24
50% & above	9

% of workforce in Britain

Scale

☐ = 250 000 people

Semiskilled & Labourers 1981–1991

change in ward workforces

% change in workforce who are semiskilled & labourers

up to -8%	18
-8% to -6%	11
-6% to -4%	16
-4% to 0%	32
0% & above	23

% of workforce in Britain

Scale

☐ = 250 000 people

6.18: Some Characteristics of Households by Socioeconomic Group in Britain 1991, 1981–1991

	Distribution of socioeconomic groups between households		Characteristics of the households which these groups head					
			Proportion of children in household		Proportion of adults not in the workforce		Heads a household with no car	
Socioeconomic group of the head of the household (with examples of occupations in brackets)	Share 1991	Changes (1981–1991)	1991	(1981–1991)	1991	(1981–1991)	1991	(1981–1991)
Total households with residents	21.44 million	(10.0%)	22.0%	(-2.7%)	37.2%	(0.3%)	33.1%	(-6.3%)
1 Employers and managers in large establishments	3.9%	(-0.8%)	26.8%	(-0.5%)	15.0%	(-13.0%)	5.6%	(-5.0%)
2 Employers and managers in small establishments	8.0%	(0.1%)	27.1%	(-0.1%)	14.4%	(-16.8%)	6.2%	(-5.1%)
3 Professional workers (architect) self-employed	0.9%	(0.1%)	31.1%	(-0.0%)	19.5%	(-14.5%)	2.0%	(-2.2%)
4 Professional workers (solicitor) - employees	3.2%	(-0.3%)	26.4%	(-2.7%)	15.3%	(-13.6%)	6.0%	(-2.7%)
5.1 Ancillary workers and artists (teacher, nurse)	6.8%	(0.6%)	25.4%	(-0.3%)	11.5%	(-14.1%)	12.6%	(-7.7%)
5.2 Foremen and supervisors - non-manual (clerk)	0.5%	(-0.3%)	24.1%	(-0.2%)	10.9%	(-17.9%)	15.1%	(-8.7%)
6 Junior non-manual workers (check-out operator)	7.1%	(-2.5%)	23.4%	(1.4%)	9.8%	(-19.1%)	23.4%	(-11.2%)
7 Personal service workers (chef, waiter/ress)	1.4%	(-0.5%)	28.4%	(4.4%)	9.9%	(-14.1%)	45.8%	(-20.5%)
8 Foremen and supervisors - manual (storekeeper)	1.8%	(-1.5%)	24.9%	(0.4%)	13.8%	(-16.2%)	12.4%	(-13.6%)
9 Skilled manual workers (builder, baker, driver)	10.3%	(-8.0%)	26.1%	(-1.6%)	14.2%	(-14.4%)	17.2%	(-15.8%)
10 Semi-skilled manual workers (care assistant)	6.5%	(-4.5%)	24.4%	(0.9%)	13.9%	(-17.7%)	30.8%	(-18.2%)
11 Unskilled manual workers (road sweeper)	2.6%	(-1.9%)	24.6%	(0.9%)	14.1%	(-18.9%)	47.6%	(-18.5%)
12 Self-employed non-professionals without employees	5.1%	(1.0%)	27.6%	(-3.2%)	16.0%	(-11.7%)	7.3%	(-6.6%)
13 Farmers - employers and managers (who own/rent)	0.3%	(-0.3%)	25.0%	(1.0%)	19.8%	(-19.4%)	1.6%	(-4.6%)
14 Farmers - own account (has only family employees)	0.3%	(-0.2%)	22.3%	(0.0%)	20.5%	(-20.9%)	2.5%	(-6.9%)
15 Agricultural workers (forester, fishing worker)	0.4%	(-0.4%)	23.9%	(-0.3%)	16.5%	(-19.0%)	13.7%	(-15.8%)
16 Members of armed forces (all ranks & occupations)	0.6%	(-0.1%)	34.4%	(-1.8%)	16.8%	(-14.0%)	8.8%	(-11.2%)
17 Inadequately described; plus people having no occupation	1.9%	(0.5%)	28.3%	(-3.0%)	19.1%	(-2.8%)	56.7%	(-1.3%)
Economically inactive (e.g. retired, looking after home)	38.3%	(19.0%)	12.3%	(-2.5%)	85.0%	(5.4%)	57.8%	(-17.7%)

Note: change estimates are slightly biased as the 1981 census tables allocated 1.2 million households headed by someone who was retired to the socioeconomic group to which their last occupation was assigned. These people and their households were excluded from the socioeconomic group classifications in the 1991 census tables and placed, instead, in the economically inactive group, thus inflating the increase reported for that group and having a smaller but significant effect on the magnitudes of the other changes reported.

6.19: Mortality of Men by Social Class in England and Wales 1930–1983

standardized mortality ratios for men aged 15 to 64 in each social class

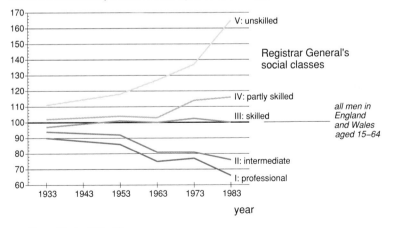

Source: Blaxter, 1991, p.72

Supervisors & Artisans

Supervisors & artisans include workers in occupations ranging from foremen to own account farmers and thus represent a middle income group who have more control over their work than do those who are paid less. This second largest social group has also been decreasing in size in recent decades, although more slowly than has the group comprising labourers & semiskilled workers. In 1971 supervisors & artisans made up 35.4% of the workforce. This fell to 34.6% in 1981 and 33.8% by 1991. The proportion of this group who were women rose from two out of ten in 1971 to three out of ten in 1991. Geographically there is also little variation in this group, with the key to the map opposite showing that three quarters of the population live in wards where between 30% and 40% of all workers are in this group. Supervisors & artisans are least likely to be found in the centres of cities or in the Home Counties west of London, but are clearly found around concentrations of industries requiring their labour — the pottery wards in Staffordshire for instance. The very gradual decline in the size of this group has been reflected in a speckled pattern of change over the 1980s shown in the second map opposite. The majority of the wards in which this group is growing are in the south of the country, whilst former mining areas have experienced the most dramatic falls.

Just as social groups are unevenly spread among different family types and ethnic groups (see page 186), almost all other aspects of life in Britain reveal strong divides in the experiences of these people and their households. Previous chapters have explored how different groups travel (Figure 3.16), work (Figures 3.19 and 3.28), are housed (Figures 4.19 and 4.22) and suffer from illness (Figure 5.2). Some more differences are shown in Figure 6.18 which concentrates on households rather than individuals and also looks at how these differences have been changing during the last decade. The figure shows that most socioeconomic groups have been declining in terms of the number who head households. The only increases have been in households headed by a person with no occupation, someone who is self-employed, an ancillary worker (such as a technician) or the manager of a small establishment. The biggest increase has been in the number of households headed by a person not in the workforce (although the available data exaggerates this rise — see note). The figure also shows the proportions (and changes in the proportions) of households without access to a car, household members who are children and adult household members who are not in the workforce.

One perennial research concern with social groups has been the divergence in their life chances over time, most clearly illustrated by the relative changes in mortality rates shown in Figure 6.19. Unfortunately, the social groups on which this figure is based use the old Registrar General's social class codings and are known to be increasingly unreliable over time. This figure cannot be updated with confidence until information from the Longitudinal Study is released from the 1991 census (Goldblatt and Fox 1988).

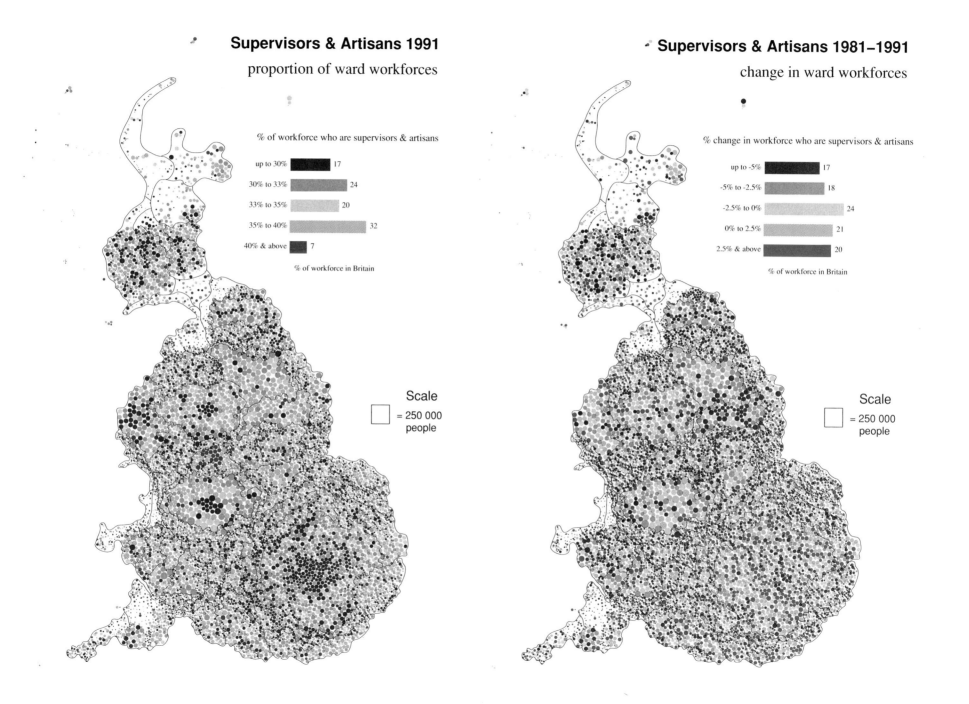

Supervisors & Artisans 1991

proportion of ward workforces

% of workforce who are supervisors & artisans

up to 30%	17
30% to 33%	24
33% to 35%	20
35% to 40%	32
40% & above	7

% of workforce in Britain

Scale

= 250 000
people

Supervisors & Artisans 1981–1991

change in ward workforces

% change in workforce who are supervisors & artisans

up to -5%	17
-5% to -2.5%	18
-2.5% to 0%	24
0% to 2.5%	21
2.5% & above	20

% of workforce in Britain

Scale

= 250 000
people

6.20: Residents in Socioeconomic Groups by Degree Qualification in Britain 1971, 1991

socioeconomic group of the workforce (with other groups separately identified): SEG number

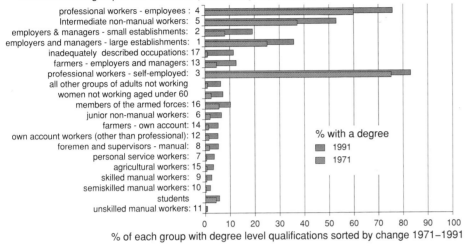

% of each group with degree level qualifications sorted by change 1971–1991

6.21: Social Group of Graduates by Subject of Degree in Britain 1991

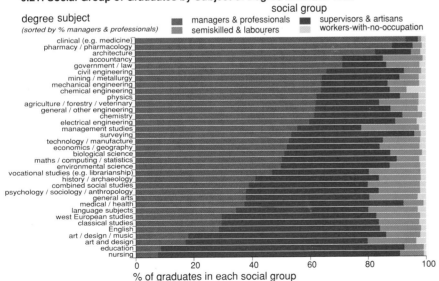

% of graduates in each social group

Managers & Professionals

Of the four social groups which are studied individually in this atlas, the group with the highest status has been growing most quickly — managers & professionals. In 1971 only one worker in eight was included in this group; by 1981 this proportion had risen to one worker in seven, and by 1991 one worker in five was a manager and/or professional. Although this rapid rise may be partly due to the re-labelling of jobs over time it is unlikely that cosmetic changes account for most of the increase. A rise in women's participation from 16% to 27% of this group between 1971 and 1991 has fuelled part of the growth. Geographically this group is the most unevenly distributed section of society, with a quarter of the population of Britain living in areas where either less than one in ten, or more than one in three, of all workers in their ward are managers & professionals. The first map drawn opposite reveals the distinctive belt of affluent wards which runs down through central London and around the Home Counties as well as the ribbons of higher status workers that are found clustered in smaller colonies further north. The second map shows how this pattern is being reinforced by the social changes which took place during the 1980s. In some parts of London, Manchester and a few other major cities the beginnings of gentrification can be seen, as areas with formerly low proportions of workers in this group have experienced rapid rises in their numbers.

The passport for most to enter this social group is a university degree, and this is increasingly a necessity, as Figure 6.20 demonstrates. The largest increases in the proportions of workers with a degree by 1991 have been predominantly in those socioeconomic groups which already had the highest proportions in 1971. Most of these groups are in the high status managers & professionals social group mapped here and, whilst for every socioeconomic group the proportion of workers holding a degree has increased, this increase has been slowest for members of the least well paid group: semiskilled & labourers. Conversely, many members of the lowest status social group (of workers-with-no-occupation) now have degrees and this group experienced the fifth largest increase in graduates over the twenty year period! The implications of this finding are that although a degree may be increasingly necessary to secure membership of the highest status social group, it no longer guarantees exclusion from the lowest status group. However, the type of degree an individual has is important in determining his/her likely social group, as is demonstrated by Figure 6.21 which shows how graduates with clinical degrees (medicine or dentistry) are most likely to be in the highest status group, whilst workers with nursing qualifications are least likely to be in this group. In 1991 it was chemical engineers who were most likely to have no occupation, management studies graduates who were most likely to be in semiskilled & labouring occupations, and workers with their highest qualification in education who were most likely to be supervisors & artisans (which, by the official classification, includes teaching).

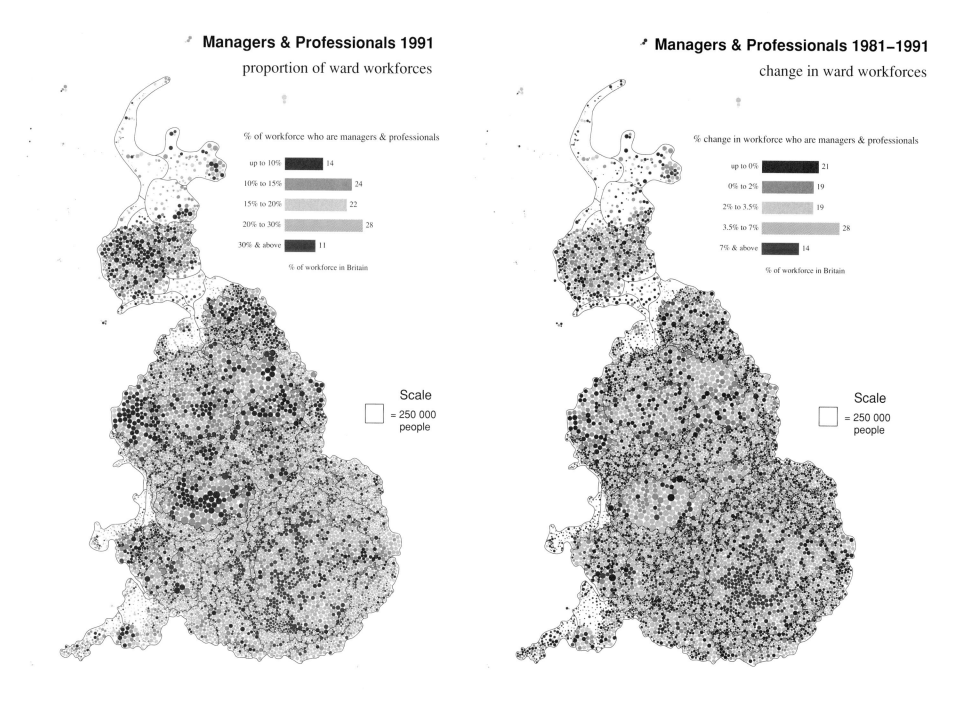

Managers & Professionals 1991

proportion of ward workforces

% of workforce who are managers & professionals

up to 10%	14
10% to 15%	24
15% to 20%	22
20% to 30%	28
30% & above	11

% of workforce in Britain

Scale
☐ = 250 000
people

Managers & Professionals 1981–1991

change in ward workforces

% change in workforce who are managers & professionals

up to 0%	21
0% to 2%	19
2% to 3.5%	19
3.5% to 7%	28
7% & above	14

% of workforce in Britain

Scale
☐ = 250 000
people

6.22: Distribution of Workers by Social Group in Britain 1991 by Ward

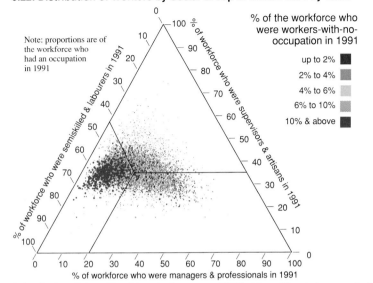

% of the workforce who were workers-with-no-occupation in 1991

- up to 2%
- 2% to 4%
- 4% to 6%
- 6% to 10%
- 10% & above

the axes in the triangle mark the position of the national average ward (5.7% of the workforce had no occupation)

6.23: Change in Semiskilled Workers by Change in Managers in Britain 1981–1991 by Ward

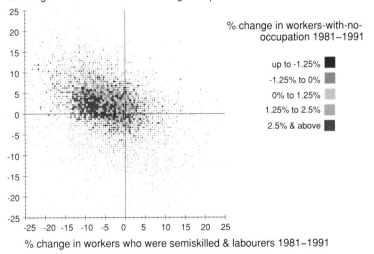

% change in workers-with-no-occupation 1981–1991

- up to -1.25%
- -1.25% to 0%
- 0% to 1.25%
- 1.25% to 2.5%
- 2.5% & above

% change in workers who were semiskilled & labourers 1981–1991

Social Groups

Having looked at each of the four social groups individually, the aggregate pattern of social status through occupation in Britain is now examined and a guide to how that pattern might be changing is also given. The first map opposite categorizes each ward by one of the four social groups according to which group is most over-represented in that ward as compared with the national average (workers-with-no-occupation: 6%, semiskilled & labourers: 41%, supervisors & artisans: 34%, managers & professionals: 20%). Because managers & professionals have the most diverse geographical spread they categorize the highest proportion of wards by population, dominating the south east of the country. The second largest group are the semiskilled & labourers. These wards intersperse with the areas of highest professional & managerial employment, dominating the north of the country where they appear to form the background of the picture, whereas in the south these wards are in the foreground. Wards with high numbers of supervisors & artisans are most abundant in the midlands, whilst 13% of the population live in wards where the greatest absolute excess is in workers-with-no-occupation.

The relationship of these four social groups within wards is shown in Figure 6.22 in which each of the ten thousand wards are placed in the triangle according to the proportions of their workforce in each of the three social groups with occupations, the ward being coloured according to the proportion of its workforce with no occupation. The figure demonstrates that managers & professionals are less likely to live in wards with a high proportion of workers who are semiskilled & labourers, but all wards are mixed and many very much so. Social segregation is more apparent across smaller areas.

The second map drawn opposite shows how the geography of social status in Britain changed over the 1980s. To draw the map, each ward was categorized according to the most over-represented social group in 1981 as well as in 1991. Each social group was then given a number ranging from one for the lowest status group to four for the highest, for each of the two censuses. The map plots the difference between these two numbers. Thus 60% of the population in Britain live in wards in which the same social group has been most over-represented at both censuses. A fifth of the population have dropped in status by one category and a tenth have risen by one category. The remaining 10% of the population have experienced more dramatic changes, of which the clearest cluster is of a large group of wards in south west London which has jumped up two or more categories in one decade. The within-ward variations behind some of these changes are shown in Figure 6.23 which concentrates on the inter-relationship between the top and the largest social group. Increases in the number of managers & professionals in wards have been matched by falls in the number of semiskilled & labourers, and by growth in the bottom social group due to the increase in the numbers of people in the workforce who have never had an occupation or have been out of work for over ten years.

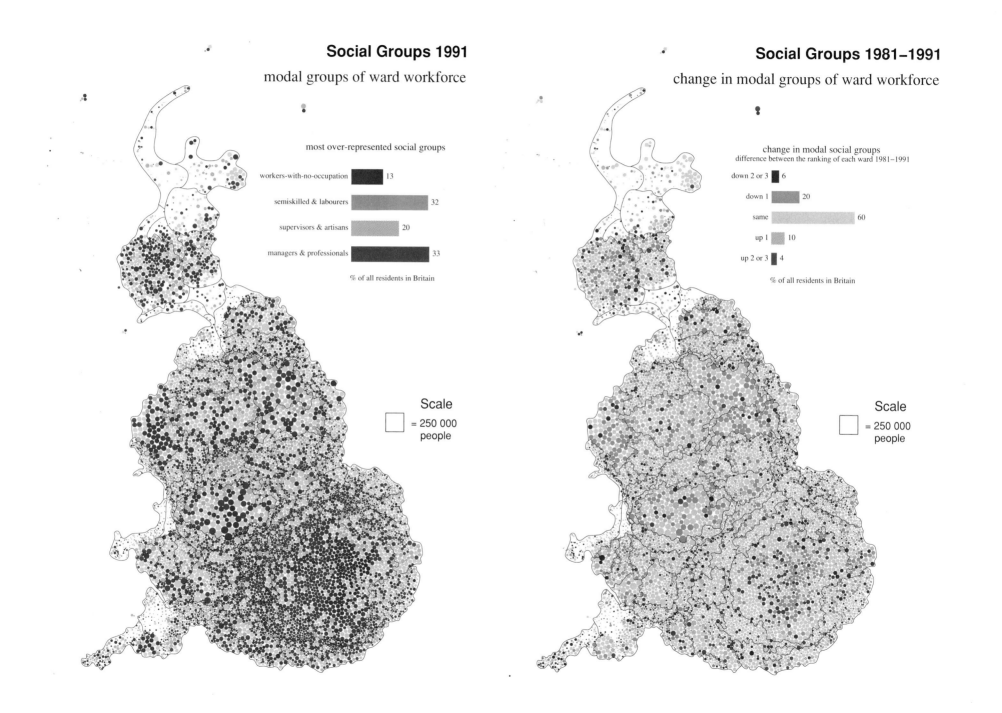

Social Groups 1991

modal groups of ward workforce

most over-represented social groups

workers-with-no-occupation		13
semiskilled & labourers		32
supervisors & artisans		20
managers & professionals		33

% of all residents in Britain

Scale

☐ = 250 000 people

Social Groups 1981–1991

change in modal groups of ward workforce

change in modal social groups
difference between the ranking of each ward 1981–1991

down 2 or 3		6
down 1		20
same		60
up 1		10
up 2 or 3		4

% of all residents in Britain

Scale

☐ = 250 000 people

6.24: Households With Surplus Cars by Households with No Cars in Britain 1991 by Ward

% of households with no cars and two or more residents aged 17 or over in 1991

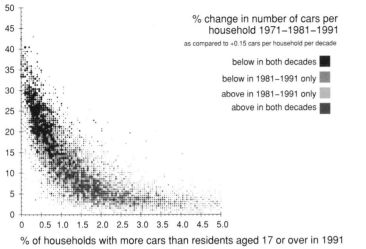

% change in number of cars per
household 1971–1981–1991

as compared to +0.15 cars per household per decade

below in both decades ■
below in 1981–1991 only ▨
above in 1981–1991 only ▨
above in both decades ■

% of households with more cars than residents aged 17 or over in 1991

6.25: Adults With Cars Not Using Them to Travel to Work 1991, 1981–1991

workers in households with more than
one car not travelling to work by car

up to 17%	■
17% to 20%	▨
20% to 25%	▨
25% to 33%	▨
33% & above	■

1991

change in workers in households with more
than one car not travelling to work by car

up to -6%	■
-5% to -6%	▨
-4% to -5%	▨
-3% to -4%	▨
-3% & above	■

1981–1991

Car Availability

The socioeconomic status of occupations is only one facet of social division in Britain. There can be great differences between the social status of two people doing the same kind of job, while people who do not work can hold any level in the hierarchy. Many aspects of social status (including inherited position, accent and access to exclusive education) are difficult to quantify. If status were only measured from answers to the census, then some members of the royal family might be recorded in the lowest social group because they have no classifiable occupation, live in subsidised accommodation and are largely reliant on the state for their income! The next few pages look at one alternative indicator of social status — *wealth*: those assets a person owns which can be bought or sold (Royal Commission on the Distribution of Income and Wealth 1980: 20). Suitable available data for this atlas relate to cars, property and shares.

How many cars a household has access to is the clearest census measure of wealth but, because many people need cars (to do their work or because they live in areas without public transport), it is not a particularly good surrogate. However, households who have access to more cars and vans than there are people aged 17 or over living in the household may well be relatively wealthy. The first map drawn opposite shows where these households with "surplus" cars are most and least likely to live. The second map shows the locations of households with two or more adults who had no access to a car in 1991. Although these "deficit" households do not live in completely different places from households with surplus cars, the inverse relationship is strong, as Figure 6.24 demonstrates. Very few wards contain an unusual number of both wealthy and poor households using these two measures of car availability. The figure also shows that the differences which do exist have been increasing in magnitude over time. Car availability has been growing most slowly in those areas where there are the most households which have no access to a car and faster where there are often more cars than drivers.

Another way in which cars may be classed as surplus to requirement is if a household has access to more than one car, but someone in that household does not use a car to get to work. Figure 6.25 shows that these households are located predominantly in London, where there are extensive alternative means of travelling to work and where road congestion is most serious (page 81). Towns such as Oxford and Cambridge are also included in the top shading category (as are some rural areas where farmers are often classified as walking to work). The second map in Figure 6.25 shows how this situation has changed since 1981. Then, of the six million workers who lived in households with more than one car, 27% travelled to work by some other means. By 1991, ten million workers lived in households with more than one car, but only 23% travelled to work by some other means. Car use increased most rapidly in cities such as Bristol, Birmingham and London. Over time, car ownership has become less of a luxury.

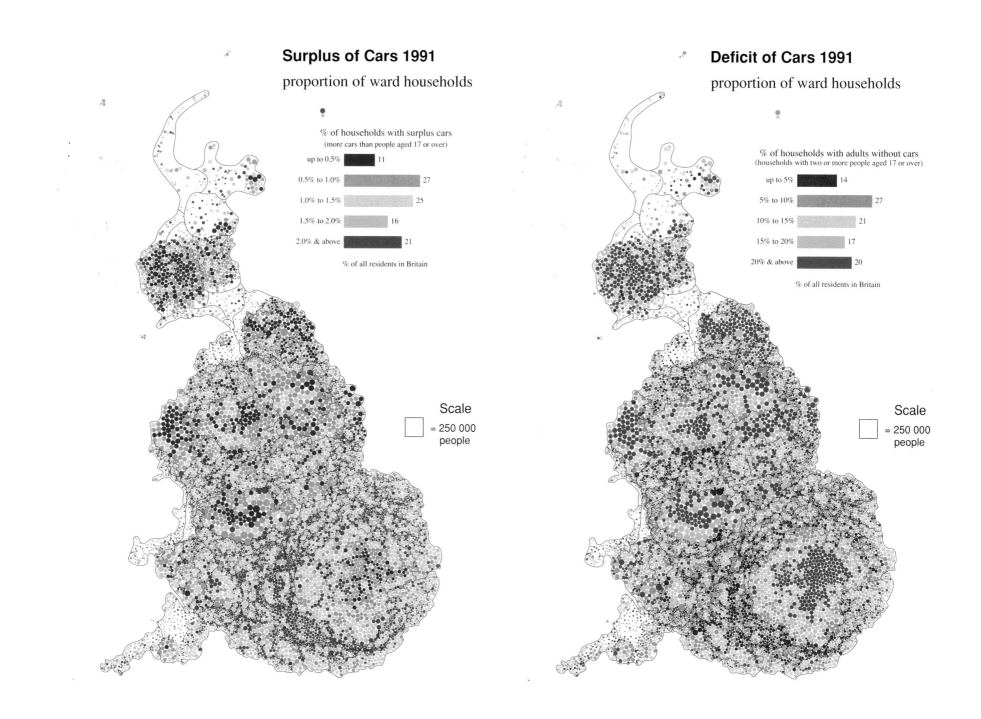

Surplus of Cars 1991

proportion of ward households

% of households with surplus cars
(more cars than people aged 17 or over)

up to 0.5%	11
0.5% to 1.0%	27
1.0% to 1.5%	25
1.5% to 2.0%	16
2.0% & above	21

% of all residents in Britain

Scale

☐ = 250 000
people

Deficit of Cars 1991

proportion of ward households

% of households with adults without cars
(households with two or more people aged 17 or over)

up to 5%	14
5% to 10%	27
10% to 15%	21
15% to 20%	17
20% & above	20

% of all residents in Britain

Scale

☐ = 250 000
people

6.26: Availability of Cars to Households by District Type 1971, 1981, 1991

average number of cars per household

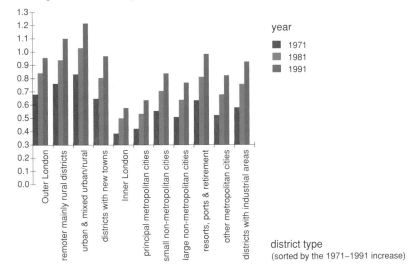

year
- 1971
- 1981
- 1991

district type
(sorted by the 1971–1991 increase)

6.27: Change in Households with No Access to a Car by Tenure 1981–1991

% change in households in owner occupation with no access to a car

% change in households in local authority tenure with no access to a car

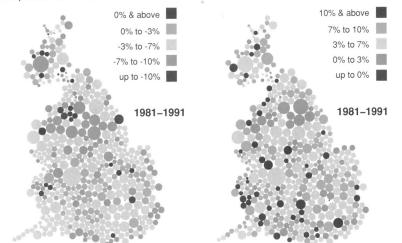

| 0% & above |
| 0% to -3% |
| -3% to -7% |
| -7% to -10% |
| up to -10% |

1981–1991

| 10% & above |
| 7% to 10% |
| 3% to 7% |
| 0% to 3% |
| up to 0% |

1981–1991

Changes in Car Availability

In Britain as a whole there are now almost as many cars as households (97 cars for every 100 households) while in 1981 there were four cars for every five households and in 1971 there were only two cars for every three households. However, this availability and its increase has not been evenly spread across the country. The variation is illustrated by Figure 6.26. The differences are due to different levels of need for a car in different areas, the proportion of households that can afford any car, and the extent of wealth which allows many households to have more than one vehicle. Between 1971 and 1991 average numbers of cars per household have increased most in those areas which had most cars to begin with. These changes reflect the build-up of wealth in different parts of the country and so the maps drawn here show change — to reflect this accumulation.

The first map examines average numbers of cars per household. Two thirds of the population are split between wards with consistently low or consistently high increases over the past two decades and there is a clear geographical pattern to this polarization. However, the map also shows that the rise in car ownership slowed in many suburbs during the 1980s. This map should be compared with that of change in car use (page 83).

The second map looks at households with two or more cars. In 1971 9% of households had two or more cars, rising to 16% in 1981 and 23% in 1991. But, by this measure, three quarters of the population were split between wards with consistently low or consistently high increases over the past two decades. An even starker contrast between the increasingly affluent and the relatively poor halves of Britain is seen to be growing. There are half as many households in the middle two categories than would be the case if the changes over time were not related. Similarly, the geographical clustering of areas is unlikely to be due to chance. For example, the cluster in south west London of recent over-average growth may signify gentrification.

Changes in the proportion of households which have no access to a car can also be drawn. These changes can be shown for subsets of the population, and in Figure 6.27 the geographies of the 1980s decline in car availability amongst local authority tenants and the increase in car availability amongst owner occupiers in Britain are shown side by side. In 1981 24% of owner occupiers and 62% of local authority tenant households had no access to a car. By 1991 these proportions had altered to 19% and 68% respectively, suggesting that those households who exercised their right to buy were more likely to be car owners. However, as the figure shows, the areas where the growth in car ownership amongst owner occupiers has been strongest are very similar to those areas where the decline in ownership amongst local authority tenants has been weakest, suggesting that these changes are not explained mainly by tenure transfer but by changes in the average wealth of whole districts and of tenure groups. For instance, ownership declined for both groups in Knowsley, Harlow and Crawley, and increased for both groups in Chichester.

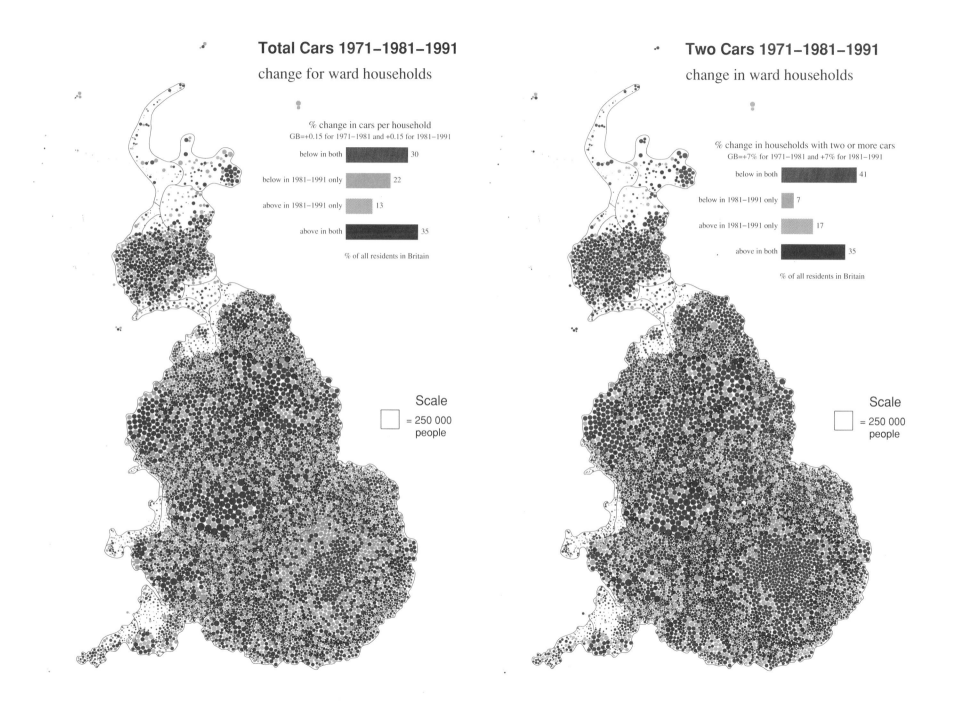

Total Cars 1971–1981–1991

change for ward households

% change in cars per household
GB=+0.15 for 1971–1981 and +0.15 for 1981–1991

below in both 30

below in 1981–1991 only 22

above in 1981–1991 only 13

above in both 35

% of all residents in Britain

Scale

☐ = 250 000 people

Two Cars 1971–1981–1991

change in ward households

% change in households with two or more cars
GB=+7% for 1971–1981 and +7% for 1981–1991

below in both 41

below in 1981–1991 only 7

above in 1981–1991 only 17

above in both 35

% of all residents in Britain

Scale

☐ = 250 000 people

6.28: Equity Held in Housing by Region and Year of Purchase in Britain by 1993

£ '000s average equity of house buyers who bought 1988–1991 with positive equity in 1993

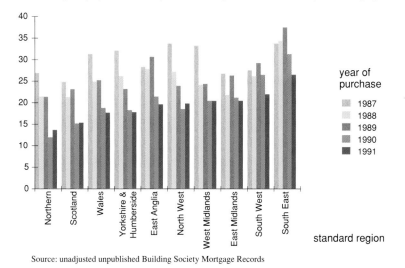

Source: unadjusted unpublished Building Society Mortgage Records

6.29: First-time Buyers' Deposit by Average Borrowers' Income at 1991 Prices by Ward in Britain

£ '000s average first-time buyers' deposit towards property purchase at 1991 prices

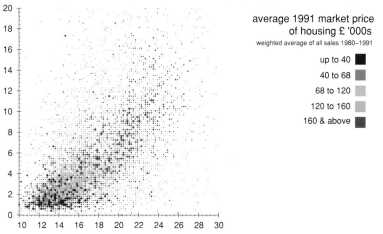

£ '000s average of all home buyers' annual household incomes in that ward

Housing Equity

The second type of wealth which is considered here is that held in the form of housing. House prices and home-owner debt have already been addressed in this atlas (in Chapter 4) and the geography of negative equity has been drawn using data from a building society. Here the same data are employed to map positive equity in housing — showing where the wealth held in "bricks and mortar" is concentrated net of mortgage commitments. It is important to note that these estimates exclude the even greater wealth of people who own outright the property they live in, or other property they own.

Positive housing equity is strongly related to the deposit which buyers were able to place towards the purchase of property for which they also borrowed money. Second time buyers built up the majority of this money from the positive equity in their previous property, but first time buyers have to raise it from savings or gifts, and thus the initial deposit which home buyers are able to put down in different areas gives a better indication of wealth in those areas. The first map opposite shows how these deposits varied from averaging under two thousand pounds inside northern cities to over eight thousand pounds in west London. Part of the reason for higher deposits in the south is that they may have been required from building societies as prices are higher in the south and buyers are only permitted to borrow a certain multiple of their income. Nevertheless the map gives an impression of where people are somehow able to raise these sums of money. Figure 4.24 showed how these deposits have changed since 1981 by region.

The second map drawn opposite is of the average positive equity in 1993 held by all borrowers who took out a mortgage between 1988 and 1991 with the building society. These dates are chosen so that the map is comparable with that of negative equity shown on page 129. Despite the large house price falls which have occurred in recent years, one person in four still lives in a ward where the average borrower has over thirty thousand pounds worth of wealth tied up in his or her home. Traditionally, buyers who have held their property for the longest would be expected to have most positive equity, as housing inflation increased their wealth, but as Figure 6.28 illustrates this relationship has become less regular in those regions experiencing erratic price changes.

The building society data set can also be used to estimate borrowers' incomes as is described on page 204. The geographical relationship between all borrowers' incomes, the average deposits of first time buyers in an area and the average price of housing in that area are shown in Figure 6.29. All three variables are strongly positively related, as would be expected, although there are some areas where borrowers have relatively high incomes but low deposits, or relatively low incomes but high deposits — and house prices in these areas tend to be lower. Thus housing wealth cannot be seen in isolation from other forms of wealth as savings or inheritance are needed to buy housing. Housing equity can also be used to raise loans to purchase other assets — such as cars.

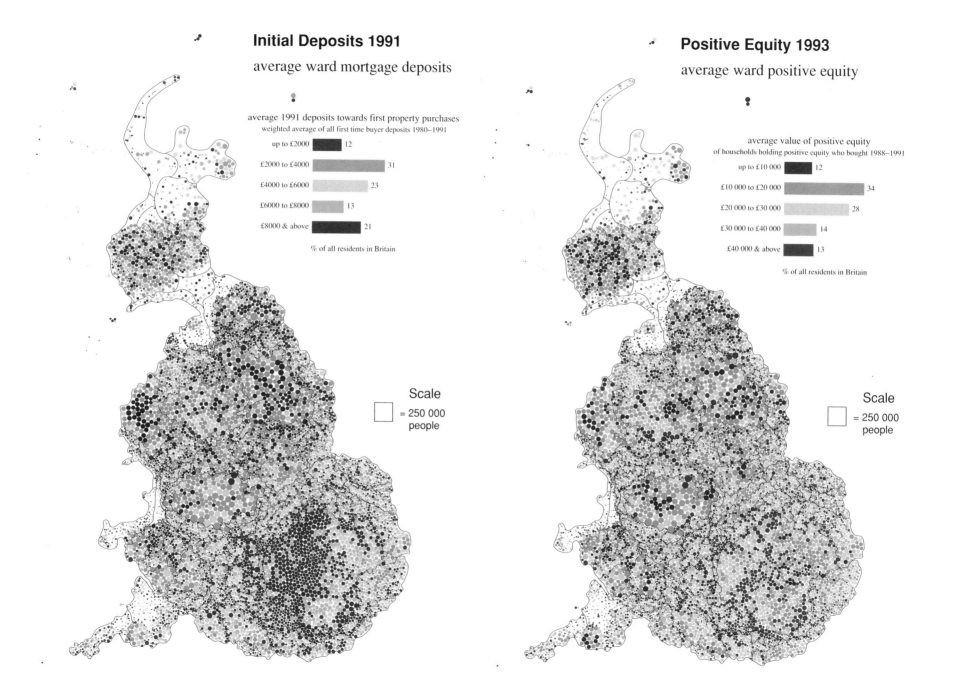

Initial Deposits 1991

average ward mortgage deposits

average 1991 deposits towards first property purchases
weighted average of all first time buyer deposits 1980–1991

up to £2000	12
£2000 to £4000	31
£4000 to £6000	23
£6000 to £8000	13
£8000 & above	21

% of all residents in Britain

Scale

☐ = 250 000 people

Positive Equity 1993

average ward positive equity

average value of positive equity
of households holding positive equity who bought 1988–1991

up to £10 000	12
£10 000 to £20 000	34
£20 000 to £30 000	28
£30 000 to £40 000	14
£40 000 & above	13

% of all residents in Britain

Scale

☐ = 250 000 people

6.30: Composition of the Net Wealth of the UK Personal Sector 1971–1993

the proportion of all wealth held by individuals in each form at each year (and total value at contemporary prices)

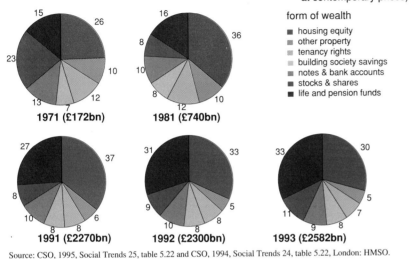

1971 (£172bn)

1981 (£740bn)

1991 (£2270bn)

1992 (£2300bn)

1993 (£2582bn)

form of wealth

■ housing equity
▨ other property
▨ tenancy rights
▨ building society savings
▨ notes & bank accounts
■ stocks & shares
■ life and pension funds

Source: CSO, 1995, Social Trends 25, table 5.22 and CSO, 1994, Social Trends 24, table 5.22, London: HMSO.

6.31: Different Forms of Wealth in Britain — Gini Curves

% residents living in wards orded by wealth (10% = richest tenth)

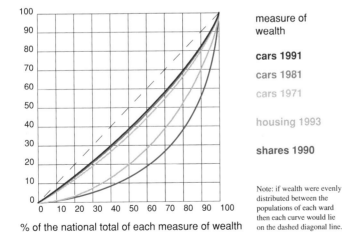

% of the national total of each measure of wealth

measure of
wealth

cars 1991

cars 1981

cars 1971

housing 1993

shares 1990

Note: if wealth were evenly distributed between the populations of each ward then each curve would lie on the dashed diagonal line.

Share Ownership

At the time of the 1991 census over a third of all personal wealth was held in the form of housing, whilst only a twentieth was held in other assets such as cars (see Figure 6.30). The second largest repository of wealth was in life and pension funds (although it is arguable how marketable this wealth is) and the third was savings mainly held in bank and building society accounts. The fourth largest store of personal wealth in Britain was in *stocks and shares* — money invested in government bonds or in the ownership of companies which entitles the owners to fixed interest or to a share of the profits respectively. The gains from share ownership can be high, by 1993 shares had become the third largest store of personal wealth, as much of the wealth stored in housing disappeared. Although in recent years individuals have invested very much more in life and pension funds which are less volatile. In 1971 share ownership was the second largest store of personal wealth in Britain. The recession of the early 1970s caused substantial falls in share prices. Share ownership is thus a gamble in which the rewards can, and usually are, high, but through which large sums of money can also be lost.

In 1990 shareholding peaked at around 11 million people following privatization of the electricity companies. Data, collected by a consultancy company, from a large sample of individual shareholders has been used here to give an indication as to how this form of wealth is distributed amongst the population of Britain. The first map opposite shows the proportion of the population that was found to be holding shares in each ward. The proportion is highest and lowest where this would be expected. The second map shows the average value of the shares held by each shareholder in the sample in each ward. Again the pattern is as expected although it is interesting to find such large differences between the wealth of shareholders living in different areas even after ignoring the different proportions holding shares. The shading categories used in this map were chosen to contain equal numbers of shareholders. Thus 28% of the population live in areas containing the least wealthy 20% of shareholders who, between them, own on average less than £2387 of shares valued at 1990 prices.

One way in which the inequality between areas due to the distribution of different forms of wealth can be measured is through drawing a Gini curve (as described on page 8). The five Gini curves drawn in Figure 6.31 show the degree of geographical concentration of wealth in terms of share ownership in 1990, housing equity in 1993 and car ownership in 1971, 1981 and 1991. Thus the richest fifth of ward populations holds over 60% of the share wealth of the country, 50% of the housing equity of the country, but less than a third of the cars in the country, and inequality in car ownership measured in this way has been decreasing over time. But the very slow movement of the car curve shows how slowly this form of inequality has been changing. This curve is, of course, based on the availability of cars as measured by the census, not on their value.

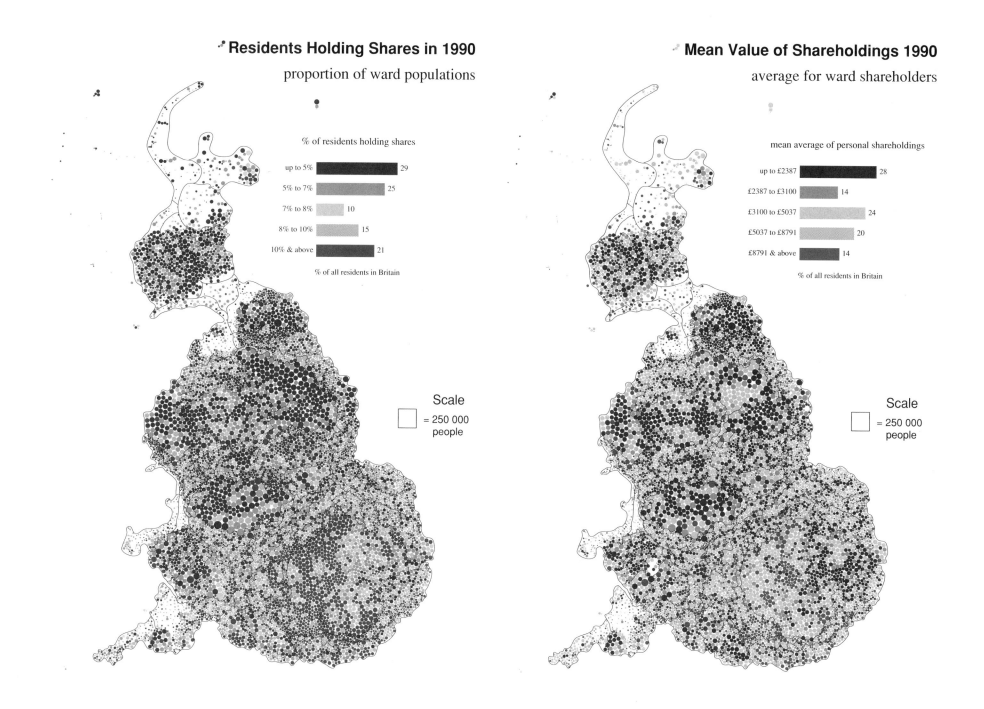

Residents Holding Shares in 1990

proportion of ward populations

% of residents holding shares

up to 5%		29
5% to 7%		25
7% to 8%		10
8% to 10%		15
10% & above		21

% of all residents in Britain

Scale

☐ = 250 000 people

Mean Value of Shareholdings 1990

average for ward shareholders

mean average of personal shareholdings

up to £2387		28
£2387 to £3100		14
£3100 to £5037		24
£5037 to £8791		20
£8791 & above		14

% of all residents in Britain

Scale

☐ = 250 000 people

6.32: Composition of Wealth by Amount of Wealth held by UK Adults 1991

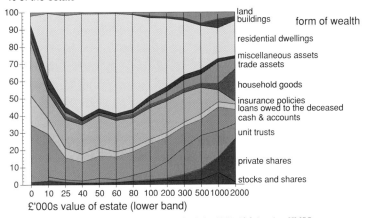

% of the estate

land
buildings   form of wealth

residential dwellings

miscellaneous assets
trade assets

household goods

insurance policies
loans owed to the deceased
cash & accounts

unit trusts

private shares

stocks and shares

£'000s value of estate (lower band)

Source: Inland Revenue, 1993, Inland Revenue Statistics, Table 13.3, London: HMSO.

Note: the form of wealth is known only for adults whose estate would require a grant of representation before it could be administered.

6.33: Absolute Value of the Personal Wealth of Adults in the UK 1976–1991

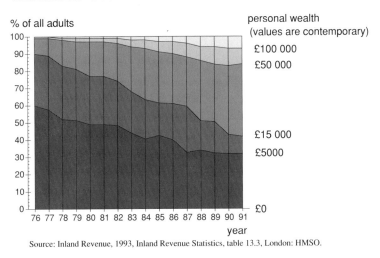

% of all adults

personal wealth
(values are contemporary)

£100 000

£50 000

£15 000

£5000

£0

year

Source: Inland Revenue, 1993, Inland Revenue Statistics, table 13.3, London: HMSO.

Extreme Wealth

What differentiates share ownership from other forms of wealth most clearly is that it has traditionally been the preserve of the very rich to hold substantial proportions of their wealth in this form. Figure 6.32 demonstrates this by showing how millionaires hold the highest proportion of their wealth in publicly quoted shares, whilst multi-millionaires hold the largest single portion of their wealth as shares in private companies. Interestingly, even for millionaires, the bulk of most people's wealth is held in residential property — which accounts for the majority of the wealth of those who are "worth" between £25 000 and £100 000. These estimates are based on the value of wealth notified to the Inland Revenue when people die and so are not truly representative of the poor, many of whom die with negligible wealth or with debts.

A robust measure of average share wealth in a ward is to take the median wealth of all shareholders in that ward. This has been done in the first map opposite. Median values of wealth tend to be lower than mean values as share wealth is unevenly distributed amongst shareholders, but the geographical distribution of median share wealth is similar to that for the mean which was shown on the previous page. The main noticeable discrepancy is that there is a clear contrast between the inner cities of the south and the north of England by this measure. Shareholders in the poorer parts of the north tend, taking the median measure, to hold only a few hundred pounds worth of shares.

The second map drawn opposite shows a much less robust measures of wealth — the maximum value of the shares held by the richest shareholder in the sample in each ward in Britain. By this estimate, 7% of the population live in wards where at least one person is a millionaire shareholder, whilst 8% of the population live in wards in which nobody owned as much as £25 000 of shares in 1990. The geographical distribution which this variable shows is recognizable, as the pattern of prosperity and relative poverty which can be traced back to the concentrations of positive housing equity, to the areas with surplus car ownership, to the residential locations of managers & professionals, through to the destinations of university graduates, to the areas where school children can expect to pass exams, and right back to the locations of children who live with adults who earn. There is thus a geography to wealth, which starts with the many places where children do not rely on social security benefits and which narrows down to the locations of the homes of millionaires, but which reflects a single pattern of where the poor and rich in 1990s Britain live.

It would be wrong to see this pattern as unchanging, but change is very slow. Figure 6.33 shows how people appear to become more wealthy over time estimated from the money they leave when they die, but this rise is largely due to inflation. In 1991 a third of the population was "worth" less than £5000, whilst one person in fourteen was worth more than £100 000. There is little equality in wealth in Britain today.

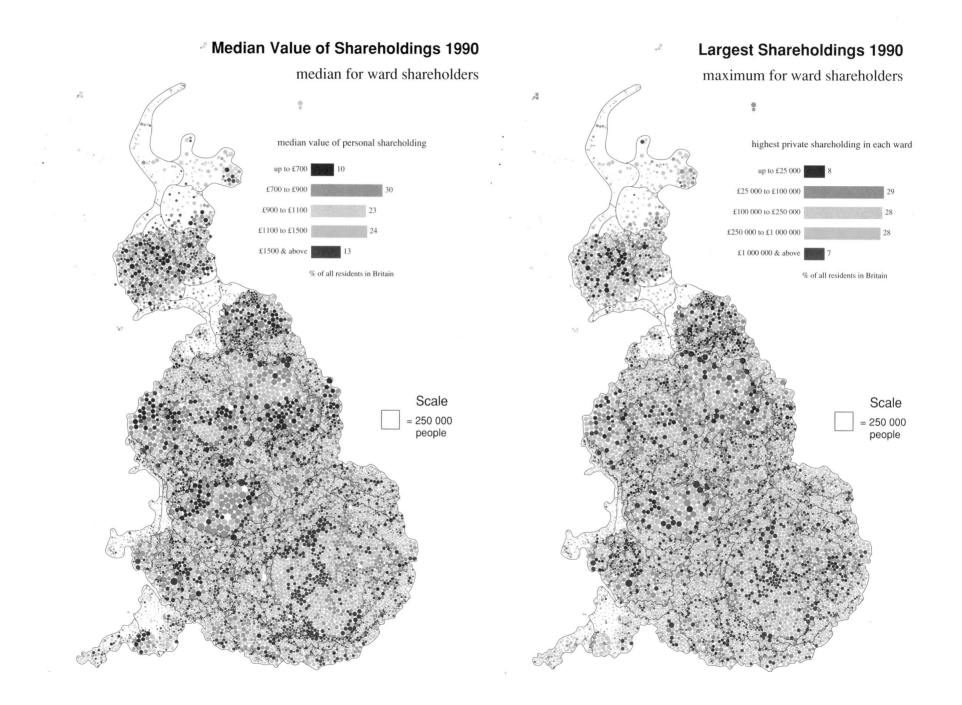

Median Value of Shareholdings 1990

median for ward shareholders

median value of personal shareholding

up to £700	10
£700 to £900	30
£900 to £1100	23
£1100 to £1500	24
£1500 & above	13

% of all residents in Britain

Scale

☐ = 250 000
people

Largest Shareholdings 1990

maximum for ward shareholders

highest private shareholding in each ward

up to £25 000	8
£25 000 to £100 000	29
£100 000 to £250 000	28
£250 000 to £1 000 000	28
£1 000 000 & above	7

% of all residents in Britain

Scale

☐ = 250 000
people

6.34: Distribution of Income for Households by Region in Britain 1991

% of households in each weekly income group in each region

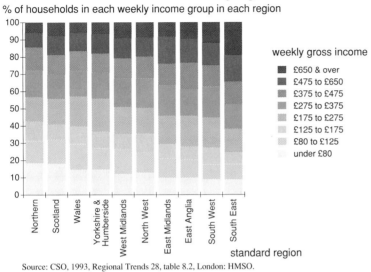

weekly gross income

■ £650 & over
■ £475 to £650
■ £375 to £475
■ £275 to £375
▨ £175 to £275
▨ £125 to £175
▨ £80 to £125
□ under £80

standard region

Source: CSO, 1993, Regional Trends 28, table 8.2, London: HMSO.

6.35: Composition of Income for Households by Region in Britain 1991

% of income from each source for households in each region

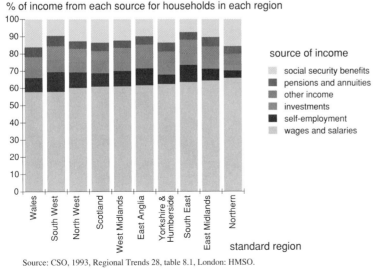

source of income

□ social security benefits
■ pensions and annuities
■ other income
■ investments
■ self-employment
□ wages and salaries

standard region

Source: CSO, 1993, Regional Trends 28, table 8.1, London: HMSO.

Household Income

For the majority of people who do not have recourse to substantial wealth, what matters most for their standard of living and social standing is income. However, in more than one household in three no one earns a salary or wage. People in these households will be largely reliant on pensions, unemployment benefit or various social security benefits. The geographical distribution of households without earners is shown in the first map drawn opposite. Over 40% of all households in Tyne and Wear, Merseyside, South Yorkshire and Wales have no earners, while in most of the South East fewer than a quarter of all households are in this position. The differences between the regional profiles of all earners are shown in Figure 6.34, in which the regions are sorted according to the proportion of households receiving less than £125 per week to live on. Some areas, such as Scotland, contain disproportionate numbers of people on both very high and very low incomes, while regions such as Yorkshire & Humberside have a slightly more equitable income distribution.

Unfortunately, official data, even on estimates of average incomes, are not available below the county level, but the far map opposite shows ward level estimates of average incomes. These are the average incomes of people who applied to take out a mortgage with the building society from which house price and housing wealth data have already been analysed (see pages 124 and 198). To estimate ward level average incomes, the incomes of all borrowers from 1980 to 1989 have been pooled, with salaries adjusted to 1989 levels. It is important to remember that these are just the incomes of a subset of the population who can afford to buy homes but are not so affluent that they can buy them outright (or prefer to borrow from a bank). The average incomes of these borrowers are not dissimilar to the average household incomes quoted in official statistics for all households, while the wage inflation which these borrowers have experienced has again been similar to that seen for all households. What the map shows most clearly is the effect of "London weighting" on average salaries in the capital and the high proportion of two earner households who live there, which together raises the average gross household income in most parts of London for borrowers to above £20 000 per annum. Patterns of wealth and poverty can be seen in the distribution of income over the rest of the country but it is the situation within London which is most dramatic. Note the contrast there between those households with no earners shown in the near map and the incomes of those who are earning shown by the far map.

Although wages and salaries are the most important component of household income, other factors matter. Figure 6.35 shows how wages make up a smaller proportion of all income in Wales and a higher proportion in the Northern Region, even though social security benefits are very significant in both areas. Other income comes from self-employment, letting property, investments and retirement pensions.

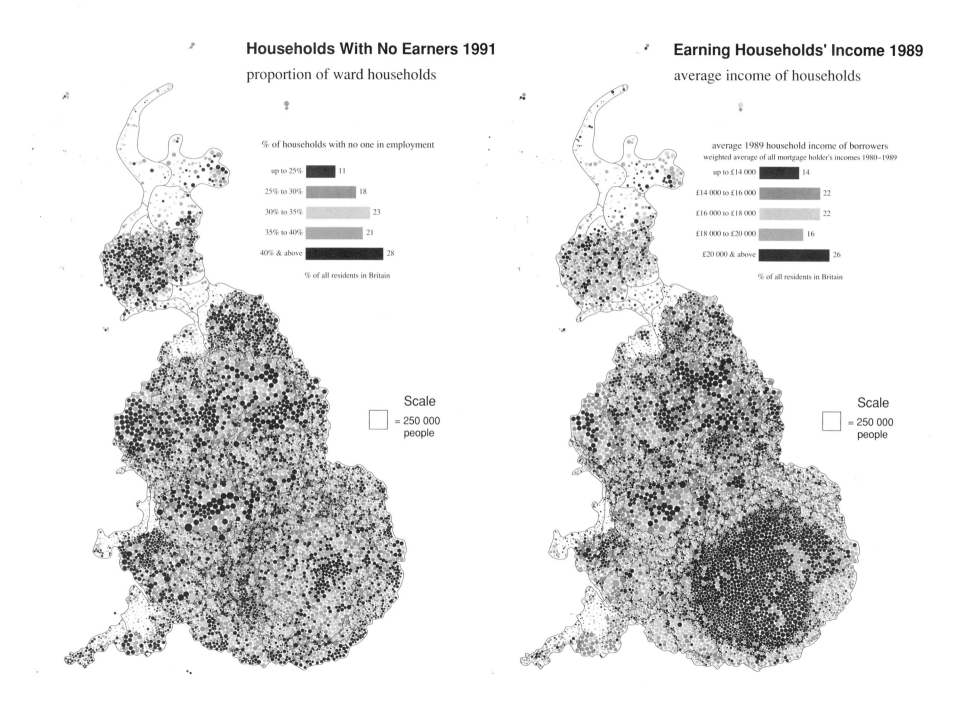

Households With No Earners 1991

proportion of ward households

% of households with no one in employment

up to 25%	11
25% to 30%	18
30% to 35%	23
35% to 40%	21
40% & above	28

% of all residents in Britain

Scale

☐ = 250 000 people

Earning Households' Income 1989

average income of households

average 1989 household income of borrowers

weighted average of all mortgage holder's incomes 1980–1989

up to £14 000	14
£14 000 to £16 000	22
£16 000 to £18 000	22
£18 000 to £20 000	16
£20 000 & above	26

% of all residents in Britain

Scale

☐ = 250 000 people

6.36: Change in the Composition of Average Weekly Income for Households by Region in England and Wales 1981–1991

£s change in income from each source: deviation from national average increase

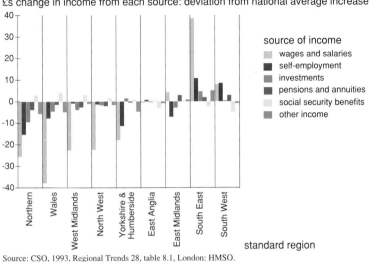

source of income
- wages and salaries
- self-employment
- investments
- pensions and annuities
- social security benefits
- other income

standard region

Source: CSO, 1993, Regional Trends 28, table 8.1, London: HMSO.

6.37: Share of Income Among Residents in the UK 1979–1991

% of income (net housing costs) of quintile groups of individuals

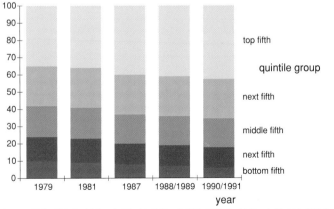

quintile group

top fifth

next fifth

middle fifth

next fifth

bottom fifth

year

Source: CSO, 1995, Social Trends 25, table 5.19 and CSO, 1994, Social Trends 24, table 5.20, London: HMSO.

Income Change

Through analysing the mortgage applications of buyers in each district in each year from 1980 to 1989 a partial picture of the geography of wage inflation in Britain can be drawn. That picture is shown in the nine maps opposite which depict the average increases between the incomes reported by borrowers in one calendar year and the next. Again it is important to remember that the maps are based on the experiences of a sample of home buyers but, again, at a regional level these statistics appear to follow closely official estimates derived from the Family Expenditure Survey (which is not a large enough sample from which to produce estimates for smaller areas). The patterns these maps contain are complex and it is worth comparing the geography of wage inflation which they reveal with the geography of house price inflation, which increases in salaries often precede (page 127). In the first period shown here the economy was still in recession and average salaries rose very slowly, falling in real terms in many places. Between 1981 and 1982 a recovery began, particularly in the south of England (which was reflected a year later by house price increases there). In the subsequent year whole swathes of districts in the Home Counties, East Anglia and elsewhere experienced wage inflation of over 12%, which spread to areas further north during the 1983–1984 period, but which was confined to the London area for the following two years. These years also saw wages rise so slowly in Wales, the North and Scotland that in real terms they were falling. However, by 1988 the wage inflation of the South East was spreading across the country. Then, by 1989, average wages in central London stopped rising for the first year in a decade.

Figure 6.36 shows, using official statistics, how these changes altered the composition of household income in different areas. In comparison to the national average change, households in the South East of England were taking home £40 more a week in their pay packet at the end of the decade than they did at the beginning, whilst the average household in Wales was almost £40 a week worse off. In Wales, the Northern Region, the North West and the West Midlands only income from social security benefits rose above the national average rate during the 1980s. In Yorkshire & Humberside income from investments also rose, while in East Anglia income from self-employment rose as well as social security benefits. Wages rose above the national average increase only in the East Midlands, the South East and the South West (the only regions in which there were also above average increases in income from pensions and annuities).

The changing geographical and social distribution of income has had accumulative effects over the years. Figure 6.37 shows that, for each period for which estimates of income have been made since 1979, the share of income of the poorest quintile of households (net housing costs) has fallen, whilst the net income of the richest fifth of households has risen, now to more than seven times the income of the poorest fifth in society. Ten years ago the rich each gained "only" three and a half times more.

Income of Earning Households 1980–1989

change in average income of households by district

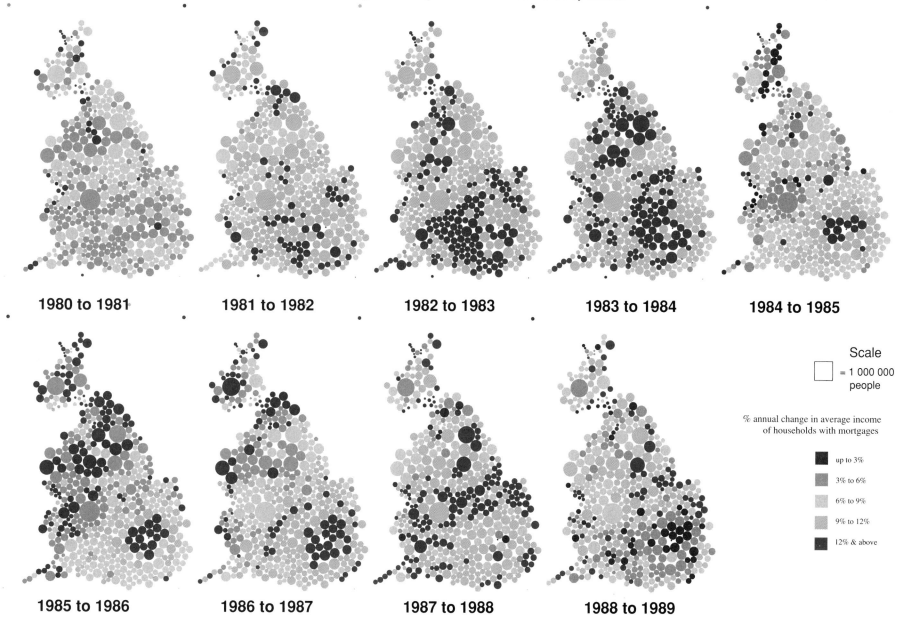

1980 to 1981   **1981 to 1982**   **1982 to 1983**   **1983 to 1984**   **1984 to 1985**

1985 to 1986   **1986 to 1987**   **1987 to 1988**   **1988 to 1989**

Scale

☐ = 1 000 000 people

% annual change in average income of households with mortgages

■ up to 3%

▨ 3% to 6%

▨ 6% to 9%

▨ 9% to 12%

■ 12% & above

6.38: Dependency Ratio by Average Borrower's Income at 1991 Prices in Britain by Ward

£ '000s average of all home buyers' household incomes in that ward

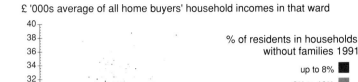

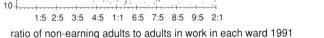

ratio of non-earning adults to adults in work in each ward 1991

6.39: Distribution of Adults In and Out of Work in Britain by Ward 1981–1991

% change in the proportion of the population living in each kind of ward

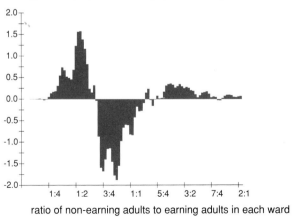

ratio of non-earning adults to earning adults in each ward

Dependency

If the rich and the poor lived in similar places then some of the problems caused by income polarization might be dissipated. Local demand for goods and services would increase as the incomes of the better-off rose, and so employment in these areas would rise. More importantly, perhaps, it would be more difficult for each group to misjudge the other. However, in many ways the rich and poor increasingly live apart in British society. There is little unemployment around the homes of the rich and increasingly numbers of people without work live in the neighbourhoods of the poor. One of the simplest means of illustrating this is to divide all adults into two groups depending on whether or not they are earning and then to compare the ratio of these two group to one another across different places. This statistic is termed the *dependency ratio* and in Britain in 1991 there were five adults in work for every four adults not in work. However, in the highest earning quarter of the country there were more than three adults in work for every two not in work, whilst in most of the wards in the lowest earning quarter there were more adults not in work than in work. The first map drawn opposite shows the detailed geography of dependency in Britain in 1991. This picture would show even greater contrasts if children were added (see page 179 to gauge the effect).

Figure 6.38 shows how the dependency ratio is related to the average home buyers' incomes. In those areas where fewer adults work these incomes tend to be low, although the relationship shown here is not rigid. The figure also shows how these two variables are related to the first distribution to be shown in this chapter — the proportion of people who are in families in each ward. Areas where average incomes are high or where few adults are in work tend to have a high proportion of their residents living outside families, whereas wards where a high proportion of residents are in families tend to be areas where a high proportion of adults are in work, but they earn relatively low wages. Incomes, family structure and dependency are strongly interrelated.

The far map opposite shows changes in the dependency ratio. Nationally, adult dependency has decreased by 1.3% since 1981 as more adults are in work now than were ten years ago. However, almost half the population now live in wards where the dependency ratio has increased, and it has increased by over 10% for a fifth of the population, mostly the fifth for which it was already high. A fifth of the population has experienced falls of 10% or more in the dependency ratio in these ten years, often when they lived in areas with relatively low ratios to begin with. Figure 6.39 illustrates more precisely how this polarization of the population has occurred, by showing which categories of wards, according to their dependency ratios, have become more or less numerous in Britain. This figure shows increases in the number of people living in wards classified to be in the extremes, and falls in the numbers of people living in wards with dependency ratios which lie near the national average.

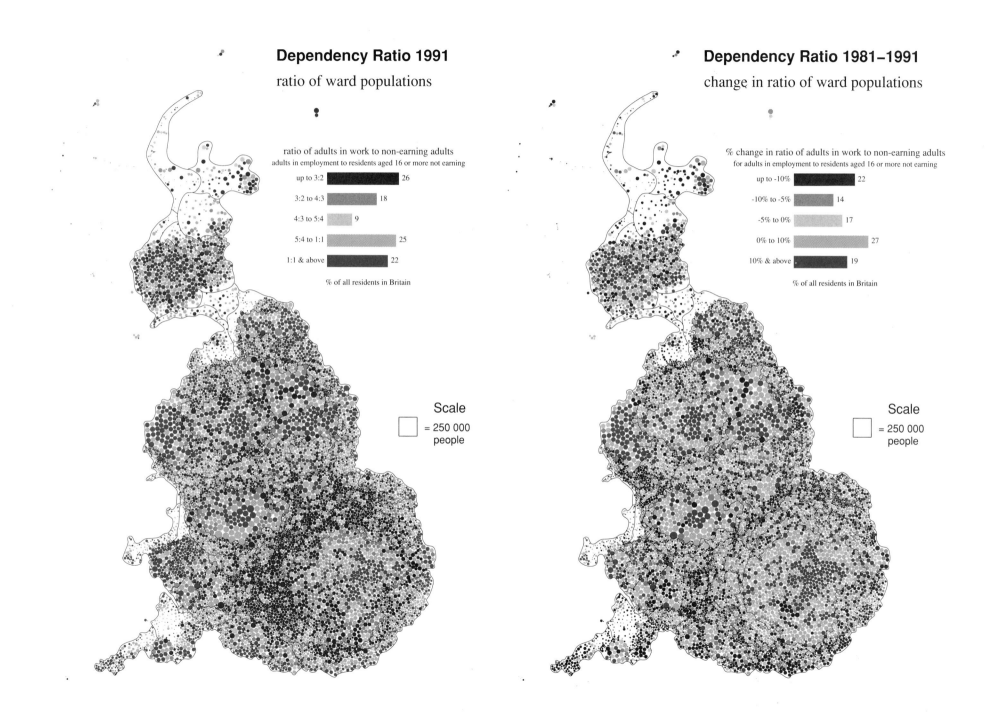

Dependency Ratio 1991

ratio of ward populations

ratio of adults in work to non-earning adults

adults in employment to residents aged 16 or more not earning

	%
up to 3:2	26
3:2 to 4:3	18
4:3 to 5:4	9
5:4 to 1:1	25
1:1 & above	22

% of all residents in Britain

Scale

☐ = 250 000 people

Dependency Ratio 1981–1991

change in ratio of ward populations

% change in ratio of adults in work to non-earning adults

for adults in employment to residents aged 16 or more not earning

	%
up to -10%	22
-10% to -5%	14
-5% to 0%	17
0% to 10%	27
10% & above	19

% of all residents in Britain

Scale

☐ = 250 000 people

Conclusion: Family and Society

Home and School

In the year of the last census, 780 000 babies were born in Britain (Figure 2.2). The kinds of families and homes into which those babies were born depended, to an extent, on the places where they were born (page 174, Figure 6.4). A geographical division has grown between the areas where parents are almost certainly married, and still together, and those places where a substantial minority of children are growing up in households with only one parent (page 175). Similarly, the number of siblings with which a child is likely to be growing up is associated with geographical location. Children in city centres are many times more likely to be growing up in large families as compared to children in more rural areas (page 177). They are also many times more likely to be living in households in which no adult is earning, just as their more affluent counterparts are now more likely to have both their parents in work (page 179). The type of family which declined most rapidly over the 1980s was the "traditional family", consisting of two adults, one of whom was in work, and two children (Figure 6.10).

The year in which this atlas is published will also be the year in which most of the children born just before the last census first go to school. It is also the year in which the babies enumerated in 1981, the children who grew up through the social changes shown here, take their first formal school examinations. Whether they receive any results at all is largely a product of where they grow up (Figure 6.11), as are the results of those who do achieve — which are strongly influenced by the school they attend (page 181). The school they attend depends, of course, largely on where their parents live which, in turn, depends on their income (page 125). Thus the qualifications which the class of '95 are awarded this year will closely reflect the economic circumstances of the families into which they were born. This process is self-perpetuating as many of the children who achieve go on to university (page 32) from where most of them proceed into well remunerated work (Figure 6.21) and then live in much the same areas as those places from where their parents came. Slowly, however, this pattern is changing (page 183); for as the babies of 1971 start to have children of their own they face choices and constraints which are very different from their parents. They are less likely to be married, and more likely to be working if they are female (Figure 2.11). For the young, and for young men in particular, unemployment is increasingly likely (Figure 3.23), while problems of housing deter many young people from settling in particular areas (page 132).

Class and Status

Almost by definition, society expects adults of "working age" to be employed. This is particularly true for men, less than 1% of whom said they were not working for a reason other than unemployment, education, retirement or sickness in 1991; this compares with almost a quarter of all women of working age (most of whom would have been looking after children). For those who have it, paid work provides more than financial reward and something to do; it confers social status. This is reflected through the incomes which different people are paid. Four aggregations of socioeconomic groups by different levels of status have been used in this chapter to show the geographical dimension to the class division of Britain. The young are most likely to have no occupation (Figure 6.15), particularly in London which has seen the largest fall in people in semiskilled & labouring occupations (page 187). Supervisors & artisans are most likely to be married (Figure 6.16) and to live in the north. Managers & professionals are the social group which grew most rapidly over the 1980s (Figure 6.14) and which has experienced most of the benefits of university expansion since 1971 (Figure 6.20). Peoples' social group is a relatively good predictor of issues such as where they are most likely to live and how they get to work (Figures 3.13, 3.14), and is an even better correlate of whether they own their home (Figure 4.22), will be ill, unemployed or lack basic amenities (Figure 5.2). There is obviously more to social status in Britain than can be shown by the types of jobs people do. Cultural and ethnic divisions (page 60) as well the differences in opportunity between the sexes and between different groups of pensioners can be just as important as occupation. Nevertheless, occupational class status increasingly divides the elderly by dependence on occupational pensions, and determines the opportunities of different groups of women in work. Geographically, class differences underlie most patterns.

Mapping Mixing: Colour Print G

One further advantage of basing social classifications upon occupations is that the census provides detailed breakdowns of people in these groups for very small areas. It is thus possible to collate the information needed to map the degree to which different groups are mixed in each ward in Britain. With four social groups, it is difficult to reduce the complex pattern of social segregation to a single statistic simple enough to be used to colour each ward. One statistic which can be used is a measure of whether the number of people in each social group is higher or lower than the national average proportion. With four social groups this results in 14 permutations (not 2^4 as all groups cannot be simultaneously over- or under-represented). Each social group can be assigned a colour and mixes of these colours have been used to shade Colour Print G to show the type of social mixing in each ward. A paint-box of four colours — light-red, yellow, light-blue and black — are used to shade the 28% of wards in which only one social group is over-represented. A mix of two of these colours, shows where two of the social groups are over represented, for instance, light-orange for the 16% of the population living in wards with above average proportions of people working as supervisors & artisans or as semiskilled & labourers. In total, 59% of the population live in wards in which two groups are over-represented, and hence in which the other two social groups are under-represented. The remaining 13% of the population live in wards in which three social groups are over-represented and just one is under-represented. Most of these wards are shaded dark orange (light-red mixed with yellow and black), the under-represented group being managers & professionals. Thus the geographical pattern to social structure can be shown in a way which conveys a great deal more information than could be achieved by showing simply the most over-represented group (page 193). A fourteen-fold classification can show the direction in which a ward is out of line, but not the extent (Figure 6.22). However, the Colour Print does show that workers with no occupation or with semiskilled & labouring jobs are typically concentrated in cities, although they merge with managers & professionals in London. The latter group are most over-represented in the Home Counties, but here too are found many light-red wards where high numbers of people in semiskilled & labouring occupations live, often to service the blue majority. Wards coloured light-orange (dominated by the largest two social groups) are found mainly in the north and Wales, but are also numerous around the southern coast and clustered in east London. Between these groups lie the largest remaining mix of people in wards coloured light-green, in which the most affluent two social groups dominate. This Colour Print shows a spatial pattern that is more complex than the distributions of wealth and health shown in Colour Prints E and F. There is a more subtle structure to the geography of class than is seen in single attributes of the population, even when these are closely related to class. This may well be because where the less affluent are in a minority, they benefit from the advantages of the wealthy and so, for example, enjoy better health than do people in similar occupations in other parts of the country. Within each social group relative affluence will also vary geographically.

Income and Wealth

The geography of wealth, whether measured in terms of cars (page 195), housing equity (page 199) or shares (page 201) shows a simpler geographical pattern to that of the mixing of social groups. Wealth is amassed over generations and so even slight differences between areas become exacerbated over time (page 197). Thus a relatively simple geographical spread of wealth can emerge from a complex mix of people. Similarly, as so much wealth is tied up in fixed assets such as property (Figure 6.30), the geographical distribution of wealth cannot change at all quickly, although the housing market crash has reduced the proportion of wealth held in the form of housing from 37% in 1991 down to 30% in 1993, to the detriment of the more affluent in society (CSO 1995: 96). Conversely, patterns of income can change more quickly than can the distribution of social groups, as differences between the salaries and wages widen for different occupations (page 207). By the end of the last decade the rise of incomes in the South East of England, and the increase in the number of families relying on social security benefits across the country (Figure 6.36), had widened income differentials considerably (Figure 6.37). It is important to realise that this separation was not reflected by a dramatic spatial polarization between social groups, which in many ways became less segregated during the 1980s (page 193). Increased employment volatility (Figure 3.23) has lead to both increased income differentials and increased mobility between income groups (DSS 1994). For instance, although most households experienced little change in their income levels between 1991 and 1992, at the extremes a quarter of households in the bottom decile (of individuals by income) in 1991 rose by two deciles or more by 1992, while one in seven households in the top decile fell by more than one decile in the same period (CSO 1995: 95). The social change which is followed most closely by changes in the distribution of incomes is the ratio of adults in and out of work (Figure 6.39). In 1990s Britain being in work at all has become more important than the kind of work people do, in terms of their social well being and for the prospects of their families, and for the communities in which they live.

References

Blaxter, M., 1991, Fifty Years On — Inequalities in Health, in M. Murphy and J. Hobcraft, *Population Research in Britain, A Supplement to Population Studies,* 45, Cambridge: Cambridge University Press.

CSO, 1993, *Regional Trends* 28, London: HMSO.

CSO, 1994, *Social Trends* 24, London: HMSO.

CSO, 1995, *Social Trends* 25, London: HMSO.

Dorling, D., 1995, Visualizing changing social structure from a census, *Environment and Planning A,* 27/2: 353–378.

DSS, 1994, *Households Below Average Incomes: 1979–1991/1992,* London: HMSO.

Goldblatt, P. and Fox, J., 1988, Mortality of Men by Occupation, *Longitudinal Study Working Paper* No. 59, Social Statistics Research Unit, London: City University.

Goodman, A. and Webb, S., 1994, For Richer, For Poorer: The Changing Distribution of Income in the United Kingdom, 1961-1991, *Institute for Fiscal Studies Commentary* No. 42, London: IFS.

Hamnett, C., 1994, Social Polarisation in Global Cities: Theory and Evidence, *Urban Studies,* 32/3: 401–424.

Inland Revenue, 1993, *Inland Revenue Statistics,* London: HMSO.

JRF, 1993, Young People at Risk of Homelessness, *Housing Research Findings* No. 89, York: Joseph Rowntree Foundation.

OPCS, 1992, *1991 Census Definitions,* London: HMSO.

Royal Commission on the Distribution of Income and Wealth, 1980, *An A to Z of Income and Wealth,* London: HMSO.

7: Politics

Politics has been reserved for the final chapter because the maps here do not show something about how people live, but something about what people think about how they live, what they believe in and how they want things to change. For mapping purposes this chapter concentrates on a single aspect of politics — electoral geography. Although there are many surveys which, unlike the census, ask people for their opinions on society, and many studies have been conducted on how government operates in different areas, none of these sources contains sufficient information to be comparable with the detailed human geography shown so far. The one consistent clue to political opinions which is available across many small areas is how people choose to vote in elections.

Electoral geography uses terms which are not always clearly understood and so are defined here. *Electors* are people who have the right to vote. In Britain this includes almost all adults with a few exceptions (for instance peers and adults committed involuntarily to psychiatric hospitals). However, to be able to vote, an elector must be *registered* by having completed a form stating where he or she lives, and by having lived there for a short length of time. The group of electors who are registered are called the *electorate*. The process of election is often termed the *poll*, meaning "the counting of voters". However, that term can also be used to mean the number of votes a candidate receives. To avoid ambiguity the phrase *the vote* is used here to mean the sum of all votes won by all candidates standing. All those electors who did not vote in an election are said to have *abstained*. The words *margin* or *majority* are used to mean the number of votes by which an election was won. In the British first past the post system this is the difference between the votes for the first and second placed candidates. Candidates usually stand for the Conservative party, the Labour party, the Liberal Democrat party, the Scottish Nationalist Party or Plaid Cymru (the last two are combined from here on as *Nationalists*). Votes for all other parties are combined in the analyses which follow and are labelled *other parties*, except for votes for candidates standing for the Social Democrats, Alliance or Liberals which are combined with the Liberal Democrat vote and labelled as *Liberal parties* or *Liberal* from here on. Elections are either local or general. In local elections each candidate contests a ward to be elected to the local council. In general elections each successful candidate represents a parliamentary constituency (consisting of well over a dozen wards) and is elected to national government.

The primary purpose of elections is, of course, not to elicit political views but to create governments, either local or national. It is important to bear this in mind when viewing each map. Electors in Britain are often presented with a very limited choice of candidates to vote for, and so voting figures can reflect the political options which voters had when they voted, as much as their opinions. For instance, in many local elections only two candidates stand. Although it is interesting to look at the share of the vote gained by each party in each place (bearing in mind these constraints), under the electoral system in Britain only the party polling most votes in each ward or constituency wins. Thus the most important electoral map is that of which party won in each area and so the chapter begins by showing this distribution of party strength for the results of all local elections held in wards immediately preceding the 1991 census. The results of all general elections since 1955 are mapped at the parliamentary constituency level later.

People can vote only if they are registered as electors and so an attempt is next made to estimate how many adults are not registered in each ward. In many wards more than one adult in ten is not registered to vote. The importance of low rates of electoral registration in determining which party wins an election is returned to at the end of the chapter. For those adults who can vote, the pattern of their votes is then examined for each of the three main political parties at British local elections and for all other parties combined. An indication of how the political geography of Britain may be changing is shown by the change in votes for each party in local elections since the census. Similarly, the map and recent pattern of change is drawn for the electorate who choose to abstain at local elections. Each of these patterns is also shown at the district level, as it is for the election of district local authorities that these elections are held.

The local election data used in this atlas only cover the period 1987 to 1994. To be able to look at longer term changes, and at results which affect the national government of Britain, general elections have to be studied. The results of all general elections which took place from 1955 to 1992 have been collected at the level of the parliamentary constituencies in which they were held. The second half of this chapter maps these elections in a variety of ways using cartograms based on constituencies. The number and size (electorate) of constituencies changes over time and so the cartograms drawn here change shape slightly between each pair of elections. Constituencies are drawn as hexagons rather than as circles which were used in the district cartograms (see index maps). The patterns of which party won and which party came second in each seat at each election are drawn, as well as the changing geographical distribution of abstentions. The chapter ends by looking in detail at the most recent changes between the general elections of 1987 and 1992 and then at the pattern of marginal seats which those changes produced. The future electoral map of Britain is considered by speculating over how individual voters will react to the changes that have occurred in their lives over recent years and on how the geographical patterns which those changes followed translate onto the electoral map of Britain. How are political changes related to the shifts in where and how people choose to live, how they are housed, how they work, in their health and in changes to the social structure of this country as a whole?

Winning Party

Local election results are not simple to map. This is because these elections are held at different times in different parts of the country and because more than one candidate can be elected from some wards. To alleviate these problems the votes in all local elections which took place in each ward between 1987 and 1990 have been combined here, as have the votes for all candidates standing for the same party in a ward. The result is to produce a single set of results, as if each and every ward had had just one local election with just one candidate standing for each party. This produces an election result simple enough to map, which also smoothes out minor changes.

Figure 7.1 shows the national share of the vote between the three main parties at the local elections held each year between 1986 and 1991 in both metropolitan districts which (apart from London boroughs) hold elections three years out of four, and in those non-metropolitan districts which also observe this pattern of voting. In 1989, local voting was for county councils and so has not been included. The graph shows that between each of the three years combined here, the Labour share of the three party vote increased and the Conservative and Liberal shares of the vote decreased. However, taken together, the average of these three years is representative of the general level of support each party had among the electorate during the second half of the last decade.

The ordinary map of which party had the most votes in each ward is dominated by the colours of the Conservative and other parties (which here include the Nationalists). In many wards in rural parts of England and Wales no Conservative candidate stands, but an "un-aligned" candidate is voted in who subsequently votes with Conservative members in the local council, thus the map can be misleading. Most misleading, however, is the use of an equal-area base to map election results. The cartogram demonstrates this, making visible the 42% of people who were living in wards in which the Labour party won most votes. In this data set results were not recorded for wards in the Scottish Islands, the Scilly Isles or in the City of London. These are areas which contain a tiny proportion of the electorate but one of which covers a significant land area.

How comfortably each ward is won by a particular party varies from place to place and Figure 7.2 shows how the distribution of votes within wards were shared between the three main parties. Each ward is shown as a dot in the *electoral triangle*. From the position of the ward the vote shares can be read off. The overall pattern of dots gives a picture of how much wards vary between each other in the performance of each party. There are distinct clusters of wards around the axis which separates seats won by either the Conservative or the Liberal parties, and around the Labour/Conservative axis. The figure also shows the average level of abstention in each ward at these elections. Abstentions can be seen to be at high levels in many of the safe Labour wards which occupy the bottom left-hand corner of the electoral triangle.

7.1: Share of the Vote Won at Local Elections in England and Wales 1986–1991

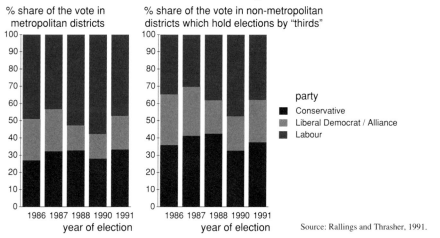

% share of the vote in metropolitan districts

% share of the vote in non-metropolitan districts which hold elections by "thirds"

party
- Conservative
- Liberal Democrat / Alliance
- Labour

year of election

Source: Rallings and Thrasher, 1991.

7.2: Distribution of the Three Party Vote in England and Wales by Ward

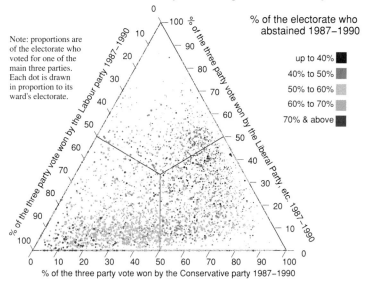

Note: proportions are of the electorate who voted for one of the main three parties. Each dot is drawn in proportion to its ward's electorate.

% of the electorate who abstained 1987–1990

- up to 40%
- 40% to 50%
- 50% to 60%
- 60% to 70%
- 70% & above

% of the three party vote won by the Conservative party 1987–1990

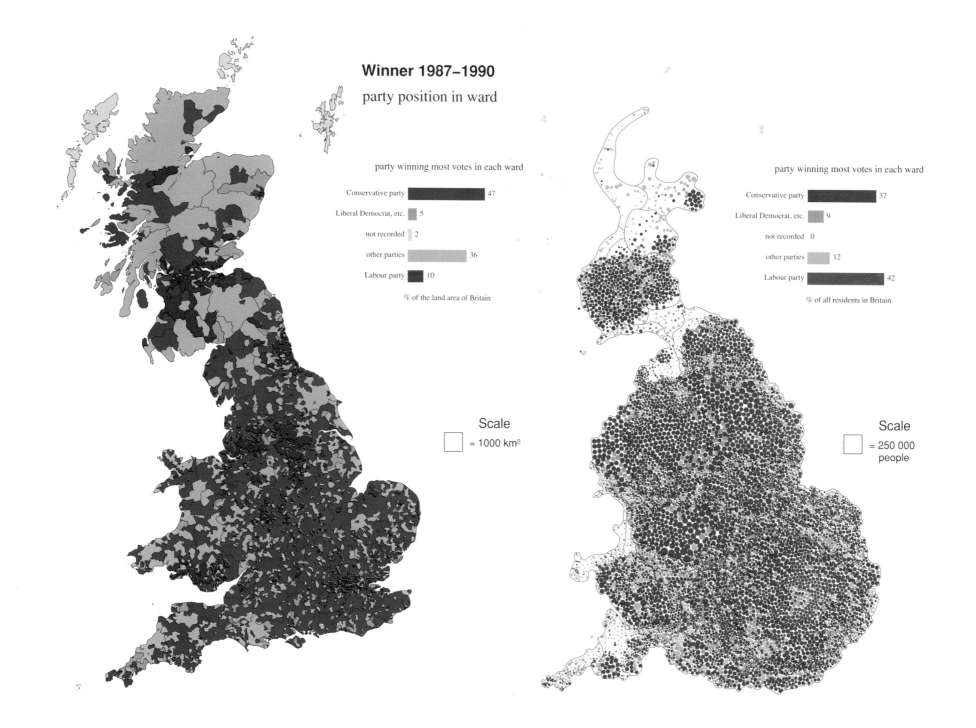

Winner 1987–1990

party position in ward

party winning most votes in each ward

	% of the land area of Britain
Conservative party	47
Liberal Democrat, etc.	5
not recorded	2
other parties	36
Labour party	10

% of the land area of Britain

party winning most votes in each ward

	% of all residents in Britain
Conservative party	37
Liberal Democrat, etc.	9
not recorded	0
other parties	12
Labour party	42

% of all residents in Britain

Scale

☐ = 1000 km²

Scale

☐ = 250 000 people

7.3: Voter Registration by Country in Britain 1981–1993

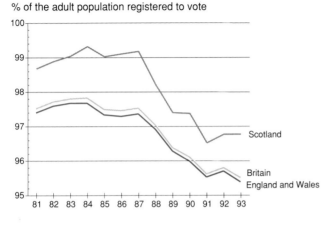

% of the adult population registered to vote

registration year

Source: OPCS, 1993, Electoral Statistics no. 20, Appendix B, London: HMSO

7.4: Voter Registration in Britain by Characteristics of Voters 1991

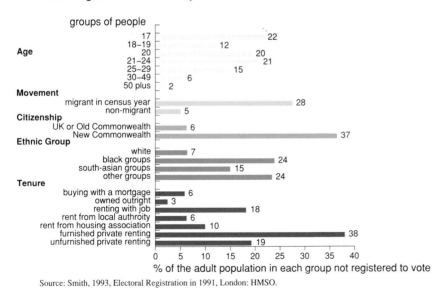

% of the adult population in each group not registered to vote

Source: Smith, 1993, Electoral Registration in 1991, London: HMSO.

Electoral Registration

In 1991 almost two million adults eligible to be on the electoral register were not registered to vote in Britain (OPCS 1993). This has been the result of a steady rise in the proportion of all eligible adults not registered to vote since the early 1980s, a rise which may have been accelerated by the introduction of the poll tax (in 1989 in Scotland and in 1990 in England and Wales, see Figure 7.3). The unadjusted census results cannot be used to find where these non-registered adults live because the census itself failed to enumerate over a million adults in Britain (see Figure 1.10). However, recent research has been conducted to estimate where the people missing from the census lived (Simpson 1994). This research has assigned those people estimated to be missing from the census in each district (subdivided by age and sex) to the wards within each district. Using the preliminary results of this work, which does not cover Scotland, the first map opposite has been drawn. This map shows the net proportion of people living in each ward in 1991 who were not recorded as being residents of that ward by the census. *People* is used to mean everyone living in an area regardless of whether they were recorded as resident in the census. There is a clear geographical pattern as to who has been excluded from the census, although in no ward was under-enumeration estimated to exceed 10%.

The second map opposite compares the number of people living in each ward aged 20 or over with the average number of adults registered to vote in local elections in the 1991 to 1994 period. The age limit of 20 was chosen rather than 18 because the preliminary population estimates divide the population up by five year age bands. In simple terms, therefore, the electorate should always be higher than this subset of adults. However, it is possible for adults to be registered to vote in more than one place and for members of the armed forces not to be registered to vote where they are living. So the number of electors could be much higher or lower than the number of adults in any area, despite no people ineligible to vote being registered. Even given this situation, however, the pattern in the map cannot easily be explained. In central London, Liverpool, Leicester and in much of Wales and Bristol over 10% of the adult population are not registered to vote. Conversely, in central Birmingham, Manchester and Tyneside there are at least 10% more electors than these adults. This may be because the electoral register was more out of date in those latter areas and contained many people who had migrated since registration. These areas also contain many students aged 18 or 19 who were eligible to vote but who would be excluded from the count of adults aged over 19 which is used here (see page 33, Figure 7.19). Reconciling adults and voters is not a simple process.

It is possible to gain an impression of what kind of adults are likely not to be registered nationally from a random sample that was taken from the 1991 census forms of people who were eligible to register. This sample was checked against the electoral register (Smith 1993). A summary of the results of the study are shown in Figure 7.4.

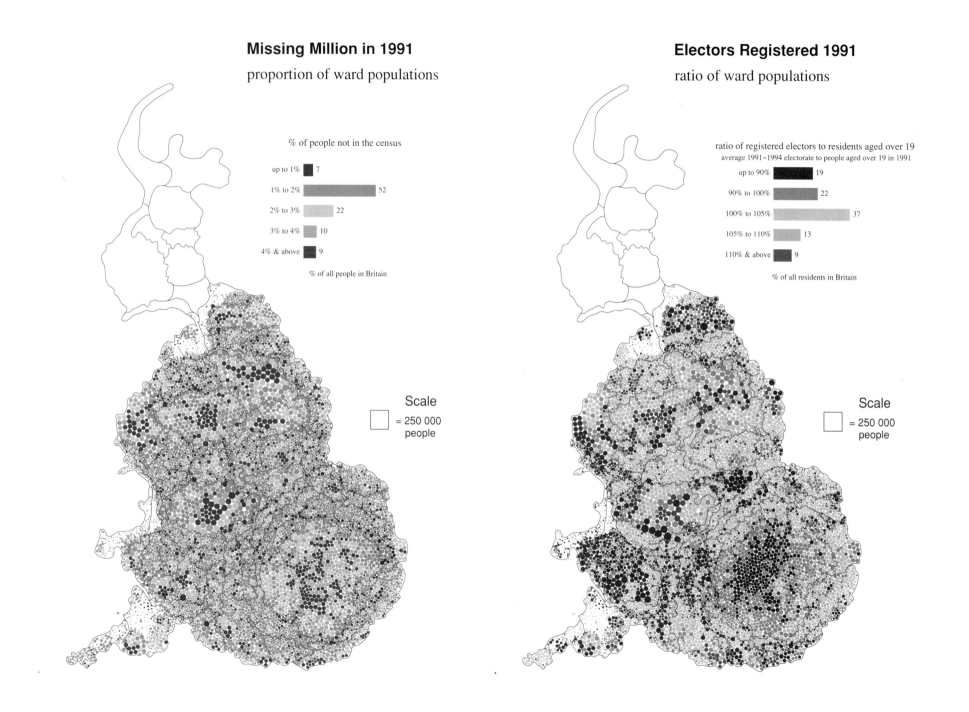

Missing Million in 1991

proportion of ward populations

% of people not in the census

up to 1%	7
1% to 2%	52
2% to 3%	22
3% to 4%	10
4% & above	9

% of all people in Britain

Scale

☐ = 250 000 people

Electors Registered 1991

ratio of ward populations

ratio of registered electors to residents aged over 19
average 1991–1994 electorate to people aged over 19 in 1991

up to 90%	19
90% to 100%	22
100% to 105%	37
105% to 110%	13
110% & above	9

% of all residents in Britain

Scale

☐ = 250 000 people

Conservative Vote

Of those adults who were eligible to vote, under 16% voted for a candidate standing for the Conservative party at local elections across all of Britain between 1987 and 1990. It is important to remember that only a minority of electors vote in local elections and that many Conservative party supporters vote for candidates who do not label themselves as Conservative at local elections. The first map opposite shows where those voters who did vote for a Conservative candidate lived. The areas in which no Conservative stood and where 13% of the population lived, such as much of Wales, contain most of the "unlabelled Conservatives". There is a distinct geography to the places where this party enjoys the support of more than a fifth of the electorate locally. This map contains a pattern similar to that of managers & professionals shown on page 191, and to the distribution of wealth shown on page 203, but discrepancies to the general trend for the more affluent to vote for the Conservative party can be found across the country.

The second map opposite shows the change in the proportion of the electorate voting for this party between the averaged result of the 1987 to 1990 set of elections and the average of the subsequent 1991 to 1994 set. The map excludes Scotland because recent local voting data were not available for that country at the time of writing. In England and Wales as a whole the Conservative share of the electorate fell from 16% to 14% in four years. The map shows some very clear patterns emerging from a variable which expresses the short-term change in the support gained from a minority of the population. The Conservatives can be seen to have suffered their highest losses in Outer London while increasing their vote most strongly in parts of the West Midlands, the Wirral and in several isolated clusters of wards grouped in particular districts. Figure 7.5 shows the changing distribution of the electorate voting for this party in graphical form, the first graph illustrating that the modal share of the electorate voting Conservative by ward was between 20% and 22% in the 1987–1990 period. The second graph in the figure shows how the proportion of the electorate living in wards grouped by (2% bands of) the Conservative vote changed in the four year period following the census. More people now live in wards in which the Conservatives win less than 20% of the electorate, and less people live in each category of ward in which they win a higher proportion than this due to the fall in their support over the period studied. The graph shows the effect of an aggregate decline in the Conservative vote in most wards in England and Wales.

The bunching of wards exhibiting similar changes into district groups on the far map opposite stresses the importance of local government and party organization in voting. For instance, electors may be more willing to vote where their vote has more chance of changing the composition of the council. Figure 7.6 shows the distribution and change in the Conservative poll aggregated to each district. A simpler pattern to that of the detailed ward level is revealed. This can be compared with other district level changes.

7.5: Conservative Vote in England and Wales by Ward 1987–1990, 1987–1990 to 1991–1994

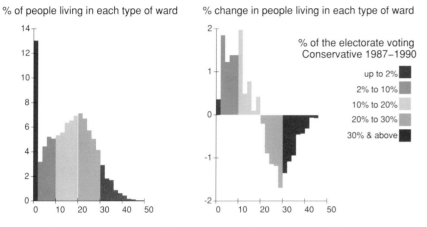

% of people living in each type of ward

% change in people living in each type of ward

% of the electorate voting Conservative 1987–1990

up to 2%
2% to 10%
10% to 20%
20% to 30%
30% & above

% of electorate voting for the Conservative party between 1987 and 1990

7.6: Conservative Vote by District 1987–1990 and Change in the Vote to 1991–1994

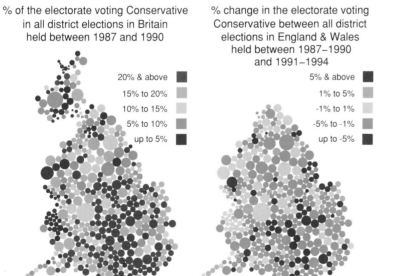

% of the electorate voting Conservative in all district elections in Britain held between 1987 and 1990

20% & above
15% to 20%
10% to 15%
5% to 10%
up to 5%

% change in the electorate voting Conservative between all district elections in England & Wales held between 1987–1990 and 1991–1994

5% & above
1% to 5%
-1% to 1%
-5% to -1%
up to -5%

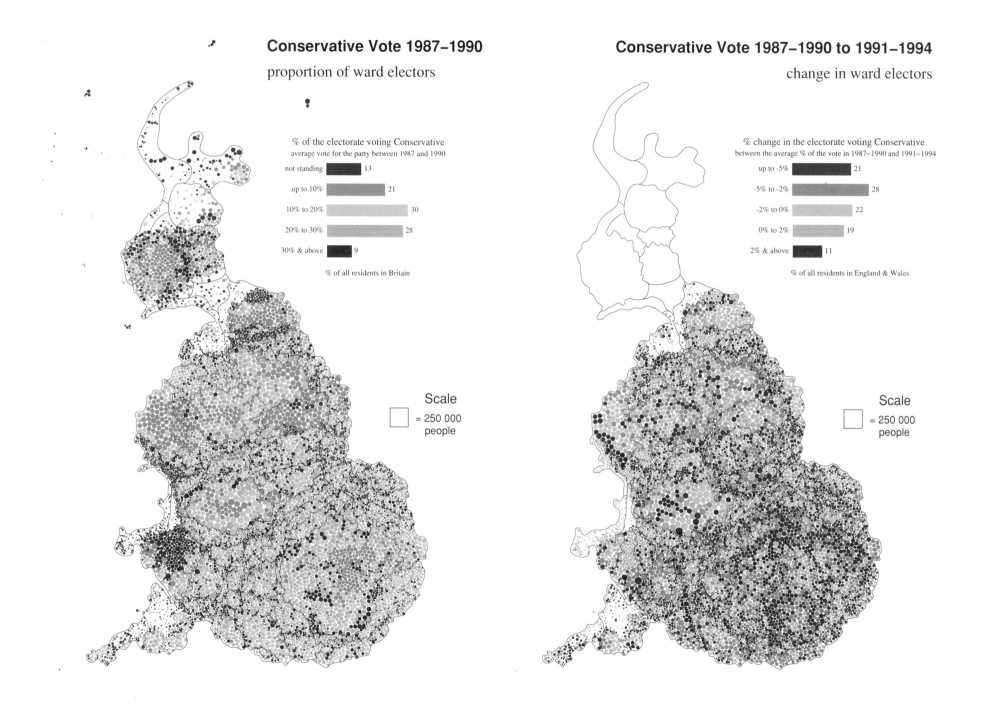

Conservative Vote 1987–1990

proportion of ward electors

% of the electorate voting Conservative
average vote for the party between 1987 and 1990

not standing	13
up to 10%	21
10% to 20%	30
20% to 30%	28
30% & above	9

% of all residents in Britain

Scale

☐ = 250 000 people

Conservative Vote 1987–1990 to 1991–1994

change in ward electors

% change in the electorate voting Conservative
between the average % of the vote in 1987–1990 and 1991–1994

up to -5%	21
-5% to -2%	28
-2% to 0%	22
0% to 2%	19
2% & above	11

% of all residents in England & Wales

Scale

☐ = 250 000 people

7.7: Labour Vote in England and Wales by Ward 1987–1990, 1987–1990 to 1991–1994

% of people living in each type of ward

% change in people living in each type of ward

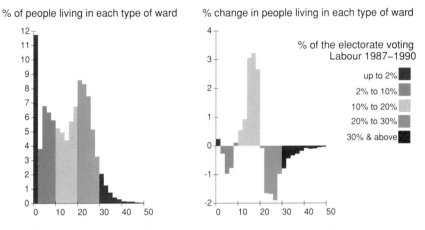

% of the electorate voting
Labour 1987–1990

up to 2%
2% to 10%
10% to 20%
20% to 30%
30% & above

% of electorate voting for the Labour party between 1987 and 1990

7.8: Labour Vote by District 1987–1990 and Change in the Vote to 1991–1994

% of the electorate voting Labour in all district elections in Britain held between 1987 and 1990

% change in the electorate voting Labour between all district elections in England & Wales held between 1987–1990 and 1991–1994

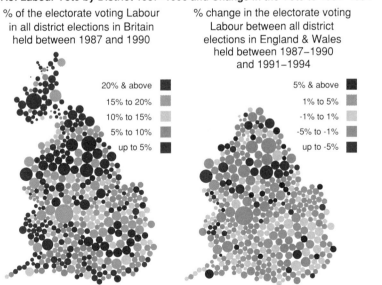

20% & above
15% to 20%
10% to 15%
5% to 10%
up to 5%

5% & above
1% to 5%
-1% to 1%
-5% to -1%
up to -5%

Labour Vote

The same maps and graphs of share of the electorate have been produced on these pages for the Labour party as were produced for the Conservative party on the last two pages and as are produced for the other parties and for voters abstaining on the following pages. This is so that the position of each party can be judged on a consistent basis. In the 1987 to 1990 period 16% of all electors voted for Labour at local elections in Britain. This is only marginally higher than the Conservative vote and both of the main two parties were quite evenly matched at this time. Geographically, the areas where the Labour party wins most votes are very much the same as those where the Conservatives do most poorly, as is shown by the first map opposite. The geography of social groups which the Labour party vote most closely matches is that of workers who are semiskilled & labourers (page 187), although this connection is not as strong as that seen for the Conservatives with the managers & professionals social group. The Labour party vote was particularly high in parts of Strathclyde, Merseyside and South Wales, and the party did not put a candidate forward in many small rural wards at this time.

The geography of the change in the vote for Labour shown on the second map opposite is much less predictable. Between 1987 to 1990 and 1991 to 1994 the party won increasing support in the East Midlands and in many parts of the South East, as well as improving on an already strong position in large parts of the north. Their vote declined, however, in the centres of many northern conurbations, in the Welsh Valleys and in specific districts such as Lambeth. In England and Wales as a whole their share of the electorate fell from 15% to 14%. This was a slower fall than for the Conservatives so that, even excluding Scotland, more electors who voted in local elections were voting Labour by 1994. Most important for the Labour party was the fact that they were now picking up votes in areas where they needed votes to win power. Figure 7.7 shows how there used to be a bimodal distribution of votes for the Labour party, which traditionally won one group of wards in which they usually gained well over a fifth of the electorate, and then did poorly in another large group of wards in which they gained less than a tenth of the electorate, with relatively few marginal wards. In the four years following this period their declining vote in safe wards and rising vote in wards in which they used to have little chance of victory has meant that this bimodal pattern has disappeared, and the Labour party now seriously contests many more areas.

Figure 7.8 shows the simplified geography at the district scale. The Labour party now controls many more district councils, but increases in their vote have only been marginally responsible for this rise. The severe decline in the Conservative vote in these same districts (as shown in Figure 7.6) is the main reason why that party no longer controls so many local authorities. The severe decline in the Labour vote in many northern metropolitan districts is mainly attributable to rising abstentions (Figure 7.14).

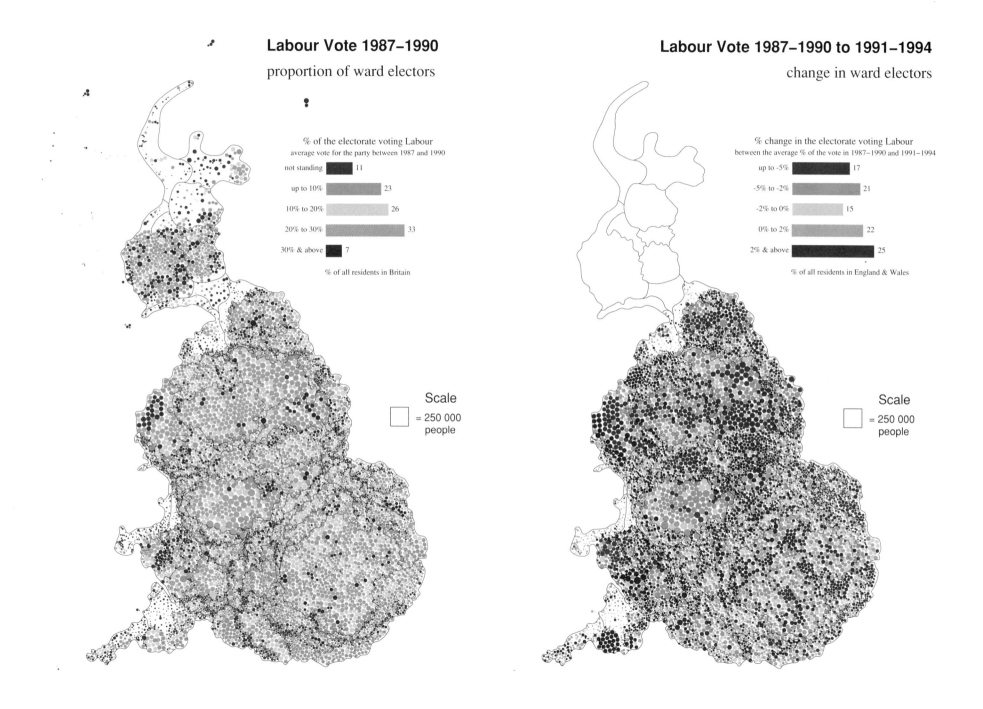

Labour Vote 1987–1990

proportion of ward electors

% of the electorate voting Labour
average vote for the party between 1987 and 1990

not standing	11
up to 10%	23
10% to 20%	26
20% to 30%	33
30% & above	7

% of all residents in Britain

Scale

☐ = 250 000 people

Labour Vote 1987–1990 to 1991–1994

change in ward electors

% change in the electorate voting Labour
between the average % of the vote in 1987–1990 and 1991–1994

up to -5%	17
-5% to -2%	21
-2% to 0%	15
0% to 2%	22
2% & above	25

% of all residents in England & Wales

Scale

☐ = 250 000 people

7.9: Liberal Vote in England and Wales by Ward 1987–1990, 1987–1990 to 1991–1994

% of people living in each type of ward

% change in people living in each type of ward

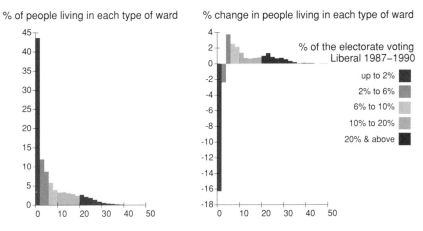

% of the electorate voting
Liberal 1987–1990

up to 2%

2% to 6%

6% to 10%

10% to 20%

20% & above

% of electorate voting for the centre parties between 1987 and 1990

7.10: Liberal Vote by District 1987–1990 and Change in the Vote to 1991–1994

% of the electorate voting Liberal, etc. in all district elections in Britain held between 1987 and 1990

20% & above

15% to 20%

10% to 15%

5% to 10%

up to 5%

% change in the electorate voting Liberal between all district elections in England & Wales held between 1987–1990 and 1991–1994

5% & above

1% to 5%

-1% to 1%

-5% to -1%

up to -5%

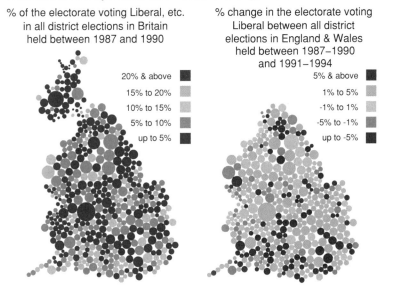

Liberal Vote

In the 1987–1990 period the Liberal vote was shared between the Liberal Democrat party and the alliance of Liberals and the SDP at various places and varying times. Between them they won support from, on average, 6% of the electorate in all local elections held in wards at this time. Support for the Liberal parties on the first map opposite shows the most chequered pattern drawn so far. In over a third of all British wards, by population, they did not put a candidate forward, while in a tenth of all wards (by population) they put a candidate forward who secured over a fifth of the vote. The clear clustering of these wards suggests that support was strongest where the Liberal parties had a chance of significantly affecting local council compositions. Although these parties are seen as having their strongest support in the south, there are clearly pockets of Liberal success right across the country. However, the first graph in Figure 7.9 illustrates the uphill struggle the Liberal Democrat party will have if it is to contest more seriously for power. Also note that a different shading scheme had to be used on the map because of the lower overall Liberal vote as compared to the two main political parties.

The change in the four years to 1991–1994 may give a clue as to how the Liberal Democrats could increase their hold on power. Nationally, the proportion of the electorate who voted for them in England and Wales rose from 7% to 9% over this period, but that rise was mainly concentrated around the areas where they already had power, as the second map opposite shows. There are a few anomalies where their vote increased in areas where they had very low support before, such as Lambeth, but these were exceptional. It is interesting to compare this map of rising support with some of the indicators of economic difficulty in the south, such as unsecured debt (page 129) or year of highest unemployment (Figure 3.31). The second graph in Figure 7.9 shows how the Liberal parties have seen both a rise in the proportion of the population living in wards which they can now win, and a huge decline in the number of seats in which they were not standing over the period.

In terms of political power, however, the Liberal parties still control only a small minority of local councils. Figure 7.10 shows those districts in which a high share of the electorate voted for them between 1987 and 1990, and how that pattern has changed since then. In the first period they won over a fifth of the vote in only ten districts: Richmond upon Thames, Sutton, Shepway, Medina, Alnwick, Yeovil, Winchester, Lewes, East Hampshire and Chelmsford. After the 1991–1994 set of local elections they had won over a fifth of the vote in another twenty districts adding Oadby & Wigston, Taunton Deane, Brentwood, Restormel, Wear Valley, Eastbourne, Torbay, Carrick, Bath, Kingston upon Thames, Mole Valley, New Forest, South Norfolk, Newbury, Waverley, North Wiltshire, Tandridge, Cheltenham, Rother and South Wight to their tally. By concentrating their vote geographically this (now united) party is gaining more power.

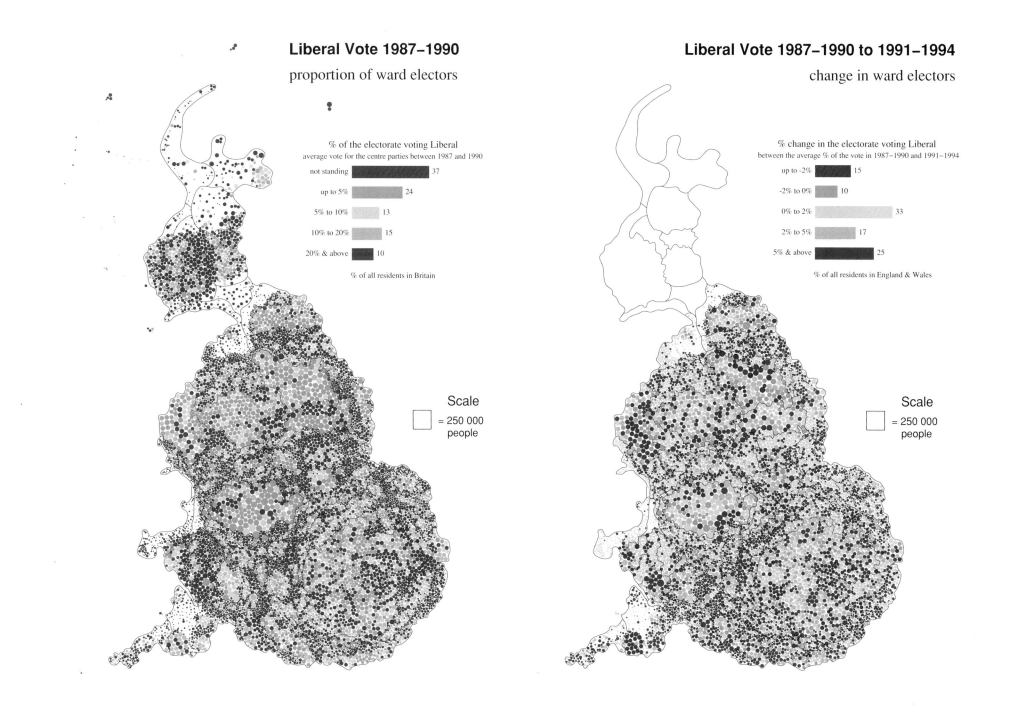

Liberal Vote 1987–1990

proportion of ward electors

% of the electorate voting Liberal

average vote for the centre parties between 1987 and 1990

not standing		37
up to 5%		24
5% to 10%		13
10% to 20%		15
20% & above		10

% of all residents in Britain

Scale

☐ = 250 000 people

Liberal Vote 1987–1990 to 1991–1994

change in ward electors

% change in the electorate voting Liberal

between the average % of the vote in 1987–1990 and 1991–1994

up to -2%		15
-2% to 0%		10
0% to 2%		33
2% to 5%		17
5% & above		25

% of all residents in England & Wales

Scale

☐ = 250 000 people

Other Party Votes

Many candidates stand for parties other than the main three at both local and general elections. At local elections these people have been, in aggregate, more successful than the Liberal parties, winning over an average 8% of the electorate in Britain between 1987 and 1990 and having a majority of the vote in wards containing 12% of the people (and three times as much of the land, see page 215). However, where more than one candidate from other parties stood, their votes have been combined, so it would be wrong to think that other parties had won this proportion of seats. The votes for these candidates can only be treated as a group to give a general indication of dissatisfaction with the main political parties, and even that can be misleading as many of the other parties' candidates in the Home Counties and North Yorkshire are standing in lieu of an official Conservative candidate. In Scotland other party candidates are likely to be members of the Scottish Nationalist party; in Wales, Plaid Cymru; and in many parts of England they are likely to be Green party members, British National party members, members of various residents associations or even members of the Monster Raving Loony party.

The first map drawn opposite shows where these various parties were most successful between 1987 and 1990. The same shading scheme is used as for the Liberal parties on the last page. This map should be compared with the map of the Conservative vote on page 219 to see where the candidates are most likely to be standing in lieu of that party. In areas like Cornwall it is obvious that candidates from other parties are contesting the Conservative party for seats, whereas in much of Northumberland "independent" candidates are standing instead of Conservatives. Support for alternative parties is lowest in the main metropolitan cities, where they are least likely to put forward candidates. The exception to this is the success of some of these parties in small areas of London.

Figure 7.11 shows that other parties gained more than 2% of the vote in a majority of wards between 1987 and 1990, but achieved this in only a third of all wards (by population) between 1991 and 1994. Nationally, their share of support from the English and Welsh electorate fell from 8% to 5% in four years. One reason for this dramatic change may be that many of the "independent" candidates were replaced by official Conservative candidates in the latter period. The far map opposite provides evidence for that shift in some of those areas where the other parties' vote declined by over 10% of the electorate. However, in many of the centres of metropolitan counties support for candidates from other parties has been growing, albeit from a very low base. Figure 7.12 shows how the latter changes have had an insignificant effect upon the aggregate district level vote for other parties, which has only risen dramatically in a few small rural districts. Now that Conservative party candidates are standing in most of England, only in Wales and Scotland are there many districts in which the aggregate vote for parties other than the main three is at all high.

7.11: Other Parties Vote in England and Wales by Ward 1987–1990, 1987–1990 to 1991–1994

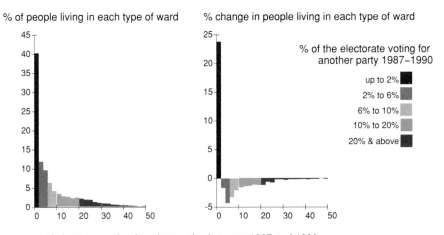

% of people living in each type of ward

% change in people living in each type of ward

% of the electorate voting for another party 1987–1990

up to 2%
2% to 6%
6% to 10%
10% to 20%
20% & above

% of electorate voting for other parties between 1987 and 1990

7.12: Other Party Vote by District 1987–1990 and Change in the Vote to 1991–1994

% of the electorate voting for other parties in all district elections in Britain held between 1987 and 1990

% change in the electorate voting for other parties between all district elections in England & Wales held between 1987–1990 and 1991–1994

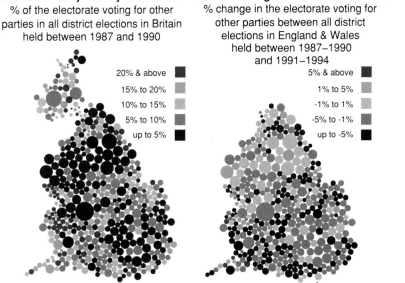

20% & above
15% to 20%
10% to 15%
5% to 10%
up to 5%

5% & above
1% to 5%
-1% to 1%
-5% to -1%
up to -5%

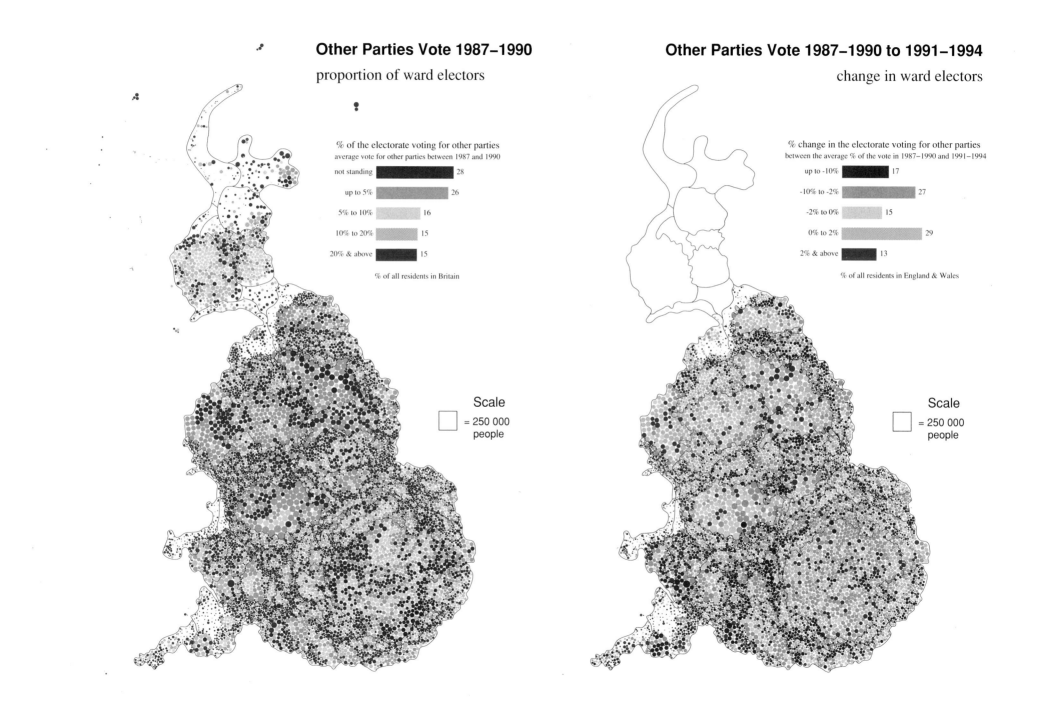

Other Parties Vote 1987–1990

proportion of ward electors

% of the electorate voting for other parties
average vote for other parties between 1987 and 1990

not standing		28
up to 5%		26
5% to 10%		16
10% to 20%		15
20% & above		15

% of all residents in Britain

Scale

☐ = 250 000 people

Other Parties Vote 1987–1990 to 1991–1994

change in ward electors

% change in the electorate voting for other parties
between the average % of the vote in 1987–1990 and 1991–1994

up to -10%		17
-10% to -2%		27
-2% to 0%		15
0% to 2%		29
2% & above		13

% of all residents in England & Wales

Scale

☐ = 250 000 people

7.13: Abstention in England and Wales by Ward 1987–1990, 1987–1990 to 1991–1994

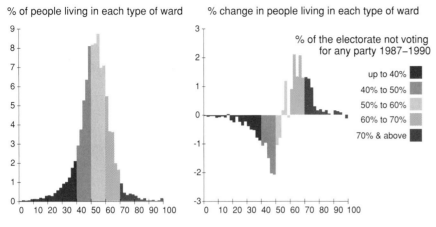

% of people living in each type of ward

% change in people living in each type of ward

% of the electorate not voting for any party 1987–1990

up to 40%
40% to 50%
50% to 60%
60% to 70%
70% & above

% of electorate not voting for any parties between 1987 and 1990

7.14: Abstention by District 1987–1990 and Change in Abstention to 1991–1994

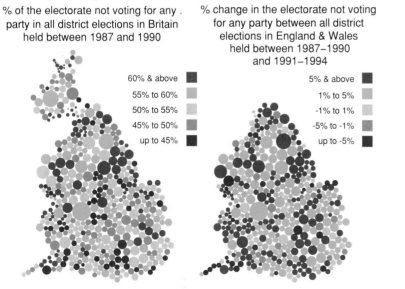

% of the electorate not voting for any party in all district elections in Britain held between 1987 and 1990

% change in the electorate not voting for any party between all district elections in England & Wales held between 1987–1990 and 1991–1994

60% & above
55% to 60%
50% to 55%
45% to 50%
up to 45%

5% & above
1% to 5%
-1% to 1%
-5% to -1%
up to -5%

Electorate Not Voting

The largest share of the electorate (categorized by political allegiance) does not vote for any of the political parties at local elections in Britain; it abstains. In Britain between 1987 and 1990, 54% of the electorate who were registered to vote did not usually vote. It is because of the size of this group that most of the figures presented in this chapter have been of shares of the electorate, rather than of shares of people who vote (which is the usual convention). The electorate not voting are too large a group to ignore. A majority of electors vote in local elections in only just over a third of all wards by population, while 7% of the population live in wards where over seven out of ten electors abstain at local elections. These statistics are shown in the key to the first map opposite which illustrates how rates of abstention vary across Britain by ward. The geographical distribution is very smooth, with few areas of high abstention rates abutting places where a high proportion of electors vote. In London, for instance, voting rates are highest in the south west and lowest in two clusters of wards in the east and centre of the capital. Between these places the rate changes very evenly. The social group distribution which most closely matches the pattern of abstention is that of workers-with-no-occupation shown on page 185. Voters who abstain may well also share some of the characteristics of adults who are not registered to vote; they certainly tend to live in the same places and so it is useful to compare the pattern of abstention with the maps and figures given on pages 216 and 217. The first graph in Figure 7.13 shows how even the distribution of abstention rates by population was in England and Wales between 1987 and 1990, with the modal rate of abstention being 55% of the electorate at that time.

The second graph in Figure 7.13 shows how the distribution of abstention rates has changed in England and Wales in the four years to 1991–1994. Abstention rates rose from 54% to 58%, and the graph indicates how (a proportion equivalent to) over four million more electors now live in areas where a majority of the electorate abstains than did in the previous period. Almost three quarters of all residents in England and Wales live in wards where abstentions rose, as the key to the second map opposite shows. This map contains a much less even pattern than the static rate of abstentions. For example, abstention rates tended to fall only in district clusters of wards where it is likely that parties campaigned strongly and that control of the council was marginal. Abstentions tended to rise most inside the largest cities, but also in areas where the rate of abstention had been very low in the previous period. In general, however, the pattern of inner city lack of interest in the political process is becoming clearer. This summary is supported by the maps shown in Figure 7.14, in which already high district aggregate abstention rates appear to have been rising most strongly. The figure also shows other features, such as high rates of abstention in very rural areas and low rates in the Welsh Valleys and much of southern England, with abstentions falling in the South West.

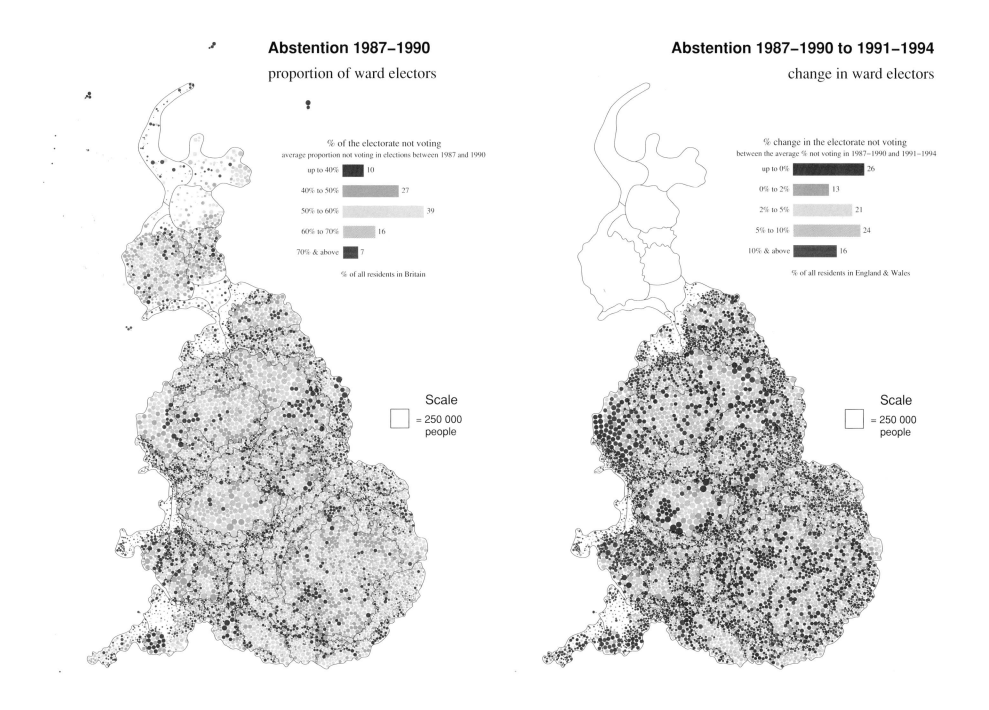

Abstention 1987–1990

proportion of ward electors

% of the electorate not voting

average proportion not voting in elections between 1987 and 1990

up to 40%		10
40% to 50%		27
50% to 60%		39
60% to 70%		16
70% & above		7

% of all residents in Britain

Scale

☐ = 250 000 people

Abstention 1987–1990 to 1991–1994

change in ward electors

% change in the electorate not voting

between the average % not voting in 1987–1990 and 1991–1994

up to 0%		26
0% to 2%		13
2% to 5%		21
5% to 10%		24
10% & above		16

% of all residents in England & Wales

Scale

☐ = 250 000 people

7.15: Seats Won by Party at each British General Election 1955–1992

number of seats won by each party in the house of commons

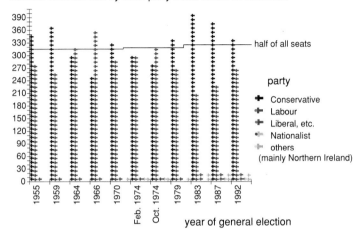

7.16: Votes Won by Party at each British General Election 1955–1992

millions of votes won by each party in the house of commons

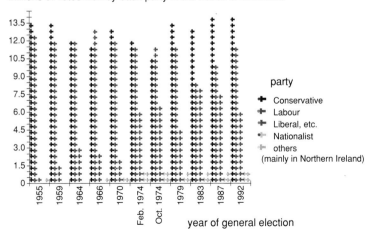

Winning General Elections

Local elections provide a great deal of geographical detail about the political preferences of the electorate, but they are not the best measure of these preferences because only a minority of electors vote for district councils. It is also very difficult to collate information about a long series of local elections because the boundaries of wards are altered so frequently and because this information was not systematically collected until relatively recently. To be able to study long term changes to the geography of voting in Britain, and to be able to include the preferences of a majority of electors, general elections need to be studied. These are held in parliamentary constituencies, of which in the United Kingdom there were 630 between 1955 and 1970, 635 between 1974 and 1979, 650 between 1983 and 1987, and 651 in 1992. The candidate of the party winning the most votes in each constituency becomes (or remains) a Member of Parliament, holding a seat in the House of Commons. Figure 7.15 shows how many members each party in Britain has returned at each general election since 1955, and thus which party won at each election, and by what margin. Before this date the electoral system was more complex (prior to the 1948 and 1954 redistributions of seats).

The maps opposite show where these constituencies were won at each election and also, for each election since 1955, whether the seat had changed hands since the previous election. To map this, the constituencies had to be linked over the two periods of redistribution (further details are given in Cornford *et al.* 1995). The shape of the cartograms changed over time as seats were destroyed and created and as the sizes of their electorates changed. Because the vast majority of seats are won by the main two parties, seats won by all other parties have been given a single shade on these maps. Together, the maps illustrate how the electoral system of the United Kingdom has evolved over four decades. Although the basic pattern has remained fairly constant, a distinct geography has emerged of those changes which have occurred. In general, the two main parties tend to win seats near to those which they already hold when they are being successful, and tend to lose seats on the edges of their "territories" when their national vote declines. In 1955 only eight seats were won by a party other than the Conservatives or the Labour party, and six of those were Liberal victories. By 1992 this total had risen to forty four, only twenty of which were held by the Liberal Democrats. Scottish and Welsh Nationalists between them won seven seats in their respective countries. The remaining seventeen seats are in Northern Ireland, where, since 1974, all seats have been held by various parties unique to that province.

Because of the nature of the first past the post electoral system the distribution of seats over-emphasizes the lead in votes of the two main parties as Figure 7.16 demonstrates. The Liberal parties fare particularly badly under this system because of the more even geographical distribution of their support.

Winner 1955–1992

party position in constituency

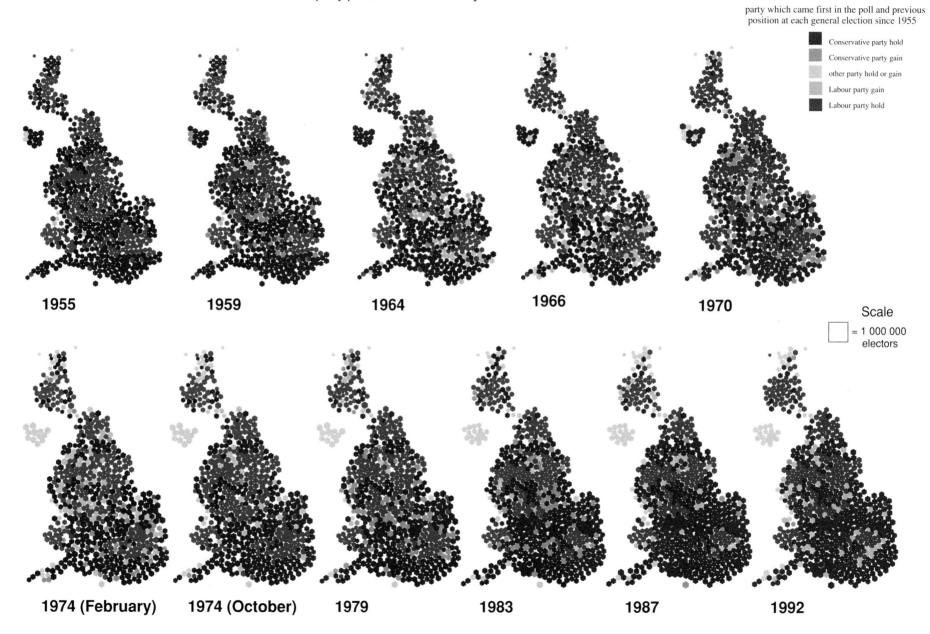

party which came first in the poll and previous
position at each general election since 1955

■ Conservative party hold
■ Conservative party gain
□ other party hold or gain
■ Labour party gain
■ Labour party hold

1955   1959   1964   1966   1970

1974 (February)   1974 (October)   1979   1983   1987   1992

Scale

☐ = 1 000 000 electors

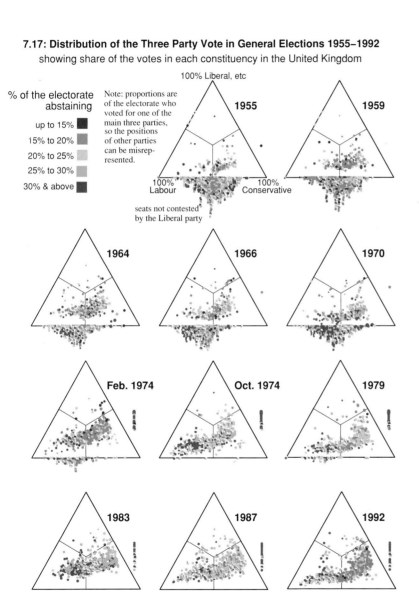

7.17: Distribution of the Three Party Vote in General Elections 1955–1992

showing share of the votes in each constituency in the United Kingdom

Runner Up 1955–1992

To understand better how votes are converted into seats at general elections it is necessary to look at the distribution of votes within constituencies and, to appreciate how potentially volatile the electoral system is, it is useful to consider which party came second in each constituency at each election. The distribution of votes within constituencies can be shown using the electoral triangle in which each seat is drawn as a dot, placed in the triangle according to the share of the vote won by each of the three main parties. This method is explained further in the text accompanying Figure 7.2 which showed how the vote is distributed within wards at recent local elections. In Figure 7.17 an electoral triangle is drawn to show the distribution of votes within constituencies at each general election from 1955 to 1992. Here the triangles have been embellished further by drawing a histogram on their base to show the distribution of votes within constituencies which were not contested by the Liberal party. This is because the Liberal party did not put a candidate forward in many constituencies during the beginning of this period. Only in 1983 did the three main parties field a candidate in every constituency in mainland Britain. The seats drawn by the side of each triangle are those in which none of the three main parties stood, being mainly Northern Ireland constituencies. The changing pattern of constituencies within the triangle illustrates how the electorate has changed its allegiances over time, and how these changes have been transformed into the changing distribution of seats held in the House of Commons. The triangle is divided into three sectors and each sector contains seats in which one of the three main parties won the most votes (a Conservative candidate did not stand in five of the six constituencies won by the Liberals in 1955, so those dots appear on the Labour/Liberal axis of the triangle). The margin of victory by which each seat was won can be measured from the distance between the seat and the nearest of the three lines subdividing the triangle. Thus, by the general election of October 1974, the Labour party had many more "safe" seats than did the Conservative party. The Liberal parties saw their votes rise dramatically in the elections of February 1974 and 1983, but the dots did not rise far enough in the triangles for the change in votes to be transformed into many changes of seats. If the triangles are divided into six sections by adding three more lines (from the corners to the centre), those sections subdivide every first and second party permutation. The geographical distribution of parties coming second is shown in the maps on the opposite page and displays a much more dramatic picture of change than is presented by merely viewing the winner of each contest. In recent years the Liberal parties have come to contest a majority of seats in the south of England, while the Scottish Nationalists are the main contender (to Labour) north of the border, as they were after the second general election in 1974. Thus there have been substantial changes beneath the surface of British politics in recent years.

Runner Up 1955–1992

party position in constituency

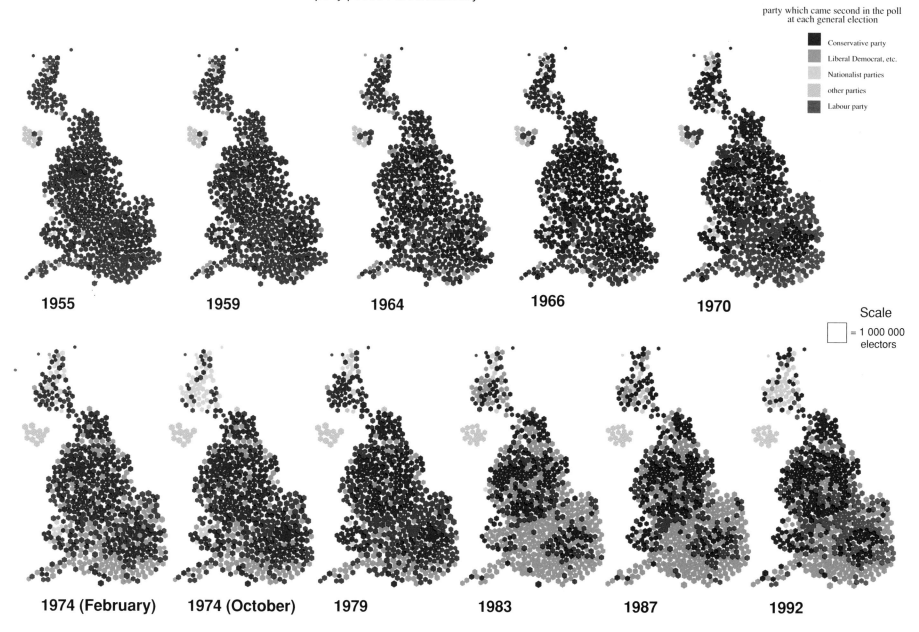

party which came second in the poll
at each general election

- Conservative party
- Liberal Democrat, etc.
- Nationalist parties
- other parties
- Labour party

1955   **1959**   **1964**   **1966**   **1970**

Scale

☐ = 1 000 000 electors

1974 (February)   **1974 (October)**   **1979**   **1983**   **1987**   **1992**

7.18: Voting and Abstaining at each British General Election 1955–1992

% of the electorate voting for each party or abstaining

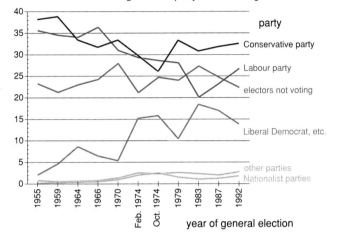

year of general election

7.19: Electors and Adults in Constituencies in England & Wales in 1991

the number of persons registered to vote in the general election of 1992 ('000s)

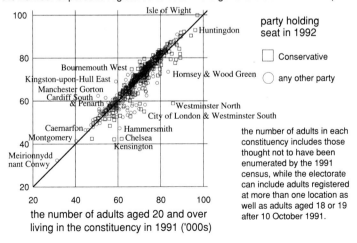

party holding
seat in 1992

☐ Conservative

◯ any other party

the number of adults in each
constituency includes those
thought not to have been
enumerated by the 1991
census, while the electorate
can include adults registered
at more than one location as
well as adults aged 18 or 19
after 10 October 1991.

the number of adults aged 20 and over
living in the constituency in 1991 ('000s)

Abstaining 1955–1992

Rates of abstention are much lower in general elections than in local elections. However, if only a small proportion of the electorate who usually do not vote did choose to vote, and voted differently from current voters, the electoral map of Britain would be radically redrawn (see page 236). Figure 7.18 shows what proportion of the electorate did not vote at each general election between 1955 and 1992 and how that proportion compared to the total share of the electorate voting for each party. Between 21% and 28% of the electorate do not vote at these general elections, with turnouts being highest in February 1974 and lowest in the general election of 1970, and low again in 1983. This pattern is reflected in the maps of abstention rates shown on the opposite page, which all use the same scale so that they can be compared. Turnout was high in 1992, and in eight seats more than six voters out of every seven went to the polls. In general, abstention rates tend to be low when the national contest is close (see Figure 7.15).

Geographically, the areas where abstention rates are high have remained much the same over these four decades. This geographical pattern is probably due to many of the same reasons which were raised in the discussion of abstention in local elections (page 226). However, some factors clearly operate more strongly at general elections where, for example, abstention rates are high along the south coast in constituencies which contain many elderly people who may find it difficult to get to the polls. Another strong correlate with abstention rates in a constituency is how marginal the seat is. This effect is illustrated by the shading of the dots in Figure 7.17. Constituencies where the Conservative and Labour shares of the vote are very similar tend to have higher turnouts (and in recent years have seen falls in the Liberal share of the vote attributable to tactical voting, see Upton 1994). More important than all these factors, however, is the underlying social geography of Britain which changes so slowly that almost exactly the same places have abstention rates of above 30% in 1992 as had those rates in 1955, despite the replacement of one generation of electors with another and the changing socioeconomic shape of the country. Again, it is probable that the same factors which are related to adults not registering to vote are linked to the high rates of abstention of those who are registered in each area. Figure 7.19 shows how the number of people on the electoral register compares with the number of adults aged over 19 living in each constituency (see page 216 for definitions). The constituencies labelled are those in which registration rates were lowest or highest, and in which the electorate was smallest or largest at the last general election. Seats with high rates of migration tend to have the largest undercounts of electors, and the voters who are registered in these seats tend to return Conservative members of parliament to the House of Commons. Conversely, seats in which there are more registered electors than usual residents aged over 19 often contain universities and return Labour members to the House of Commons.

Abstention 1955–1992

proportion of constituency electors

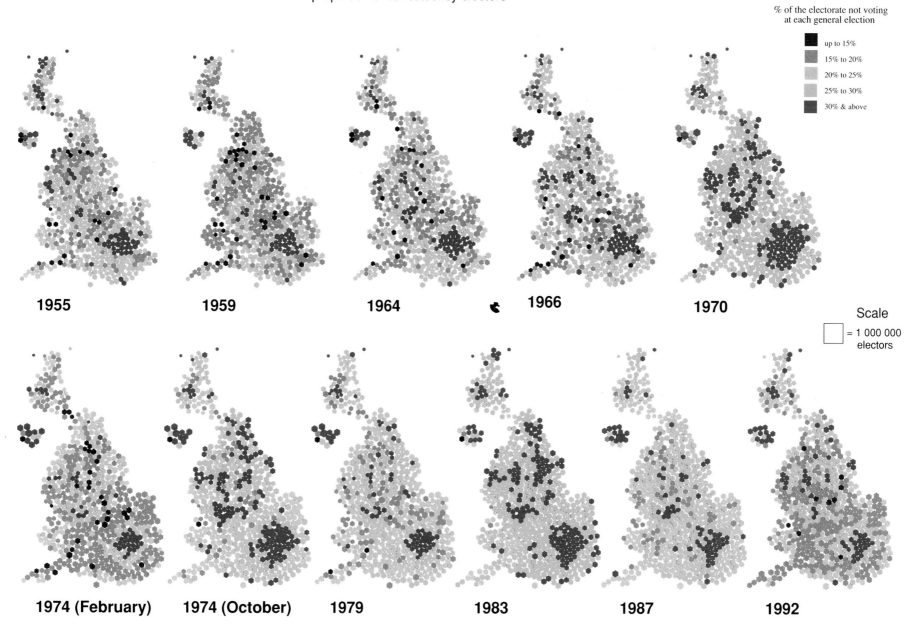

% of the electorate not voting
at each general election

- up to 15%
- 15% to 20%
- 20% to 25%
- 25% to 30%
- 30% & above

1955 **1959** **1964** **1966** **1970**

1974 (February) **1974 (October)** **1979** **1983** **1987** **1992**

Scale

☐ = 1 000 000 electors

Voting 1979–1992

Many of the maps in other chapters in this atlas have compared changes between the two census dates of 1981 and 1991, and the latest period of voting is of particular interest, so here the share of the vote won by each party in each constituency at the 1992 general election is mapped, and the change to the vote from 1979 to 1992 is also drawn. This is the longest recent period for which votes can be compared using a consistent set of seats as the votes cast in the 1979 election have been redistributed to the constituencies which have been in place since 1983 to conduct research such as this (BBC/ITN 1983).

The top row of maps opposite shows what proportion of the electorate voted for each party or abstained in each constituency at the general election of 1992. The southern ring of Conservative loyalty with its associated northern pockets of support has been a familiar pattern in many of the maps in this atlas. The Conservative party won majority support (of over half the electorate) in only sixteen seats at the last general election, mainly in the Home Counties. The pattern of Labour party support is largely the mirror image of this, although that party won the support of a majority of electors in eighteen seats, with the safest being in South Wales. The geographical pattern of Liberal party support is similar to that of the Conservatives, but at a lower level, and in no seat did this party win a majority of the electorate. The Scottish and Welsh Nationalists are confined to their respective countries and receive most support in the north of each; while combined other party support is very high in Northern Ireland, but stands at below 10% in almost every seat on the mainland. The pattern of the electorate abstaining was shown on the last page. Here the most extreme group of constituencies is highlighted, with between a third and a half of its electors abstaining at the last general election.

The second set of maps shows how much of the pattern of voting described above can be attributed to changes which took place over the last decade. In general, the existing electoral division of the country was strengthened (Johnston *et al.* 1988), but there were exceptions to this trend. The Conservatives stood in Northern Ireland for the first time in two decades in 1992 and so automatically gained support there. Labour increased its support in a ring of southern coastal towns over the decade. The Liberal party saw the most dramatic changes, as illustrated opposite, and the Nationalists and other parties all gained greater support. Abstentions, which rose in general, fell dramatically in central London constituencies. Figure 7.20 shows a summary of these changes for votes aggregated by standard region, extracting metropolitan counties, and sorted by the change in the rate of abstention over the period, with Greater London seeing the strongest fall and South Yorkshire experiencing the fastest rise. Conservative support fell most in Merseyside, while Liberal support increased most in the South West. A more precise picture of the changes in the share of the vote held by each of the three main parties over this period is given in Figure 7.21 at the constituency level.

7.20: Change in the Party Votes by Region and Metroplitan County 1979–1992

standard regions of Britain with metropolitan counties shown separately

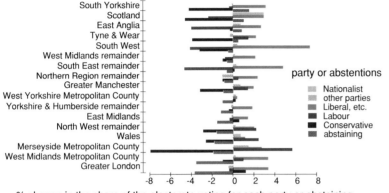

party or abstentions

■ Nationalist
▨ other parties
■ Liberal, etc.
■ Labour
■ Conservative
■ abstaining

% change in the share of the electorate voting for each party or abstaining

7.21: Change in the Three Party Vote in the General Elections of 1979 and 1992

% change in the Labour share of the three party vote for each constituency in Britain

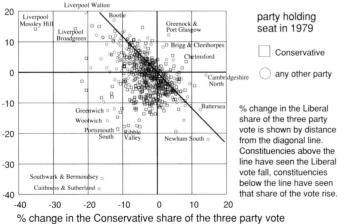

party holding seat in 1979

☐ Conservative

◯ any other party

% change in the Liberal share of the three party vote is shown by distance from the diagonal line. Constituencies above the line have seen the Liberal vote fall, constituencies below the line have seen that share of the vote rise.

% change in the Conservative share of the three party vote

Voting 1992, 1979–1992

proportion of constituency electors

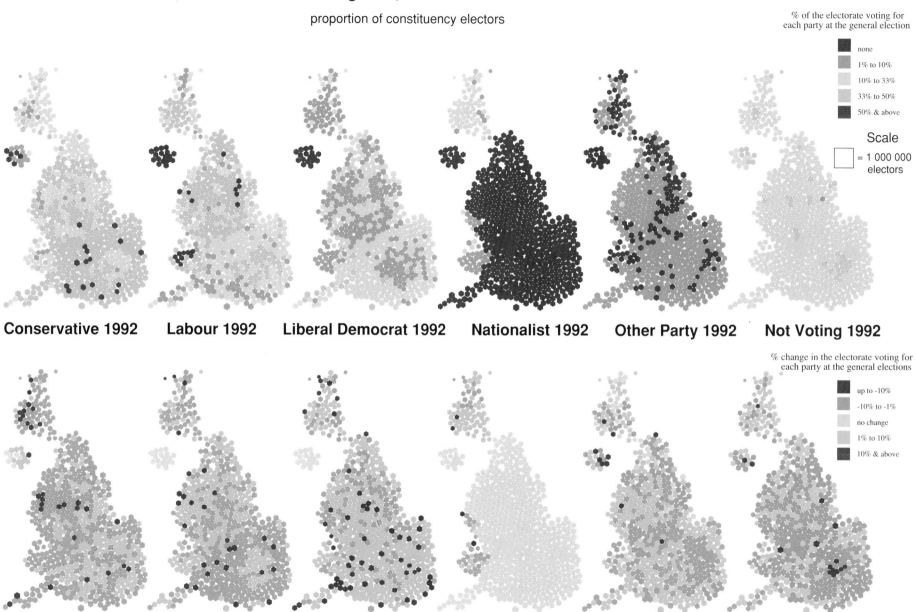

% of the electorate voting for
each party at the general election

- none
- 1% to 10%
- 10% to 33%
- 33% to 50%
- 50% & above

Scale

= 1 000 000
electors

Conservative 1992   **Labour 1992**   **Liberal Democrat 1992**   **Nationalist 1992**   **Other Party 1992**   **Not Voting 1992**

% change in the electorate voting for
each party at the general elections

- up to -10%
- -10% to -1%
- no change
- 1% to 10%
- 10% & above

Conservative 79–92   **Labour 79–92**   **Liberal/Democrat 79–92**   **Nationalist 79–92**   **Other Party 79–92**   **Not Voting 79–92**

7.22: The Fifty Most Marginal Constituencies in Britain after the 1992 General Election

Marginal Rank	Constituency Name	Margin (%) after 1992	Conservative '92% ('87%)		Labour '92% ('87%)		Liberal '92% ('87%)		Nationalist '92% ('87%)		Other '92% ('87%)	
Conservative seats which are Labour targets												
1	Vale of Glamorgan	0.0	36.3	(37.1)	36.3	(27.5)	7.6	(13.2)	1.7	(1.4)	0.0	(0.0)
2	Bristol North West	0.1	34.9	(37.0)	34.8	(27.4)	11.7	(14.9)	0.0	(0.0)	1.0	(0.0)
3	Hayes and Harlington	0.1	35.8	(36.7)	35.7	(26.4)	8.2	(11.4)	0.0	(0.0)	0.0	(0.0)
4	Ayr	0.1	33.9	(31.5)	33.7	(31.2)	6.2	(11.8)	9.1	(5.3)	0.2	(0.0)
10	Bolton North East	0.3	36.9	(34.9)	36.6	(33.6)	8.5	(10.2)	0.0	(0.0)	0.3	(0.0)
13	Norwich North	0.4	35.4	(36.3)	35.0	(23.9)	10.6	(19.0)	0.0	(0.0)	0.8	(0.0)
14	Corby	0.5	36.9	(35.3)	36.4	(32.5)	8.5	(11.8)	0.0	(0.0)	1.1	(0.0)
17	Slough	0.7	34.9	(35.6)	34.2	(30.1)	5.5	(10.2)	0.0	(0.0)	3.7	(0.0)
20	Tynemouth	0.8	37.0	(33.8)	36.2	(30.3)	6.5	(14.0)	0.0	(0.0)	0.7	(0.0)
21	Southampton Test	0.8	33.6	(34.8)	32.8	(25.4)	10.1	(16.2)	0.0	(0.0)	0.9	(0.0)
25	Edmonton	0.9	35.0	(37.2)	34.1	(26.1)	6.2	(9.3)	0.0	(0.0)	0.3	(0.0)
26	Amber Valley	1.0	39.1	(41.8)	38.1	(27.9)	7.5	(11.5)	0.0	(0.0)	0.0	(0.0)
28	Luton South	1.1	35.5	(34.8)	34.4	(27.6)	8.2	(12.8)	0.0	(0.0)	1.0	(0.0)
30	Bury South	1.2	37.8	(36.7)	36.6	(32.6)	7.3	(10.4)	0.0	(0.0)	0.3	(0.0)
31	Stirling	1.2	32.9	(30.4)	31.7	(28.8)	5.7	(11.8)	11.3	(8.5)	0.7	(0.0)
32	Dover	1.2	36.8	(36.7)	35.6	(27.3)	9.0	(15.9)	0.0	(0.0)	2.1	(0.0)
33	North West Leicestershire	1.4	39.2	(39.5)	37.8	(28.4)	8.8	(14.2)	0.0	(0.0)	0.3	(0.8)
37	Bolton West	1.5	37.1	(35.5)	35.6	(28.9)	10.6	(15.7)	0.0	(0.0)	0.3	(0.0)
39	City of Chester	1.7	36.9	(35.8)	35.2	(28.4)	10.8	(15.6)	0.0	(0.0)	0.9	(0.0)
41	Batley and Spen	1.8	36.2	(34.3)	34.3	(32.5)	8.3	(11.3)	0.0	(0.0)	0.8	(0.9)
44	Langbaurgh	2.0	37.7	(32.9)	35.8	(30.3)	9.6	(15.7)	0.0	(0.0)	0.0	(0.0)
49	Basildon	2.2	35.7	(31.9)	33.6	(28.0)	10.3	(13.3)	0.0	(0.0)	0.0	(0.0)
50	Coventry South West	2.3	36.6	(34.0)	34.3	(29.1)	7.4	(15.5)	0.0	(0.0)	1.9	(0.0)
Conservative seats which are Liberal targets												
7	Brecon and Radnor	0.3	31.0	(29.3)	22.6	(24.7)	30.8	(29.4)	0.8	(1.1)	0.8	(0.0)
9	Portsmouth South	0.3	29.4	(30.8)	10.1	(9.2)	29.1	(30.6)	0.0	(0.0)	0.6	(0.6)
34	Hazel Grove	1.4	38.1	(37.1)	9.9	(9.7)	36.6	(34.3)	0.0	(0.0)	0.3	(0.5)
35	Edinburgh West	1.5	30.6	(29.7)	14.8	(17.6)	29.1	(27.7)	7.0	(4.5)	1.1	(0.0)
40	Isle of Wight	1.8	38.2	(40.7)	4.8	(4.7)	36.4	(34.2)	0.0	(0.0)	0.4	(0.0)
42	Conwy	1.9	26.6	(29.8)	20.3	(17.1)	24.7	(24.0)	5.8	(6.0)	1.4	(0.0)
Labour seats which are Conservative targets												
5	Rossendale and Darwen	0.2	36.3	(37.4)	36.4	(30.7)	9.4	(12.1)	0.0	(0.0)	0.9	(0.0)
6	Warrington South	0.2	35.6	(32.5)	35.8	(27.8)	10.3	(17.2)	0.0	(0.0)	0.4	(0.0)
8	Birmingham Yardley	0.3	26.9	(31.5)	27.2	(27.1)	23.6	(15.3)	0.0	(0.0)	0.4	(0.0)
12	Ipswich	0.4	34.8	(34.2)	35.2	(32.9)	9.2	(9.7)	0.0	(0.0)	1.1	(0.3)
15	Halifax	0.7	33.6	(32.1)	34.2	(33.7)	10.0	(11.9)	0.0	(0.0)	0.9	(0.0)
18	Ilford South	0.7	34.1	(34.7)	34.8	(26.9)	7.4	(10.1)	0.0	(0.0)	0.5	(0.0)
19	Southampton Itchen	0.8	33.1	(33.6)	33.8	(24.4)	10.0	(17.9)	0.0	(0.0)	0.0	(0.0)
22	Cambridge	0.8	28.2	(31.2)	29.0	(22.1)	14.5	(23.9)	0.0	(0.0)	1.4	(0.9)
23	Dewsbury	0.9	34.3	(32.8)	35.1	(33.4)	9.0	(12.6)	0.0	(0.0)	1.8	(0.0)
24	Birmingham Northfield	0.9	34.3	(32.8)	34.6	(28.5)	7.7	(11.3)	0.0	(0.0)	0.0	(0.0)
27	Pembroke	1.0	34.8	(33.1)	35.9	(25.0)	9.1	(21.1)	2.2	(1.6)	0.9	(0.0)
38	Thurrock	1.7	34.1	(30.4)	35.8	(29.3)	7.4	(11.8)	0.0	(0.0)	0.7	(0.0)
43	Lewisham East	1.9	32.0	(33.3)	33.9	(25.3)	8.5	(15.3)	0.0	(0.0)	0.3	(0.0)
45	North Warwickshire	2.0	36.6	(36.0)	38.6	(32.0)	8.6	(11.9)	0.0	(0.0)	0.0	(0.0)
47	Cannock and Burntwood	2.1	36.7	(35.5)	38.8	(31.5)	8.1	(12.8)	0.0	(0.0)	0.6	(0.0)
Liberal seats which are Conservative targets												
11	Gordon	0.3	27.3	(23.5)	8.3	(8.5)	27.7	(36.4)	10.5	(5.3)	0.0	(0.0)
29	North Devon	1.2	38.6	(41.6)	4.9	(5.1)	39.7	(35.0)	0.0	(0.0)	1.1	(0.0)
48	Cheltenham	2.1	35.9	(39.6)	5.1	(5.9)	38.0	(33.4)	0.0	(0.0)	1.2	(0.0)
Liberal seats which are Labour targets												
16	Inverness, Nairn and Lochaber	0.7	16.6	(16.3)	18.4	(18.0)	19.1	(26.1)	18.1	(10.5)	1.1	(0.0)
Nationalist seats which are Labour targets												
36	Angus East	1.5	28.6	(29.5)	9.5	(8.1)	6.2	(5.9)	30.1	(32.0)	0.7	(0.0)
46	Ynys Mon	2.1	27.9	(27.1)	19.0	(13.8)	3.5	(5.4)	29.9	(35.3)	0.3	(0.0)

Marginal After 1992

The most recent general election results are always of great interest because they not only show which party has support where, but also give an indication of how firm is their grip on power, and thus of how likely it is for there to be a change of government in the near future. The 1992 general election produced the closest result, in terms of seats won for the main two parties for 18 years (see Figure 7.15). The Conservative party had a majority of seats in the House of Commons of only 21 after it won the election. This has subsequently been reduced even further in by-elections and by Conservative rebellions. In fourteen seats it won with margins of 1% of the electorate or less. These seats are shown in Figure 7.22, which lists all the most marginal constituencies in the country by this measure. The figure shows that after the 1992 general election the Conservative party held more marginal seats at this level than did all the other parties combined. Most importantly, only one seat — Inverness, Nairn & Lochaber — was a marginal being contested between the two main opposition parties (and this seat is unique in that all four parties are effectively contesting there, as the voting statistics in Figure 7.22 illustrate). Thus, the party of government is in a very weak position and faces two opposition parties which are not a great threat to each other in terms of electoral geography.

The first map opposite is shaded to show where marginal and safe seats are most often found using this definition of marginality. The size of the margin of victory of each party is also given as a figure within each constituency. The areas of traditional party loyalty, identified as having high support for particular parties on the last page, can be seen to contain the largest majorities. After 1992 it was generally suburban seats which were most marginal, a great many of which were in the midlands and the north of the country. The most marginal seats in absolute as well as relative terms were Vale of Glamorgan (won by 19 votes), Bristol North West (45 votes), Hayes and Harlington (53 votes) and Ayr (85 votes). All of these seats were won by the Conservative party, as Figure 7.22 shows. Thus, in theory, 103 voters, voting differently out of an electorate of 43 238 935 could have nearly halved the government majority, and a change in allegiance of a further (carefully selected) 1141 voters would have resulted in a hung parliament!

Well over nine million registered electors did not vote at the last election and almost another two million eligible adults were not registered to vote. The second map opposite gives an indication of how important these people could be in the future. Constituencies are shaded according to the ratio of adults not voting to the margin of victory in a seat. The key to the map shows that one elector in six in Britain lives in a seat where more than five times as many adults failed to vote than were needed by the runner-up to win that seat at the last general election. The figures within each constituency show the proportion of adults not voting. The scope for a great deal of electoral change obviously exists if, and when, enough people decide that they want to effect that change.

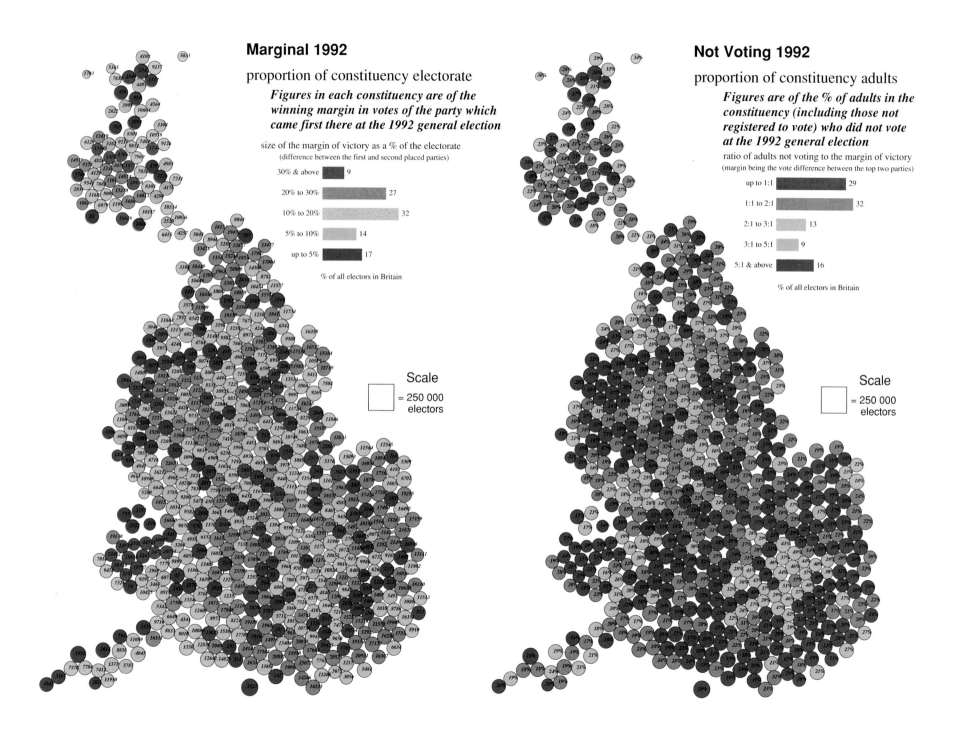

Marginal 1992

proportion of constituency electorate

Figures in each constituency are of the winning margin in votes of the party which came first there at the 1992 general election

size of the margin of victory as a % of the electorate
(difference between the first and second placed parties)

30% & above	9
20% to 30%	27
10% to 20%	32
5% to 10%	14
up to 5%	17

% of all electors in Britain

Scale

☐ = 250 000 electors

Not Voting 1992

proportion of constituency adults

Figures are of the % of adults in the constituency (including those not registered to vote) who did not vote at the 1992 general election

ratio of adults not voting to the margin of victory
(margin being the vote difference between the top two parties)

up to 1:1	29
1:1 to 2:1	32
2:1 to 3:1	13
3:1 to 5:1	9
5:1 & above	16

% of all electors in Britain

Scale

☐ = 250 000 electors

Conclusion: Votes and Parties

Local Elections

The geographically specific way in which politicians are elected in Britain is a demonstration of the importance given to local problems and solutions in this society. At any one time more than fifteen thousand individuals are in political office in Britain following European, Parliamentary, County or District elections. All of these people are elected to represent specific areas, and the majority of these people represent the residents of the ten thousand plus wards which have been mapped throughout this atlas. Thus there is a constitutional acknowledgement of the importance of local issues and governance. You may be constrained to send your children to a local school, but you also have the choice of which councillors to elect, some of whom will govern that school. However, as local politics has become more popular, with a gradual increase in turnout and electoral completion over time (Rallings and Thrasher 1991), the powers of local government have been reduced so that elected councillors have less control over spending and are being removed from positions of influence over local services such as schools, colleges and hospitals. The number of wards with very low turnouts is now growing (Figure 7.13) as, with the shrinking power of local authorities, local elections become more of a referendum and less a means of changing the management of services and amenities in particular localities.

Aspects of the social structure of Britain can be seen through the snapshots of local political opinion which were presented in this chapter. Locally, the Conservative party generally fared well only where the rich (page 203) and those in work (page 69) were most numerous. The Labour party shows much the opposite pattern, representing areas containing most of the ill (page 137) and those most reliant on local services in Britain (page 119). The pattern of Liberal (and other) party support is more complex. Third and Fourth party voters are most numerous in wards in districts where they can make a difference to the balance of the council. In many ways the first-past-the-post electoral system prevents subtle expressions of local opinion, reducing most debates to two-way contests, and thus simplifying more complex social interests. Voting change is even more difficult to account for, particularly over quite short periods of time. Already, though, the impact of issues such as rising negative equity (page 129) and the new pattern of unemployment (Figure 3.31) can be seen in changes such as the collapse of the Conservative vote in Outer London (page 219), and the rise of Labour in the East Midlands (page 221). The continued spread of the Liberals out from their strongholds in the periphery of Britain (Figure 7.10), and the increased support for alternative parties in the city centres (page 225), may both reflect some of the particular combinations of social change and realignment which took place in the early 1990s.

Political Colours: Colour Print H

Although the voting system itself simplifies political opinion and preference, the way in which voting patterns are portrayed smoothes them even further. The cartogram of which party wins in each seat (page 215) hides large variations in the degree of success of different candidates standing in different places (Figure 7.2). With colour a more subtle picture of British electoral geography can be painted. Colour Print H groups wards into fifteen categories on the basis of which party won, which party came second and the difference between their two votes. Only the votes of the three main parties are used to colour this map. It is fortunate that each of these political parties have chosen primary colours to represent them. Thus all wards in which the Conservative candidate won most votes can be given a shade of blue, all wards where Labour did best can be given a shade of red, and all wards where the Liberals had the largest poll are coloured a shade of yellow. In wards which are considered not to be safe, a hint of the colour of the party coming second is added. Liberal seats where Labour came second are light-orange, whereas close Labour victories over the Conservatives are a shade of magenta. Here, safe wards are defined as wards in which the first placed party was forty (percentage) points ahead of the second placed party in terms of shares of the three party vote. Safe wards are given the clearest or darkest shade of each of the three primary colours. Conversely wards are classified as marginal, here, if the difference between the first placed two parties is less than ten points. Light pastel shades are used to show the six possible types of marginal into which each of these wards falls.

The key to Colour Print H shows what proportion of the population of Britain live in each ward by electoral type, as well as the relative positions of each shading category in "electoral space" (using the same scale as in Figure 7.2). The largest group of wards are classed as safe Labour victories, although it is important to realise that in places such as Scotland a Nationalist or other party candidate may well have won the ward. There, Labour may simply have polled much more than the candidates of the other main two parties (assuming they stood). The next largest group of wards by population live in areas comfortably won by the Labour party where the Conservative candidate came second. One person in six lives in an area like this, mostly in cities. Safe Conservative seats are the next largest group, encompassing 11% of the population. Rural and suburban areas contain most of these people, but there are also clear concentrations in areas such as south west London. In terms of wards which are marginal between these two parties, they both hold equal numbers containing, in total, a tenth of the population. Almost as many people live in wards where the Liberal party and the Conservative party are effectively contesting one another, but only 3% of the population are involved in serious contests between Labour and the Liberals. Geographically, the Liberal party has one of the most interesting distributions. Where the Liberal party does well in rural areas its wards are tinted green as the Conservative party tends to come second. Inside cities such as London and Liverpool its wards have an orange tint as Labour are the main alternative there. In terms of increasing their vote, three times as many people live in marginal Conservative wards which the Liberals have a good chance of winning as live in similar marginal Labour wards. Thus the local electoral geography of Britain reflects something of the nature of contests being held for national government, as well as the greater complexity that is revealed at this spatial resolution.

General Elections

Increasingly it is general elections which matter. As powers are taken away from local government, and as the state plays a more active role in determining who gets what, the prospects of people in local areas become more and more dependent on decisions taken in Westminster. It is central government which now decides how much social housing to build, how many schools to support, how health care should be organized and which local industries are promoted. Central government now collects and spends more money less fairly than it has done at any time since the war (Social Justice Commission 1994).

Because national politics is so dominated by the two main parties it is possible to draw simple maps which simultaneously show both the static picture and voting change in constituencies (page 229). The rise of the third and fourth placed parties over recent elections has made this mapping more difficult (Figure 7.16), so that it is now necessary to show which party came second in every seat to demonstrate the variation in the types of political competition which now take place (page 231). Over the last forty years the electoral geography of Britain has changed dramatically. The Liberal party is now significant as well as Labour from the point of view of the government losing seats (Figures 7.17 and 7.22). However, electoral geography means that the only party which can hope to gain majority power other than the Conservatives is Labour, and its chances of achieving that at the next election are still only slight (Cornford et al. 1995).

It is worth comparing some district-level economic changes with the more recent changes to the political map of Britain (page 229). The Conservative gains in 1983 corresponded with widespread falls in unemployment outside London (page 97), as did their victories in 1987, which were concentrated in the south. In 1992, when Labour regained many of these seats, unemployment was rising in most districts. A similar pattern is found when the general election maps are compared with the house price changes preceding election years (page 127). House price rises in 1982–1983 and 1986–1987 correspond geographically with government victories, while price falls before the last election were deepest around suburban London, where Labour made most

gains. The Liberal party has also gained from some of these changes which is shown most clearly by the recent rise in its local vote in those areas which have suffered most from the latest recession (Figure 7.10). Between the 1979 and 1992 general elections the Liberal vote grew most strongly in the South West and South East (excluding London), Labour saw its largest fall in these two regions and gained most in Merseyside, Wales and the North West as a whole, whereas the Conservatives saw their largest falls in Merseyside, Scotland and South Yorkshire, their vote only rising noticeably in London over the decade, where turnout too rose most strongly (Figure 7.20).

Registration and Representation

Just as most of the press coverage of the 1991 census has concentrated on who was not included, so who is not included in elections is equally, if not more, important. These issues are inextricably linked, as the maps on page 217 show, because it is much the same people missing from social statistics who are excluded from the political process. But because the electoral register does not impute voters, almost twice as many adults are not eligible to vote as were not counted by government statisticians. These people are known to be more likely to be young, renting, not to be white (Figure 7.4) and to be living in particular parts of particular cities. Their absence from the political process will have a much more marked effect than if they were evenly distributed amongst the population. Most seriously, they have not been included in the current reorganisation of parliamentary constituencies, so future generations of people living in places like central London will have far fewer members of parliament than they are entitled to.

References

BBC/ITN, 1983, *The BBC/ITN Guide to the New Parliamentary Constituencies*, Chichester: Parliamentary Research Services.

Cornford, J., Dorling, D. and Tether, B., 1995, Historical precedent and British electoral prospects, *Electoral Studies,* 14/2: 123–142.

Johnston, R.J., Pattie, C.J. and Allsopp, J.G., 1988, *A Nation Dividing? The Electoral Map of Great Britain 1979–1987*, London: Longman.

OPCS, 1993, *Electoral Statistics*, No. 20, London: HMSO.

Rallings, C. and Thrasher, M., 1991, *1991 Local Elections Handbook*, Polytechnic South West: Plymouth Local Government Chronicle Elections Centre.

Simpson, S., 1994, Editorial: Coverage of the Great Britain Census of Population and Housing, *Journal of the Royal Statistical Society* A, 157/3: 313–316.

Smith, S., 1993, *Electoral Registration in 1991*, London: HMSO.

Social Justice Commission, 1994, *Social Justice: Strategies for National Renewal*, London: Vintage.

Upton, G., 1994, Picturing the 1992 British General Election, *Journal of the Royal Statistical Society* A, 157/2: 231-252.

Index

Note: references to *Colour Prints* refer to the full colour prints which follow page xxxii.